sed & awk

sed & awk

Dale Dougherty

O'Reilly & Associates, Inc.
103 Morris Street, Suite A
Sebastopol, CA 95472

sed & awk
by Dale Dougherty

Editor: Tim O'Reilly

Printing History:

November 1990:	First Edition.
March 1991:	Minor corrections.
July 1992:	Minor corrections.
November 1992:	Minor corrections.

Nutshell Handbook and the Nutshell Handbook logo are registered trademarks of O'Reilly & Associates, Inc.

This book is printed on acid-free paper with 50% recycled content, 10-15% post-consumer waste. O'Reilly & Associates is committed to using paper with the highest recycled content available consistent with high quality.

ISBN: 0-937175-59-5

[8/94]

Table of Contents

Figures

Tables

The following is a list of the programs in the book, with a brief description of each:

README — this file.
acronyms — program to read and substitute acronyms; Chapter 7 & 8.
awkro — acronym processor from Chapter 8.
bitmap.awk — awk script that demonstrates multi-dimensional arrays; Chapter 8.
contrib/ — subdirectory containing programs from Chapter 12.
contrib2/ — subdirectory containing additional contributed programs.
date-month — convert numeric month to name of month; Chapter 8.
do.outline.awk — awk script to create numbered outline.
do.outline.sed — sed script to extract outline from document; Chapter 4.
factorial — program to derive factorials; Chapter 8.
filesum — program to list size of files in directory; Chapter 7.
getmac — program for extracting troff macro definitions; Chapter 4.
glossary — sample glossary file for lookup program.
grades.awk — script to average student grades; Chapter 8.
gres — sed script for command line substitution command; Chapter 3.
index.edit — sed script for correcting index entries; Chapter 5.
index/ — subdirectory that contains index programs in Chapter 11.
invoke — nawk menu-based command generator; Chapter 10.
lookup — program to read glossary file and print definition; Chapter 8.
lotto — quick-pick lottery program; Chapter 9.
match — nawk program that outputs string matched by regular expresssion; Chapter 9.
phone — nawk program that looks up phone number; Chapter 8.
phones.data — data file for phone program.
phrase — sed script to match more than one word over more than one line; Chapter 6.
romanum — decimal to Roman numeral conversion; Chapter 8.
runsed — shell script to invoke sed; Chapter 4.
sedman — sed script to strip nroff'd man pages; Chapter 5.
soelim.awk — nawk script that simulates soelim program; Chapter 10.
spellcheck — shell script that involves spellcheck.awk; Chapter 11.
spellcheck.awk — nawk script for interactive spellchecker; Chapter 11.
words — awk program for stripping macros prior to word count; Chapter 10.

Preface

This book is about a set of uncommonly named UNIX utilities, **sed** and **awk**. These utilities have many things in common, including the use of regular expressions for pattern matching. Since pattern matching is such an important part of the use of these utilities, this book explains UNIX regular expression syntax very thoroughly. Because there is a natural progression in learning from **grep** to sed to awk, we will be covering all three programs, although the focus is on sed and awk.

Sed and awk are tools used by users, programmers, and system administrators —anyone working with text files. Sed, so called because it is a stream editor, is perfect for applying a series of edits to a number of files. Awk, named after its developers Aho, Weinberger, and Kernighan, is a programming language that permits easy manipulation of structured data and the generation of formatted reports. This book covers the original awk; the new awk, which became available as **nawk** starting with UNIX System V Release 3; and the Free Software Foundation GNU project's version of awk, **gawk**.

The focus of this book is on writing scripts for sed and awk that quickly solve an assortment of problems for the user. Many of these scripts could be called "quick-fixes." In addition, we'll cover scripts that solve larger problems that require more careful design and development.

Scope of this Handbook

Chapter 1, *Power Tools for Editing*, is an overview of the features and capabilities of sed and awk.

Chapter 2, *Understanding Basic Operations*, demonstrates the basic operations of sed and awk, showing a progression in functionality from sed to awk. Both share a similar command line syntax, accepting user instructions in the form of a script.

Chapter 3, *Understanding Regular Expression Syntax*, describes UNIX regular expression syntax in full detail. New users are often intimidated by these strange expressions, used for pattern matching. It is important to master regular expression syntax to get the most from sed and awk. The pattern-matching examples in this chapter largely rely on **grep** and **egrep**.

Chapter 4, *Writing Sed Scripts*, begins a three-chapter section on sed. This chapter covers the basic elements of writing a sed script using only a few sed commands. It also presents a shell script that simplifies invoking sed scripts.

Chapter 5, *Basic Sed Commands*, and Chapter 6, *Advanced Sed Commands*, divide the sed command set into basic and advanced commands. The basic commands are ones that parallel manual editing actions, while the advanced commands introduce simple programming capabilities. Among the advanced commands are those that manipulate the hold space, a set-aside temporary buffer.

Chapter 7, *Writing Scripts for Awk*, begins a four-chapter section on awk. This chapter presents the primary features of this scripting language. A number of scripts are explained, including one that modifies the output of the ls command.

Chapter 8, *Conditionals, Loops, and Arrays*, describes how to use common programming constructs such as conditionals, loops, and arrays.

Chapter 9, *Functions*, describes how to use awk's built-in functions as well as how to write user-defined functions (a feature introduced in new awk).

Chapter 10, *The Bottom Drawer*, covers a set of miscellaneous awk topics. It describes how to execute UNIX commands from an awk script and how to direct output to files and pipes. It presents **awkcc**, an awk-to-C translator. This chapter also offers some (meager) advice on debugging awk scripts.

Chapter 11, *Full-featured Scripts*, presents two longer, more complex awk scripts that together demonstrate nearly all the features of the language. The first script is an interactive spell checker. The second script processes and formats the index for a book or a master index for a set of books.

Chapter 12, *A Miscellany of Scripts*, presents a number of user-contributed scripts that show different styles and techniques of writing scripts for sed and awk.

Appendix A, *Sed Quick Reference*, is a quick reference describing sed's commands and command-line options.

Appendix B, *Awk Quick Reference*, is a quick reference to awk's command-line options and a full description of its scripting language.

Appendix C, *Supplement for Chapter 11*, presents the full listings for the **spellcheck.awk** script and the **masterindex** shell script described in Chapter 11, *Full-featured Applications*.

Availability of Sed and Awk

Sed and awk were part of UNIX's seventh edition and have been part of the standard distribution ever since. Sed has been unchanged since it was introduced.

In 1985, the authors of awk extended the language, adding many useful features. Unfortunately, this new version remained inside AT&T for several years. Now it is finally part of AT&T's System V as of Release 3.1. It can be found under the name of nawk, for new awk; the older version still exists under its original name. Otherwise, source code is available for a licensing fee from AT&T's UNIX Toolchest.* The Free Software Foundation GNU project's version of awk, gawk, implements all the features of the new awk. It is freely available, although not technically in the public domain. If your UNIX system does not offer nawk, I highly recommend that you obtain gawk.†

---

*The UNIX Toolchest offers source code for a variety of programs. There is a registration fee for non-System V licensees and programs are individually priced. You can reach the UNIX Toolchest (in New Jersey) via modem at 908-522-6900; login as *guest*. In Europe, the number is 44-1-567-7711 (London). In the Far East, dial 81-3-431-3670 (Tokyo). The UNIX Toolchest also carries **awkcc**, an awk-to-C translator for producing compiled programs from awk scripts.

†For information on obtaining gawk, contact the Free Software Foundation, Inc., 675 Massachusetts Avenue, Cambridge, MA 02139. The telephone number is 617-876-3296.

NOTE

In this book, you can assume that what is true for nawk is true for gawk, unless gawk is explicitly called out. Scripts written for nawk are 100 percent compatible with gawk. There are a few areas where gawk has introduced gawk-specific features; however, recent versions of nawk support many of these features, suggesting that the remaining differences are really very minor.

DOS Versions

egrep, sed, and awk are available for MS-DOS-based machines as part of the MKS Toolkit (Mortice Kern Systems, Inc., Ontario, Canada). Their implementation of awk supports the features of nawk.

The MKS Toolkit also includes the Korn Shell, which means that many shell scripts written for the Bourne shell on UNIX systems can be run on a PC. While most users of the MKS Toolkit have probably already discovered these tools in UNIX, we hope that the benefits of these programs will be obvious to PC users who have not ventured into UNIX.

We have used a PC on occasion because Ventura Publisher is a terrific formatting package. One of the reasons we like it is that we can continue to use **vi** to create and edit the text files and use sed for writing editing scripts. We have used sed to write conversion programs that translate **troff** macros codes into Ventura stylesheet tags. We have also used it to insert tags in batch mode. This can save having to tag manually repeated elements in a file.

Sed and awk are also useful for writing conversion programs that handle different file formats.

Other Sources of Information About Sed and Awk

For a long time, the main source of information on these utilities was two articles contained in Volume 2 of the *UNIX Programmer's Guide*. The article *awk—A Pattern Scanning and Processing Language* (September 1, 1978) was written by the language's three authors. In ten pages, it offers a brief tutorial and discusses several design and implementation issues. The article *SED—A Non-interactive Text Editor* (August 15, 1978) was written by Lee E. McMahon. It is a reference that gives a full description of each function and includes some useful examples (using Coleridge's *Xanadu* as sample input). Homogenized versions of both these articles are presently distributed with most UNIX systems.

In trade books, the most significant treatment of sed and awk appears in *The UNIX Programming Environment* by Brian W. Kernighan and Rob Pike

(Prentice-Hall, 1984). The chapter entitled "Filters" not only explains how these programs work but shows how they can work together to build useful applications.

The authors of awk collaborated on a book describing the enhanced version: *The AWK Programming Language* (Addison-Wesley, 1988). It contains many full examples and demonstrates the broad range of areas where awk can be applied. It follows in the style of the *UNIX Programming Environment*, which at times makes it too dense for some readers who are new users

Most general introductions to UNIX introduce sed and awk in a long parade of utilities. Of these books, Henry McGilton and Rachel Morgan's *Introducing the UNIX System* offers the best treatment of basic editing skills, including use of all UNIX text editors.

UNIX Text Processing (Hayden Books, 1987) by the author of this handbook and Tim O'Reilly, covers sed and awk in full, although we did not include the new version of awk. Readers of that book will find some parts that are the same as in this book, but in general a different approach has been taken here. Whereas in the textbook we treated sed and awk separately, expecting advanced users only to tackle awk, here we try to present both programs in relation to one another. They are different tools that can be used individually or together to provide interesting opportunities for text processing.

Sample Programs

The sample programs in this book were written and tested on a Mac IIci running A/UX 2.0 (UNIX System V Release 2) and a SparcStation 1 running SunOS 4.0. Programs requiring nawk were generally tested using gawk (2.10beta 07 Apr 1989) as well as nawk.

The full-length example programs in this book are available free of charge from UUNET (that is, except for UUNET's connect-time charges). If you have access to UUNET, you can retrieve the source code using **uucp** or **ftp**.

For uucp transfer, the filename is *~/published/oreilly/nutshell/sedawk/progs.tar.Z*. For ftp transfer, **cd** to */published/oreilly/nutshell/sedawk*, specify binary transfer and get */progs.tar.Z*. You will need to uncompress the files and extract them from the archive.

Obtaining the Example Programs

The example programs in this book are available electronically in a number of ways, including ftp and uucp. Use *ftp* if you are directly on the Internet. Use UUCP if you have a modem.

FTP

To use FTP, you need a machine with direct access to the Internet. A sample session is shown, with what you should type in boldface.

```
% ftp ftp.uu.net
Connected to ftp.uu.net.
220 FTP server (Version 6.21 Tue Mar 10 22:09:55 EST 1992) ready.
Name (ftp.uu.net:kismet): anonymous
331 Guest login ok, send domain style e-mail address as password.
Password: kismet@ora.com (use your user name and host here)
230 Guest login ok, access restrictions apply.
ftp> cd /published/oreilly/nutshell/sedawk
250 CWD command successful.
ftp> binary (Very important! You must specify binary transfer for compressed files.)
200 Type set to I.
ftp> get progs.tar.Z
200 PORT command successful.
150 Opening BINARY mode data connection for xlibprgs2.tar.Z.
226 Transfer complete.
ftp> quit
221 Goodbye.
%
```

If the file is a compressed tar archive, extract the files from the archive by typing:

```
% zcat progs.tar.Z | tar xf -
```

System V systems require that you add the *o* option to the tar command.

If *zcat* is not available on your system, use separate uncompress and tar commands.

UUCP

You can get the examples from UUNET whether you have an account or not. If you or your company has an account with UUNET, you will have a system with a direct UUCP connection to UUNET. The basic syntax for uucp is:

```
uucp source yourhost\!~/yourname/
```

The *source* is a pathname to the file on the remote machine. In this case, it is:

```
uunet\!~/published/oreilly/nutshell/sedawk/progs.tar.Z/
```

The backslashes can be omitted if you use the Bourne shell (*sh*) instead of *csh*. The file should appear some time later (up to a day or more) in the directory

*/usr/spool/uucppublic/**yourname***. If you don't have an account but would like one so that you can get electronic mail, then contact UUNET at 703-204-8000.

If you don't have a UUNET account, you can set up a UUCP connection to UUNET using the phone number 1-900-468-7727. As of this writing, the cost is 50 cents per minute. The charges will appear on your next telephone bill. The login name is "uucp" with no password. For example, an *L.sys/Systems* entry might look like:

```
uunet Any ACU 19200 1-900-468-7727 ogin:--ogin: uucp
```

Your entry may vary depending on your UUCP configuration. If you have a PEP-capable modem, make sure s50=255s111=30 is set before calling.

Once you've got the desired file, follow the directions under FTP to extract the files from the archive.

Conventions Used in this Handbook

The following conventions are used in this book:

Bold   is used for statements and functions, identifiers, and program names.

Italic   is used for file and directory names when they appear in the body of a paragraph as well as for data types and to emphasize new terms and concepts when they are introduced.

`Constant Width`   is used in examples to show the contents of files or the output from commands.

`Constant Bold`   is used in examples to show command lines and options that should be typed literally by the user.

Quotes   are used to identify a code fragment in explanatory text. System messages, signs, and symbols are quoted as well.

$ is the Bourne Shell prompt.

%   is the C Shell prompt.

[]   surrounds optional elements in a description of program syntax. (The brackets themselves should never be typed.)

Acknowledgements

To say that this book has been long anticipated is no understatement. I published three articles on awk in UNIX/World in the spring and summer of 1987, making the mistake of saying that these articles were from the upcoming Nutshell Handbook, "Sed & Awk." I proposed to Tim O'Reilly that I adapt the articles and create a book as a project I could work on at home shortly after the birth of my son, Benjamin. I thought I'd finish it in several months. Well, my son turned three recently, around the time I was completing the first draft. Cathy Brennan and the customer service representatives have been patiently handling requests for the book ever since the UNIX/World articles appeared. Cathy said that she even had people call to order the book, swearing it was available because they knew other people who had read it. I owe a debt of gratitude to her and her staff and to the readers I've kept waiting.

My thanks to Tim O'Reilly for creating a great company in which one can easily get sidetracked by a number of interesting projects. As editor, he pushed me to complete the book but would not allow it to be complete without his writing all over it. As usual, his suggestions made me work to improve the book.

Thanks to all the writers and production editors at O'Reilly & Associates, who presented interesting problems to be solved with sed and awk. Thanks to Ellie Cutler who was the production editor for the book and also wrote the index. Thanks to Lenny Muellner for allowing me to quote him throughout the book. Thanks as well to Sue Willing and Donna Woonteiler for their efforts in getting the book into print. Thanks to Chris Reilly who did the illustrations. Thanks to the individual contributors of the sed and awk scripts in Chapter 12. Thanks also to Kevin C. Castner, Tim Irvin, Mark Schalz, Alex Humez, Glenn Saito, Geoff Hagel, Tony Hurson, Jerry Peek, Mike Tiller, and Lenny Muellner, who sent me mail pointing out typos and errors.

Finally, dearest thanks to Nancy and Katie, Ben and Glenda.

We'd Like to Hear From You

To ask technical questions, report errors, or comment on the book, send email to:

bookquestions@ora.com (via the Internet)

To be put on the mailing list or request a catalog, send email to:

info@ora.com   (via the Internet)
uunet!ora!info   (via UUCP)

1

Power Tools for Editing

May You Solve Interesting Problems
A Stream Editor
A Pattern-matching Programming
    Language
Three Hurdles to Mastering Sed and Awk

My wife won't let me buy a power saw. She is afraid of an accident if I use one. So I rely on a hand saw for a variety of weekend projects like building shelves. However, if I made my living as a carpenter, I would have to use a power saw. The speed and efficiency provided by power tools would be essential to being productive.

For people who create and modify text files, sed and awk are power tools for editing. Most of the things that you can do with these programs can be done interactively with a text editor. However, using sed and awk can save many hours of repetitive work in achieving the same result.

Sed and awk are peculiar and it takes time to learn them, but the capabilities they provide can repay the learning many times over, especially if text editing is a normal part of your trade.

May You Solve Interesting Problems

The primary motivation for learning sed and awk is that they are useful for devising general solutions to text editing problems.* For some people, myself included, the satisfaction of solving a problem is the difference between work and drudgery. Given the choice of using **vi** or sed to make a series of repeated edits over a number of files, I will choose sed, simply because it makes the problem more interesting to me. I am refining a solution instead of repeating a series of keystrokes. Besides, once I accomplish my task, I congratulate myself on being clever. I feel like I have done a little bit of magic and spared myself some dull labor.

Initially, using sed and awk will seem like the long way to accomplish a task. After several attempts you may conclude that the task would have been easier to do manually. Be patient. You not only have to learn how to use sed and awk but you also need to learn to recognize situations where using them pays off. As you become more proficient, you will solve problems more quickly and solve a broader range of problems.

You will also begin to see opportunities to find general solutions to specific problems. There is a way of looking at a problem so you see it related to a class of problems. Then you can devise a solution that can be re-used in other situations.

Let me give you an example (without showing any program code). One of our books used a cross-referencing naming scheme in which the reference was defined and processed by our formatting software (**sqtroff**). In the text file, a reference to a chapter on error handling might be coded as follows:

```
\*[CHerrorhand]
```

"CHerrorhand" is the name given the reference and "*[" and "]" are calling sequences that distinguish the reference from other text. In a central file, the names used for cross references in the document are defined as **sqtroff** strings. For instance, "CHerrorhand" is defined to be "Chapter 16, Error Handling." (The advantage of using a symbolic cross-referencing scheme like this, instead of explicit referencing, is that if chapters are added or deleted or re-ordered, only the central file needs to be edited to reflect the new organization.) When the formatting software processes the document, the references are properly resolved and expanded.

---

*I suppose this section title is a combination of the Chinese proverb "May you live in interesting times" and what Tim O'Reilly once said to me, that someone will solve a problem if he finds the problem interesting.

The problem we recently faced was that we had to use the same files to create an online version of the book. Because our **sqtroff** formatting software would not be used, we needed some way to expand the cross references in the files. In other words, we did not want files containing "*[CHerrorhand]"; instead we wanted what "CHerrorhand" referred to.

There were three possible ways to solve this problem:

1. Use a text editor to search for all references and replace each of them with the appropriate literal string.

2. Use sed to make the edits. This is similar to making the edits manually, only faster.

3. Use awk to write a program that (a) reads the central file to make a list of reference names and their definitions, (b) reads the document searching for the reference calling sequence, and (c) looks up the name of the reference on the list and replaces it with its definition.

The first method is obviously time-consuming (and not very interesting!). The second method, using sed, has an advantage in that it creates a tool to do the job. It is pretty simple to write a sed script that looks for "*[CHerrorhand]" and replaces it with "Chapter 16, Error Handling," for instance. The same script can be used to modify each of the files for the document. The disadvantage is that the substitutions are hard-coded; that is, for each cross reference, you need to write a command that makes the replacement. The third method, using awk, builds a tool that works for *any* cross reference that follows this syntax. This script could be used to expand cross references in other books as well. It spares you from having to compile a list of specific substitutions. It is the most general solution of the three and designed for the greatest possible re-use as a tool.

Part of solving a problem is knowing which tool to build. There are times when a sed script is a better choice because the problem does not lend itself to, or demand, a more complex awk script. You have to keep in mind what kinds of applications are best-suited for sed and awk.

A Stream Editor

Sed is a "non-interactive" stream-oriented editor. It interprets a script that controls the actions that sed performs. It is stream-oriented because, like many UNIX programs, input flows through the program and is directed to standard output. (vi, for instance, is not stream-oriented. Nor are most DOS applications.) Input typically comes from a file but can be directed from the keyboard. Output goes to the terminal screen by default but can be captured in a file instead.

Sed offers capabilities that seem a natural extension of interactive text editing. For instance, it offers a search-and-replace facility that can be applied globally to a single file or a group of files. While you would not typically use sed to change a term that appears once in a particular file, you will find it very useful to make a series of changes across a number of files. Think about making 20 different edits in over 100 files in a matter of minutes, and you get an idea of how powerful sed can be.

Using sed is similar to writing simple shell scripts (or batch files in DOS). You specify a series of actions to be performed in sequence. Most of these actions could be done manually from within **vi**: replacing text, deleting lines, inserting new text, etc. The advantage of sed is that you can specify all editing instructions in one place and then execute them on a single pass through the file. You don't have to go into each file to make each change. Sed can also be used effectively to edit very large files that would be slow to edit interactively.

There are many opportunities to use sed in the course of creating and maintaining a document, especially when the document consists of individual chapters, each placed in a separate file. Typically, after a draft of a document has returned from review, there are a number of changes that can be applied to all files. For instance, during the course of a software documentation project, the name of the software or its components might change, and you have to track down and make these changes. With sed, this is a simple process.

Sed can be used to achieve consistency throughout a document. You can search for all the different ways a particular term might be used and make them all the same. You can use sed to insert special typesetting codes or symbols prior to formatting by **troff**. For instance, it can be used to replace quotation marks with the ASCII character codes for forward and back double quotes ("curly quotes" instead of "straight" quotes.)

Sed also has the unique ability to be used as an editing *filter*. In other words, you could process an input file and send the output to another program. For instance, you could use sed to analyze an uncoded text file and insert **troff** macros before directing the output to **troff** for formatting. It allows you to make edits on the fly, perhaps ones that are temporary.

We use sed to write numerous conversion programs—translating formatting codes in Scribe or TeX files into **troff**. We've also written conversion programs for PC word processing files, such as WordStar. Later on, we will look at a sed script that converts **troff** macros into stylesheet tags for use in Ventura Publisher. (Perhaps sed could be used to translate a program written in the syntax of one language to the syntax of another language.) Sun Microsystems recently released a conversion program converting SunView programs to XView, and the program largely consisted of sed scripts, converting the names of various functions.

Sed has a few rudimentary programming constructs that can be used to build more complicated scripts. It also has the ability to work on more than one line at a time, although this is not easy to do.

All but the simplest sed scripts are usually invoked from a "shell wrapper," a shell script that invokes sed and also contains the commands that sed executes. A shell wrapper is an easy way to name and execute a single-word command. The fact that sed is being used might be transparent to other users of the command. One example of such a shell wrapper is the script **phrase**, which we'll look at later in this book. It allows you to match a pattern that might fall over two lines, addressing a specific limitation of **grep**.

In summary, use sed:

1. To automate editing actions to be performed on one or more files.
2. To simplify the task of performing the same edits on multiple files.
3. To write conversion programs.

A Pattern-matching Programming Language

Identifying awk as a programming language scares some people away from it. If you are one of them, consider awk a different approach to problem solving, one in which you have a lot more control over what you want the computer to do.

Sed is easily seen as the flip side of interactive editing. A sed procedure corresponds closely enough to how you would apply the editing commands manually. Sed limits you to the methods you use in a text editor. Awk offers a more general model for processing a file.

A typical example of an awk program is one that transforms data into a formatted report. The data might be a log file generated by a UNIX program such as **uucp**, and the report might summarize the data in a format useful to a system administrator. Another example is a data processing application consisting of separate data entry and data retrieval programs. Data entry is the process of recording data in a structured way. Data retrieval is the process of extracting data from a file and generating a report.

The key to all of these operations is that the data has some kind of structure. Let me illustrate this by making the analogy to a bureau. A bureau consists of multiple drawers, and each drawer has a certain set of contents: socks in one drawer, underwear in another, and sweaters in a third drawer. Sometimes drawers have compartments allowing different kinds of things to be stored together. These are all structures that determine where things go—when you are sorting the laundry—and where things can be found—when you are getting dressed. Awk allows you to use the structure of a text file in writing the procedures for putting things in and taking things out.

Thus, the benefits of awk are best realized when the data has some kind of structure. A text file can be loosely or tightly structured. A chapter containing major and minor sections has some structure. We'll look at a script that extracts the section headings and numbers them to produce an outline. A table consisting of tab-separated items in columns might be considered very structured. You could use an awk script to re-order columns of data, or even change columns into rows and rows into columns.

Like sed scripts, awk scripts are typically invoked by means of a shell wrapper. This is a shell script that usually contains the command line that invokes awk as well as the script that awk interprets. Of course, simple one-line awk scripts can be entered from the command line.

Some of the features of awk are:

- Ability to view a text file as made up of records and fields in a textual database.
- Use of variables to manipulate the database.
- Use of arithmetic and string operators.
- Use of common programming constructs such as loops and conditionals.
- Ability to generate formatted reports.

With nawk, additional features make it easier to write larger scripts. Using nawk, you can:

- Define functions.
- Execute UNIX commands from a script.
- Process the result of UNIX commands.
- Process command-line arguments more gracefully.
- Work more easily with multiple input streams.

Because of these new features, awk now has the power and range that users might rely upon to do the kinds of tasks performed by shell scripts. In this book, you'll see examples of a menu-based command generator, an interactive spell checker, and an index processing program, all which use the special features of nawk.

The capabilities of awk extend the idea of text editing into computation, making it possible to perform a variety of data processing tasks, including analysis, extraction, and reporting of data. These are, indeed, the most common uses of awk but there are also many unusual applications: one person told me he had written a Lisp interpreter in awk and another had written a compiler!

Three Hurdles to Mastering Sed and Awk

There are a number of introductory UNIX books that will acquaint you with sed and awk. The goal of this book is to take you much further—to help you *master* sed and awk and to reduce the amount of time and effort that it takes you to reach that goal.

There are three hurdles on the way to mastering sed and awk. You must learn:

1. *How sed and awk work.*
    This is a relatively low hurdle to clear because, fortunately, sed and awk work in a very similar manner, based on the line editor **ed**. Chapter 2, *Understanding Basic Operations*, covers the mechanics of using sed and awk.

2. *To apply UNIX regular expression syntax.*
    Using UNIX regular expression syntax for pattern matching is common to both sed and awk, and many other UNIX programs. This can be a difficult hurdle for two reasons: the syntax is arcane, and though many people have some experience using regular expressions, few have persevered to master the complete syntax. The more facile you are in using this syntax, the easier sed and awk are to use. That is why we spend a good deal of time covering regular expressions up front in Chapter 3, *Understanding Regular Expression Syntax*.

3. *The knack of script writing.*
    This is the most difficult, rather like a series of high hurdles. Because of this, the bulk of the book is devoted to script writing. With sed, you have to learn a set of single-letter commands. With awk, you have to learn the statements of a programming language. To get the knack of script writing, though, you simply must pore over lots of examples and, of course, must try your hand at writing scripts yourself.

If you were running the high hurdles, the ability to clear the hurdles does not win the race—clearing them swiftly does. In writing scripts, learning the scripting command set or language is simply clearing the hurdle. Acquiring the ability to attack interesting problems with your scripts is running fast enough to compete.

2

Understanding Basic Operations

Awk, by Sed and Grep, out of Ed
Command-line Syntax
Using Sed
Using Awk
Using Sed and Awk Together

If you are starting out to learn sed and awk, you can benefit from looking at how much they have in common.

- They are invoked using similar syntax.
- They are both stream oriented, reading input from text files one at a time and directing the result to standard output.
- They use regular expressions for pattern matching.
- They allow the user to specify instructions in a script.

One reason they have so much in common is that their origins can be found in the same line editor, **ed**. In this chapter, we begin by taking a brief look at **ed** and show how sed and awk were logical steps towards the creation of a programmable editor.

Where sed and awk differ is in the kind of instructions that control the work that is done. Make no mistake—this is a major difference, and it affects the kinds of tasks that can best be performed with these programs.

This chapter looks at the command-line syntax of sed and awk and the basic structure of scripts. It also offers a tutorial, using a mailing list, that will give you a taste of script writing. It is valuable to see sed and awk scripts side-by-side before you concentrate on any one of them.

Awk, by Sed and Grep, out of Ed

You can trace the lineage of awk to sed and **grep**, and through those two programs to **ed**, the original UNIX line editor.

Have you ever used a line editor? If so, it will be much easier for you to understand the line orientation of sed and awk. If you have used **vi**, a full screen editor, then you are familiar with a number of commands that are derived from its underlying line editor, **ex**.

Let's look at some basic operations using the line editor **ed**. Don't worry—this is an exercise intended to help you learn sed and awk, not an attempt to convince you of the wonders of line editors. The **ed** commands that are shown in this exercise are identical to the **sed** commands you'll learn later on. Feel free to experiment with **ed** on your own to get a sense of how it works. (If you're already familiar with **ed**, feel free to skip to the next section.)

To use a line editor, you work on one line at a time. It is important to know what line you are positioned at in the file. When you open a file using **ed**, it displays the number of characters in the file and positions you at the last line.

```
% ed test
339
```

There is no prompt. If you enter a command that **ed** does not understand, it prints a question mark as an error message. You can specify the print command, **p**, to display the current line.

```
p
label on the first box.
```

By default, a command affects only the current line. To make an edit, you move to the line that you want to edit and then apply the command. To move to a line, you specify its *address*. An address might consist of a line number, a symbol indicating a specific position in the file, or a regular expression. You can go to the first line by entering the line number 1. Then you can enter the delete command to remove that line.

```
1
You might think of a regular expression
d
```

Entering "1" makes the first line the current line, displaying it on the screen. The delete command in ed is "d" and here it deletes the current line. Rather than moving to a line and then editing it, you can prefix an editing command with an address that indicates which line or range of lines are the object of the command. If you enter "1d", the first line would be deleted.

You can also specify a regular expression as an address. To delete a line containing the word "regular," you could issue this command:

```
/regular/d
```

where slashes delimit the regular expression and "regular" is the string you want to match. This command deletes the first line containing "regular" and makes the line following it the current line.

- Make sure you understand that the delete command deletes the whole line. It does not just delete the word "regular" on the line.

To delete *all* the lines that contain the regular expression, you'd prefix the command with the letter "g" for global.

```
g/regular/d
```

The global command makes all lines that match the regular expression the object of the specified command. The substitution command, **s**, in **ed** is:

[*address*]s/*pattern*/*replacement*/*flag*

pattern is a regular expression that matches a string in the current line to be replaced by *replacement*. For example, the following command replaces the first occurrence of "regular" with "complex" on the current line.

```
s/regular/complex/
```

No address is specified, so it affects only the first occurrence on the current line. It is an error if "regular" is not found on the current line. To look for multiple occurrences on the *same* line, you must specify "g" as a flag:

```
s/regular/complex/g
```

This command changes all occurrences on the current line. An address must be specified to direct this command to act upon more than the current line. The following substitution command specifies an address:

```
/regular/s/regular/complex/g
```

This command affects the first line that matches the address in the file. Remember, the first "regular" is an address and the second is a pattern to match for the substitution command. To make it apply to all lines, use the global command, putting "g" before the address.

```
g/regular/s/regular/complex/g
```

Now the substitution is made everywhere—all occurrences on all lines.

- Note the different meanings of "g." The "g" at the beginning is the global command that means make the changes on all lines matched by the address. The "g" at the end is a flag that means change each occurrence on a line, not just the first.

The address and the pattern need not be the same.

```
g/regular expression/s/regular/complex/g
```

On any line that contains the string "regular expression," replace "regular" with "complex". If the address and the pattern are the same, you can tell **ed** by specifying two consecutive delimiters (*//*).

```
g/regular/s//complex/g
```

In this example, "regular" is specified as the address and the pattern to be matched for substitution is the same. If it seems that we've covered these commands quickly and that there is a lot to absorb, don't worry. We will be covering these commands again later on.

The familiar UNIX utility **grep** is derived from the following global command in **ed**:

```
g/re/p
```

which stands for "global regular expression print." grep is a line-editing command that has been extracted from **ed** and made available as an external program. It is hard-wired to perform one editing command. It takes the regular expression as an argument on the command line and uses it as the address of lines to print. Here's an example, looking for lines matching "box":

```
% grep 'box' test
You are given a series of boxes, the first one labeled "A",
label on the first box.
```

It prints any lines matching the regular expression.

One more interesting feature of **ed** is the ability to *script* your edits, placing them in a separate file and directing them as input to the line editor. For instance, if a series of commands were put in a file named *ed-script*, the following command executes the script:

```
ed test < ed-script
```

This feature makes **ed** a programmable editor—that is, you can script any action that you might perform manually.

Sed was created as a special-purpose editor that was meant to execute scripts exclusively; unlike **ed**, it cannot be used interactively. Sed differs from **ed** primarily in that it is stream-oriented. By default, all of the input to sed passes through and goes to standard output. The input file itself is not changed. To actually make edits, you typically use the shell mechanism for output redirection, and when you are satisfied with the edits you've made, replace the original file with the modified version.

ed is not stream-oriented and changes are made to the file itself. An **ed** script must contain commands to save the file and quit the editor. It produces no output to screen, except what may be generated by a specific command.

The stream-orientation of sed has a major impact on how addressing is applied. In **ed**, a command without an address affects only the current line. Sed goes through the file, a line at a time, such that each line becomes the current line, and the commands are applied to it. The result is that sed applies a command without an address to every line in the file.

Look at the following substitution command:

```
s/regular/complex/
```

If you entered this command interactively in **ed**, you'd substitute "complex" for the first occurrence of "regular" on the current line. In an **ed** script, if this was the first command in the script, it would be applied only to the last line of the file (**ed**'s default current line). However, in a sed script, the same command applies to all lines. That is, sed commands are implicitly global. In sed, the previous example has the same result as the following global command in **ed**:

```
g/regular/s//complex/
```

This command also achieves the same result in both in an **ed** script and a sed script.

- Understanding the difference between current-line addressing in **ed** and global-line addressing in sed is very important. In **ed** you use addressing to *expand* the number of lines that are the object of a command; in sed, you use addressing to *restrict* the number of lines affected by a command.

Sed also was designed with a number of additional commands that support script writing. We will look at many of these commands in Chapter 6, *Advanced Sed Commands*.

Awk was developed as a programmable editor that, like sed, is stream-oriented and interprets a script of editing commands. Where awk departs from sed is in discarding the line-editor command set. It offers in its place a programming language modeled on the C language. The **print** statement replaces the "p" command, for example. The concept of addressing is carried over, such that:

```
/regular/ { print }
```

prints those lines matching "regular". The braces ({ }) surround a series of one or more statements that are applied to the same address.

The advantage of using a programming language in scripts is that it offers a lot more ways to control what the programmable editor can do. Awk offers conditional statements, loops, and other programming constructs.

One of the most distinctive features of awk is that it *parses*, or breaks up, each input line and makes individual words available for processing with a script. Thus, awk parses the input file into records and fields so you can refer to, and manipulate, these structures. (An editor such as **vi** also recognizes words, allowing you to move word by word, or make a word the object of an action, but these features can only be used interactively.)

Although awk was designed as a programmable editor, users found that awk scripts could do a wide range of other tasks as well. The authors of awk never imagined it would be used to write large programs. But, recognizing that awk was being used in this way, the authors revised the language, creating **nawk** to offer more support for writing larger programs and tackling general-purpose programming problems.

Command-line Syntax

You invoke sed and awk in much the same way. The command-line syntax is:

> *command [options] script filename*

Like almost all UNIX programs, sed and awk can take input from standard input and send the output to standard output. If a *filename* is specified, input is taken from that file. The output contains the processed information. Standard output is the terminal display screen, and typically the output from these programs is directed there. It can also be sent to a file, using I/O redirection in the shell, but it must not go to the same file that supplies input to the program.

The *options* for each command are different. We will demonstrate many of these options in upcoming sections. (The complete list of command-line options for sed can be found in Appendix A; the complete list of options for awk is in Appendix B.)

The *script* specifies what instructions to perform. If specified on the command line, the script must be surrounded in single quotes if it contains a blank space or any characters that might be interpreted by the shell (? and * for instance).

One option common to both sed and awk is the **-f** option that allows you to specify the name of a script file. That is, as a script grows in size, it is convenient to place it in a file. Thus, you might invoke sed as follows:

   sed -f *scriptfile inputfile*

Figure 2-1 shows the basic operation of sed and awk. Each program makes a copy of an input line, which is read one at a time from the input file, and executes each instruction specified in the script on that copy. Thus, changes made to the input line do not affect the actual input file.

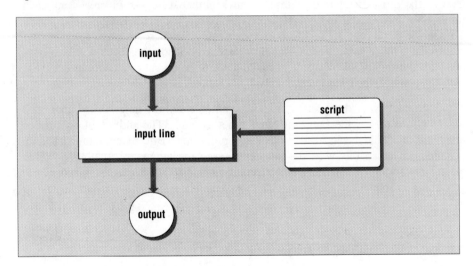

Figure 2-1. How sed and awk work

Scripting

A script is where you tell the program what to do. At least one line of instruction is required. Short scripts can be specified on the command line; longer scripts are usually placed in a file where they can be easily revised and tested. In writing a script, keep in mind the sequence in which instructions will be executed and how each instruction changes the input line.

In sed and awk, each instruction has two parts: a *pattern* and a *procedure*. The pattern is a regular expression delimited with slashes (/). A procedure specifies one or more actions to be performed.

As each line of input is read, the program reads the first instruction in the script and checks the *pattern* against the current line. If there is no match, the *procedure* is ignored and the next instruction is read. If there is a match, then the action or actions specified in the *procedure* are followed. All of the instructions are read, not just the first instruction that matches the input line.

When all the applicable instructions have been interpreted and applied for a single line, sed outputs the line and repeats the cycle for each input line.

The contents of a procedure are very different in sed and awk. In sed, the procedure consists of editing commands like those used in the line editor. Most commands consist of a single letter.

In awk, the procedure consists of programming statements and functions. A procedure must be surrounded by braces.

In the sections that follow, we'll look at a few scripts that process a sample mailing list.

Sample Mailing List

In the upcoming sections, the examples use a sample file, named *list*. It contains a list of names and addresses, as shown below.

```
$ cat list
John Daggett, 341 King Road, Plymouth MA
Alice Ford, 22 East Broadway, Richmond VA
Orville Thomas, 11345 Oak Bridge Road, Tulsa OK
Terry Kalkas, 402 Lans Road, Beaver Falls PA
Eric Adams, 20 Post Road, Sudbury MA
Hubert Sims, 328A Brook Road, Roanoke VA
Amy Wilde, 334 Bayshore Pkwy, Mountain View CA
Sal Carpenter, 73 6th Street, Boston MA
```

If you like, create this file on your system or use a similar one of your own making. Because many of the examples in this chapter are short and interactive, you can enter them at a terminal and verify the results.

Using Sed

There are two ways to invoke sed: either you specify your editing instructions on the command line or you put them in a file and supply the name of the file.

Specifying Simple Instructions

You can specify simple editing commands on the command line.

> **sed** [-e] *'instruction' file*

The -e option is necessary only when you are supplying more than one instruction on the command line. It tells sed to interpret the next argument as an instruction. When there is a single instruction, sed is able to make that determination on its own. Let's look at some examples.

Using the sample input file, *list*, the following example uses the s command for substitution to replace "MA" with "Massachusetts".

```
% sed 's/MA/Massachusetts/' list
John Daggett, 341 King Road, Plymouth Massachusetts
Alice Ford, 22 East Broadway, Richmond VA
Orville Thomas, 11345 Oak Bridge Road, Tulsa OK
Terry Kalkas, 402 Lans Road, Beaver Falls PA
Eric Adams, 20 Post Road, Sudbury Massachusetts
Hubert Sims, 328A Brook Road, Roanoke VA
Amy Wilde, 334 Bayshore Pkwy, Mountain View CA
Sal Carpenter, 73 6th Street, Boston Massachusetts
```

Three lines are affected by the instruction but all lines are displayed.

Enclosing the instruction in single quotes is not required in all cases but you should get in the habit of always doing it. The enclosing single quotes prevent the shell from interpreting special characters or blank spaces found in the editing instruction. (The shell uses spaces to determine individual arguments submitted to a program; shell metacharacters are expanded before the command is invoked.)

For instance, the first example could have been entered without them but in the next example they are required, since the substitution command contains blank spaces:

```
% sed 's/ MA/, Massachusetts/' list
John Daggett, 341 King Road, Plymouth, Massachusetts
Alice Ford, 22 East Broadway, Richmond VA
Orville Thomas, 11345 Oak Bridge Road, Tulsa OK
Terry Kalkas, 402 Lans Road, Beaver Falls PA
Eric Adams, 20 Post Road, Sudbury, Massachusetts
Hubert Sims, 328A Brook Road, Roanoke VA
Amy Wilde, 334 Bayshore Pkwy, Mountain View CA
Sal Carpenter, 73 6th Street, Boston, Massachusetts
```

In order to place a comma between the city and state, the instruction replaced the space before the two-letter abbreviation with a comma and a space.

There are three ways to specify multiple instructions on the command line:

1. Separate instructions with a semicolon.

    ```
    sed 's/ MA/, Massachusetts/; s/ PA/, Pennsylvania/' list
    ```

2. Precede each instruction by -e.   *multiple commands*

    ```
    sed -e 's/ MA/, Massachusetts/' -e 's/ PA/, Pennsylvania/' list
    ```

3. Use the multi-line entry capability of the Bourne shell. Press RETURN after entering a single quote and a secondary prompt (>) will be displayed for multi-line input.

    ```
    % sed '
    > s/ MA/, Massachusetts/
    > s/ PA/, Pennsylvania/
    > s/ CA/, California/' list
    John Daggett, 341 King Road, Plymouth, Massachusetts
    Alice Ford, 22 East Broadway, Richmond VA
    Orville Thomas, 11345 Oak Bridge Road, Tulsa OK
    Terry Kalkas, 402 Lans Road, Beaver Falls, Pennsylvania
    Eric Adams, 20 Post Road, Sudbury, Massachusetts
    Hubert Sims, 328A Brook Road, Roanoke VA
    Amy Wilde, 334 Bayshore Pkwy, Mountain View, California
    Sal Carpenter, 73 6th Street, Boston, Massachusetts
    ```

This technique will not work in the C shell. Instead, use semicolons at the end of each instruction, and you can enter commands over multiple lines by ending each line with a backslash. (Or, you could temporarily go into the Bourne shell by entering **sh** and then type the command.)

In the example above, changes were made to five lines and, of course, all lines were displayed. Remember that nothing has changed in the input file.

Command Garbled

The syntax of a sed command can be detailed, and it is easy to make a typing mistake or omit a required element. Notice what happens when incomplete syntax is entered:

```
$ sed -e 's/MA/Massachusetts' list
sed: command garbled: s/MA/Massachusetts
```

Sed will usually display any line that it cannot execute, but it does not tell you what is wrong with the command. In this instance, a slash, which marks the search and replacement portions of the command, is missing at the end of the substitute command.

Script Files

It is not practical to enter longer editing scripts on the command line. That is why it is usually best to create a script file that contains the editing instructions. The editing script is simply a list of sed commands that are executed in the order in which they appear. This form, using the **-f** option, requires that you specify the name of the script file on the command line.

> sed **-f** *scriptfile file*

All the editing commands that we want executed are placed in a file. We follow a convention of creating temporary script files named **sedscr**.

```
$ cat sedscr
s/ MA/, Massachusetts/
s/ PA/, Pennsylvania/
s/ CA/, California/
s/ VA/, Virginia/
s/ OK/, Oklahoma/
```

The following command reads all of the substitution commands in **sedscr** and applies them to each line in the input file *list*:

```
$ sed -f sedscr list
John Daggett, 341 King Road, Plymouth, Massachusetts
Alice Ford, 22 East Broadway, Richmond, Virginia
Orville Thomas, 11345 Oak Bridge Road, Tulsa, Oklahoma
Terry Kalkas, 402 Lans Road, Beaver Falls, Pennsylvania
Eric Adams, 20 Post Road, Sudbury, Massachusetts
Hubert Sims, 328A Brook Road, Roanoke, Virginia
Amy Wilde, 334 Bayshore Pkwy, Mountain View, California
Sal Carpenter, 73 6th Street, Boston, Massachusetts
```

Once again, the result is a passing fancy, displayed on the terminal screen. No change is made to the input file.

If a sed script can be used again, you should rename the script and save it. Scripts of proven value can be maintained in a personal or system-wide library.

Saving Output

Unless you are redirecting the output of sed to another program, you will want to capture the output in a file. This is done by specifying one of the shell's I/O redirection symbols followed by the name of a file:

```
$ sed -f sedscr list > newlist
```

Do not redirect the output to the file you are editing or you will clobber it. (The ">" redirection operator zeroes the file before anything else.) If you want the output file to replace the input file, you can do it as a separate step, using the **mv** command. But you better be sure your editing script has worked properly before you overwrite the original.

In Chapter 4, *Writing Sed Scripts*, we will look at a shell script named **runsed** that automates the process of creating a temporary file and using **mv** to overwrite the original file.

Suppressing Automatic Display of Input Lines

The default operation of sed is to output every input line. The **-n** option is used to suppress passing through each line of input, whether or not it has been modified. When specifying this option, each instruction must contain a print command, **p**, to produce output. Look at the following example.

```
$ sed -n -e 's/MA/Massachusetts/p' list
John Daggett, 341 King Road, Plymouth Massachusetts
Eric Adams, 20 Post Road, Sudbury Massachusetts
Sal Carpenter, 73 6th Street, Boston Massachusetts
```

Compare this output to the first example in this section. Here, only the lines that were affected by this command were printed.

Summary of Options

Table 2-1 summarizes the sed command-line options.

Table 2-1: Command Line Options for Sed

Option	Description
-e	Editing instruction follows.
-f	Filename of script follows.
-n	Suppress automatic output of input lines.

Using Awk

Like sed, awk executes a set of instructions for each line of input. You can specify instructions on the command line or create a script file. For command lines, the syntax is:

awk *'instructions' files*

Input is read a line at a time from one or more *files* or from standard input. The *instructions* must be enclosed in single quotes to protect them from the shell. (Instructions always contain curly braces which are interpreted as special characters by the shell.) Multiple command lines can be entered in the same way as shown for sed: separating commands with semicolons or using the multi-line input capability of the Bourne shell.

Awk programs are usually placed in a file where they can be tested and modified. The syntax for invoking awk with a script file is:

awk -f *'script' files*

The -f option works the same way as it does with sed.

While awk instructions have the same structure as sed, consisting of *pattern* and *procedure* sections, the procedures themselves are quite different. Here is where awk looks less like an editor and more like a programming language. There are statements and functions instead of one- or two-character command sequences. For instance, you use the **print** statement to print the value of an expression or to print the contents of the current input line.

Awk, in the usual case, interprets each input line as a record and each word on that line, delimited by blank spaces or tabs, as a field. One or more consecutive blank spaces are counted as a single delimiter. Awk allows you to reference these fields, either in patterns or procedures. $0 represents the entire input line. $1, $2, ... refer to the position of individual fields on the input line.

Normally, awk takes a newline to indicate a new record and a blank space or tab to delimit a field. These defaults can be changed. Awk splits the input record before the script is applied. Let's look at a few examples, using the sample input file *list*.

The first example contains a single instruction that prints the first field of each line in the input file.

```
$ awk '{print $1}' list
John
Alice
Orville
Terry
Eric
Hubert
Amy
Sal
```

"$1" is a special variable that references the value of the first field on each input line. Because there is no pattern specified, the print statement is applied to all lines. In the next example, a pattern "/MA/" is specified but there is no procedure. The default action is to print each line that matches the pattern.

```
$ awk '/MA/' list
John Daggett, 341 King Road, Plymouth MA
Eric Adams, 20 Post Road, Sudbury MA
Sal Carpenter, 73 6th Street, Boston MA
```

Three lines are printed. As mentioned in the first chapter, an awk program can be used more like a query language, extracting useful information from a file. We might say that the pattern placed a condition on the selection of records to be included in a report, namely that they must contain the string "MA". Now we can also specify what portion of a record to include in the report. The next example uses a **print** statement to limit the output to the first field of each record.

```
$ awk '/MA/{print $1}' list
John
Eric
Sal
```

It helps to understand the above instruction if we try to read it aloud: *Print the first word of each line containing the string "MA"*. We can say "word" because by default awk separates the input into fields using blanks or tabs as the field separator.

In the next example, we use the **-F** option to change the field separator to a comma. This allows us to retrieve any of three fields: the full name, the street address, and the city and state.

```
$ awk -F, '/MA/{print $1}' list
John Daggett
Eric Adams
Sal Carpenter
```

Do not confuse the **-F** option to change the field separator with the **-f** option to specify the name of a script file.

In the next example, we print each field on its own line. Multiple commands are separated by semicolons.

```
$ awk -F, '{print $1; print $2; print $3}' list
John Daggett
 341 King Road
 Plymouth MA
Alice Ford
 22 East Broadway
 Richmond VA
Orville Thomas
 11345 Oak Bridge Road
 Tulsa OK
Terry Kalkas
 402 Lans Road
 Beaver Falls PA
Eric Adams
 20 Post Road
 Sudbury MA
Hubert Sims
 328A Brook Road
 Roanoke VA
Amy Wilde
 334 Bayshore Pkwy
 Mountain View CA
Sal Carpenter
 73 6th Street
 Boston MA
$
```

Our examples using sed actually changed the content of incoming data. Our examples using awk rearrange the data.

Bailing Out

The following message, seen on unsuccessful attempts to execute an awk program, will become quite a familiar sight:

```
awk: syntax error near line 2
awk: bailing out near line 2
```

This message can be caused by any of the following:

- Not enclosing a procedure within braces ({ }).
- Not surrounding the instructions within apostrophes ('').
- Not enclosing regular expressions within slashes (//).

Nawk tends to be more helpful than awk in pointing to the specific source of the problem.

Summary of Options

Table 2-2 summarizes the awk command-line options.

Table 2-2: Command Line Options for Awk

Option	Description
-f	Filename of script follows.
-F	Change field separator.
-v	*var=value* follows (nawk).

Nawk introduced a -v option for specifying parameters on the command line. We discuss this option in Chapter 7, *Writing Scripts for Awk*.

Using Sed and Awk Together

In UNIX, pipes can be used to pass the output from one program as input to the next program. Let's look at a few examples that combine sed and awk to produce a report. The sed script that replaced the postal abbreviation of a state with its full name is general enough that it might be used again as a script file named **nameState**:

```
$ cat nameState
s/ CA/, California/
s/ MA/, Massachusetts/
s/ OK/, Oklahoma/
s/ PA/, Pennsylvania/
s/ VA/, Virginia/
```

Of course, you'd want to handle all states, not just five, and if you were running it on documents other than mailing lists, you should make sure that it does not make unwanted replacements.

The output for this program, using the input file *list*, is the same as we have already seen. In the next example, the output produced by **nameState** is piped to an awk program that extracts the name of the state from each record.

```
$ sed -f nameState list | awk -F, '{print $4}'
Massachusetts
Virginia
Oklahoma
Pennsylvania
Massachusetts
Virginia
California
Massachusetts
$
```

The awk program is processing the output produced by the sed script. Remember that the sed script replaces the abbreviation with a comma and the full name of the state. In effect, it splits the third field containing the city and state into two fields. "$4" references the fourth field.

What we are doing here could be done completely in sed, but probably with more difficulty and less generality. Also, with the new version of awk, which allows you to replace the string you match, you could achieve this result entirely with an awk script.

While the result of this program is not very useful, it could be passed to sort | **uniq -c**, which would sort the states into an alphabetical list with a count of the number of occurrences of each state.

Now we are going to do something more interesting. We want to produce a report that sorts the names by state and lists the name of the state followed by the name of the person residing in that state. The following example contains a listing for the **byState** program.

```
awk -F, '{
    print $4 ", " $0
    }' $* |
sort |
awk -F, '
$1 == LastState {
    print "\t" $2
    }
$1 != LastState {
    LastState = $1
    print $1
    print "\t" $2 }'
```

This shell script has three parts. The program invokes awk to produce input for the **sort** program and then invokes awk again to test the sorted input and determine if the name of the state in the current record is the same as the previous record. Let's see the script in action:

```
% sed -f nameState list | byState
California
        Amy Wilde
Massachusetts
        Eric Adams
        John Daggett
        Sal Carpenter
Oklahoma
        Orville Thomas
Pennsylvania
        Terry Kalkas
Virginia
        Alice Ford
        Hubert Sims
$
```

The names are sorted by state. This is a typical example of using awk to generate a report from structured data.

To examine how the **byState** program works, let's look at each of its parts separately. It is designed to read input from the **nameState** program and expects "$4" to be the name of the state. Let's look at the output produced by the first line of the program:

```
% sed -f nameState list | awk -F, '{print $4 ", " $0}'
Massachusetts, John Daggett, 341 King Road, Plymouth, Massachusetts
Virginia, Alice Ford, 22 East Broadway, Richmond, Virginia
Oklahoma, Orville Thomas, 11345 Oak Bridge Road, Tulsa, Oklahoma
Pennsylvania, Terry Kalkas, 402 Lans Road, Beaver Falls, Pennsylvania
Massachusetts, Eric Adams, 20 Post Road, Sudbury, Massachusetts
Virginia, Hubert Sims, 328A Brook Road, Roanoke, Virginia
California, Amy Wilde, 334 Bayshore Pkwy, Mountain View, California
Massachusetts, Sal Carpenter, 73 6th Street, Boston, Massachusetts
```

The **sort** program, by default, sorts lines in alphabetical order, looking at characters from left to right. In order to sort records by state, and not names, we insert the state as a sort key at the beginning of the record. Now the **sort** program can do its work for us. (Notice that using the **sort** utility saves us from having to write sort routines inside awk.)

The second time awk is invoked we perform a programming task. The script looks at the first field of each record (the state) to determine if it is the same as the previous record. If it is not the same (line 4), the name of the state is printed followed by the person's name. If it is the same (line 5), then only the person's name is printed.

```
$1 != LastState {
    LastState = $1
    print $1
    print "\t" $2 }
$1 == LastState {
    print "\t" $2
    }'
```

There are a couple of significant things to look at here, including the assignment of a variable, the testing of the first field of each input line to see if it contains a variable string, and the printing of a tab to align the output data. Note that we are able to test a variable before we assign it. This is a small script, but you'll see the same kind of routine used to compare index entries in a much larger indexing program in Chapter 11, *Full-featured Applications*. However, at this point, don't worry too much about understanding what each statement is doing. Our point here is just to give you an overview of what sed and awk can do.

In this chapter, we have covered the basic operations of sed and awk. We have looked at important command-line options and introduced you to scripting. In the next chapter, we are going to look at regular expressions, something both programs use to match patterns in the input.

3

Understanding Regular Expression Syntax

That's an Expression
A Line Up of Characters
I Never Metacharacter I Didn't Like

When my young daughter is struggling to understand the meaning of an idiomatic expression, such as "Someone let the cat out of the bag," before I tell her what it means, I have to tell her that it's an *expression*, that she's not to interpret it literally. (As a consequence, she also uses "That's just an expression" to qualify her own remarks, especially when she is unsure about what she has just said.)

An expression, even in computer terminology, is not something to be interpreted literally. It is something that needs to be evaluated. An expression is descriptive of a result.

In this chapter, we are going to look at regular expression syntax. A regular expression describes a pattern or a particular sequence of characters, although not necessarily specifying characters literally.

While regular expressions are a basic part of UNIX, not everyone has a complete understanding of the syntax. In fact, it can be quite confusing to look at an expression such as:

```
^  *.*
```

which uses *metacharacters* or special symbols to match a line with one or more leading blanks.

If you use any UNIX text editor on a routine basis, you are probably somewhat familiar with regular expression syntax. **grep**, sed and awk all use regular expressions. However, not all of the metacharacters used in regular expression syntax are available for all three programs. The basic set of metacharacters were introduced with the **ed** line editor, and made available in **grep**. Sed uses the same set of metacharacters. Later a program named **egrep** was introduced and it offered an *extended* set of metacharacters. Awk uses the same set of metacharacters as **egrep**.

To understand regular expression syntax, you have to learn the functions performed by various metacharacters. But you also have to see many examples of them working in various combinations. That is our approach in this chapter, to introduce each metacharacter and provide a lot of examples, that for the most part use **grep**, and its cousin, **egrep**, to demonstrate practical applications.

If you already understand regular expression syntax, feel free to skip this chapter. A complete listing of regular expression metacharacters can be found in Table 3-1, as well as in Appendix A for sed and Appendix B for awk.

That's an Expression

You are probably familiar with the kinds of expressions that a calculator interprets. Look at the following arithmetic expression:

```
2+4
```

"Two plus four" consists of several constants or literal values and an operator. A calculator program must recognize, for instance, that "2" is a numeric constant and that the plus sign represents an operator, not to be interpreted as the "+" character.

An expression tells the computer how to produce a result. Although it is the result of "two plus four" that we really want, we don't simply tell the computer to return a six. We instruct the computer to evaluate the expression and return a value.

An expression can be more complicated than "2+4"; in fact, it might consist of multiple simple expressions, such as the following:

```
2 + 3 * 4
```

A calculator normally evaluates an expression from left to right. However, certain operators have precedence over others: that is, they will be performed first. Thus, the above expression will evaluate to 14 and not 20 because multiplication takes precedence over addition. Precedence can be overridden by placing the simple expression in parentheses. Thus, (2+3)*4 or "the sum of two plus three times four" will evaluate to 20. The parentheses are symbols that instruct the calculator to change the order in which the expression is evaluated.

A regular expression, by contrast, is descriptive of a pattern or sequence of characters. Concatenation is the basic operation implied in every regular expression. That is, a pattern matches adjacent characters. Look at the following example of a regular expression:

```
ABE
```

Each literal character is a regular expression that matches only that single character. This expression describes an "A followed by a B then followed by an E" or simply "the string ABE". The term "string" means each character concatenated to the one preceding it. That a regular expression describes a *sequence* of characters can't be emphasized enough. (Novice users are inclined to think in higher-level units such as words, and not individual characters.) Regular expressions are case-sensitive; "A" does not match "a".

Programs such as **grep** that accept regular expressions must first evaluate the syntax of the regular expression to produce a pattern. They then read the input line-by-line trying to match the pattern. An input line is a string, and to see if a string matches the pattern, a program compares the first character in the string to the first character of the pattern. If there is a match, it compares the second character in the string to the second character of the pattern. Whenever it fails to make a match, it compares the next character in the string to the first character of the pattern. Figure 3-1 illustrates this process, trying to match the pattern "ABE" on an input line.

A regular expression is not limited to literal characters. There is, for instance, a metacharacter—the dot (.)—that can be used as a "wildcard" to match any single character. You can think of this wildcard as analogous to a blank tile in Scrabble™ where it means any letter. Thus, we can specify the regular expression

"A.E" and it will match "ACE," "ABE", and "ALE". It will match any character in the position following "A".

The metacharacter "*", the asterisk, is used to match zero or more occurrences of the *preceding* regular expression, which typically is a single character. You may be familiar with "*" as a *shell* metacharacter, where it means "one or more characters." But that meaning is very different from "*" in a regular expression. By itself, the asterisk metacharacter does not match anything; it modifies what goes before it. The regular expression ".*" matches any number of metacharacters, whereas in the shell, "*" has that meaning. (For instance, in the shell, ls * will list all the files in the current directory.) The regular expression "A.*E" matches any string that matches "A.E" but it will also match any number of characters between "A" and "E": "AIRPLANE," "A FINE," "AFFABLE," or "A LONG WAY HOME," for example.

If you understand the difference between "." and "*" in regular expressions, you already know about the two basic types of metacharacters: those that can be evaluated to a single character, and those that modify how characters that precede it are evaluated.

It should also be apparent that by use of metacharacters you can expand or limit the possible matches. You have more control over what is matched and what is not.

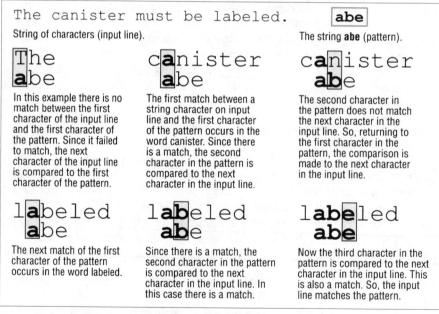

Figure 3-1. Interpreting a regular expression

A Line Up of Characters

We have seen two basic elements in an expression:

1. A value expressed as a literal or a variable.

2. An operator.

A regular expression is made up of these same elements. Any character, except those listed as metacharacters in Table 3-1, is interpreted as a literal that matches only itself.

Table 3-1. Summary of Metacharacters

Special Characters	Usage
.	Matches any *single* character except *newline*.
*	Matches any number (including zero) of the single character (including a character specified by a regular expression) that immediately precedes it.
[...]	Matches any *one* of the class of characters enclosed between the brackets. A circumflex (ˆ) as first character inside brackets reverses the match to all characters except newline and those listed in the class. A hyphen (-) is used to indicate a range of characters. The close bracket (]) as the first character in class is a member of the class. All other metacharacters lose their meaning when specified as members of a class.
ˆ	First character of regular expression, matches the beginning of the line.
$	As last character of regular expression, matches the end of the line.
\{n,m\}	Matches a range of occurrences of the single character (including a character specified by a regular expression) that immediately precedes it. \{n\} will match exactly n occurrences, \{n,\} will match at least n occurrences, and \{n,m\} will match any number of occurrences between n and m. (sed and **grep** only.)
\	Escapes the special character that follows.

Extended Metacharacters (egrep and awk)	
Special Characters	**Usage**
+	Matches one or more occurrences of the preceding regular expression.
?	Matches zero or one occurrences of the preceding regular expression.
|	Specifies that either the preceding or following regular expression can be matched.
()	Groups regular expressions.

Metacharacters have a special meaning in regular expressions, much the same way as "+" and "*" have special meaning in arithmetic expressions. Several of the metacharacters (+ ? () |) are available only as part of the extended set used by programs such as **egrep** and awk. We will look at what each metacharacter does in upcoming sections, beginning with the backslash.

The Ubiquitous Backslash

The backslash (\) metacharacter transforms metacharacters into ordinary characters. It forces the literal interpretation of any metacharacter such that it will match itself. For instance, the dot (.) is a metacharacter that needs to be escaped with a backslash if you want to match a period. This regular expression matches a period followed by three spaces.

```
\.□□□
```

A square box (□) is used to make blank spaces visible in our examples.

The backslash is typically used to match **troff** requests or macros that begin with a dot.

```
\.nf
```

You can also use the backslash to escape the backslash. For instance, the font change request in **troff** is \f. To search for lines containing this request, you'd use the following regular expression:

```
\\f
```

In addition, sed uses the backslash to cause a group of ordinary characters to be interpreted as metacharacters, as shown in Figure 3-2.

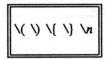

Figure 3-2. Escaped metacharacters in sed

A Wildcard

The *wildcard* metacharacter, or dot (.), might be considered equivalent to a variable. A variable represents any value in an arithmetic expression. In a regular expression, a dot (.) is a wildcard that represents any character except the newline.

Given that we are describing a sequence of characters, the wildcard metacharacter allows you to specify a position that any character can fill.

For instance, if we were searching a file containing a discussion of the Intel family of microprocessors, the following regular expression:

```
80.86
```

would match lines containing references to "80286" or "80386". To match a decimal point or a period, you must escape the dot with a backslash.

It is seldom useful to match just any character at the beginning or end of a pattern. Therefore, the wildcard character is usually preceded and followed by a literal character or other metacharacter. For example, the following regular expression might be written to search for references to chapters:

```
Chapter .
```

It searches for "the string 'Chapter' followed by any character." In a search, this expression would turn up virtually the same matches as the fixed string pattern "Chapter". Look at the following example:

```
% grep 'Chapter .' sample
you will find several examples in Chapter 9.
"Quote me 'Chapter and Verse'," she said.
Chapter Ten
```

Searching for the string "Chapter" as opposed to "Chapter ." would have matched all of the same lines. However, there is one case that would be different—if "Chapter" appeared at the end of a line. The wildcard does not match the newline, so "Chapter ." would not match that line, while the fixed-string pattern would match the line.

Writing Regular Expressions

For all practical purposes, you can rely on a program to produce the correct result. However, that doesn't mean the program always works correctly as far as you are concerned. Most of the time, you can bet that if a program does not produce the output that you expected, the real problem (putting aside input or syntax errors) is how you described what you wanted.

In other words, the place to look to correct the problem is the expression where you described the result you wanted. Either the expression is incomplete or the expression is improperly formulated. For instance, if a program evaluates the following expression:

```
WEEKLY.SALARY*52=PAY
```

and knows the values of these variables, it will calculate the correct result. But someone might object that the formula did not account for sales people, who also receive a commission. To describe this instance, the expression would need to be re-formulated as:

```
WEEKLY.SALARY*52+COMMISSION=PAY
```

You could say that whoever wrote the first expression did not fully understand the scope of the problem and thus, did not describe it well. It is important to know just how detailed a description must be. If you ask someone to bring you a book, and there are multiple books in view, you need to describe more specifically the book that you want (or be content with an indeterminate selection process).

The same is true with regular expressions. What makes regular expressions difficult to write is that you have to learn how to describe patterns and recognize the context in which they appear. Writing regular expressions involves more than learning the mechanics of regular expressions. It involves recognizing the level of description that is necessary in a regular expression, based on the context in which the pattern will be applied.

A program such as **grep** is simple and easy to use. Understanding the elements of regular expressions is not all so hard, either. Regular expressions allow you to write simple or complex descriptions of patterns. However, what makes writing regular expressions difficult (and interesting) is the complexity of the application: the variety of occurrences or contexts in which a pattern appears. This complexity is inherent in language itself, just as you can't always understand an expression by looking up each word in the dictionary.

The process of writing a regular expression involves three steps:

1. Knowing what it is you want to match and how it might appear in the text.
2. Writing a pattern to describe what you want to match.
3. Testing the pattern to see what it matches.

This process is virtually the same kind of process that a programmer follows to develop a program. Step 1 might be considered the specification, which should reflect an understanding of the problem to be solved as well as how to solve it. Step 2 is analogous to the actual coding of the program, and Step 3 involves running the program and testing it against the specification. Steps 2 and 3 form a loop that is repeated until the program works satisfactorily.

Testing your description of what you want to match ensures that the description works as expected. It usually uncovers a few surprises. Carefully examining the results of a test, comparing the output against the input, will greatly improve your understanding of regular expressions. You might consider evaluating the results of a pattern matching operation as follows:

Hits	*The lines that I wanted to match.*
Misses	*The lines that I didn't want to match.*
Misses that should be hits	*The lines that I didn't match but wanted to match.*
Hits that should be misses	*The lines that I matched but didn't want to match.*

Trying to perfect your description of a pattern is something that you work at from opposite ends: you try to eliminate the "hits that should be misses" by limiting the possible matches and you try to capture the "misses that should be hits" by expanding the possible matches.

The difficulty is especially apparent when you must describe patterns using fixed strings. Each character you remove from the fixed-string pattern increases the number of possible matches. For instance, while searching for the string "what", you determine that you'd like to match "What" as well. The only fixed-string pattern that will match "What" and "what" is "hat", the longest string common to both. It is obvious, though, that searching for "hat" will produce unwanted matches. Each character you add to a fixed-string pattern decreases the number of possible matches. The string "them" is going to produce fewer matches than the string "the".

Using metacharacters in patterns provides greater flexibility in extending or narrowing the range of matches. Metacharacters, used in combination with literals or other metacharacters, can be used to expand the range of matches while still eliminating the matches that you do not want.

Character Classes

A character class is a refinement of the wildcard concept. Instead of matching *any* character at a specific position, we can list the characters to be matched. The square bracket metacharacters ([]) enclose the list of characters, any of which can occupy a single position.

Character classes are useful for dealing with uppercase and lowercase letters, for instance. If "what" might appear with either an initial capital letter or a lower-case letter, you can specify:

```
[Ww]hat
```

This regular expression can match "what" or "What". It will match any line that contains this four-character string, the first character of which is either "W" or "w". Therefore, it could match "Whatever" or "somewhat".

If a file contained structured heading macros, such as .H1, .H2, .H3, etc., you could extract any of these lines with the regular expression:

```
\.H[12345]
```

This pattern matches a three-character string, where the last character is any number from 1 to 5.

The same syntax is used by the UNIX shell. Thus, you can use character classes to specify filenames in UNIX commands. For example, to extract headings from a group of chapter files, you might enter:

```
% grep '\.H[123]' ch0[12]
ch01:.H1 "Contents of Distribution Tape"
ch01:.H1 "Installing the Software"
ch01:.H1 "Configuring the System"
ch01:.H2 "Specifying Input Devices"
ch01:.H3 "Using the Touch Screen"
ch01:.H3 "Using the Mouse"
ch01:.H2 "Specifying Printers"
ch02:.H1 "Getting Started"
ch02:.H2 "A Quick Tour"
 .  .
    .
    .
```

Note that you have to quote the pattern so that it is passed on to **grep** rather than interpreted by the shell. The output produced by **grep** identifies the name of the file for each line printed. As another example of a character class, assume you want to specify the different punctuation marks that end a string:

```
.[!?;:,".]□□.
```

This expression matches "any character followed by an exclamation mark or question mark or semicolon or colon or comma or quotation mark or period and then followed by two blank spaces and any character." It could be used to show that two spaces had been left between the end of a sentence and the beginning of the next sentence, when this occurs on one line. Notice that there are three dots in this expression. The first and last dots are wildcard metacharacters, but the second dot is interpreted literally. Inside square brackets, the standard metacharacters lose their meaning. Thus, the dot inside the square brackets indicates a period. Figure 3-3 lists the characters that have a special meaning inside square brackets.

```
\    Escapes any special character.
-    Indicates a range when not in the first or last position.
^    Indicates a reverse match only when in the first position.
```

Figure 3-3. Special characters in character classes

The backslash (\) performs its usual escape function, allowing you to specify that "-" or "^" should be interpreted literally.

A Range of Characters

The hyphen character (-) allows you to specify a range of characters. For instance, the range of all uppercase letters can be specified as:

```
[A-Z]
```

A range of single-digit numbers can be specified as:

```
[0-9]
```

This character class helps solve an earlier problem of matching chapter references. Look at the following regular expression:

```
[cC]hapter [1-9]
```

It matches the string "chapter" or "Chapter" followed by a space and then followed by any single digit number from 1 to 9. Each of the following lines match the pattern:

```
you will find the information in chapter 9
and chapter 12.
Chapter 4 contains a summary at the end.
```

Depending upon the task, the second line in this example might be considered "a hit that should be a miss." You might add a space following "[1-9]" to avoid matching two-digit numbers. You could also specify a class of characters not to be matched at that position, as we'll see in the next section. Multiple ranges can be specified as well as intermixed with literal characters:

```
[0-9a-z?,.;:'"]
```

This expression will match "any single character that is numeric, lowercase alphabetic, or a question mark, comma, period, semicolon, colon, apostrophe, or quotation mark." Remember that each character class matches a single character. If you specify multiple classes, you are describing two consecutive characters such as:

```
[a-zA-Z][.?!]
```

This expression will match "any lowercase or uppercase letter followed by either a period, a question mark, or an exclamation mark."

The close bracket (]) is interpreted as a member of the class if it occurs as the first character in the class. The hyphen loses its special meaning within a class if it is the first or last character. Therefore, to match arithmetic operators, put the minus sign (-) first in the following example:

```
[-+*/]
```

You could also use the backslash to escape the hyphen wherever it occurs in the range, but the syntax is messier.

Trying to match dates with a regular expression is an interesting problem. Here are two possible formats:

```
MM-DD-YY
MM/DD/YY
```

The following regular expression indicates the possible range of values for each character position:

```
[0-1][0-9][-/][0-3][0-9][-/][0-9][0-9]
```

Either "-" or "/" could be the delimiter. Putting the hyphen in the first position ensures that it will be interpreted in a character class literally, as a hyphen, and not as indicating a range.

Excluding A Class of Characters

Normally, a character class includes all the characters that you want to match at that position. The circumflex (^) as the first character in the class excludes all of the characters in the class from being matched. Instead any character except newline that is not listed in the square brackets will be matched. The following pattern will match any non-numeric character:

```
[^0-9]
```

It matches all uppercase and lowercase letters of the alphabet and all special characters such as punctuation marks.

Excluding specific characters is sometimes more convenient than explicitly listing all the characters you want to match. For instance, if you wanted to match any consonant, you could simply exclude vowels:

```
[^aeiou]
```

This expression would match any consonant, any vowel in uppercase, and any punctuation mark or special character.

Look at the following regular expression:

```
\.DS "[^1]"
```

This expression reads the string ".DS" followed by a quote followed by any character other than the number "1" followed by a quote. It is designed to avoid matching the following line:

```
.DS "1"
```

while matching lines such as:

```
.DS "I"
.DS "2"
```

This syntax can also be used to limit the extent of a match, as we'll see up ahead.

Repeated Occurrences of a Character

The asterisk (*) metacharacter indicates that the preceding regular expression may occur zero or more times. That is, if it modifies a single character, the character may be there or not, but if it is, there may be more than one of them.

You could use the asterisk metacharacter to match a word that might appear in quotes.

```
□"*hypertext"*□
```

The word "hypertext" will be matched regardless of whether it appears in quotes or not.

Also, if the literal character modified by the asterisk does exist, there could be more than one occurrence. For instance, let's examine a series of numbers:

```
1
5
10
50
100
500
1000
5000
```

The regular expression:

```
[15]0*
```

would match all lines, whereas the regular expression:

```
[15]00*
```

would match all but the first two lines. The first zero is a literal, but the second is modified by the asterisk, meaning it might or might not be present. A similar technique is used to match consecutive blanks because you usually want to match one or more, not zero or more blanks. You can use the following expression to do that:

```
□□*
```

When preceded by a dot metacharacter, the asterisk metacharacter matches any number of characters. It can be used to identify a span of characters between two fixed strings. If you wanted to match any string inside of quotation marks, you could specify:

```
".*"
```

This would match all characters between the first and last quotation marks on the line. The span matched by ".*" is always the longest possible. This may not seem important now but it will be once you learn about replacing the string that was matched.

As another example, a pair of angle brackets is a common notation for enclosing formatting instructions used in markup languages, such as SGML and Ventura Publisher.

You could print all lines with these marks by specifying:

```
% grep '<.*>' sample
```

When used to modify a character class, the asterisk can match any number of a character in that class. For instance, look at the following five-line sample file:

```
I can do it
I cannot do it
I can not do it
I can't do it
I cant do it
```

If we wanted to match each form of the negative statement, but not the positive statement, the following regular expression would do it:

```
can[ no']*t
```

The asterisk causes any of the characters in the class to be matched in any order and for any number of occurrences. Here it is:

```
% grep "can[ no']*t" sample
I cannot do it
I can not do it
I can't do it
I cant do it
```

There are four hits and one miss, the positive statement. Notice that had the regular expression tried to match any number of characters between the string "can" and "t", as in the following example:

```
can.*t
```

it would have matched all lines.

The extended set of metacharacters used by **egrep** and awk provides several variations of closure which can be quite useful. The plus sign (+) matches one or more occurrences of the preceding regular expression. Our earlier example of matching one or more blank spaces can be simplified as such:

```
□+
```

The plus sign metacharacter can be thought of as "at least one" of the preceding character. In fact, it better corresponds to how many people think "*" works.

The question mark (?) matches zero or one occurrences. For example, in a previous example, we used a regular expression to match "80286" and "80386". What if we also wanted to match the string "8086"? Here's a regular expression that could be used with **egrep** or awk:

```
80[23]?86
```

It matches the string "80" followed by either a "2" or a "3" or no character followed by the string "86". Don't confuse the "?" in a regular expression with the "?" wildcard in the shell. The latter represents a single character, equivalent to "." in a regular expression.

What's the Word? Part I

As you have probably figured out, it is sometimes difficult to match a complete word. For instance, if we wanted to match the pattern "book", our search would hit lines containing the word "book" and "books" but also the words "bookish", "handbook", and "booky". The obvious thing to do to limit the matching is to surround "book" with blank spaces.

```
□book□
```

However, this expression would only match the word "book"; it would miss the plural "books". To match either the singular or plural word, you could use the asterisk metacharacter:

```
□books*□
```

This will match "book" or "books". However, it will not match "book" if it is followed by a period, a comma, a question mark, or a quotation mark.

When you combine this metacharacter with the wildcard metacharacter (.), you can match zero or more occurrences of any character. In the previous example, we might write a fuller regular expression as:

```
□book.*□
```

This expression matches the string "book" followed by "any number of characters or none followed by a blank space." Here are a few lines that would match:

```
Here are the books that you requested
Yes, it is a good book for children
It is amazing to think that it was called a "harmful book" when
once you get to the end of the book, you can't believe
```

(Note that only the second line would be matched by the fixed string "□book□".) The expression "□book.*□" matches lines containing words such as "booky", "bookworm", and "bookish". We could eliminate two of these matches by using a different modifier. The question mark (?), which is part of the extended set of metacharacters, matches 0 or 1 occurrences of the preceding character. Thus, the expression:

```
□book.?□
```

would match "book", "books", and "booky" but not "bookish" and "bookworm". To eliminate a word like "booky", we would have to use character classes to specify all the characters in that position that we want to match. Furthermore, since the question mark metacharacter is not available with sed, we would have to resort to character classes anyway, as you'll see later on.

Trying to be all inclusive is not always practical with a regular expression, especially when using **grep**. Sometimes it is best to keep the expression simple and allow for the misses. However, as you use regular expressions in sed for making replacements, you will need to be more careful that your regular expression is complete. We will look at a more comprehensive regular expression for searching for words in Part II of "What's the Word?" later in this chapter.

Positional Metacharacters

There are two metacharacters that allow you to specify the context in which a string appears, either at the beginning of a line or at the end of a line. The circumflex (^) metacharacter is a single-character regular expression indicating the beginning of a line. The dollar sign ($) metacharacter is a single-character regular expression indicating the end of a line.

You could print lines that begin with a tab:

```
^<tab>
```

Without the ^ metacharacter, this expression would print any line containing a tab.

Normally, using **vi** to input text to be processed by troff, you do not want blank spaces appearing at the end of lines. If you wanted to find (and remove) them, the following regular expression will match lines with one or more spaces at the end of a line:

□□*$

troff requests and macros must be input at the beginning of a line. They are two-character strings, preceded by a dot and followed by a space. The regular expression used to search for them is:

^\...□

This expression matches "a dot at the beginning of a line followed by any two-character string, and then followed by a space.

You can use both positional metacharacters together to match blank lines:

^$

You might use this pattern with the count option, **-c**, to **grep** to count the number of blank lines in a file:

```
% grep -c '^$' ch03
2
```

This regular expression is useful if you want to delete blank lines using sed. The following regular expression can be used to match a blank line even if it contains blank spaces:

^□*$

Similarly, you can match the entire line:

^.*$

which is something you might possibly want to do with sed. Note that ^ and $ are interpreted as metacharacters only if they appear at the beginning and end of the pattern.

Phrases

A pattern-matching program such as **grep** does not match a string if it extends over two lines. For all practical purposes, it is difficult to match phrases with assurance. Remember that text files are basically unstructured and line breaks are quite random. If you are looking for any sequence of words, it is possible that they might appear on one line but they may be split up over two.

You can write a series of regular expression to capture a phrase:

```
Almond Joy
Almond$
^Joy
```

This is not perfect, as the second regular expression will match "Almond" at the end of a line, regardless of whether or not the next line begins with "Joy". A similar problem exists with the third regular expression.

Later, when we look at sed, you'll learn how to match patterns over multiple lines and you'll see a shell script incorporating sed that makes this capability available in a general way.

A Span of Characters

The metacharacters that allow you to specify repeated occurrences of a character (*+?) indicate a span of undetermined length. Consider the following expression:

```
11*0
```

It will match each of the following lines:

```
10
110
111110
111111111111111111111111111110
```

These metacharacters give elasticity to a regular expression.

Now let's look at a pair of metacharacters that also allow you to indicate a span but moreover let you determine the length of the span. In other words, you can specify the minimum and maximum number of occurrences of a literal character or regular expression.

Escaped curly braces, \{ and \}, are available in **grep** and sed, but not awk and **egrep**. They enclose one or two arguments.

$$\backslash\{n,m\backslash\}$$

n and m are integers between 0 and 256. If you specify $\backslash\{n\backslash\}$ by itself, then exactly n occurrences of the preceding character or regular expression will be matched. If you specify $\backslash\{n,\backslash\}$, then at least n occurrences will be matched. If you specify $\backslash\{n,m\backslash\}$, then any number of occurrences between n and m will be matched.

For example, the following expression:

```
10\{2,4\}1
```

will match "1001", "10001", and "100001" but not "101" or "1000001".

This metacharacter pair can be useful for matching data in fixed-length fields, data that perhaps was extracted from a database. It can also be used to match formatted data such as phone numbers, social security numbers, inventory part IDs, etc. For instance, the format of a social security number is three digits, a hyphen, followed by two digits, a hyphen, and then four digits. That pattern could be described as follows:

```
[0-9]\{3\}-[0-9]\{2\}-[0-9]\{4\}
```

Similarly, a local phone number could be described with the following regular expression:

```
[0-9]\{3\}-[0-9]\{4\}
```

If you are using awk, where you do not have escaped braces available, you can simply repeat the character classes the appropriate number of times:

```
[0-9][0-9][0-9]-[0-9][0-9][0-9][0-9]
```

Alternative Operations

The vertical bar (|) metacharacter, part of the extended set of metacharacters, allows you to specify a union of regular expressions. A line will match the pattern if it matches any one of the regular expressions. For instance, the following regular expression:

```
UNIX|XENIX
```

will match lines containing either the string "UNIX" or the string "XENIX". More than one alternative can be specified:

```
UNIX|XENIX|AIX
```

A line matching any of these three patterns will be printed by **egrep**.

In sed, lacking the union metacharacter, you would specify each pattern separately. In the next section, where we look at grouping operations, we will see additional examples of this metacharacter.

Grouping Operations

Parentheses, (), are used to group regular expressions and establish precedence. They are part of the extended set of metacharacters. Let's say that a company's name in a text file is referred to as "BigOne" or "BigOne Computer":

```
BigOne( Computer)?
```

This expression will match the string "BigOne" by itself or followed by a single occurrence of the string " Computer".

Similarly, if a term is sometime spelled out and at other times abbreviated:

```
% egrep "Lab(oratorie)?s" mail.list
AT&T Bell Laboratories
Bell Labs
```

You can use parentheses with a vertical bar to group alternative operations. In the following example, we use it to specify a match of the singular or plural of the word "company".

```
compan(y|ies)
```

What's the Word? Part II

Let's re-evaluate the regular expression for searching for a single word in light of the new metacharacters we've discussed. Our first attempt at writing a regular expression to search for a word concluded with the following expression:

```
□book.*□
```

This expression is fairly simple, matching a space followed by the string "book" followed by any number of characters followed by a space. However, it does not match all possible occurrences and it does match a few nuisance words.

The following test file contains numerous occurrences of "book". I've added a notation, which is not part of the file, to indicate whether the input line should be a "hit" (>) and included in the output or a "miss" (<). I've tried to include as many different examples as possible.

```
% cat bookwords
> This file tests for book in various places, such as
> book at the beginning of a line or
> at the end of a line book
> as well as the plural books and
< handbooks.  Here are some
< phrases that use the word in different ways:
> "book of the year award"
> to look for a line with the word "book"
```

```
> A GREAT book!
> A great book? No.
> told them about (the books) until it
> Here are the books that you requested
> Yes, it is a good book for children
> amazing that it was called a "harmful book" when
> once you get to the end of the book, you can't believe
< A well-written regular expression should
< avoid matching unrelated words,
< such as booky
< and bookish and
< bookworm and so on.
```

As we search for occurrences of the word "book", there are thirteen lines that should be matched and seven lines that should not be matched. First, let's run the previous regular expression on the sample file and check the results.

```
% grep '□book.*□' bookwords
This file tests for book in various places, such as
as well as the plural books and
A great book? No.
told them about (the books) until it
Here are the books that you requested
Yes, it is a good book for children
amazing that it was called a "harmful book" when
once you get to the end of the book, you can't believe
such as booky
and bookish and
```

It only prints eight of the 13 lines that we want to match and it prints two of the lines that we don't want to match. The expression matches lines containing the words "booky" and "bookish". It ignores "book" at the beginning of a line and at the end of a line. It ignores "book" when there are certain punctuation marks involved.

To restrict the search even more, we must use character classes. Generally, the list of characters that might end a word are punctuation marks, such as:

```
? . , ! ; : '
```

In addition, quotation marks, parentheses, braces, and brackets might surround a word or open or close with a word:

```
" () {} []
```

You would also have to accommodate the plural or possessive forms of the word.

Thus, you would have two different character classes: before and after the word. Remember that all we have to do is list the members of the class inside square brackets. Before the word, we now have:

```
["[{(]
```

and after the word:

```
[]})"?!.,;:'s]
```

Note that putting the closing square bracket as the first character in the class makes it a member of the class rather than closing the set. Putting the two classes together, we get the expression:

```
□["[{(]*book[]})"?!.,;:'s]*□
```

Show this to the uninitiated, and they'll throw up their hands in despair! But now that you know the principles involved, you can not only understand this expression, but could easily reconstruct it. Let's see how it does on the sample file:

```
% grep '□["[{(]*book[]})"?!.,;:'s]*□' bookwords
This file tests for book in various places, such as
as well as the plural books and
to look for a line with the word "book"
A great book? No.
told them about (the books) until it
Here are the books that you requested
Yes, it is a good book for children
amazing that it was called a "harmful book" when
once you get to the end of the book, you can't believe
```

We eliminated the lines that we don't want but there are four lines that we're not getting. Let's examine the four lines:

```
book at the beginning of a line or
at the end of a line book
"book of the year award"
A GREAT book!
```

All of these are problems caused by the string appearing at the beginning or end of a line. Because there is no blank space at the beginning or end of a line, the pattern is not matched. We can use the positional metacharacters, ^ and $. Since we want to match either a blank space or beginning or end of a line, we can use egrep and specify the "or" metacharacter along with parentheses for grouping. For instance, to match either the beginning of a line or a space, you could write the expression:

```
(^| )
```

(Because | and () are part of the extended set of metacharacters, if you were using sed, you'd have to write different expressions to handle each case.)

Here's the revised regular expression:

```
(^|□) ["[{(]*book[]})"?!.,;:'s]*(□|$)
```

Now let's see how it works:

```
% grep '(^|□) ["[{(]*book[]})"?!.,;:'s]*(□|$)' bookwords
This file tests for book in various places, such as
book at the beginning of a line or
at the end of a line book
as well as the plural books and
"book of the year award"
to look for a line with the word "book"
A GREAT book!
A great book? No.
told them about (the books) until it
Here are the books that you requested
Yes, it is a good book for children
amazing that it was called a "harmful book" when
once you get to the end of the book, you can't believe
```

This is certainly a complex regular expression; however, it can be broken down into parts. This expression may not match every single instance, but it can be easily adapted to handle other occurrences that you may find.

You could also create a simple shell script to replace "book" with a command-line argument. The only problem might be that the plural of some words is not simply "s." By sleight of hand, you could handle the "es" plural by adding "e" to the character class following the word; it would work in many cases.

As a further note, the **ex** and **vi** text editors have a special metacharacter for matching a string at the beginning of a word, \<, and one for matching a string at the end of a word, \>. Used as a pair, they can match a string only when it is a complete word. Matching a word is such a common case that these metacharacters would be widely used, if they were available for all regular expressions. I'm not sure who might make such an enhancement to standard UNIX, but it would be a welcome one, along with making the extended regular expression character set standard to all programs that use regular expressions (i.e., sed).

Your Replacement is Here

When using **grep**, it seldom matters how you match the line as long as you match it. When you want to make a replacement, however, you have to consider the extent of the match. In other words, what characters on the line did you actually match?

In this section, we're going to look at several examples that demonstrate the extent of a match. Then we'll introduce a program that works like **grep** but also allows you to specify a replacement string. Lastly, we will look at a several meta-characters used to describe the replacement string.

The Extent of the Match

Let's look at the following regular expression:

```
A*Z
```

This matches "zero or more occurrences of A followed by Z." It will produce the same result as simply specifying "Z". The letter "A" could be there or it could not be; in fact, the letter "Z" is the only character matched. Here's a sample two-line file:

```
All of us, including Zippy, our dog
Some of us, including Zippy, our dog
```

If we try to match the previous regular expression, both lines would print out. Interestingly enough, the actual match in both cases is made on the "Z" and only the Z. We can use the **gres** command (see insert "A Program for Making Single Replacements") to demonstrate the extent of the match.

```
$ gres "A*Z" "00" test
All of us,including 00ippy, our dog
Some of us,including 00ippy, our dog
```

We would have expected the extent of the match on the first line to be from the "A" to the "Z" but only the "Z" is actually matched. This result may be more apparent if we change the regular expression slightly:

```
A.*Z
```

".*" can be interpreted as "zero or more occurrences of any character," which means that "any number of characters" can be found, including none at all. The entire expression can be evaluated as "an A followed by any number of characters followed by a Z." An "A" is the initial character in the pattern and "Z" is the last character; anything or nothing might occur in between. Running **grep** on the same two-line file produces one line of output. We've added a line of carets (^) underneath to mark what was matched.

```
All of us, including Zippy, our dog
^^^^^^^^^^^^^^^^^^^^^^^^^^^^^
```

The extent of the match is from "A" to "Z". The same regular expression would also match the following line:

```
I heard it on radio station WVAZ 1060.
                            ^^
```

The string "AZ" matches "A followed by any number of characters (including zero) followed by Z." Now, let's look at a similar set of sample lines that contain multiple occurrences of "A" and "Z".

```
All of us, including Zippy, our dog
All of us, including Zippy and Ziggy
All of us, including Zippy and Ziggy and Zelda
```

The regular expression "A.*Z" will match the longest possible extent in each case.

```
All of us, including Zippy, our dog
^^^^^^^^^^^^^^^^^^^^^^^^^^
All of us, including Zippy and Ziggy
^^^^^^^^^^^^^^^^^^^^^^^^^^^^^^^^^^
All of us, including Zippy and Ziggy and Zelda
^^^^^^^^^^^^^^^^^^^^^^^^^^^^^^^^^^^^^^^^^^^^^^
```

This can cause problems if what you want is to match the shortest extent possible.

A Program for Making Single Replacements

The MKS Toolkit, a set of UNIX utilities for DOS by Mortice-Kern Systems, Inc., contains a very useful program called **gres** (*g*lobal *r*egular *e*xpression *s*ubstitution). Just like **grep**, it searches for a pattern in a file; however, it allows you to specify a replacement for the string that you match. This program is in fact a simplified version of sed, and like sed, it prints all lines regardless of whether or not a replacement was made. It does not make the replacement in the file itself. You have to redirect the output from the program into a file if you want to save the changes.

gres is not part of standard UNIX but it would be a nice tool to have. It can be created using a simple shell script that invokes sed to do the work.

A Program for Making Single Replacements *(continued)*

```
% cat gres
if [ $# -lt "3" ]
then
      echo Usage: gres pattern replacement file
      exit
fi
pattern=$1
replacement=$2
if [ -f $3 ]
then
      file=$3
else
      echo $3 is not a file.
      exit
fi
A="`echo | tr '\012' '\001'`"
sed -e "s$A$pattern$A$replacement$A" $file
```

Throughout the rest of the chapter, we will use **gres** to demonstrate the use of replacement metacharacters. Remember that whatever applies to **gres** applies to sed as well. Here we replace the string matched by the regular expression "A.*Z" with double zero (00).

```
% gres "A.*Z" "00" sample
00ippy, our dog
00iggy
00elda
```

Limiting the Extent

Earlier we said that a regular expression tries to match the longest string possible and that can cause unexpected problems. For instance, look at the regular expression to match any number of characters inside of quotation marks:

```
".*"
```

Let's look at a **troff** macro that has two quoted arguments, as shown below:

```
.Se "Appendix" "Full Program Listings"
```

To match the first argument, we might describe the pattern with the following regular expression:

```
\.Se ".*"
```

However, it ends up matching the whole line because the second quotation mark in the pattern matches the last quotation mark on the line. If you know how many arguments there are, you can specify each of them:

```
\.Se ".*" ".*"
```

Although this works as you'd expect, each line might not have the same number of arguments, causing misses that should be hits—you simply want the first argument. Here's a different regular expression that matches the shortest possible extent between two quotation marks:

```
"[^"]*"
```

It matches "a quote followed by any number of characters that do not match a quote followed by a quote":

```
% gres '"[^"]*"' '00' sampleLine
.Se 00 "Appendix"
```

Now let's look at a few lines with a dot character (.) used as a leader between two columns of numbers:

```
1........5
5........10
10.......20
100......200
```

The difficulty in matching the leader characters is that there are a variable number of them. Let's say that you wanted to replace all of the leaders with a single tab. You might write a regular expression to match the line as follows:

```
[0-9][0-9]*\.\.*[0-9]\[0-9]*
```

This expression might unexpectedly match the line:

```
see Section 2.3
```

To restrict matching, you could specify the minimum number of dots that are common to all lines:

```
[0-9][0-9]*\.\{5,\}[0-9][0-9]*
```

This expression uses braces available in sed to match "a single digit followed by at least five dots and then followed by a single digit." To see this in action, we'll show a sed command that replaces the leader dots with a hyphen. However, we have not covered the syntax of sed's replacement metacharacters—\(and \) to save a part of a regular expression and \1 and \2 to recall the saved portion. This command, therefore, may look rather complex (it is!) but it does the job.

```
% sed 's/\([0-9][0-9]*\)\.\{5,\}\([0-9][0-9]*\)/\1-\2/' sample
1-5
5-10
10-20
100-200
```

A similar expression can be written to match one or more leading tabs or tabs between columns of data. You could change the order of columns as well as replacing the tab with another delimiter. You should experiment on your own by making simple and complex replacements, using sed or **gres**.

I Never Metacharacter I Didn't Like

Figure 3-4 lists interesting examples of regular expressions, many of which have been described in this chapter.

Postal Abbreviation for State	□[A-Z][A-Z]□
City, State	^.*, [A-Z][A-Z]
City, State, Zip	^.*, [A-Z][A-Z] [0-9]\{5\}(-[0-9]\{4\})?
Month, Day, Year	[A-Z][a-z]\{3,9\} [0-9]\{1,2\}, [0-9]\{4\}
Social Security Number	[0-9]\{3\}-[0-9]\{2\}-[0-9]\{4\}
Local Telephone	[0-9]\{3\}-[0-9]\{4\}
Formatted Dollar Amounts	\$[0-9]*\.[0-9]\{2\}
troff In-line Font Requests	\f[(BIRP][C]*[BW]*
troff Requests	\.[a-z]\{2\}□
troff Macros	\.[A-Z12]□
troff Macro with arguments	\.[A-Z12]□".*"
Ventura Publisher In-line Codes	<.*>
Ventura-style Codes	^@.* = .*
Match blank lines	^$
Match entire line	^.*$
Match one or more spaces	□□*

Figure 3-4. Useful regular expressions

4

Writing Sed Scripts

Applying Commands in a Script
A Global Perspective on Addressing
Testing and Saving Output
Four Types of Sed Scripts
Making Changes Across a Set of Files
Getting to the PromiSed Land

To use sed, you write a script that contains a series of editing actions and then you run the script on an input file. Sed allows you to take what would be a *hands-on* procedure in an editor such as **vi** and transform it into a *look-no-hands* procedure that is executed from a script.

When performing edits manually, you get to trust the cause-and-effect relationship of entering an editing command and seeing the immediate result. There is usually an "undo" command that allows you to reverse the effect of a command and return the text file to its previous state. Once you learn an interactive text editor, you have the feeling of making changes in a safe and controlled manner, one step at a time.

Most people new to sed will feel there is greater risk in writing a script to perform a series of edits than in making those changes manually. The fear is that by automating the task, something will happen that cannot be reversed. The object of learning sed is to understand it well enough to see that your results are predictable. In other words, you come to understand the cause-and-effect relationship between your editing script and the output that you get.

This requires using sed in a controlled, methodical way. In writing a script, you should follow these steps:

1. Think through what you want to do before you do it.

2. Describe, unambiguously, a procedure to do it.

3. Test the procedure repeatedly before committing to any final changes.

These steps are simply a re-statement of the same process we described for writing regular expressions in Chapter 3, *Understanding Regular Expression Syntax*. They describe a methodology for writing programs of any kind. The best way to see if your script works is to run tests on different input samples and observe the results.

With practice, you can come to rely upon your sed scripts working just as you want them to. (It occurs to me that there is something analogous in the management of one's own time, learning to trust that certain tasks can be delegated to others. You begin testing people on small tasks, and if they succeed, you give them larger tasks.)

This chapter, then, is about making you comfortable writing scripts that do your editing work for you. This involves understanding three basic principles of how sed works:

- All of the editing commands in a script are applied in order to each line of input.

- Commands are applied to all lines (globally) unless line addressing restricts the lines affected by editing commands.

- The original input file is unchanged; the editing commands modify a copy of original input line and the copy is sent to standard output.

After covering these basic principles, we'll look at four types of scripts that demonstrate different sed applications. These scripts provide the basic models for the scripts that you will write. Although there are a number of commands available for use in sed, the scripts in this chapter purposely use only a few commands. Nonetheless, you may be surprised at how much you can do with so few. (Chapter 5, *Basic Sed Commands*, and Chapter 6, *Advanced Sed Commands*, present the basic and advanced sed commands, respectively.) The idea is to concentrate from the outset on understanding how a script works and how to use a script before exploring all the commands that can be used in scripts.

Applying Commands in a Script

Combining a series of edits in a script can have unexpected results. You might not think of the consequences one edit can have on another. New users typically think that sed applies an individual editing command to all lines of input before applying the next editing command. But the opposite is true. Sed applies each command to the first input line before reading the second input line and applying the editing script to it. Because sed is always working with the the latest version of the original line, any edit that is made changes the line for subsequent commands. Sed doesn't retain the original. This means that a pattern that might have matched the original input line may no longer match the line after an edit has been made.

Let's look at an example that uses the substitute command. Suppose someone quickly wrote the following script to change "pig" to "cow" and "cow" to "horse".

```
s/pig/cow/
s/cow/horse/
```

What do you think happened? Try it on a sample file. We'll discuss what happened later, after we look at how sed works.

The Pattern Space

Sed maintains a *pattern space*, a workspace or temporary buffer where a single line of input is held while the editing commands are applied.* The transformation of the pattern space by a two-line script is shown in Figure 4-1. It changes "The Unix·System" to "The UNIX Operating System".

Initially, the pattern space contains a copy of a single input line. In Figure 4-1, that line is "The Unix System". The normal flow through the script is to execute each command on that line until the end of the script is reached. The first command in the script is applied to that line, changing "Unix" to "UNIX". Then the second command is applied, changing "UNIX System" to "UNIX Operating System".† Note that the pattern for the second substitute command

---

*One advantage of the one-line-at-a-time design is that sed can read very large files without any problems. Screen editors that have to read the entire file into memory, or some large portion of it, can run out of memory or be extremely slow to use in dealing with large files.

†Yes, we could have changed "Unix System" to "UNIX Operating System" in one step. However, the input file might have instances of "UNIX System" as well as "Unix System." So by changing "Unix" to "UNIX" we make both instances consistent before changing them to "UNIX Operating System".

does not match the original input line; it matches the current line as it has changed in the pattern space.

When all the instructions have been applied, the current line is output and the next line of input is read into the pattern space. Then all the commands in the script are applied to that line.

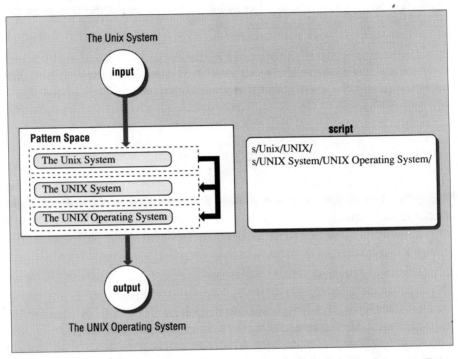

Figure 4-1. The commands in the script change the contents of the pattern space

As a consequence, any sed command might change the contents of the pattern space for the next command. The contents of the pattern space are dynamic and do not always match the original input line. That was the problem with the sample script at the beginning of this chapter. The first command would change "pig" to "cow" as expected. However, when the second command changed "cow" to "horse" on the same line, it also changed the "cow" that had been a "pig". So, where the input file contained pigs and cows, the output file has only horses!

This mistake is simply a problem of the order of the commands in the script. Reversing the order of the commands—changing "cow" into "horse" before changing "pig" into "cow"—does the trick.

```
s/cow/horse/
s/pig/cow/
```

Some sed commands change the flow through the script, as we will see in subsequent chapters. For example, the **N** command reads another line into the pattern space without removing the current line, so you can test for patterns across multiple lines. Other commands tell sed to exit before reaching the bottom of the script or to go to a labeled command.

Sed also maintains a second temporary buffer called the *hold space*. You can copy the contents of the pattern space to the hold space and retrieve it later. The commands that make use of the hold space are discussed in Chapter 6, *Advanced Sed Commands*.

A Global Perspective on Addressing

One of the first things you'll notice about sed commands is that sed will apply them to every input line. Sed is implicitly global, unlike **cd**, **ex**, or **vi**. The following substitute command will change every "CA" into "California".

```
s/CA/California/
```

If the same command were entered from the **ex** command prompt in **vi**, it would make the replacement for all occurrences on the current line only. In sed, it is as though each line has a turn at becoming the current line and so the command is applied to every line. Line addresses are used to supply context for, or *restrict*, an operation. (In short: Nothing gets done in **vi** unless you tell it which lines to work on, while sed will work on every line unless you tell it not to.) For instance, by supplying the address "Sebastopol" to the previous substitute command, we can limit the replacement of "CA" by "California" only on lines containing "Sebastopol".

```
/Sebastopol/s/CA/California/g
```

An input line consisting of "Sebastopol, CA" would match the address and the substitute command would be applied, changing it to "Sebastopol, California". A line consisting of "San Francisco, CA" would not be matched and the substitution would not be applied.

A sed command can specify zero, one, or two addresses. An address can be a regular expression that describes a pattern, a line number, or a line addressing symbol.

- If no address is specified, then the command is applied to each line.
- If there is only one address, the command is applied to any line matching the address.
- If two comma-separated addresses are specified, the command is performed on the first matching line and all succeeding lines up to and including a line matching the second address.
- If an address is followed by an exclamation mark (!), the command is applied to all lines that do *not* match the address.

To illustrate how addressing works, let's look at examples using the delete command, **d**. A script consisting of simply the **d** command and no address:

```
d
```

produces no output since it deletes *all* lines.

When a line number is supplied as an address, the command affects only that line. For instance, the following example deletes only the first line:

```
1d
```

The line number refers to an internal line count maintained by sed. This counter is not reset for multiple input files. Thus, no matter how many files were specified as input, there is only one line 1 in the input stream.

Similarly, the input stream has only one last line. It can be specified using the addressing symbol $. The following example deletes the last line of input:

```
$d
```

The $ symbol should not be confused with the $ used in regular expressions, which means the end of the line.

When a regular expression is supplied as an address, the command affects only the lines matching that pattern. The regular expression must be enclosed by slashes (/). The following delete command:

```
/^$/d
```

deletes only blank lines. All other lines are passed through untouched.

If you supply two addresses, then you specify a range of lines over which the command is executed. The following example shows hows to delete all lines blocked by a pair of macros, in this case, .TS and .TE, that mark **tbl** input.

```
/\.TS/,/\.TE/d
```

It deletes all lines beginning with the line matched by the first pattern and up to and including the line matched by the second pattern. Lines outside this range are not affected. The following command deletes from line 50 to the last line in the file:

```
50,$d
```

You can mix a line address and a pattern address:

```
1,/^$/d
```

This example deletes from the first line up to the first blank line, which, for instance, will delete a mailer header from a mail message that you have saved in a file.

You can think of the first address as enabling the action and the second address as disabling it. Sed has no way of looking ahead to determine if the second match will be made. The action will be applied to lines once the first match is made. The command will be applied to *all* subsequent lines until the second match is made. In the previous example, if the file did not contain a blank line, then all lines would be deleted.

An exclamation mark (!) following an address reverses the sense of the match. For instance, the following script deletes all lines *except* those inside **tbl** input:

```
/\.TS/,/\.TE/!d
```

This script, in effect, extracts **tbl** input from a source file.

Grouping Commands

Braces ({ }) are used in sed to nest one address inside another or to apply multiple commands at the same address. You can nest addresses if you want to specify a range of lines and then, within that range, specify another address. For example, to delete blank lines only inside blocks of **tbl** input, use the following command:

```
/\.TS/,/\.TE/{
/^$/d
}
```

The opening curly brace must end a line and the closing curly brace must be on a line by itself. Be sure there are no blank spaces after the braces.

You can apply multiple commands to the same range of lines by enclosing the editing commands within braces, as shown below.

```
/\.TS/,/\.TE/{
    /^$/d
    s/\.ps 10/.ps 8/
    s/\.vs 12/.vs 10/
}
```

This example not only deletes blank lines in **tbl** input but it also uses the substitute command, s, to change several **troff** requests. Remember, these commands are applied only to lines within the .TS/.TE block.

Testing and Saving Output

In our previous discussion of the pattern space, you saw that sed:

1. Makes a copy of the input line.

2. Modifies that copy in the pattern space.

3. Outputs the copy to standard output.

What this means is that sed has a built-in safeguard so that you don't make changes to the original file. Thus, the following command line:

```
% sed -f sedscr testfile
```

does not make the change in *testfile*. It sends all lines to the screen—the lines that were modified as well as the lines that are unchanged. You have to capture this output in a new file if you want to save it.

```
% sed -f sedscr testfile > newfile
```

The redirection symbol ">" directs the output from sed to the file *newfile*. Don't redirect the output from the command back to the input file or you will overwrite the input file.

One important reason to redirect the output to a file is to verify your results. You can examine the contents of *newfile* and compare it to *testfile*. If you want to be very methodical about checking your results (and you should be), use the **diff** program to point out the differences between the two files.

```
% diff testfile newfile
```

This command will display lines that are unique to *testfile* preceded by a "<" and lines unique to *newfile* preceded by a ">". When you have verified your results, make a backup copy of the original input file and then use the **mv** command to overwrite the original with the new version. Be sure that the editing script is working properly before abandoning the original version.

Because these steps are repeated so frequently, you will find it helpful to put them into a shell script. While we can't go into much depth about the workings of shell scripts, these scripts are fairly simple to understand and use. Writing a shell script involves using a text editor to enter one or more command lines in a file, saving the file and then using the **chmod** command to make the file executable. The name of the file is the name of the command, and it can be entered at the system prompt. If you are unfamiliar with shell scripts, follow the shell scripts presented in this book as recipes in which you make your own substitutions.

The following two shell scripts are useful for testing sed scripts and then making the changes permanently in a file. They are particularly useful when the same script needs to be run on multiple files.

testsed

The shell script **testsed** automates the process of saving the output of sed in a temporary file. It expects to find the script file, **sedscr**, in the current directory and applies these instructions to the input file named on the command line. The output is placed in a temporary file.

```
for x
do
sed -f sedscr $x > tmp.$x
done
```

The name of a file must be specified on the command line. As a result, this shell script saves the output in a temporary file with the prefix *tmp.*. You can examine the temporary file to determine if your edits were made correctly. If you approve of the results, you could then use **mv** to overwrite the original file with the temporary.

You might also incorporate the **diff** command into the shell script. (Add **diff $x tmp.$x** after the sed command.)

If you find that your script did not produce the results you expected, remember that the easiest "fix" is usually to perfect the editing script and run it again on the original input file. Don't write a new script to "undo" or improve upon changes made in the temporary file.

runsed

The shell script **runsed** was developed to make changes to an input file permanently. In other words, it is used in cases when you would want the input file and the output file to be the same. Like **testsed**, it creates a temporary file, but then it takes the next step: copying the file over the original.

```
for x
do
echo "editing $x: \c"
if test "$x" = sedscr; then
```

```
        echo "not editing sedscript!"
elif test -s $x; then
    sed -f sedscr $x > /tmp/$x
    if test -s /tmp/$x
    then
    cmp -s $x /tmp/$x && echo "file not changed: \c";\
     cp /tmp/$x $x;echo "done"
    else
    echo "Sed produced an empty file - check your sedscript."
    fi
else
    echo "original file is empty."
fi
done
echo "all done"
```

To use **runsed,** create a sed script named **sedscr** in the directory where you want to make the edits. Supply the name or names of the files to edit on the command line. Shell metacharacters can be used to specify a set of files.

> $ **runsed ch0?**

runsed simply invokes **sed -f sedscr** on the named files, one at a time, and redirects the output to a temporary file. **runsed** then tests this temporary file to make sure that output was produced before copying it over the original.

The muscle of this shell script (line 7) is essentially the same as **testsed.** The additional lines are intended to test for unsuccessful runs, for instance, when no output is produced. It compares the two files to see if changes were actually made or to see if an empty output file was produced before overwriting the original.

However, **runsed** does not protect you from imperfect editing scripts. You should use **testsed** first to verify your changes before actually making them permanent with **runsed.**

Four Types of Sed Scripts

In this section, we are going to look at four types of scripts, each one illustrating a typical sed application.

Multiple Edits to the Same File

The first type of sed script demonstrates making a series of edits in a file. The example we use is a script that converts a file created by a word processing program into a file coded for **troff**.

Once I was doing a writing project for a computer company, here referred to as BigOne Computer. In the document I was writing I had to include a product bulletin for "Horsefeathers Software." I was promised that the product bulletin was on-line and that they could send it to me. Unfortunately, when the file arrived, it contained the formatted output for a line printer. It was the only way they could give it to me. A portion of that file follows.

```
        HORSEFEATHERS SOFTWARE PRODUCT BULLETIN

    DESCRIPTION
+     _____

    BigOne Computer  offers three   software packages from the   suite
    of Horsefeathers  software products   --  Horsefeathers  Business
    BASIC, BASIC  Librarian,  and LIDO.  These software products can
    fill   your    requirements   for   powerful,   sophisticated,
    general-purpose business  software providing you with a base for
    software customization or development.

    Horsefeathers  BASIC is  BASIC optimized for use on  the  BigOne
    machine with UNIX  or MS-DOS operating systems.  BASIC Librarian
    is a full  screen program editor, which also provides the ability
```

Note that the text has been justified with spaces added between words. There are also spaces added to create a left margin.

I find that when I begin to tackle a problem using sed, I do best if I make a mental list of all the things I want to do. When I begin coding, I write a a script containing a single command that does one thing. I test that it works, then I add another command, repeating this cycle until I've done all that's obvious to do. I say what's obvious because my list is not always complete, and the cycle of implement-and-test often adds other items to the list.

It may seem to be a rather tedious process to work this way and indeed there are a number of scripts where it's fine to take a crack at writing the whole script in one pass and then begin testing it. However, the one-step-at-a-time is highly recommended for beginners because you isolate each command and get to easily see what is working and what is not. When you try to do several commands at once, you might find that when problems arise you end up re-creating the recommended process in reverse; that is, removing commands one-by-one until you locate the problem.

Here is my list of the obvious edits that need to be made to the Horsefeathers Software bulletin:

1. Replace all blank lines with a paragraph macro (.LP).

2. Remove all leading blanks from each line.

3. Remove the printer underscore line, the one that begins with a "+".

4. Remove multiple blank spaces that were added between words.

The first edit requires that we match blank lines. However, in looking at the input file, I wasn't sure whether the blank lines had leading spaces or not. As it turns out, they do not, so I can match blank lines using the pattern "^$". (If there were spaces on the line, I could write the pattern "□*$".) Thus, the first edit is fairly straightforward to accomplish:

```
s/^$/.LP/
```

It replaces each blank line with ".LP". Note that you do not escape the literal period in the replacement section of the substitute command. I put this command in a file named *sedscr* and test the command as follows:

```
% sed -f sedscr horsefeathers
                HORSEFEATHERS SOFTWARE PRODUCT BULLETIN
.LP
   DESCRIPTION
+        _____
.LP
   BigOne Computer  offers three   software packages from the   suite
   of Horsefeathers  software products   --  Horsefeathers  Business
   BASIC, BASIC  Librarian,  and LIDO.  These software products can
   fill  your    requirements   for   powerful,    sophisticated,
   general-purpose business  software providing you with a base for
   software customization or development.
.LP
   Horsefeathers  BASIC is  BASIC optimized for use on  the  BigOne
   machine with UNIX  or MS-DOS operating systems.  BASIC Librarian
   is a full  screen program editor, which also provides the ability
```

It is pretty obvious which lines have changed. (I frequently cut out a portion of a file to use for testing. It works best if the portion is small enough to fit on the screen yet is large enough to include different examples of what you want to change. After all edits have been applied successfully to the test file, a second level of testing occurs when you apply them to the complete, original file.)

The next edit that we make is to remove the line that begins with a "+" and contains a line-printer underscore. We can simply delete this line using the delete command, **d**. In writing a pattern to match this line, we have a number of choices. Each of the following would match that line:

```
/^+/
/^+□/
/^+□□*/
/^+□□*__*/
```

As you can see, each successive regular expression matches a greater number of characters. Only through testing can you determine how complex the expression needs to be to match a specific line and not others. The longer the pattern that you define in a regular expression, the more comfort you have in knowing that it won't produce unwanted matches. For this script, we'll choose the third expression:

```
/^+□□*/d
```

This command will delete any line that begins with a plus sign and is followed by at least one space. The pattern specifies two spaces, but the second is modified by "*", which means that the second space might or might not be there.

This command was added to the sed script and tested but since it only affects one line, we'll omit showing the results and move on. The next edit needs to remove the spaces that pad the beginning of a line. The pattern for matching that sequence is very similar to the address for the previous command.

```
s/^□□*//
```

This command removes any sequence of spaces found at the beginning of a line. The replacement portion of the substitute command is empty, meaning that the matched string is removed.

We can add this command to the script and test it.

```
% sed -f sedscr horsefeathers
HORSEFEATHERS SOFTWARE PRODUCT BULLETIN
.LP
DESCRIPTION
.LP
BigOne Computer  offers three  software packages from the  suite
of Horsefeathers  software products  --  Horsefeathers  Business
BASIC, BASIC  Librarian,  and LIDO.  These software products can
fill  your   requirements   for   powerful,   sophisticated,
general-purpose business  software providing you with a base for
software customization or development.
.LP
Horsefeathers  BASIC is  BASIC optimized for use on  the  BigOne
machine with UNIX  or MS-DOS operating systems.  BASIC Librarian
is a full  screen program editor, which  also provides the ability
```

The next edit attempts to deal with the extra spaces added to justify each line. We can write a substitute command to match any string of two or more spaces and replace it with a single space.

```
s/⬜⬜*/⬜/g
```

We add the global flag at the end of the command so that all occurrences, not just the first, are replaced. Note that, like previous regular expressions, we are not specifying how many spaces are there, just that two or more be found. There might be two, three, or four consecutive spaces. No matter how many, we want to reduce them to one.

Let's test the new script:

```
% sed -f sedscr horsefeathers
HORSEFEATHERS SOFTWARE PRODUCT BULLETIN
.LP
DESCRIPTION
.LP
BigOne Computer offers three software packages from the suite
of Horsefeathers software products -- Horsefeathers Business
BASIC, BASIC Librarian, and LIDO. These software products can
fill your requirements for powerful, sophisticated,
general-purpose business software providing you with a base for
software customization or development.
.LP
Horsefeathers BASIC is BASIC optimized for use on the BigOne
machine with UNIX or MS-DOS operating systems. BASIC Librarian
is a full screen program editor, which also provides the ability
```

It works as advertised, reducing two or more spaces to one. On closer inspection, though, you might notice that the script removes a sequence of two spaces following a period, a place where they belong.

We could perfect our substitute command such that it does not make the replacement for spaces following a period. The problem is that there are cases when three spaces follow a period and we'd like to reduce that to two. The best way seems to be to write a separate command that deals with the special case of a period followed by spaces.

```
s/\.⬜⬜*/.⬜⬜/g
```

This command replaces a period followed by any number of spaces with a period followed by two spaces. It should be noted that the previous command reduces multiple spaces to one, so that only one space will be found following a period. Nonetheless, this pattern works regardless of how many spaces follow the period, as long as there is at least one. (It would not, for instance, affect a filename of the form *test.ext* if it appeared in the document.) This command is placed at the end of the script and tested:

```
% sed -f sedscr basic
```

The following result is displayed on the screen:

```
HORSEFEATHERS SOFTWARE PRODUCT BULLETIN
.LP
DESCRIPTION
.LP
BigOne Computer offers three software packages from the suite
of Horsefeathers software products -- Horsefeathers Business
BASIC, BASIC Librarian, and LIDO.  These software products can
fill your requirements for powerful, sophisticated,
general-purpose business software providing you with a base for
software customization or development.
.LP
Horsefeathers BASIC is BASIC optimized for use on the BigOne
machine with UNIX or MS-DOS operating systems.  BASIC Librarian
is a full screen program editor, which also provides the ability
```

It works. Here's the completed script:

```
s/^$/.LP/
/^+□□*/d
s/^□□*//
s/□□*/□/g
s/\.□□*/.□□/g
```

As we said earlier, the next stage would be to test the script on the complete file, using **testsed**, and examine the results thoroughly. When we are satisfied with the results, we can use **runsed** to make the changes permanent:

```
% runsed hf.product.bulletin
done
```

By executing **runsed**, we have overwritten the original file.

Before leaving this script, it is instructive to point out that although the script was written to process a specific file, each of the commands in the script is one that you might expect to use again, even if you don't use the entire script again. In other words, you will probably write other scripts that delete blank lines or check for two spaces following a period. Recognizing how commands can be reused in other situations reduces the time it takes to develop and test new scripts. It's like a singer learning a song and adding it to his or her repetoire.

Making Changes Across a Set of Files

The most common use of sed is in making a set of search-and-replacement edits across a set of files. Many times these scripts aren't very unusual or interesting, just a list of substitute commands that change one word or phrase to another. Of course, such scripts don't need to be interesting as long as they are useful and save doing the work manually.

The example we look at in this section is a conversion script, designed to modify various "machine-specific" terms in a UNIX documentation set. One person went through the documentation set and made a list of things that needed to be changed. Another person worked from the list to create the following list of substitutions.

```
s/ON switch/START switch/g
s/ON button/START switch/g
s/STANDBY switch/STOP switch/g
s/STANDBY button/STOP switch/g
s/STANDBY/STOP/g
s/[cC]abinet [Ll]ight/control panel light/g
s/core system diskettes/core system tape/g
s/TERM=542[05] /TERM=PT200 /g
s/Teletype 542[05]/BigOne PT200/g
s/542[05] terminal/PT200 terminal/g
s/Documentation Road Map/Documentation Directory/g
s/Owner\/Operator Guide/Installation and Operation Guide/g
s/AT&T 3B20 [cC]omputer/BigOne XL Computer/g
s/AT&T 3B2 [cC]omputer/BigOne XL Computer/g
s/3B2 [cC]omputer/BigOne XL Computer/g
s/3B2/BigOne XL Computer/g
```

The script is straightforward. The beauty is not in the script itself but in sed's ability to apply this script to the hundreds of files comprising the documentation set. Once this script is tested, it can be executed using **runsed** to process as many files as there are at once.

Such a script can be a tremendous time-saver, but it can also be an opportunity to make big-time mistakes. What sometimes happens is that a person writes the script, tests it on one or two out of the hundreds of files and concludes from that test that the script works fine. While it may not be practical to test each file, it is important that the test files you do choose be both representative and exceptional. Remember that text is extremely variable and you cannot typically trust that what is true for a particular occurrence is true for all occurrences.

Using **grep** to examine large amounts of input can be very helpful. For instance, if you wanted to determine how "core system diskettes" appears in the documents, you could **grep** for it everywhere and pour over the listing. To be thorough, you should also **grep** for "core", "core system", "system diskettes", and "diskettes" to look for occurrences split over multiple lines. (You could also use the **phrase** script in Chapter 6, *Advanced Sed Commands*, to look for occurrences of multiple words over consecutive lines.) Examining the input is the best way to know what your script must do.

In some ways, writing a script is like devising a hypothesis, given a certain set of facts. You try to prove the validity of the hypothesis by increasing the amount of data that you test it against. If you are going to be running a script on multiple files, use **testsed** to run the script on several dozen files after you've tested it on a smaller sample. Then compare the temporary files to the originals to see if your assumptions were correct. The script might be off slightly and you can revise it. The more time you spend testing, which is actually rather interesting work, the less chance you will spend your time being frustrated by unraveling problems caused by a botched script.

Extracting Contents of a File

One type of sed application is used for extracting relevant material from a file. In this way, sed functions like grep, with the additional advantage that the input can be modified prior to output. This type of script is a good candidate for a shell script.

Here are two examples: extracting a macro definition from a macro package and displaying the outline of a document.

Extracting a Macro Definition

troff macros are defined in a macro package, often a single file that's located in a directory such as */usr/lib/macros*. A **troff** macro definition always begins with the string ".de", followed by an optional space and the one- or two-letter name of the macro. The definition ends with a line beginning with two dots (..). The script we show in this section extracts a particular macro definition from the macro packages. (It saves you from having to locate and open the file with an editor and search for the lines that you want to examine.)

The first step in designing this script is to write one that extracts a specific macro, in this case, the BL (Bulleted List) macro in the **-mm** package.

```
% sed -n   "/^\.deBL/,/^\.\.$/p" /usr/lib/macros/mmt
.deBL
.if\\n(.$<1 .)L \\n(Pin 0 1n 0 \\*(BU
.if\\n(.$=1 .LB 0\\$1 0 1 0 \\*(BU
.if\\n(.$>1 \{.ie !w\\$1 .)L \\n(Pin 0 1n 0 \\*(BU 0 1
.el.LB 0\\$1 0 1 0 \\*(BU 0 1 \}
..
```

Sed is invoked with the **-n** option to keep it from printing out the entire file. With this option, sed will print only the lines it is explicitly told to print via the print command. The sed script contains two addresses: the first matches the start of the macro definition ".deBL" and the second matches its termination, ".." on a line by itself. Note that dots appear literally in the two patterns and are escaped using the backslash.

The two addresses specify a range of lines for the print command, **p.** It is this capability that distinguishes this kind of search script from **grep**, which cannot match a range of lines.

We can take this command line and make it more general by placing it in a shell script. One obvious advantage of creating a shell script is that it saves typing. Another advantage is that a shell script can be designed for more general usage. For instance, we can allow the user to supply information from the command line. In this case, rather than hard-code the name of the macro in the sed script, we can use a command-line argument to supply it. You can refer to each argument on the command line in a shell script by positional notation: the first argument is $1, the second is $2, and so on. Here's the **getmac** script:

```
:
# getmac -- print mm macro definition for $1
sed -n  "/^\.de$1/,/^\.\.$/p" /usr/lib/macros/mmt
```

The first line of the shell script is a colon, forcing interpretation of the script by the Bourne shell. The second line is a comment that describes the name and purpose of the script. The sed command, on the third line, is identical to the previous example, except that "BL" is replaced by "$1", a variable representing the first command-line argument. Note that the double-quotes surrounding the sed script are necessary. Single quotes would not allow interpretation of "$1" by the shell.

This script, **getmac**, can be executed as follows:

```
% getmac BL
```

where **BL** is the first command-line argument. It produces the same output as the previous example.

This script can be adapted to work with any of several macro packages. The following version of **getmac** allows the user to specify the name of a macro package as the second command-line argument.

```
:
#getmac - read macro definition for $1 from package $2
file=/usr/lib/macros/mmt
mac="$1"
case $2 in
 -ms) file="/work/macros/current/tmac.s";;
 -mm) file="/usr/lib/macros/mmt";;
 -man) file="/usr/lib/macros/an";;
esac
sed -n "/^\.de *$mac/,/^\.\.$/p" $file
```

What is new here is a **case** statement that tests the value of $2 and then assigns a value to the variable **file**. Notice that we assign a default value to **file** so if the user does not designate a macro package, the **-mm** macro package is searched. Also, for clarity and readability, the value of $1 is assigned to the variable **mac.**

73

In creating this script, we discovered a difference among macro packages in the first line of the macro definition. The **-ms** macros includes a space between ".de" and the name of the macro, while **-mm** and **-man** do not. Fortunately, we are able to modify the pattern to accommodate both cases.

```
/^\.de *$mac/
```

Following ".de", we specify a space followed by an asterisk, which means the space is optional.

The script prints the result on standard output, but it can easily be redirected into a file, where it can become the basis for the redefinition of a macro.

Generating an Outline

Our next example not only extracts information; it modifies it to make it easier to read. We create a shell script named **do.outline** that uses sed to give an outline view of a document. It processes lines containing coded section headings, such as the following:

```
.Ah "Shell Programming"
```

The macro package we use has a chapter heading macro named "Se" and hierarchical headings named "Ah", "Bh", and "Ch". In the **-mm** macro package, these macros might be "H", "H1", "H2", "H3", etc. You can adapt the script to whatever macros or tags identify the structure of a document. The purpose of the do.outline script is to make the structure more apparent by printing the headings in an indented outline format.

The result of **do.outline** is shown below:

```
% do.outline ch13/sect1

CHAPTER   13 Let the Computer Do the Dirty Work
        A.   Shell Programming
             B.   Stored Commands
             B.   Passing Arguments to Shell Scripts
             B.   Conditional Execution
             B.   Discarding Used Arguments
             B.   Repetitive Execution
             B.   Setting Default Values
             B.   What We've Accomplished
```

It prints the result to standard output (without, of course, making any changes within the files themselves).

Let's look at how to put together this script. The script needs to match lines that begin with the macros for:

- Chapter title (.Se)
- Section heading (.Ah)
- Subsection heading (.Bh)

We need to make substitutions on those lines, replacing macros with a text marker (A, B, for instance) and adding the appropriate amount of spacing to indent each heading.

Here's the basic script:

```
sed -n '
s/^\.Se /Chapter /p
s/^\.Ah / A. /p
s/^\.Bh /     B. /p' $*
```

do.outline operates on all files specified on the command line ("$*"). The **-n** option suppresses the default output of the program. The sed script contains three substitute commands that replace the codes with the letters and indent each line. Each substitute command is modified by the **p** flag that indicates the line should be printed.

When we test this script, the following results are produced:

```
CHAPTER   "13" "Let the Computer Do the Dirty Work"
      A.   "Shell Programming"
          B.   "Stored Commands"
          B.   "Passing Arguments to Shell Scripts"
```

The quotation marks which surround the arguments to a macro are passed through. We can write a substitute command to remove the quotation marks.

```
s/"//g
```

It is necessary to specify the global flag, **g**, to catch all occurrences on a single line. However, the key decision is where to put this command in the script. If we put it at the end of the script, it will remove the quotation marks after the line has already been output. We have to put it at the top of the script and perform this edit for all lines, regardless of whether or not they are output later in the script.

```
sed -n '
s/"//g
s/^\.Se /Chapter /p
s/^\.Ah / A. /p
s/^\.Bh /     B. /p' $*
```

This script now produces the results that were shown earlier.

You can modify this script to search for almost any kind of coded format. For instance, here's a rough version for a TeX file:

```
sed -n '
s/[{}]//g
s/\\section/          A. /p
s/\\subsection/          B.  /p' $*
```

Edits To Go

Let's consider an application that shows sed in its role as a true stream editor, making edits in a pipeline—edits that are never written back into a file.

On a typewriter-like device (including a CRT), an em-dash is typed as a pair of hyphens (--). In typesetting, it is printed as a single, long dash (—). **troff** provides a special character name for the em-dash, but it is inconvenient to type "\(em."

The following command changes two consecutive dashes into an em-dash.

```
s/--/\\(em/g
```

We double the backslashes in the replacement string for \(em, since the backslash has a special meaning to sed.

Perhaps there are cases in which we don't want this substitute command to be applied. What if someone is using hyphens to draw a horizontal line? We can refine this command to exclude lines containing three or more consecutive hyphens. To do this, we use the ! address modifier:

```
/---/!s/--/\\(em/g
```

It may take a moment to penetrate this syntax. What's different is that we use a pattern address to restrict the lines that are affected by the substitute command, and we use ! to reverse the sense of the pattern match. It says, simply, "If you find a line containing three consecutive hyphens, don't apply the edit." On all other lines, the substitute command will be applied.

We can use this command in a script that automatically inserts em-dashes for us. To do that, we will use sed as a pre-processor for a **troff** file. The file will be processed by sed and then piped to troff.

```
sed '/---/!s/--/\\(em/g' file | troff
```

In other words, sed changes the input file and passes the output directly to **troff**, without creating an intermediate file. The edits are made on-the-go, and do not affect the input file. You might wonder why not just make the changes permanently in the original file? One reason is simply that it's not necessary — the input remains consistent with what the user typed but **troff** still produces what looks best for typeset-quality output. Furthermore, because it is embedded in a larger shell script, the transformation of hyphens to em-dashes is transparent to the user, and not an additional step in the formatting process.

We use a shell script named **format** that uses sed for this purpose. Here's what the shell script looks like:

```
eqn="";pic="";macros="ms";col="";roff="ditroff -Tps"
sed="| sed '/---/!s/--/\\(em/g'
while [ $# -gt 0 ]
do
    case $1 in
      -E) eqn="| eqn";;
      -P) pic="| pic";;
      -N) roff="nroff";col="| col";sed="";;
      -*) options="$options $1";;
       *) if [ -f $1 ]; then
          files="$files $1"
          else echo "format: $1: file not found"; exit
          fi;;
    esac
    shift
done
eval "cat $files $sed | tbl $eqn $pic | $roff $options $col | lp"
```

This script assigns and evaluates a number of variables (prefixed by a dollar sign) that construct the command line that is submitted to format and print a document. (Notice that we've set up the **-N** option for **nroff** so that it sets the sed variable to null, since we only want to make this change if we are using **troff**.)

Changing hyphens to em-dashes is not the only "prettying up" edit we might want to make when typesetting a document. For example, most keyboards do not allow you to type open and close quotation marks (**troff**, you can indicate a open quotation mark as \'\' and a close quotation mark as \'\'. We can use sed to change each double-quote character to a pair of single open-quotes or close-quotes (depending on context), which, when typeset, will produce the appearance of a proper "double quote".

This is a considerably more difficult edit to make, since there are many separate cases involving punctuation marks, space, and tabs. Our script might look like the following:

```
s/^"/\'\'/
s/"$/\'\'/
s/"? /\'\'? /g
s/"?$/\'\'?/g
s/ "/ \'\'/g
s/" /\'\'  /g
s/.        "/         \'\'/g
```

```
s/"        /\'\'      /g
s/")/\'\')/g
s/"]/\'\']/g
s/("/(\'\'/g
s/\["/\[\'\'/g
s/";/\'\';/g
s/":/\'\':/g
s/,"/,\'\'/g
s/",/\'\',/g
s/\."/.\\\&\'\'/g
s/"\./\'\'.\\\&/g
s/"\(em/\'\'\(em/g
s/\(em"/\(em\'\'/g
```

The first substitute command looks for a quotation mark at the beginning of a line and changes it to an open-quote. The second command looks for a quotation mark at the end of a line and changes it to a close-quote. The remaining commands look for the quotation mark in different contexts, before or after a punctuation mark, a space, a tab, or an em-dash. We put these commands in a "cleanup" script, along with the command changing hyphens to dashes, and invoke it in the pipeline that formats and prints documents using **troff**.

Getting to the PromiSed Land

You have now seen four different types of sed scripts, as well as how they are embedded inside shell scripts to create easy-to-use applications. More and more, as you work with sed, you will develop methods for creating and testing sed scripts. You will come to rely upon these methods and gain confidence that you know what your script is doing and why.

Here are a few tips:

1. *Know thy Input!*
   Carefully examine your input file, using **grep**, before designing your script.

2. *Use the Whitman Sampler Approach!*
   Start with a small sample of occurrences in a test file. Run your script on the sample and make sure the script is working. Remember, it's just as important to make sure the script *doesn't* work where you *don't* want it to. Then increase the size of the sample. Try to increase the complexity of the input.

3. *Sedimentary, My Dear Watson.*
   Work carefully, testing each command that you add to a script. Compare the output against the input file to see what has changed. Prove to yourself that your script is complete. Your script may work perfectly, based on your assumptions of what is in the input file, but your assumptions may be wrong.

4. *Be pragmatic!*

Try to accomplish what you can with your sed but it doesn't have to do 100 percent of the job. If you encounter difficult situations, check and see how frequently they occur. Sometimes it's better to do a few remaining edits manually.

If you can add to these tips with your experience, tack them on.

5

Basic Sed Commands

The sed command set consists of 25 commands. In this chapter, we introduce four new editing commands: **d** (delete), **a** (append), **i** (insert), and **c** (change). We also look at ways to change the flow control (i.e., determine which command is executed next) within a script.

About the Syntax of Sed Commands

Before looking at individual commands, there are a couple points to review about the syntax of all sed commands. We covered most of this material in the previous chapter.

A line address is optional with any command. It can be a pattern described as a regular expression surrounded by slashes, a line number, or a line-addressing symbol. Most sed commands can accept two comma-separated addresses that indicate a range of lines. For these commands, our convention is to specify:

> [*address*]*command*

A few commands accept only a single line address. They cannot be applied to a range of lines. The convention for them is:

> [*line-address*]*command*

Remember also that commands can be grouped at the same address by surrounding the list of commands in braces:

> *address* {
>
> > *command1*
> > *command2*
> > *command3*
>
> }

The first command can be placed on the same line with the opening brace but the closing brace must appear on its own line. Each command can have its own address and multiple levels of grouping are permitted. Also, as you can see from the indentation of the commands inside the braces, blanks, and tabs at the beginning of lines are permitted.

When sed is unable to understand a command, it prints the message "Command garbled." One common syntax error is to allow blank spaces at the end of a command line. A newline must follow immediately at the end of a command. Extra spaces at the end are not permitted.

Proof of this restriction is offered by an "undocumented" feature: multiple sed commands can be placed on the same line if each one is separated by a semicolon. The following example is syntactically correct:

```
n;d
```

However, putting a space after the **n** command causes a syntax error. Putting a space *before* the **d** command is okay.

Placing multiple commands on the same line is highly discouraged because sed scripts are difficult enough to read even when each command is written on its own line. (Note that the change, insert, and append commands must be specified over multiple lines and cannot be specified on the same line.)

Comment

You can use a comment to document a script by describing its purpose. Starting in this chapter, our full script examples begin with a comment line. A comment line can appear as the first line of a script. In System V's version of sed, a comment is permitted only on the first line. On some versions, including sed running under Sun OS 4.1 and with gsed, you can place comments anywhere in the script, even on a line following a command. The examples in this book will follow the more restrictive case of System V sed, limiting comments to the first line of the script. However, the ability to use comments to document your script is valuable and you should make use of it if your version of sed permits it.

An octothorpe (#) must be the first character on the line. The syntax of a comment line is:

#[n]

The following example shows the first line of a script:

```
# wstar.sed: convert WordStar files
```

If necessary, the comment can be continued on multiple lines by ending the preceding line with a backslash. For consistency, you might begin the continuation line with an # so that the line's purpose is obvious.

If the next character following # is **n**, the script will not automatically produce output. It is equivalent to specifying the command-line option -**n**. The rest of the line following the **n** is treated as a comment.

Substitution

We have already demonstrated many uses of the substitute command. Let's look carefully at its syntax:

[*address*]s/*pattern*/*replacement*/*flags*

where the *flags* that modify the substitution are:

n   A number (1 to 512) indicating that a replacement should be made for only the *n*th occurrence of the *regexp*.

g   Make changes globally on all occurrences in pattern space. Normally only the first occurrence is replaced.

p   Print the contents of the pattern space.

w *file*   Write the contents of pattern space to *file*.

The substitute command is applied to the lines matching the *address*. If no address is specified, it is applied to all lines that match the *pattern*, a regular expression. If a regular expression is supplied as an address, and no *pattern* is specified, the substitute command matches what is matched by the address. This can be useful when the substitute command is one of multiple commands applied at the same address. For an example, see the section "Checking Out Reference Pages" in this chapter.

Unlike addresses, which require a slash (/) as a delimiter, the regular expression can be delimited by any character except a blank or a newline. Thus, if the pattern contained slashes, you could choose another character, such as an exclamation mark, as the delimiter.

```
s!/usr/mail!/usr2/mail!
```

Note that the delimiter appears three times and is required after the *replacement*. Regardless of which delimiter you use, if it does appear in the regular expression, use a backslash (\) to escape it.

A regular expression can also use "\n" to match an *embedded* newline. This occurs, as you will see in the next chapter, in the special case when another line is appended to the current line in the pattern space. See Chapter 2, *Understanding Basic Operations*, for a discussion of line addressing and Chapter 3, *Understanding Regular Expression Syntax*, for a discussion of regular expression syntax.

The *replacement* is a string of characters that will replace what is matched by the regular expression. (See "The Extent of the Match" in Chapter 3.) In the *replacement* section, only the following characters have special meaning:

&   Replaced by the string matched by the regular expression.

\n   Matches the *n*th substring (*n* is a single digit) previously specified in the *regexp* using "\(" and "\)".

****   Used to escape the ampersand (&) and the backslash (\) when they are used literally in the replacement section. In addition, it can be used to escape the newline and create a multi-line *replacement* string.

See the next section, "Replacement Metacharacters," for examples of using the replacement metacharacters.

Flags can be used in combination where it makes sense. For instance, **gp** makes the substitution globally on the line and prints the line. The global flag is by far the most commonly used. Without it, the replacement is made only for the first occurrence on the line. The print flag and the write flag both provide the same functionality as the print and write commands (which are discussed later on in this chapter) with one important difference. These actions are contingent upon a successful substitution occurring. In other words, if the replacement is made, the line is printed or written to file. Because the default action is to pass through all lines, regardless of whether any action is taken, the print and write flags are typically used when the default output is suppressed (the **-n** option). In addition, if a script contains multiple substitute commands that match the same line, multiple copies of that line will be printed or written to file.

The numeric flag can be used in the somewhat rare instances where the regular expression repeats itself on a line and the replacement must be made for only one of those occurrences by position. For instance, a line, perhaps containing **tbl** input, might contain multiple tabs. Let's say that there are three tabs per line, and you'd like to replace the second tab with ">". The following substitute command would do it:

```
s/|—|/>/2
```

"|—|" represents an actual tab character, which is otherwise invisible on the screen. If the input is a one-line file such as the following:

```
Column1    Column2    Column3    Column4
```

the output produced by running the script on this file will be:

```
Column1    Column2>Column3    Column4
```

Note that without the numeric flag, the substitute command would replace only the first tab. (Therefore "1" can be considered the default numeric flag.)

Replacement Metacharacters

The replacement metacharacters are backslash (\\), ampersand (&), and \\n. The backslash is generally used to escape the other metacharacters but it is also used to include a newline in a replacement string.

We can do a variation on the previous example to replace the second tab on each line with a newline.

```
s/|—|/\
/2
```

Note that no spaces are permitted after the backslash. This script produces the following result:

```
Column1    Column2
Column3    Column4
```

Another example comes from the conversion of a file for **troff** to an ASCII input format for Ventura Publisher™. It converts the following line for **troff**:

```
.Ah "Major Heading"
```

to a similar line for Ventura Publisher:

```
@A Head = Major Heading
```

The twist in this problem is that the line needs to be preceded and followed by a blank line. It is an example of writing a multi-line replacement string.

```
/^.Ah/{
s/.Ah */\
\
@A HEAD = /
s/""//g
s/$/\
/
}
```

The first substitute command replaces ".Ah" with two newlines and "@A HEAD". Each backslash at the end of the line is necessary to escape the newline. The second substitution removes the quotation marks. The last command matches the end of line in the pattern space (not the embedded newlines) and adds a newline after it.

In the next example, the backslash is used to escape the ampersand, which appears literally in the replacement section.

```
s/ORA/O'Reilly \& Associates, Inc./g
```

It's easy to forget about the ampersand appearing literally in the replacement string. If we had not escaped it in this example, the output would have been "O'Reilly ORA Associates, Inc."

As a metacharacter, the ampersand (&) represents the extent of the pattern match, not the line that was matched. It's easy to forget about the ampersand appearing literally in the replacement string. If we had not escaped it in this example, the output would have been "O'Reilly ORA Associates, Inc."

You might use the ampersand to match a word and surround it by **troff** requests. The following example surrounds a word with point-size requests:

```
s/UNIX/\\s-2&\\s0/g
```

Because backslashes are also replacement metacharacters, two backslashes are necessary to output a single backslash. The "&" in the replacement string refers to "UNIX". If the input line is:

```
on the UNIX Operating System.
```

then the substitute command produces:

```
on the \s-2UNIX\s0 Operating System.
```

The ampersand is particularly useful when the regular expression matches variations of a word. It allows you to specify a variable replacement string that corresponds to what was actually matched. For instance, let's say that you wanted to surround with parentheses any cross reference to a numbered section in a document. In other words, any reference such as "See Section 1.4" or "See Section 12.9" should appear in parentheses, as "(See Section 12.9)". A regular expression can match the different combination of numbers, so we use "&" in the replacement string and surround whatever was matched.

```
s/See Section [1-9][1-9]*\.[1-9][1-9]*/(&)/
```

The ampersand makes it possible to reference the entire match in the replacement string.

Now let's look at the metacharacters that allow us to select any individual portion of a string that is matched and recall it in the replacement string. A pair of escaped parentheses are used in sed to enclose any part of a regular expression and save it for recall. Up to nine "saves" are permitted for a single line. "\n" is used to recall the portion of the match that was saved, where *n* is a number from 1 to 9 referencing a particular "saved" string in order of use.

For example, to embolden the section numbers when they appeared as a cross reference, we could write the following substitution:

```
s/\(See Section \)\([1-9][1-9]*\.[1-9][1-9]*\)/\1\\fB\2\\fP/
```

Two pairs of escaped parentheses are specified. The first captures "See Section" (because this is a fixed string, it could have been simply retyped in the replacement string). The second captures the section number. The replacement string recalls the first saved substring as "\1" and the second as "\2," which is surrounded by bold-font requests.

We can use a similar technique to match parts of a line and swap them. For instance, let's say there are two parts of a line separated by a colon. We can

match each part, putting them within escaped parentheses and swapping them in
the replacement.

```
% cat test1
first:second
one:two
% sed 's/\(.*\):\(.*\)/\2:\1/' test1
second:first
two:one
```

The larger point is that you can recall a saved substring in any order, and multiple
times, as you'll see in the next example.

Correcting Index Entries

Later, in the awk section of this book, we will present a program for formatting an
index, such as the one for this book. The first step in creating an index is to place
index codes in the document files. We use an index macro named .XX, which
takes a single argument, the index entry. For example, a sample index entry
might be:

```
.XX "sed, substitution command"
```

Each index entry appears on a line by itself. When you run an index, you get a
collection of index entries with page numbers that are then sorted and merged in a
list. An editor pouring over that list will typically find errors and inconsistencies
that need to be corrected. It is, in short, a pain to have to track down the file
where an index entry resides and then make the correction, particularly when
there are dozens of entries to be corrected.

Sed can be a great help in making these edits across a group of files. One can
simply create a list of edits in a sed script and then run it on all the files. A key
point is that the substitute command needs an address that limits it to lines beginning ".XX". Your script should not make changes in the text itself.

Let's say that we wanted to change the index entry above to "sed, substitute command." The following command would do it:

```
/^.XX /s/sed, substitution command/sed, substitute command/
```

The address matches all lines that begin with ".XX" and only on those lines does
it attempt to make the replacement. You might wonder, why not specify a shorter
regular expression? For example:

```
/^.XX /s/substitution/substitute/
```

The answer is simply that there could be other entries which use the word "substitution" correctly and which we would not want to change.

We can go a step further and provide a shell script that creates a list of index entries prepared for editing as a series of sed substitute commands.

```
:
#index.edit -- compile list of index entries for editing.
grep "^\.XX" $* | sort -u |
sed '
s/^\.XX \(.*\)$/\/^\\.XX \/s\/\1\/\1\//'
```

The **index.edit** shell script uses grep to extract all lines containing index entries from any number of files specified on the command line. It passes this list through **sort** which, with the **-u** option, sorts and removes duplicate entries. The list is then piped to sed, and the one-line sed script builds a substitution command. Let's look at it more closely. Here's just the regular expression:

```
^\.XX \(.*\)$
```

It matches the entire line, saving the index entry for recall. Here's just the replacement string:

```
\/^\\.XX \/s\/\1\/\1\/
```

It generates a substitute command beginning with an address: a slash, followed by two backslashes—to output one backslash to protect the dot in the ".XX" that follows—then comes a space, then another slash to complete the address. Next we output an "s" followed by a slash, and then recall the saved portion to be used as a regular expression. That is followed by another slash and a second time we recall the saved substring as the replacement string. A slash finally ends the command.

When the **index.edit** script is run on a file, it creates a listing similar to the following:

```
% index.edit ch05
/^.XX /s/"append command(a)"/"append command(a)"/
/^.XX /s/"change command"/"change command"/
/^.XX /s/"change command(c)"/"change command(c)"/
/^.XX /s/"commands:sed, summary of"/"commands:sed, summary of"/
/^.XX /s/"delete command(d)"/"delete command(d)"/
/^.XX /s/"insert command(i)"/"insert command(i)"/
/^.XX /s/"line numbers:printing"/"line numbers:printing"/
/^.XX /s/"list command(l)"/"list command(l)"/
```

This output could be captured in a file. Then you can delete the entries that don't need to change and you can make changes by editing the replacement string. At that point, you can use this file as a sed script to correct the index entries in all document files.

If you were doing a large book and there were lots of entries, you might use **grep** again to extract particular entries from the output of **index.edit** and direct into their own file for editing. It saves you from having to wade through numerous entries.

There is one small failing in this program. It should look for metacharacters that might appear literally in index entries and protect them in regular expressions. For instance, if an index entry contains an asterisk, it will not be interpreted as such, but as a metacharacter. To make that change effectively requires the use of several advanced commands so we'll put off improving this script until the next chapter.

Delete

We have previously demonstrated examples of the delete command (**d**). It takes an address and deletes the contents of the pattern space if the line matches the address.

The delete command is also a command that can change the flow of control in a script. That is because once it is executed, no further commands are executed on the "empty" pattern space.* The delete command causes a new line of input to be read and a new pass on the editing script to begin from the top. (In this behavior, it is the same as the **next** command, which you'll encounter later in this chapter.)

The important thing to remember is: if the line matches the address, the entire line is deleted, not just the portion of the line that is matched. (Use the substitute command to delete a portion of a line by specifying an empty replacement.)

In the previous chapter, we showed a command to delete blank lines:

```
/^$/d
```

Another use of the delete command could be to strip out certain **troff** requests, such as those that add spacing, break the page, and turn fill mode off and on:

```
/^.sp/d
/^.bp/d
/^.nf/d
/^.fi/d
```

These commands delete an entire line. For instance, the first command will delete the line ".sp 1" or ".sp .03v".

---

*UNIX documentation reads "no further commands are attempted on the corpse of a deleted line." R.I.P.

The delete command can be used to delete a range of lines. In the previous chapter, there is an example of deleting all tables from a file by deleting the lines between the .TS and .TE macros.

There is also a delete command (**D**) used to delete a portion of a multi-line pattern space. This advanced command is presented in the next chapter.

Append, Insert and Change

The append (**a**), insert (**i**), and change (**c**) commands provide editing functions that are commonly performed with an interactive editor, such as **vi**. You may find it strange to use these same commands to "enter" text using a non-interactive editor. The syntax of these commands is unusual for sed because they must be specified over multiple lines. The syntax follows:

append	[*line-address*]a\
	text
insert	[*line-address*]i\
	text
change	[*address*]c\
	text

The insert command places the supplied text before the current line in the pattern space. The append command places it after the current line. The change command replaces the contents of the pattern space with the supplied text.

Each of these commands requires a backslash following it to escape the first end of line. The *text* must begin on the next line. To input multiple lines of text, each successive line must end with a backslash, with the exception of the very last line. For example, the following insert command inserts two lines of text at a line matching "<Larry's Address>":

```
/<Larry's Address>/i\
4700 Cross Court\
French Lick, IN
```

Also, if the text contains a literal backslash, add an extra backslash to escape it.*

The append and insert commands can be applied only to a single line address, not a range of lines. The change command, however, can address a range of lines. In

---

*UNIX documentation says that any leading tabs or blank spaces in the supplied text will disappear on output. I do not find that to be true. If they disappear on your system, the solution is to put a backslash at the beginning of the line, preceding the first tab or space. The backslash is not output.

this case, it replaces *all* addressed lines with a single copy of the text. In other words, it deletes each line in the range but the supplied text is output only once. For example, the following script, when run on a file containing a mail message:

```
/From /,/^$/c\
<Mail Header Removed>
```

removes the entire mail-message header and replaces it with the the line "<Mail Header Removed>." Note that you will see the opposite behavior when the change command is one of a group of commands, enclosed in braces, that act on a range of lines. For instance, the following script:

```
/From /,/^$/{
    s/From //p
    c\
<Mail Header Removed>
}
```

will output "<Mail Header Removed>" for each line in the range. So, while the former example output the text once, this example will output it ten times if there are ten lines in the range.

The change command clears the pattern space, having the same effect on the pattern space as the delete command. No command following the change command in the script is applied.

The insert and append commands do not affect the contents of the pattern space. The supplied text will not match any address in subsequent commands in the script, nor can those commands affect the text. No matter what changes occur to alter the pattern space, the supplied text will still be output appropriately. This is also true when the default output is suppressed—the supplied text will be output even if the pattern space is not. Also, the supplied text does not affect sed's internal line counter.

Let's look at an example of the insert command. Suppose we wanted to source a local file of macros in all the files of a particular document. In addition, we'd like to define a page header string that identifies the document as a draft. The following script inserts two new lines of text before the first line of a file:

```
1i\
.so macros\
.ds CH First Draft
```

After sed executes this command, the pattern space remains unchanged. The new text is output before the current line. A subsequent command could not successfully match "macros" or "First Draft".

A variation of the previous example shows the append command adding a line to the end of a file:

```
$a\
End of file
```

The $ is a line-addressing symbol that matches the last line of a file. The supplied text will be output after the current line, so it becomes the last line in the output. Note that even though only one line is output, the supplied text must start on a line by itself and cannot be on the same line as the append command.

The next example shows the insert and append commands used in the same script. The task here is to add a few **troff** requests before the macro that initializes a list, and several after the macro that closes the list.

```
/\.Ls/i\
.in 5n\
.sp .3
/.Le/a\
.in 0\
.sp .3
```

The insert command puts two lines before the .Ls macro and the append command puts two lines after the .Le macro.

The insert command can be used to put a blank line before the current line, or the append command to put one after, by leaving the line following it blank.

The change command replaces the contents of the pattern space with the text you provide. In effect, it deletes the current line and puts the supplied text in its place. It can be used when you want to match a line and replace it entirely. Let's say for instance that a file contains a lot of explicit **troff** spacing requests with different amounts of spacing. Look at the following series:

```
.sp 1.5
.sp
.sp 1
.sp 1.5v
.sp .3v
.sp 3
```

If you wanted to change all the arguments to ".5", it is probably easier to use the change command than try to match all the individual arguments and make the proper substitution.

```
/^.sp/c\
.sp .5
```

This command allows us to ignore the arguments and replace them regardless of what they are.

The list command (l) displays the contents of the pattern space, showing non-printing characters as two-digit ASCII codes. It is similar in function to the list (:l) command in **vi**. You can use this command to detect "invisible" characters in the input.

```
$ cat test/spchar
Here is a string of special characters: ^A  ^B
^M ^G


$ sed -n -e "l" test/spchar
Here is a string of special characters: \01 \02
\15 \07
```

Because the list command causes immediate output, we suppress the default output or we would get duplicate copies of the lines.

You cannot match a character by ASCII value (nor can you match octal values) in sed.* Instead, you have to find a key combination in **vi** to produce it. Use CTRL-V to quote the character. For instance, you can match an ESC character (^[). Look at the following script:

```
# list line and replace ^[ with "Escape"
l
s/^[/Escape/
```

Here's a one-line test file:

```
The Great ^[ is a movie starring Steve McQueen.
```

Running the script produces the following output:

```
The Great 33 is a movie starring Steve McQueen.
The Great Escape is a movie starring Steve McQueen.
```

The ^[character was produced in **vi** by entering CTRL-V and then pressing the ESC key.

---

*You can do this in nawk, however.

Stripping Out Non-Printable Characters from nroff Files

The UNIX formatter **nroff** produces output for line printers and CRT displays. To achieve such special effects as emboldening, it outputs the character followed by a backspace and then outputs the same character again. A sample of it viewed with a text editor might look like:

```
N^HN^HN^HNA^HA^HA^HAM^HM^HM^HME^HE^HE^HE
```

which emboldens the word "NAME". There are three overstrikes for each character output. Similarly, underlining is achieved by outputting an underscore, a backspace and then the character to be underlined. The following example is the word "file" surrounded by a sequence for underscoring it.

```
_^Hf_^Hi_^Hl_^He
```

It might be necessary at times to strip these printing "special-effects" perhaps if you are given this type of output as a source file. The following line removes the sequences for emboldening and underscoring:

```
s/.^H//g
```

It removes any character preceding the backspace along with the backspace itself. In the case of underlining, "." matches the underscore; for emboldening, it matches the overstrike character. Because it is applied repeatedly, multiple occurrences of the overstrike character are removed, leaving a single character for each sequence. Note that **^H** is entered in **vi** by pressing CTRL-V followed by CTRL-H.

A sample application is "de-formatting" an nroff-produced **man** page found on a System V UNIX system. (Berkeley UNIX systems usually provide the coded source to man pages, whereas System V provides formatted files.) If you should want to access the formatted pages with a text editor, you'd want to get a clean version. (In many ways, this is a similar problem to one we solved in converting a word processing file in the previous chapter.) A formatted **man** page captured in a file looks like this:

```
^[9     who(1)                                              who(1)


^[9 N^HN^HN^HNA^HA^HA^HAM^HM^HM^HME^HE^HE^HE
        who - who is on the system?

  S^HS^HS^HSY^HY^HY^HYN^HN^HN^HNO^HO^HO^HOP^HP^HP^HPS^HS^HS^HSI^HI
        who [-a] [-b] [-d] [-H] [-l] [-p] [-q] [-r] [-s] [-t] [-T]
        [-u] [_^Hf_^Hi_^Hl_^He]
```

```
who am i

who am I
```

```
D^HD^HD^HDE^HE^HE^HES^HS^HS^HSC^HC^HC^HCR^HR^HR^HRI^HI^HI^HIP^HP
        who can list the user's name, terminal line, login time,
        elapsed time since activity occurred on the line, and the
...
```

In addition to stripping out the emboldening and underlining sequences, there are strange escape sequences that produce form feeds or various other printer functions. You can see the sequence "^[9" at the top of the formatted man page. This escape sequence can simply be removed:

```
s/^[9//g
```

Once again, the Esc character is entered in **vi** by typing CTRL-V followed by pressing the Esc key. The number 9 is literal. There are also what looks to be leading spaces that supply the left margin and indentation. On further examination, it turns out that leading spaces precede the heading such as "NAME" but a single tab precedes each line of text. Also, there are tabs that unexpectedly appear in the text, which have to do with how **nroff** optimizes for display on a CRT screen.

To eliminate the left margin and the unwanted tabs, we add two commands to our previous two:

```
#sedman -- deformat nroff-formatted man page
s/.^H//g
s/^[9//g
s/^[□|—|]*//g
s/|—|/ /g
```

The third command looks for any number of tabs or spaces at the beginning of a line. (A tab is represented by "|—|" and a space by "□".) The last command looks for a tab and replaces it with a single space. Running this script on our sample **man** page output produces a file that looks like this:

```
who(1)                                                           who(1)



NAME
who - who is on the system?

SYNOPSIS
who [-a] [-b] [-d] [-H] [-l] [-p] [-q] [-r] [-s] [-t] [-T]
[-u] [file]
```

```
who am i

who am I

DESCRIPTION
who can list the user's name, terminal line, login time,
elapsed time since activity occurred on the line, and the
...
```

This script does not eliminate the unnecessary blank lines caused by paging. We will look at how to do that in the next chapter, as it requires a multi-line operation.

Transform

The transform command is peculiar, not only because it is the least mnemonic of all sed commands. This command transforms each character by position in string *abc* to its equivalent in string *xyz*. Its syntax follows:

> [*address*]y/*abc*/*xyz*/

The replacement is made by character position. Therefore, it has no idea of a "word". Thus, "a" is replaced by "x" anywhere on the line, regardless of whether or not it is followed by a "b". One possible use of this command is to reverse uppercase and lowercase letters.

```
/.*/y/abcdefghijklmnopqrstuvwxyz/ABCDEFGHIJKLMNOPQRSTUVWXYZ/
```

This command affects the entire contents of the pattern space. If you want to convert a single word on the input line, you could do it by using the hold space. See the next chapter for more details on how to use the hold space. (The process is not trivial: you output the line up to the word you want to change, delete that portion of the line, copy the line after the word to the hold space, transform the word, and then append the contents of the hold space back to the pattern space.)

Print

The print command (**p**) causes the contents of the pattern space to be output. It does not clear the pattern space nor does it change the flow of control in the script. However, it is frequently used before commands (**d,N,b**) that do change flow control. Unless the default output is suppressed, the print command will cause duplicate copies of a line to be output. It can be used when default output is suppressed or when the flow control through the program avoids reaching the bottom of the script.

Let's look at a script that shows how the print command might be used for debugging purposes. It is used to show what the line looked like before you made any changes.

```
#n Print line before and after changes.
/^\.Ah/{
p
s/"//g
s/\.Ah //p
}
```

Note that the print flag is supplied to the substitute command. The substitute command's print flag differs from the print command in that it is conditional upon a successful substitution.

Here's a sample run of the above script:

```
% sed -f sed.debug ch05
.Ah "Comment"
Comment
.Ah "Substitution"
Substitution
.Ah "Delete"
Delete
.Ah "Append, Insert and Change"
Append, Insert and Change
.Ah "List"
List
```

Each affected line is printed twice.

We'll see additional examples of the print command in the next chapter. see also the multi-line print command (**P**) in the next chapter.

Print Line Number

An equal sign (=) following an address prints the line number of the matched line. Unless you suppress the automatic output of lines, both the line number and the line itself will be printed. Its syntax is:

> [*line-address*]=

This command cannot operate on a range of lines.

A programmer might use this to print certain lines in a source file. For instance, the following script prints the line number followed by the line itself for each line containing a tab followed by the string "if". Here's the script:

```
#n print line number and line with if statement
/	if/{
=
p
}
```

Note the "#n" suppresses the default output of lines. Now let's see how it works on a sample program, *random.c*:

```
$ sed -f sedscr.= random.c
192
        if(  rand_type  ==  TYPE_0  )  {
234
        if(  rand_type  ==  TYPE_0  )  state[ -1 ] = rand_type;
236
        if(  n  <  BREAK_1  )  {
252
            if(  n  <  BREAK_3  )  {
274
        if(  rand_type  ==  TYPE_0  )  state[ -1 ] = rand_type;
303
        if(  rand_type  ==  TYPE_0  )  state[ -1 ] = rand_type;
```

The line numbers might be useful in finding problems reported by the compiler, which typically lists the line number.

Next

The next command (**n**) outputs the contents of the pattern space and then reads the next line of input *without* returning to the top of the script. Its syntax is:

[*address*]**n**

The next command changes the normal flow control, which doesn't output the contents of the pattern space until the bottom of the script is reached and which always begins at the top of the script after reading in a new line. In effect, the next command causes the next line of input to replace the current line in the pattern space. The current line, however, is output normally, although subsequent commands in the script are not applied.

Of course, if the default output of sed is suppressed, then executing the next command does not automatically output the current line.

Let's look at an example of the next command in which we delete a blank line only when it follows a pattern matched on the previous line. In this case, a writer has inserted a blank line after a section heading macro (.H1). We want to remove that blank line without removing all blank lines in the file. Here's the sample file:

```
.H1 "On Egypt"

Napolean, pointing to the Pyramids, said to his troops:
"Soldiers, forty centuries have their eyes upon you."
```

The following script removes that blank line:

```
/^.H1/{
n
/^$/d
}
```

You can read this script as follows: "Match any line beginning with the string ".H1", then print that line and read in the next line. If that line is blank, delete it." The braces are used to apply multiple commands at the same address.

In a longer script, you should be aware that commands occuring before the next command will not be applied to the new input line, nor will commands occuring after it be applied to the old input line.

You'll see additional examples of the **next** command in Chapter 6, *Advanced Sed Commands*, along with a multi-line version of this command.

Reading and Writing Files

The read (**r**) and write (**w**) commands allow you to work directly with files. Both take a single argument, the name of a file. The syntax follows:

> [*line-address*]**r** *file*

> [*address*]**w** *file*

The read command reads the contents of *file* into the pattern space after the addressed line. It cannot operate on a range of lines. The write command writes the contents of the pattern space to the *file*.

You must have a single space between the command and the filename. (Everything after that space and up to the newline is taken to be the filename. Thus, leading or embedded blank spaces will become part of the filename.) The read command will not complain if the file does not exist. The write command will create a file if it does not exist; if the file already exists, the write command will overwrite it each time the script is invoked. If there are multiple instructions writing to the same file in one script, then each write command appends to the file. Also, be aware that you can only open up to 10 files per script.*

The read command can be useful for inserting the contents of one file at a particular place in another file. For instance, let's say that there a set of files and each file should close with the same one or two paragraph statement. A sed script would allow you to maintain the closing separately while inserting it as needed, for instance, when sending the file to the printer.

```
sed '
$r closing' $* | pr | lp
```

The $ is an addressing symbol specifying the last line of the file. The contents of the file named *closing* are placed after the contents of pattern space and output with it. This example does not specify a pathname, assuming the file to be in the same directory as the command. A more general-purpose command should use the full pathname.

You may want to test out a few quirks of the read command. Let's look at the following command:

```
/^<Company-list>/r company.list
```

That is, when sed matches a line beginning with the string "<Company-list>", it is going to append the contents of the file *company.list* to the end of the matched line. No subsequent command will affect the lines read from the file. For instance, you can't make any changes to the list of companies that you've read into the file. However, commands that address the original line will work. For instance, the previous command could be followed by a second command:

```
/^<Company-list>/d
```

to delete the original line. So that if the input file was as follows:

```
For service, contact any of the following companies:
<Company-list>
Thank you.
```

running the two-line script would produce:

```
For service, contact any of the following companies:
        Allied
        Mayflower
        United
Thank you.
```

---

*The same restriction applies to the original version of awk.

Even if you suppress the automatic output, using the **-n** option or **#n** script syntax, the result of a read command will still be sent to standard output. However, the original line in the pattern space will not be output.

Now let's look at examples of the write command. One use is to extract information from one file and place it in its own file. For instance, imagine that we had a file listing the names of salespeople alphabetically. For each person, the listing designates which of the four regions the person is assigned. Here's a sample:

```
Adams, Henrietta      Northeast
Banks, Freda          South
Dennis, Jim           Midwest
Garvey, Bill          Northeast
Jeffries, Jane        West
Madison, Sylvia       Midwest
Sommes, Tom           South
```

Writing a script for a seven-line file, of course, is ridiculous. Yet such a script can potentially handle as many names as you can put together, and is reusable.

If all we wanted was to extract the names for a particular region, we could easily use **grep** to do it. The advantage with sed is that we can break up the file into four separate files in a single step. The following four-line script does it:

```
/Northeast$/w region.northeast
/South$/w region.south
/Midwest$/w region.midwest
/West$/w region.west
```

All of the names of salespeople that are assigned to the Northeast region will be placed in a file named *region.northeast*.

The write command writes out the contents of the pattern space when the command is invoked, not when end of the script is reached. In the previous example, we might want to remove the name of the region before writing it to file. For each case, we could handle it as we show for the Northeast region:

```
/Northeast$/{
    s///
    w region.northeast
    }
```

The substitute command matches the same pattern as the address and removes it. There are many different uses for the write command. Once I used this command in a script to generate three customized versions of the same source file.

Checking Out Reference Pages

Like many programs, a sed script often starts out small, and is simple to write and simple to read. In testing the script, you may discover specific cases for which the general rules do not apply. To account for these, you add lines to your script, making it longer, more complex, and more complete. While the amount of time you spend refining your script may cancel out the time saved by not doing it manually, at least during that time your mind has been engaged by your own seeming sleight-of-hand: "See! The computer did it."

We encountered one such problem in preparing a formatted copy of command pages that the writer had typed as a text file without any formatting information. Although the files had no formatting codes, headings were used consistently to identify the format of the command pages. A sample file is shown below.

```
********************************************************************

NAME:     DBclose - closes a database

SYNTAX:
    void DBclose(fdesc)
        DBFILE *fdesc;

USAGE:
    fdesc      - pointer to database file descriptor

DESC:
DBclose() closes a file when given its database file descriptor.
Your pending writes to that file will be completed before the
file is closed.  All of your update locks are removed.
*fdesc becomes invalid.

Other users are not effected when you call DBclose().  Their update
locks and pending writes are not changed.

Note that there is no default file as there is in BASIC.
*fdesc must specify an open file.

DBclose() is analogous to the CLOSE statement in BASIC.

RETURNS:
    There is no return value

********************************************************************
```

The task was to format this document for the laser printer, using the reference header macros we had developed. Because there were perhaps forty of these command pages, it would have been utter drudgery to go through and add codes by hand. However, because there were that many, and even though the writer was generally consistent in entering them, there would be enough differences from command to command to have required several passes.

We'll examine the process of building this sed script. In a sense, this is a process of looking carefully at each line of a sample input file and determining whether or not an edit must be made on that line. Then we look at the rest of the file for similar occurrences. We try to find specific patterns that mark the lines or range of lines that need editing.

For instance, by looking at the first line, we know that we need to eliminate the row of asterisks separating each command. We specify an address for any line beginning and ending with an asterisk and look for zero or more asterisks in between. The regular expression uses an asterisk as a literal and as a metacharacter:

```
/^\*\**\*$/d
```

This command deletes rows of asterisks anywhere they occur in the file. We saw that blank lines were used to separate paragraphs, but replacing every blank line with a paragraph macro would cause other problems. In many cases, the blank lines can be removed because spacing has been provided in the macro. This is a case where we put off deleting or replacing blank lines on a global basis until we have dealt with specific cases. For instance, some blank lines separate labeled sections, and we can use them to define the end of a range of lines. The script, then, is designed to delete unwanted blank lines as the last operation.

Tabs were a similar problem. Tabs were used to indent syntax lines and in some cases after the colon following a label, such as "NAME". Our first thought was to remove all tabs by replacing them with eight blank spaces but there were tabs we wanted to keep, such as those inside the syntax line. So we removed only specific cases, tabs at the beginning of lines and tabs following a colon.

```
/^|-|/s///
/:|-|/s//:/
```

The next line we come across has the name of the command and a description.

```
NAME:     DBclose - closes a database
```

We need to replace it with the macro .Rh 0. Its syntax is:

.Rh 0 *"command" "description"*

We insert the macro at the beginning of the line, remove the hyphen, and surround the arguments with quotation marks.

```
/NAME:/{
        s//.Rh 0 "/
        s/ - /" "/
        s/$/"/
        }
```

We can jump ahead of ourselves a bit here and look at what this portion of our script does to the sample line:

```
.Rh 0 "DBclose" "Closes a database file"
```

The next part that we examine begins with "SYNTAX". What we need to do here is put in the .Rh macro, plus some additional **troff** requests for indentation, a font change, and no-fill and no-adjust. (The indentation is required because we stripped the tabs at the beginning of the line.) These requests must go in before and after the syntax lines, turning the capabilities on and off. To do this, we define an address that specifies the range of lines between two patterns, the label and a blank line. Then, using the change command, we replace the label and the blank line with a series of formatting requests.

```
/SYNTAX:/,/^$/{
        /SYNTAX:/c\
.Rh Syntax\
.in +5n\
.ft B\
.nf\
.na
        /^$/c\
.in -5n\
.ft R\
.fi\
.ad b
        }
```

Following the change command, each line of input ends with a backslash except the last line. As a side effect of the change command, the current line is deleted from the pattern space.

The USAGE portion is next, consisting of one or more descriptions of variable items. Here we want to format each item as an indented paragraph with a hanging italicized label. First, we output the .Rh macro; then we search for lines having two parts separated by a tab and a hyphen. Each part is saved, using backslash-parentheses, and recalled during the substitution.

```
/USAGE:/,/^$/{
        /USAGE:/c\
```

```
.Rh Usage
    /\(.*\)|-|- \(.*\)/s//.IP "\\fI\1\\fR" 15n\
\2./
      }
```

This is a good example of the power of regular expressions. Let's look ahead, once again, and preview the output for the sample.

```
.Rh Usage
.IP "\fIfdesc\fR" 15n
pointer to database file descriptor.
```

The next part we come across is the description. We notice that blank lines are used in this portion to separate paragraphs. In specifying the address for this portion, we use the next label, "RETURNS".

```
/DESC:/,/RETURNS:/{
i\
.LP
s/DESC:$/.Rh Description/
s/^$/.LP/
}
```

The first thing we do is insert a paragraph macro because the preceding USAGE section consisted of indented paragraphs. (We could have used the variable-list macros from the **mm** package in the USAGE section; if so, we would insert the **.LE** at this point.) Then we substitute the label "DESC" with the .Rh macro and replace all blank lines in this section with a paragraph macro.

When we tested this portion of the sed script on our sample file, it didn't work because there was a single space following the DESC label. We changed the regular expression to look for zero or more spaces following the label. Although this worked for the sample file, there were other problems when we used a larger sample. The writer was inconsistent in his use of the "DESC" label. Mostly, it occurred on a line by itself; sometimes, though, it was included at the start of the second paragraph. So we had to add another pattern to deal with this case. It searches for the label followed by a space and one or more characters.

```
s/DESC: *$/.Rh Description/
s/DESC: \(.*\)/.Rh Description\
\1/
```

In the second case, the reference header macro is output followed by a newline.

The next section, labeled "RETURNS", is handled in the same way as the SYNTAX section.

We do make minor content changes, replacing the label "RETURNS" with "Return Value" and consequently adding this substitution:

```
s/There is no return value.*/None./
```

The very last thing we do is delete remaining blank lines.

```
/^$/d
```

Our script is put in a file named **refsed**. Here it is in full.

```
# refsed -- add formatting codes to reference pages
/^\*\**\*$/d
/^|-|/s///
/:|-|/s//:/
/NAME:/{
      s//.Rh 0 "/
      s/ - /" "/
      s/$/"/
      }
/SYNTAX:/,/^$/{
      /SYNTAX:/c\
.Rh Syntax\
.in +5n\
.ft B\
.nf\
.na
      /^$/c\
.in -5n\
.ft R\
.fi\
.ad b
      }
/USAGE:/,/^$/{
      /USAGE:/c\
.Rh Usage
      /\(.*\)|-|- \(.*\)/s//.IP "\\fI\1\\fR" 15n\
2./
      }
/DESC:/,/RETURNS/{
i\
.LP
s/DESC: *$/.Rh Description/
s/DESC: \(.*\)/.Rh Description\
\1/
s/^$/.LP/
}
/RETURNS:/,/^$/{
      /RETURNS:/c\
.Rh "Return Value"\
i\
```

```
.LP
s/There is no return value\.*/None./
}
/^$/d
```

As we have remarked, you should not have sed overwrite the original. It is best to redirect the output of sed to another file or let it go to the screen. If the sed script does not work properly, you will find that it is generally easier to change the script and re-run it on the original file than write a new script to correct the problems caused by a previous run.

```
% sed -f refsed refpage
.Rh 0 "DBclose " " closes a database"
.Rh Syntax
.in +5n
.ft B
.nf
.na
void DBclose(fdesc)
     DBFILE *fdesc;
.in -5n
.ft R
.fi
.ad b
.Rh Usage
.IP "\fIfdesc\fR" 15n
pointer to database file descriptor.
.LP
.Rh Description
DBclose() closes a file when given its database file descriptor.
Your pending writes to that file will be completed before the
file is closed.  All of your update locks are removed.
*fdesc becomes invalid.
.LP
Other users are not effected when you call DBclose().  Their update
locks and pending writes are not changed.
.LP
Note that there is no default file as there is in BASIC.
*fdesc must specify an open file.
.LP
DBclose() is analogous to the CLOSE statement in BASIC.
.LP
.Rh "Return Value"
.LP
None.
```

Quit

The quit command (q) causes sed to stop reading new input lines (and stop sending them to the output). Its syntax is:

[*line-address*]q

It can take only a single-line address. Once the line matching *address* is reached, the script will be terminated.* For instance, the following one-liner uses the quit command to print the first 100 lines from a file:

```
% sed '100q' test
...
```

It prints each line until it gets to line 100 and quits. In this regard, this script functions similar to the UNIX **head** command.

Another possible use of **quit** is to quit the script after you've extracted what you want from a file. For instance, in an application like **getmac** (presented in Chapter 4, *Writing Sed Scripts*), there is some inefficiency in continuing to scan through a large file after sed has found what it is looking for.

So, for example, we could revise the sed script in the **getmac** shell script as follows:

```
sed -n "
/^\.de *$mac/,/^\.\./{
p
/^\.\./q
}" $file
done
```

The grouping of commands keeps the line:

```
/^\.\./q
```

from being executed until sed reaches the end of the macro we're looking for. (This line by itself would terminate the script at the conclusion of the first macro definition.) The sed program quits on the spot, and doesn't continue through the rest of the file looking for other possible matches.

---

*You need to be very careful not to use **q** in any program that writes its edits back to the original file. After **q** is executed, no further output is produced. It should not be used in any case where you want to edit the front of the file and pass the remainder through unchanged. Using **q** in this case is a very dangerous beginner's mistake.

Because the macro definition files are not that long, and the script itself not that complex, the actual time saved from this version of the script is negligible. However, with a very large file, or a complex, multi-line script that needs to be applied to only a small part of the file, this script could be a significant timesaver.

If you compare the following two shell scripts, you should find that the first one performs better than the second. The following simple shell program prints out the top ten lines of a file and then quits:

```
for file
do
sed 10q $file
done
```

The next example also prints the first ten lines using the print command and suppressing default output:

```
for file
do
sed -n 1,10p $file
done
```

If you haven't already done so, you should practice using the commands presented in this chapter before going on to the advanced commands in the next chapter.

6

Advanced Sed Commands

Multi-line Pattern Space
A Case for Study
Hold That Line
Advanced Flow Control Commands
To Join a Phrase

In this chapter, we cover the remaining sed commands. These commands require more determination to master and are more difficult to learn from the standard documentation than any of the basic commands. You can consider yourself a true sed-master once you understand the commands presented here.

The advanced commands fall into three groupings:

1. Working with a multi-line pattern space (**N,D,P**).

2. Using the *hold space* to preserve the contents of the pattern space and make it available for subsequent commands (**H,h,G,g,x**).

3. Writing scripts that use branching and conditional instructions to change the flow of control (**:,b,t**).

If the advanced scripts in this chapter have one thing in common, it is that they alter the sequential flow of execution or control. Normally, a line is read into the pattern space and each command in the script, one right after the other, is applied to that line. When the bottom of the script is reached, the line is output and the pattern space is cleared. Then a new line is read into the pattern space and control passes back to the top of the script. That is the normal flow of control in a sed script.

The scripts in this chapter interrupt or break the normal flow of control for various reasons. They might want to prevent commands in the script from executing except under certain circumstances, or to prevent the contents of the pattern space from being cleared out. Altering the flow of control makes a script much more difficult to read and understand. In fact, the scripts may be easier to write than they are to read. When you are writing a difficult script, you have the benefit of testing it to see how and why commands work.

I'd recommend that you test the scripts presented in this chapter and experiment by adding or removing commands to understand how the script is working. Seeing the results for yourself will help you understand the script much better than simply reading about it.

Multi-line Pattern Space

We have emphasized in previous discussions of regular expressions that pattern matching is line-oriented. A program like **grep** attempts to match a pattern on a single line of input. This makes it difficult to match a phrase, for instance, which can start at the end of one line and finish at the beginning of the next line. Other patterns might be significant only when repeated on multiple lines.

Sed has the ability to look at more than one line in the pattern space. This allows you to match patterns that extend over multiple lines. In this section, we will look at commands that create a multi-line pattern space and manipulate its contents. The three multi-line commands (**N,D,P**) all correspond to lowercase basic commands (**n,d,p**) that were presented in the previous chapter. The Delete (**D**) command, for instance, is a multi-line version of the delete command (**d**). The difference is that while **d** deletes the contents of the pattern space, **D** deletes only the first line of a multi-line pattern space.

Append Next Line

The multi-line Next (**N**) command creates a multi-line pattern space by reading a new line of input and appending it to the contents of the pattern space. The original contents of pattern space and the new input line are separated by a newline. The embedded newline character can be matched in patterns by the escape sequence \n. In a multi-line pattern space, only the metacharacter "^" matches the newline at the beginning of the pattern space and "$" matches the newline at the end. After the Next command is executed, control is then passed to subsequent commands in the script.

The Next command differs from the next command, which outputs the contents of the pattern space and then reads a new line of input. The next command does not create a multi-line pattern space.

For our first example, let's suppose that we wanted to change "Owner and Operator Guide" to "Installation Guide" but we found that it appears in the file on two lines, splitting between "Operator" and "Guide." For instance, here's a few lines of sample text:

```
Consult Section 3.1 in the Owner and Operator
Guide for a description of the tape drives
available on your system.
```

The following script looks for "Operator" at the end of a line, reads the next line of input and then makes the replacement.

```
/Operator$/{
N
s/Owner and Operator\nGuide/Installation Guide/
}
```

In this example, we know where the two lines split and where to specify the embedded newline. When the script is run on the sample file, it produces the two lines of output, one of which combines the first and second lines and is too long to show here. This happens because the substitute command matches the embedded newline but does not replace it. Unfortunately, you cannot use "\n" to insert a newline in the replacement string. You must use the backslash to escape the newline, as follows:

```
s/Owner and Operator\nGuide /Installation Guide\
/
```

This command restores the newline after "Installation Guide." It is also necessary to match a blank space following "Guide" so the new line won't begin with a space. Now we can show the output:

```
Consult Section 3.1 in the Installation Guide
for a description of the tape drives
available on your system.
```

Remember, you don't have to replace the newline but if you don't it can make for some long lines.

What if there are other occurrences of "Owner and Operator Guide" that break over multiple lines in different places? You could modify the regular expression to look for a space or a newline between words, as shown below:

```
/Owner/{
N
s/Owner *\n*and *\n*Operator *\n*Guide/Installation Guide/
}
```

The asterisk indicates that the space or newline is optional. This seems like hard work, though, and indeed there is a more general way. We have also changed the address to match "Owner," the first word in the pattern instead of the last. We can read the newline into the pattern space and then use a substitute command to remove the embedded newline, wherever it is.

```
s/Owner and Operator Guide/Installation Guide/
/Owner/{
N
s/ *\n/ /
s/Owner and Operator Guide */Installation Guide\
/
}
```

The first line matches "Owner and Operator Guide" when it appears on a line by itself. (See the discussion after the example about why this is necessary.) If we match the string "Owner", we read the next line into the pattern space, and replace the embedded newline with a space. Then we attempt to match the whole pattern and make the replacement followed by a newline. This script will match "Owner and Operator Guide" regardless of how it is broken across two lines. Here's our expanded test file:

```
Consult Section 3.1 in the Owner and Operator
Guide for a description of the tape drives
available on your system.

Look in the Owner and Operator Guide shipped with your system.

Two manuals are provided including the Owner and
Operator Guide and the User Guide.

The Owner and Operator Guide is shipped with your system.
```

Running the above script on the sample file produces the following result:

```
% sed -f sedscr sample
Consult Section 3.1 in the Installation Guide
for a description of the tape drives
available on your system.

Look in the Installation Guide shipped with your system.

Two manuals are provided including the Installation Guide
and the User Guide.

The Installation Guide is shipped with your system.
```

In this sample script, it might seem redundant to have two substitute commands that match the pattern. The first one matches it when the pattern is found already on one line and the second matches the pattern after two lines have been read into the pattern space. Why the first command is necessary is perhaps best demonstrated by removing that command from the script and running it on the sample file:

```
% sed -f sedscr2 sample
Consult Section 3.1 in the Installation Guide
for a description of the tape drives
available on your system.

Look in the Installation Guide
shipped with your system.
Two manuals are provided including the Installation Guide
and the User Guide.
```

Do you see the two problems? The most obvious problem is that the last line did not print. The last line matches "Owner" and when **N** is executed, there is not another input line to read, so sed quits. It does not even output the line. If this is the normal behavior, the Next command should be used as follows to be safe:

```
$!N
```

It excludes the last line ($) from the Next command. As it is in our script, by matching "Owner and Operator Guide" on the last line, we avoid matching "Owner" and applying the **N** command. However, if the word "Owner" appeared on the last line we'd have the same problem unless we implement the "$!N" syntax.

The second problem is a little less conspicuous. It has to do with the occurrence of "Owner and Operator Guide" in the second paragraph. In the input file, it is found on a line by itself:

```
Look in the Owner and Operator Guide shipped with your system.
```

In the output shown above, the blank line following "shipped with your system" is missing. The reason for this is that this line matches "Owner" and the next line, a blank line, is appended to the pattern space. The substitute command removes the embedded newline and the blank line has in effect vanished. (If the line were not blank, the newline would still be removed but the text would appear on the same line with "shipped with your system.") The best solution seems to be to avoid reading the next line when the pattern can be matched on one line. So, that is why the first instruction attempts to match the case where the string appears all on one line.

Converting an Interleaf File

Frame and Interleaf make WYSIWYG technical publishing packages. Both of them have the ability to read and save the contents of a document in an ASCII-coded format as opposed to their normal binary file format. In this example, we convert an Interleaf file into **troff**; however, the same kind of script could be applied to convert a **troff**-coded file to Interleaf format. The same is true of Frame. Both place coding tags in the file, surrounded by angle brackets.

In this example, our conversion demonstrates the effect of the change command on a multi-line pattern space. In the Interleaf file, "<para>" marks a paragraph. Before and after the tag are blank lines. Look at the sample file:

```
<para>

This is a test paragraph in Interleaf style ASCII.   Another line
in a paragraph.   Yet another.

<Figure Begin>

v.1111111111111111111111111100000000000000000000011111111111111000000
100001000100100010001000001000000000000000000000000000000000000000
000000

<Figure End>

<para>

More lines of text to be found after the figure.
These lines should print.
```

This file also contains a bitmap figure, printed as a series of 1s and 0s. To convert this file to **troff** macros, we must replace the "<para>" code with a macro (.LP). However, there's a bit more to do because we need to remove the blank line that follows the code. There are several ways to do it, but we will use the Next command to create a multi-line pattern space, consisting of "<para>" and the blank line, and then use the change command to replace what's in the pattern space with a paragraph macro. Here's the part of the script that does it:

```
/<para>/{
     N
     c\
.LP
```

The address matches lines with the paragraph tag. The Next command appends the next line, which should be blank, to the pattern space. We use the Next command (**N**) instead of next (**n**) because we don't want to output the contents of the pattern space. The change command overwrites the previous contents ("<para>" followed by a newline) of the pattern space, even when it contains multiple lines.

In this conversion script, we'd like to extract the bit-mapped figure data and write it to a separate file. In its place, we insert figure macros that mark the the figure in the file.

```
/<Figure Begin>/,/<Figure End>/{
                w fig.interleaf
                /<Figure End>/i\
.FG\
<insert figure here>\
.FE
                d
                }
```

This procedure matches the lines between "<Figure Begin>" and "<Figure End>" and writes them to the file named *fig.interleaf*. Each time this instruction is matched, the delete command will be executed, deleting the lines that have been written to file. When "<Figure End>" is matched, a pair of macros are inserted in place of the figure in the output. Notice that the subsequent delete command does not affect the text output by the insert command. It does, however, delete "<Figure End>" from the pattern space.

Here's the entire script:

```
/<para>/{
      N
      c\
.LP
}
/<Figure Begin>/,/<Figure End>/{
                w fig.interleaf
                /<Figure End>/i\
.FG\
<insert figure here>\
.FE
                d
                }
/^$/d
```

The third instruction simply removes unnecessary blank lines. (Note that this instruction could be depended upon to delete the blank line following the "<para>" tag; but you don't always want to remove all blank lines, and I wanted to demonstrate the change command across a multi-line pattern space.)

The result of running this script on the test file produces:

```
$ sed -f sed.interleaf test.interleaf
.LP
This is a test paragraph in Interleaf style ASCII.   Another line
in a paragraph.   Yet another.
.FG
<insert figure here>
```

```
.FE
.LP
More lines of text to be found after the figure.
These lines should print.
```

Multi-line Delete

The delete command (**d**) deletes the contents of the pattern space and causes a new line of input to be read with editing resuming at the top of the script. The Delete command (**D**) works slightly differently: it deletes a portion of the pattern space, up to the first embedded newline. It does not cause a new line of input to be read; instead, it returns to the top of the script, applying these instructions to what remains in the pattern space. We can see the difference by writing a script that looks for a series of blank lines and outputs a single blank line. The version below uses the delete command:

```
# reduce multiple blank lines to one; version using d command
/^$/{
     N
     /^\n$/d
}
```

When a blank line is encountered, the next line is appended to the pattern space. Then we try to match the embedded newline. Note that the positional metacharacters, ^ and $, match the beginning and the end of the pattern space, respectively. Here's a test file:

```
This line is followed by 1 blank line.

This line is followed by 2 blank lines.


This line is followed by 3 blank lines.



This line is followed by 4 blank lines.



This is the end.
```

Running the script on the test file produces the following result:

```
% sed -f sed.blank test.blank
This line is followed by 1 blank line.

This line is followed by 2 blank lines.          .
This line is followed by 3 blank lines.


This line is followed by 4 blank lines.
This is the end.
```

Where there was an even number of blank lines, all the blank lines were removed. Only when there was an odd number was a single blank line preserved. That is because the delete command clears the entire pattern space. Once the first blank line is encountered, the next line is read in, and both are deleted. If a third blank line is encountered, and the next line is not blank, the delete command is not applied, and thus a blank line is output.

If we use the multi-line Delete command, we get a different result, and the one that we wanted:

```
/^\n$/D
```

The reason the multi-line Delete command gets the job done is that when we encounter two blank lines, the Delete command removes only the first of the two. The next time through the script, the blank line will cause another line to be read into the pattern space. If that line is not blank, then both lines are output, thus ensuring that a single blank line will be output. In other words, when there are two blank lines in the pattern space, only the first one is deleted. When there is a blank line followed by text, the pattern space is output normally.

Multi-line Print

The multi-line Print command differs slightly from its lowercase cousin. This command outputs the first portion of a multi-line pattern space, up to the first embedded newline.

After the last command in a script is executed, the contents of the pattern space are automatically output. (The **-n** option or **#n** suppress this default action.) Therefore, print commands (**P** or **p**) are used when the default output is suppressed or when flow of control in a script changes such that the bottom of the script is not reached.

The Print command frequently appears after the Next command and before the Delete command. These three commands can set up an input/output loop that maintains a two-line pattern space yet outputs only one line at a time. The purpose of this loop is to output only the first line in the pattern space, then return to the top of the script to apply all commands to what had been the second line in the pattern space. Without this loop, when the last command in the script was executed, both lines in the pattern space would be output.

The flow through a script that sets up an input/output loop using the Next, Print, and Delete commands is illustrated in Figure 6-1. A multi-line pattern space is created to match "UNIX" at the end of the first line and "System" at the beginning of the second line. If "UNIX System" is found across two lines, we change it to "UNIX Operating System." The loop is set up to return to the top of the script and look for "UNIX" at the end of the second line.

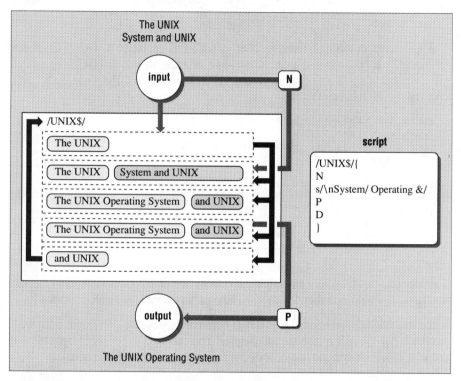

Figure 6-1. The Next, Print, and Delete commands used to set up input/output loop

The Next command appends a new input line to the current line in the pattern space. After the substitute command is applied to the multi-line pattern space, the first part of the pattern space is output by the Print command and then removed by the Delete command. That means the current line is output and the new line becomes the current line. The Delete command prevents the script from reaching bottom, which would output both lines and clear the contents of the pattern space. The Delete command allows us to preserve the second portion of the pattern space and pass control to the top of the script where all the editing commands can now be applied to that line. One of those commands is the Next command which reads another new line into the pattern space.

The following script implements the same loop.

```
/UNIX$/{
        N
        /\nSystem/{
        s// Operating &/
        P
        D
        }
}
```

The substitute command matches "\nSystem" and replaces it with " Operating \nSystem." It is important that the newline be maintained, or else there will be only a single line in the pattern space. Note the order of the Print and Delete commands. Here's our test file:

```
Here are examples of the UNIX
System.  Where UNIX
System appears, it should be the UNIX
Operating System.
```

Running the script on the test file produces:

```
% sed -f sed.Print test.Print
Here are examples of the UNIX Operating
System.  Where UNIX Operating
System appears, it should be the UNIX
Operating System.
```

The input/output loop lets us match the occurrence of UNIX at the end of the second line. It would be missed if the two-line pattern space was output normally.

If the relationship between the **P** and **D** commands remains unclear to you, we'll have another go at it in the next example. You can also experiment by removing either command from the above script or try using their lowercase cousins.

A Case for Study

Lenny, on our staff, was having difficulty converting a document coded for Scribe™ to our **troff** macro package, because of font changes. The problems he encountered are quite interesting, apart from the task he was trying to do.

The Scribe convention for putting text in a bold font is:

```
@f1(put this in bold)
```

This font change command can appear in-line and may begin on one line and end on a subsequent line. It can also appear more than once on a line. Here's a sample file that shows several different occurrences:

```
% cat test
I want to see @fl(what will happen) if we put the
font change commands @fl(on a set of lines).  If I understand
things (correctly), the @fl(third) line causes problems. (No?).
Is this really the case, or is it (maybe) just something else?

Let's test having two on a line @fl(here) and @fl(there) as
well as one that begins on one line and ends @fl(somewhere
on another line).  What if @fl(is here) on the line?
Another @fl(one).
```

The sample file shows the different contexts in which the font-change commands appear. The script must match "@fl(anything)" when it occurs on a single line or multiple times on the same line or when it extends across more than one line.

The easiest way to make a single match is:

```
s/@fl(\(.*\))/\\fB\1\\fR/g
```

The regular expression matches '@fl(.*)' and saves anything inside parentheses using \(and \). In the replacement section, the saved portion of the match is recalled as "\1".

Putting this command in a sed script, we will run it on the first paragraph of our sample file.

```
% sed -f sed.len test
I want to see \fBwhat will happen\fR if we put the
font change commands \fBon a set of lines\fR.  If I understand
things (correctly), the \fBthird) line causes problems. (No?\fR.
Is this really the case, or is it (maybe) just something else?

Let's test having two on a line \fBhere) and @fl(there\fR as
well as one that begins on one line and ends @fl(somewhere
on another line).  What if \fBis here\fR on the line?
```

The substitute command works properly in the first two lines. It fails on the third line. It also fails in the first line of the second paragraph where there are multiple occurrences on the same line.

Because a regular expression always makes the longest match possible, ".*" matches all the characters from "@fl(" to the *last* closing parenthesis on the line. In other words, the span indicated by ".*" ends with the last close parenthesis it finds, not the first. (It might help to keep in mind that a pattern-matching operation looks for the character that ends a span at the end of the line; if it is not found, it looks at the next to last character on the line, backing up along the line, one character at a time, to look for the end of the span.)

We can fix this problem by modifying the regular expression ".*" to zero or more occurrences of any character except ")".

```
[^)]*
```

In a character class, the caret (^) reverses the sense of the operation so it matches all characters except those specified in the brackets. Here's how the revised command looks:

```
s/@f1(\(([^)]*\))/\\fB\1\\fR/g
```

Now we have a command that handles one or more occurrences on a single line.

```
I want to see \fBwhat will happen\fR if we put the
font change commands \fBon a set of lines\fR.  If I understand
things (correctly), the \fBthird\fR line causes problems. (No?).
Is this really the case, or is it (maybe) just something else?

Let's test having two on a line \fBhere\fR and \fBthere\fR as
well as one that begins on one line and ends @f1(somewhere
on another line).  What if \fBis here\fR on the line?
```

This command gets all instances except the one in the second paragraph that extends over two lines. Before solving this problem, it is interesting to look at Lenny's first solution to it and why it fails. Here's Lenny's first script:

```
/@f1(/,/)/{
        s/@f1(/\\fB/g
        s/)/\\fR/g
}
```

He tried to attack the problem of matching an occurrence over multiple lines by specifying a range of lines. Here's the result of running the script on the test file:

```
% sed -f sed.len test.len
I want to see \fBwhat will happen\fR if we put the
the font commands \fBon a set of lines\fR.  If I understand
things (correctly\fR, the \fBthird\fR line causes problems. (No?
\fR Is this really the case, or is it (maybe\fR just something else?

Let's test having two on a line \fBhere\fR and \fBthere\fR as
well as one that begins on one line and ends \fBsomewhere
on another line\fR.  What if \fBis here\fR on the line?
```

Matching lines containing ")" makes unwanted matches on lines containing only parentheses.

The solution to matching the pattern over more than two lines is to create a multi-line pattern space. If we match "@f1" and no closing parenthesis is found, we need to read (**N**) another line into the buffer and try to make the same kind of match as the first case (the \n represents the newline).

```
s/@f1(\([^)]*\))/\\fB\1\\fR/g
/@f1(.*/{
N
s/@f1(\(.*\n[^)]*\))/\\fB\1\\fR/g
}
```

We can test it out:

```
$ sed -f sednew test
I want to see \fBwhat will happen\fR if we put the
the font commands \fBon a set of lines\fR.  If I understand
things (correctly), the \fBthird\fR line causes problems. (No?)
Is this really the case, or is it (maybe) just something else?

Let's test having two on a line \fBhere\fR and \fBthere\fR as
well as one that begins on one line and ends \fBsomewhere
on another line\fR.  What if @f1(is here) on the line?
```

As you can see, we have caught all but the very last one. The **N** command reads a second line into the pattern space. The script matches the pattern across two lines and then outputs *both* lines from the pattern space. What about the second line? It needs a chance to have all the commands in the script applied to it from top to bottom. Now, perhaps you understand why we need to set up a multi-line input/output loop like the one discussed in the previous section. We add the multi-line Print and multi-line Delete to the script.

```
# Scribe font change script.
s/@f1(\([^)]*\))/\\fB\1\\fR/g
/@f1(.*/{
N
s/@f1(\(.*\n[^)]*\))/\\fB\1\\fR/g
P
D
}
```

This can be translated as: Once making a substitution across two lines, print the first line and then delete it from the pattern space. With the second portion remaining in the pattern space, control passes to the top of the script where we see if there is an @f1 remaining on the line.

The revised script matches all occurrences in the sample file. However, it's not perfect, so we'll hear from Lenny again.

Hold That Line

The pattern space is a buffer that contains the current input line. There is also a set-aside buffer called the *hold space*. The contents of the pattern space can be copied to the hold space and the contents of the hold space can be copied to the pattern space. A group of commands allows you to move data between the hold space and the pattern space. The hold space is used for temporary storage, and that's it. Individual commands can't address the hold space or alter its contents.

The most frequent use of the hold space is to have it retain a duplicate of the current input line while you change the original in the pattern space. The commands that affect the pattern space are:

Hold	**h or H**	Copy or append contents of pattern space to hold space.
Get	**g or G**	Copy or append contents of hold space to pattern space.
Exchange	**x**	Swap contents of hold space and pattern space.

Each of these commands can take an address that specifies a single line or a range of lines. The hold (**h,H**) commands move data into the hold space and the get (**g,G**) commands move data from the hold space back into the pattern space. The difference between the lowercase and uppercase versions of the same command is that the lowercase command overwrites the contents of the target buffer, while the uppercase command appends to the existing contents. The hold command replaces the contents of the hold space with the contents of the pattern space. The get command replaces the contents of the pattern space with the contents of the hold space.

The Hold command puts a newline followed by the contents of the pattern space after the contents of the hold space. (The newline is appended to the hold space even if the hold space is empty.) The Get command puts a newline followed by the contents of the hold space after the contents of the pattern space.

The exchange command swaps the contents of the two buffers. It has no side effects on either buffer.

Let's use a trivial example to illustrate putting lines into the hold space and retrieving them later. We are going to write a script that reverses pairs of lines. For a sample file, we'll use a list of numbers:

```
1
2
11
22
111
222
```

The object is to reverse the order of the lines beginning with 1 and the lines beginning with 2. Here's how we use the hold space: we copy the first line to the hold space—and hold on to it—while we clear the pattern space. Then we get the second line and append the line in the hold space to it. Look at the script:

```
#Reverse flip
/1/{
h
d
}
/2/{
G
}
```

Any line matching a "1" is copied to the hold space and deleted from the pattern space. Control passes to the top of the script and the line is not printed. When the next line is read, it matches the pattern "2" and the line which had been copied to the hold space is now appended to the pattern space. Then both lines are printed. In other words, we save the first line of the pair and don't output it until we match the second line.

Here's the result of running the script on the sample file:

```
% sed -f sed.flip test.flip
2
1
22
11
222
111
```

The hold command followed by the delete command is a fairly common pairing. Without the delete command, control would reach the bottom of the script and the contents of the pattern space would be output. If the script used the next (n) command, instead of the delete command, the contents of the pattern space would also be output. You can experiment with this script by removing the delete command altogether or by putting a next command in its place. You could also see what happens if you use g instead of G.

Note that the logic of this script is poor, though the script is useful for demonstration purposes. If a line matches the first instruction and the next line fails to match the second instruction, the first line will not be output. This is a hole down which lines disappear.

A Capital Transformation

In the previous chapter, we introduced the transform command (y) and described how it can exchange lowercase letters for uppercase letters on a line. Since this command acts on the entire contents of the pattern space, it is something of a chore to do a letter-by-letter transformation of a portion of the line. But it is possible, though convoluted, as the following example will demonstrate.

While working on a programming guide, we found that the names of statements were entered inconsistently. They needed to be uppercase, but some were lowercase while others had an initial capital letter. While the task was simple—to capitalize the name of the statement—there were nearly a hundred statements and it seemed a tedious project to write that many explicit substitutions of the form:

```
s/find the Match statement/find the MATCH statement/g
```

The transform command could do the lowercase-to-uppercase conversion but it applies the conversion to the entire line. The hold space makes this task possible because we use it to store a copy of the input line while we isolate and convert the statement name in that the pattern space. Look at the script first:

```
# capitalize statement names
/the .* statement/{
h
s/.*the \(.*\) statement.*/\1/
y/abcdefghijklmnopqrstuvwxyz/ABCDEFGHIJKLMNOPQRSTUVWXYZ/
G
s/\(.*\)\n\(.*the \).*\( statement.*\)/\2\1\3/
}
```

The address limits the procedure to lines that match "the .* statement". Let's look at what each command does:

h   The hold command copies the current input line into the hold space. Using the sample line "find the Match statement", we'll show what the contents of the pattern space and hold space contain. After the "h" command, both the pattern space and the hold space are identical.

> *Pattern Space*: `find the Match statement`
> *Hold Space*: `find the Match statement`

`s/.*the \(.*\) statement.*/\1/`
    The substitute command extracts the name of the statement from the line and replaces the entire line with it.

> *Pattern Space*: `Match`
> *Hold Space*: `find the Match statement`

`y/abcdefghijklmnopqrstuvwxyz/ABCDEFGHIJKLMNOPQRSTUVWXYZ/`
    The transform command changes each lowercase letter to an uppercase letter.

> *Pattern Space*: `MATCH`
> *Hold Space*: `find the Match statement`

G   The Get command appends the line saved in the hold space to the pattern space.

> *Pattern Space*: `MATCH\nfind the Match statement`
> *Hold Space*: `find the Match statement`

`s/\(.*\)\n\(.*the \).*\( statement.*\)/\2\1\3/`

The substitute command matches three different parts of the pattern space: 1) all characters up to the embedded newline, 2) all characters following the embedded newline and up to and including "the" followed by a space, and 3) all characters beginning with a space and followed by "statement" up to the end of the pattern space. The name of the statement as it appeared in the original line is matched but not saved. The replacement section of this command recalls the saved portions and re-assembles them in a different order, putting the capitalized name of the command in between "the" and "statement."

> *Pattern Space*: `find the MATCH statement`
> *Hold Space*: `find the Match statement`

Let's look at a test run. Here's our sample file:

```
find the Match statement
Consult the Get statement.
using the Read statement to retrieve data
```

Running the script on the sample file produces:

```
find the MATCH statement
Consult the GET statement.
using the READ statement to retrieve data
```

As you can see from this script, the hold space can be skillfully used to isolate and manipulate portions of the input line.

Correcting Index Entries (Part II)

In the previous chapter, we looked at a shell script named **index.edit**. This script extracts index entries from one or more files and automatically generates a sed script consisting of a substitute command for each index entry. We mentioned that a small failing of the script was it did not look out for regular expression metacharacters that appeared as literals in an index entry, such as the following:

```
.XX "asterisk (*) metacharacter"
```

After processing this entry, the original **index.edit** generated the following substitute command:

```
/^\.XX /s/asterisk (*) metacharacter/asterisk (*) metacharacter/
```

While it "knows" to escape the period before ".XX", it doesn't protect the meta-character "*". The problem is the pattern "(*)" does not match "(*)" and the substitute command would fail to be applied. The solution is to modify the **index.edit** script so that it looks for metacharacters and escapes them. There is one more twist: there are a different set of metacharacters recognized in the replacement string.

We have to maintain two copies of the index entry. The first copy we edit to escape regular expression metacharacters and then use for the pattern. The second copy we edit to escape the metacharacter special to the replacement string. The hold space keeps the second copy while we edit the first copy, then we swap the two and edit the second copy. Here's the script:

```
:
# index.edit -- compile list of index entries for editing
#         new version that matches metacharacters
grep "^\.XX" $* | sort -u |
sed '
h
s/[][\\*.]/\\&/g
x
s/[\\&]/\\&/g
s/^\.XX //
s/$/\//
x
s/^\\\.XX \(.*\)$/\/^\\.XX \/s\/\1\//
G
s/\n//'
```

The hold command puts a copy of the current index entry into the hold space. Then the substitute command looks for any of the following metacharacters: "]", "[", "\", "*" or ".". This regular expression is rather interesting: 1) if the close bracket is the first character in a character class, it is interpreted literally, not as the closing delimiter of the class; and 2) of the metacharacters specified, only the backslash has a special meaning in a character class and must be escaped. Also, there is no need to escape the metacharacters "^" and "$" because they only have special meaning if in the first or last positions in a regular expression, respectively, which is impossible given the syntax of the index entry. After escaping the metacharacters, the exchange command swaps the contents of the pattern space and the hold space.

Starting with a new copy of the line, the substitute command adds a backslash to escape either a backslash or an ampersand for the replacement string. Then another substitute command removes the the ".XX " from the line and one after that appends a slash (/) to the end of the line, preparing a replacement string that looks like:

```
"asterisk (*) metacharacter"/
```

Once again, the exchange command swaps the pattern space and the hold space. With the first copy in the pattern space, we need to prepare the pattern address and the substitute pattern. The substitute command saves the index entry, and replaces the line with the first part of the syntax for the substitute command:

```
\/^\\.XX \/s\/\1\//
```

Using the sample entry, the pattern space would have the following contents:

```
/^\.XX /s/"asterisk (\*) metacharacter"/
```

Then the Get command takes the replacement string in the hold space and appends it to the pattern space. Because the Get command also inserts a newline, the substitute command is necessary to remove it. The following line is output at the end:

```
/^\.XX /s/"asterisk (\*) metacharacter"/"asterisk (*) metacharacter"/
```

Building Blocks of Text

The hold space can be used to collect a block of lines before outputting them. Some **troff** requests and macros are block-oriented, in that commands must surround a block of text. Usually a code at the beginning enables the format and one at the end disables the format. SGML-coded documents also contain many block-oriented constructs. For instance, "<p>" begins a paragraph and "</p>" ends it. In the next example, we'll look at placing SGML-style paragraph tags in a plain text file. For this example, the input is a file containing variable-length lines that form paragraphs; each paragraph is separated from the next one by a blank line. Therefore, the script must collect all lines in the hold space until a blank line is encountered. The contents of the hold space are retrieved and surrounded with the paragraph tags.

Here's the script:

```
/^$/!{
        H
        d
        }
/^$/{
        x
        s/^\n/<p>/
        s/$/<\/p>/
        G
        }
```

Running the script on a sample file produces:

```
<p>My wife won't let me buy a power saw.  She is afraid of an
accident if I use one.
So I rely on a hand saw for a variety of weekend projects like
building shelves.
However, if I made my living as a carpenter, I would
have to use a power
saw.  The speed and efficiency provided by power tools
would be essential to being productive. </p>

<p>For people who create and modify text files,
sed and awk are power tools for editing. </p>

<p>Most of the things that you can do with these programs
can be done interactively with a text editor.  However,
using these programs can save many hours of repetitive
work in achieving the same result.</p>
```

The script has basically two parts, corresponding to each address. Either we do one thing if the input line is *not* blank or a different thing if it is. If the input line is not blank, it is appended to the hold space (with **H**), and then deleted from the pattern space. The delete command prevents the line from being output and clears the pattern space. Control passes back to the top of the script and a new line is read. The general idea is that we don't output any line of text; it is collected in the hold space.

If the input line is blank, we process the contents of the hold space. To illustrate what the second procedure does, let's use the second paragraph in the previous sample file and show what happens. After a blank line has been read, the pattern space and the hold space have the following contents:

Pattern Space: `^$`
Hold Space: `\nFor people who create and modify text files,`
          `\nsed and awk are power tools for editing.`

A blank line in the pattern space is represented as "`^$`", the regular expression that matches it. The embedded newlines are represented in the hold space by "`\n`". Note that the Hold command puts a newline in the hold space and then appends the current line to the hold space. Even when the hold space is empty, the Hold command places a newline before the contents of the pattern space.

The exchange command (**x**) swaps the contents of the hold space and the pattern space. The blank line is saved in the hold space so we can retrieve it at the end of the procedure. (We could insert a newline in other ways, also).

Pattern Space: `\nFor people who create and modify text files,`
          `\nsed and awk are power tools for editing.`
Hold Space: `^$`

Now we make two substitutions: placing "<p>" at the beginning of the pattern space and "</p>" at the end. The first substitute command matches "\n" because a newline is at the beginning of the line as a consequence of the hold command. The second substitute command matches the end of the pattern space ("$" does not match any embedded newlines but the terminal newline.)

```
Pattern Space: <p>For people who create and modify text files,
               \nsed and awk are power tools for editing.<>
Hold Space: ^$
```

Note that the embedded newline is preserved in the pattern space. The last command, **G**, appends the blank line in the hold space to the pattern space. Upon reaching the bottom of the script, sed outputs the paragraph we had collected in the hold space and coded in the pattern space.

This script illustrates the mechanics of collecting input and holding on to it until another pattern is matched. It's important to pay attention to flow control in the script. The first procedure in the script does not reach bottom because we don't want any output *yet*. The second procedure does reach bottom, clearing the pattern space and the hold space before we begin collecting lines for the next paragraph.

This script also illustrates how to use addressing to set up exclusive addresses, in which a line must match one or the other address. You can also set up addresses to handle various exceptions in the input and thereby improve the reliability of a script. For instance, in the previous script, what happens if the last line in the input file is *not* blank? All the lines collected since the last blank line will not be output. There are several ways to handle this, but a rather clever one is to manufacture a blank line that the blank-line procedure will match later in the script. In other words, if the last line contains a line of text, we will copy the text to the hold space and clear the contents of the pattern space with the substitute command. We make the current line blank so that it matches the procedure that outputs what has been collected in the hold space. Here's the procedure:

```
${
/^$/!{
      H
      s/^.*$//
      }
}
```

This procedure must be placed in the script *before* the two procedures shown earlier. The addressing symbol "$" matches only the last line in the file. Inside this procedure, we test for all lines that are not blank. If the line is blank, we don't have to do anything with it. If current line is not blank, then we append it to the hold space. This is what we do in the other procedure that matches a non-blank line. Then we use the substitute command to create a blank line in the. pattern space.

Upon exiting this procedure, there is a blank line in the pattern space. It matches a subsequent procedure for blank lines that adds the SGML paragraph codes and outputs the paragraph.

Advanced Flow Control Commands

You have already seen several examples of changes in sed's normal flow control. In this section, we'll look at two commands that allow you to direct which portions of the script get executed and when. The branch (**b**) and test (**t**) commands transfer control in a script to a line containing a specified label. If no label is specfied, control passes to the end of the script. The branch command transfers control unconditionally while the test command is a conditional transfer, occurring only if a substitute command has changed the current line.

A label is any sequence of up to seven characters. A label is put on a line by itself and beginning with a colon:

```
:mylabel
```

There are no spaces permitted between the colon and the label. Spaces at the end of the line will be considered part of the label. When you specify the label in a branch or test command, a space is permitted between the command and the label itself:

```
b mylabel
```

Be sure you don't put a space after the label.

Branching

The branch command allows you to transfer control to another line in the script.

> [*address*]**b**[*label*]

The *label* is optional, and if not supplied, control is transferred to the end of the script. If a label is supplied, execution resumes at the line following the label.

In Chapter 4, we looked at a typesetting script that transformed quotation marks and hyphens into their typesetting counterparts. If we wanted to avoid making these changes on certain lines, then we could use the branch command to skip that portion of the script. For instance, text inside computer-generated examples marked by the .ES and .EE macros should not be changed. Thus, we could write the previous script like this:

```
/^\.ES/,/^\.EE/b
s/^"/\`\`/
s/"$/\'\'/
s/"? /\`\`? /g
            .
            .
            .
s/\\(em\\^"/\\(em`\`/g
s/"\\(em/\'\'\\(em/g
s/\\(em"/\\(em`\`/g
```

Because no label is supplied, the branch command branches to the end of the script, skipping all subsequent commands.

The branch command can be used to execute a set of commands as a procedure, one that can be called repeatedly from the main body of the script. As in the case above, it also allows you to avoid executing the procedure at all based on matching a pattern in the input.

You can have a similar effect by using ! and grouping a set of commands. The advantage of the branch command over ! for our application is that we can more easily specify multiple conditions to avoid. The ! symbol can apply to a single command, or can apply to a set of commands enclosed in braces that immediately follows. The branch command, on the other hand, gives you almost unlimited control over movement around the script.

For example, if we are using multiple macro packages, there may be other macro pairs besides .ES and .EE that define a range of lines that we want to avoid altogether. So, for example, we can write:

```
/^.ES/,/^.EE/b
/^.PS/,/^.PE/b
/^.G1/,/^.G2/b
```

To get a good idea of the types of flow control possible in a sed script, let's look at some simple but abstract examples. The first example shows you how to use the branch command to create a loop. Once an input line is read, command1 and command2 will be applied to the line; afterwards, if the contents of the pattern space match the pattern, then control will be passed to the line following the label "top", which means command1 then command2 will be executed again.

```
:top
command1
command2
/pattern/b top
command3
```

The script executes command3 only if the pattern doesn't match. All three commands will be executed, although the first two may be executed multiple times.

In the next example, command1 is executed. If the pattern is matched, control passes to the line following the label "end". This means command2 is skipped.

```
command1
/pattern/b end
command2
:end
command3
```

In all cases, command1 and command3 are executed. Now let's look at how to specify that either command2 or command3 are executed, but not both. In the next script, there are two branch commands.

```
command1
/pattern/b dothree
command2
b
:dothree
command3
```

The first branch command transfers control to command3. If that pattern is not matched, then command2 is executed. The branch command following command2 sends control to the end of the script, bypassing command3. The first of the branch commands is conditional upon matching the pattern; the second is not. We will look at a "real-world" example after looking at the test command.

The Test Command

The test command branches to a label (or the end of the script) if a successful substitution has been made on the currently addressed line. Thus, it implies a conditional branch. Its syntax follows:

> [*address*]t[*label*]

If no *label* is supplied, control falls through to the end of the script. If the label is supplied, then execution resumes at the line following the label.

Let's look at an example from Tim O'Reilly. He was trying to generate automatic index entries based on evaluating the arguments in a macro that produced the top of a command reference page. If there were three quoted arguments, he wanted to do something different than if there were two or only one.

The task was to try to match each of these cases in succession (3,2,1) and when a successful substitution was made, avoid making any further matches. Here's Tim's script:

```
/.Rh 0/{
s/"\(.*\)" "\(.*\)" "\(.*\)"/"\1" "\2" "\3"/
t
s/"\(.*\)" "\(.*\)"/"\1" "\2"/
t
s/"\(.*\)"/"\1"/
}
```

The test command allows us to drop to the end of the script once a substitution has been made. If there are three arguments on the .Rh line, the test command after the first substitute command will be true, and sed will go on to the next line. If there are fewer than three arguments, no substitution will be made, the test command will be evaluated false, and the next substitute command will be tried. This will be repeated until all the possibilities are used up.

The test command provides functionality similar to a case statement in the C programming language or the shell programming languages. You can test each case and when a case proves true, then you exit the construct.

If the above script were part of a larger script, we could use a label, perhaps tellingly named "break," to drop to the end of the command grouping where additional commands can be applied.

```
/.Rh 0/{
s/"\(.*\)" "\(.*\)" "\(.*\)"/"\1" "\2" "\3"/
t break
  .
  .
  .
}
:break
more commands
```

The next section gives a full example of the test command and the use of labels.

One More Case

Remember Lenny? He was the fellow given the task of converting Scribe documents to **troff**. I had sent him the following script:

```
# Scribe font change script.
s/@f1(\([^)]*\))/\\fB\1\\fR/g
/@f1(.*/{
N
```

```
s/@f1(\(.*\n[^)]*\)))/\\fB\1\\fR/g
P
D
}
```

He sent me the following mail after using the script:

```
Thank you so much!  You've not only fixed the script but shown
me where I was confused about the way it works.  I can repair
the conversion script so that it works with what you've done,
but to be optimal it should do two more things that I can't seem
to get working at all—maybe it's hopeless and I should be content
with what's there.

First, I'd like to reduce multiple blank lines down to one.
Second, I'd like to make sed match the pattern over more
than two (say, even only three) lines.

Thanks again.

Lenny
```

The first request to reduce a series of blank lines to one has already been shown in this chapter. The following four lines perform this function:

```
/^$/{
N
/^\n$/D
}
```

We want to look mainly at accomplishing the second request. Our previous font-change script created a two-line pattern space, tried to make the match across those lines, and then output the first line. The second line became the first line in the pattern space and control passed to the top of the script where another line was read in.

We can use labels to set up a loop that reads multiple lines and makes it possible to match a pattern across multiple lines. The following script sets up two labels: **begin** at the top of the script and **again** near the bottom. Look at the improved script:

```
# Scribe font change script.   New and Improved.
:begin
/@f1(\(([^)]*\))/{
s//\\fB\1\\fR/g
b begin
}
/@f1(.*/{
N
s/@f1(\(([^)]*\n[^)]*\)))/\\fB\1\\fR/g
t again
b begin
```

```
}
:again
P
D
```

Let's look more closely at this script, which has three parts. Beginning with the line that follows **:begin**, the first part attempts to match the font change syntax if it is found completely on one line. After making the substitution, the branch command transfers control back to the label **begin**. In other words, once we have made a match, we want to go back to the top and look for other possible matches, including the instruction that has already been applied—there could be multiple occurrences on the line.

The second part attempts to match the pattern over multiple lines. The Next command builds a multiple line pattern space. The substitution command attempts to locate the pattern with an embedded newline. If it succeeds, the test command passes control to the line following the **again** label. If no substitution is made, control is passed to the line following the label **again** so that we can read in another line. This is a loop that goes into effect when we've matched the beginning sequence of a font change request but have not yet found the ending sequence. Sed will loop back and keep appending lines into the pattern space until a match has been found.

The third part is the procedure following the label **again**. The first line in the pattern space is output and then deleted. Like the previous version of this script, we deal with multiple line in succession. Control never reaches the bottom of the script but is redirected by the Delete command to the top of the script.

To Join a Phrase

We have covered all the advanced constructs of sed and are now ready to look at a shell script named **phrase** that uses nearly all of them. This script is a general-purpose, **grep**-like program that allows you to look for a series of multiple words that might appear across two lines.

An essential element of this program is that, like **grep**, it only prints out the lines that match the pattern. You might think we'd use the **-n** to suppress the default output of lines. However, what is unusual about this sed script is that it creates an input/output loop, controlling when a line is output or not.

The logic of this script is to first look for the pattern on one line and print the line if it matches. If no match is found, we read another line into the pattern space (as in previous multi-line scripts). Then we copy the two-line pattern space to the hold space for safe-keeping. Now the new line that was read into the pattern space previously could match the search pattern on its own, so the next match we attempt is on the second line only. Once we've determined that the pattern is not found on either the first or second lines, we remove the newline between the two lines and look for it spanning those lines.

The script is designed to accept arguments from the command line. The first argument is the search pattern. All other command-line arguments will be interpreted as filenames. Let's look at the entire script before analyzing it:

```
:
# phrase -- search for words across lines
# $1 = search string; remaining args = filenames
search=$1
shift
for file
do
sed '
/'"$search"'/b
N
h
s/.*\n//
/'"$search"'/b
g
s/ *\n/ /
/'"$search"'/{
g
b
}
g
D' $file
done
```

A shell variable named **search** is assigned the first argument on the command line, which should be the search pattern. This script shows another method of passing a shell variable into a script. Here we surround the variable reference with a pair of double-quotes and then single quotes. Notice the script itself is enclosed in single quotes, which protect characters that are normally special to the shell from being interpreted. The sequence of a double-quote pair inside a single-quote pair makes sure the enclosed argument is evaluated first by the shell before the sed script is evaluated by sed.*

---

*You can also use shell variables to pass a series of commands into a sed script. This somewhat simulates a procedure call but it makes the script more difficult to read.

The sed script tries to match the search string at three different points, each marked by the address that looks for the search pattern. The first line of the script looks for the search pattern on line by itself:

```
/'"$search"'/b
```

If search pattern matches the line, the branch command, without a label, transfers control to the bottom of the script where the line is printed. This makes use of sed's normal control-flow so that the next input line is read into the pattern space and control then returns to the top of the script. The branch command is used in the same way each time we try to match the pattern.

If a single input line does not match the pattern, we begin our next procedure to create a multi-line pattern space. It is possible that the new line, by itself, will match the search string. It may not be apparent why this step is necessary—why not just immediately look for the pattern anywhere across two lines? The reason is that if the pattern is actually matched on the second line, we'd still output the pair of lines. In other words, the user would see the line preceding the matched line and might be confused by it. This way we output the second line by itself if that is what matches the pattern.

```
N
h
s/.*\n//
/'"$search"'/b
```

The Next command appends the next input line to the pattern space. The hold command places a copy of the two-line pattern space into the hold space. The next action will change the pattern space and we want to preserve the original intact. Before looking for the pattern, we use the substitute command to remove the previous line, up to and including the embedded newline. There are several reasons for doing it this way and not another way, so let's consider some of the alternatives. You could write a pattern that matches the search pattern only if it occurs after the embedded newline:

```
/\n.*'"$search"'/b
```

However, if a match is found, we don't want to print the entire pattern space, just the second portion of it. Using the above construct would prints both lines when only the second line matches.

You might want to use the Delete command to remove the first line in the pattern space before trying to match the pattern. A side effect of the Delete command is a change in flow-control that would resume execution at the top of the script. (The Delete command could conceivably be used but not without changing the logic of this script.)

So, we try to match the pattern on the second line, and if that is unsuccessful, then we try to match it across two lines:

```
g
s/ *\n/ /
/'"$search"'/{
g
b
}
```

The get command retrieves a copy of the original line from the hold space, overwriting the line we had worked with in the pattern space. The substitute command replaces the embedded newline and any spaces preceding it with a single space. Then we attempt to match the pattern. If the match is made, we don't want to print the contents of the pattern space, but rather get the duplicate from the hold space (which preserves the newline) and print it. Thus, before branching to the end of the script, the get command retrieves the copy from the hold space.

The last part of the script is executed only if the pattern has not been matched.

```
g
D
```

The get command retrieves the duplicate, that preserves the newline, from the hold space. The Delete command removes the first line in the pattern space and passes control back to the top of the script. We delete only the first part of the pattern space, instead of clearing it, because after reading another input line, it is possible to match the pattern spanning across both lines.

Here's the result when the program is run on a sample file:

```
$ phrase "the procedure is followed" sect3
If a pattern is followed by a \f(CW!\fP, then the procedure
is followed for all lines that do \fInot\fP match the pattern.
so that the procedure is followed only if there is no match.
```

As I mentioned at the outset, writing sed scripts is a good primer for programming. In the chapters that follow, we will be looking at the awk programming language. You will see many similarities to sed to make you comfortable but you will see a broader range of constructs for writing useful programs. As you begin trying to do more complicated tasks with sed, the scripts get so convoluted as to make them difficult to understand. One of the advantages of awk is that it handles complexity better, and once you learn the basics, awk scripts are easier to write and understand.

7

Writing Scripts for Awk

Hello World
Awk's Programming Model
Pattern Matching
Records and Fields
Expressions
System Variables
Relational and Boolean Operators
Formatted Printing
Passing Parameters into a Script
Information Retrieval

To write an awk script, you must become familiar with the rules of the game. The rules can be stated plainly and you will find them described in Appendix B rather than in this chapter. The goal of this chapter is not to describe the rules but to show you how to play the game. In this way, you will become acquainted with many of the features of the language and see examples that illustrate how scripts actually work. Some people prefer to begin by reading the rules, which is roughly equivalent to learning to use a program from its man page or learning to speak a language by scanning its rules of grammar—not an easy task. Having a good grasp of the rules, however, is essential once you begin to use awk regularly. But that is to say that the more you use awk, the faster the rules of the game become second nature. You learn them through trial and error—spending a long time trying to fix a silly syntax error such as a missing space or brace has a magical effect upon long-term memory. Thus, the best way to learn to write scripts is to begin writing them. As you make progress writing scripts, you will no doubt benefit from reading the rules (and re-reading them) in Appendix B or the awk man page or *The AWK Programming Language* book. You can do that later— let's get started now.

Hello World

It has become a convention to introduce a programming language by demonstrating the "Hello, world" program. Showing how this program works in awk will demonstrate just how unconventional awk is. In fact, it's necessary to show several different approaches to printing "Hello, world."

In the first example, we create a file named *test* that contains a single blank line. This example shows a script that contains the **print** statement:

```
% awk '{ print "Hello, world" }' test
Hello, world
```

This script has only a single action, which is enclosed in braces. That action is to execute the **print** statement for each line of input. In this case, the *test* file contains only a single line; thus, the action occurs once. Note that the input line is read but never output.

Now let's look at another example. Here, we use a file that contains the line "Hello, world."

```
% cat test2
Hello, world
% awk '{ print }' test2
Hello, world
```

In this example, "Hello, world" appears in the input file. The same result is achieved because the **print** statement, without arguments, simply outputs each line of input. If there were additional lines of input, they would be output as well.

Both of these examples illustrate that awk is input-driven. That is, nothing happens unless there are lines of input on which to act. When you invoke the awk program, it reads the script that you supply, checking the syntax of your instructions. Then awk attempts to execute the instructions for each line of input. Thus, the **print** statement will not be executed unless there is input from the file.

To verify this for yourself, try entering the command line in the first example but omit the filename. You'll find that because awk expects input to come from the keyboard, it will wait until you give it input to process: press RETURN several times, then type an EOF (CTRL-D on most systems) to signal the end of input. For each time that you pressed RETURN, the action that prints "Hello, world" will be executed.

There is yet another way to write the "Hello, world" message and not have awk wait for input. This method associates the action with the **BEGIN** pattern. The

BEGIN pattern specifies actions that are performed *before* the first line of input is read.

```
% awk 'BEGIN { print "Hello, world" }'
Hello, world
```

What is different here is that awk prints the message first and then looks for input. In the earlier examples, awk waited for input before printing the message.

Awk's Programming Model

It's important to understand the basic model that awk offers the programmer. Part of the reason why awk is easier to learn than many programming languages is that it offers such a well-defined and useful model to the programmer.

An awk program consists of what we will call a *main input loop*. A *loop* is a routine that is executed over and over again until some condition exists that terminates it. You don't write this loop, it is given—it exists as the framework within which the code that you do write will be executed. The main input loop in awk is a routine that reads one line of input from a file and makes it available for processing. The actions you write to do the processing assume that there is a line of input available. In another programming language, you would have to create the main input loop as part of your program. It would have to open the input file and read one line at a time. This is not necessarily a lot of work but it illustrates that awk is "setting you up," making it easier for you to write your program.

The main input loop is executed as many times as there are lines of input. As you saw in the "Hello, world" examples, this loop does not execute until there is a line of input. It terminates when there is no more input to be read.

Awk allows you to write two special routines that can be executed *before* any input is read and *after* all input is read. These are the procedures associated with the **BEGIN** and **END** rules, respectively. In other words, you can do some preprocessing before the main input loop is ever executed and you can do some postprocessing after the main input loop has been terminated. The **BEGIN** and **END** procedures are optional and they do not need to be defined.

You can think of an awk script as having potentially three major parts: what happens before, what happens during, and what happens after processing the input. Figure 7-1 shows the relationship of these parts in the flow of control of an awk script.

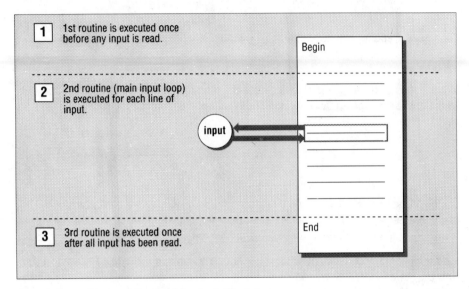

1 1st routine is executed once before any input is read.

Begin

2 2nd routine (main input loop) is executed for each line of input.

input

3 3rd routine is executed once after all input has been read.

End

Figure 7-1. Flow of Control in Awk Scripts

Of these three parts, the main input loop or "what happens during processing" is where most of the work gets done. Inside the main input loop, your instructions are written as a series of pattern/action procedures. A pattern is a rule for testing the input line to determine whether or not the action should be applied to it. The actions, as we shall see, can be quite complex, consisting of statements, functions, and expressions.

The main thing to remember is that each pattern/action procedure sits in the main input loop, which takes care of reading the input line. The procedures that you write will be applied to each input line, one line at a time.

Pattern Matching

The "Hello, world" program does not demonstrate the power of pattern-matching rules. In this section, we look at a number of small, even trivial examples that nonetheless demonstrate this central feature of awk scripts.

When awk reads an input line, it attempts to match each pattern-matching rule in a script. Only the lines matching the particular pattern are the object of an action. If no action is specified, the line that matches the pattern is printed (executing the **print** statement is the default action). Consider the following script:

```
/^$/ { print "This is a blank line." }
```

This script reads: *if the input line is blank, then print "This is a blank line."* The pattern is written as a regular expression that identifies a blank line. The action, like most of those we've seen so far, contains a single **print** statement.

If we place this script in a file named *awkscr* and use an input file named *test* that contains three blank lines, then the following command executes the script:

```
$ awk -f awkscr test
This is a blank line
This is a blank line
This is a blank line
```

(From this point on, we'll assume that our scripts are placed in a separate file and invoked using the -f command-line option.) The result tells us that there are three blank lines in *test*. This script ignores lines that are not blank.

Let's add several new rules to the script. This script is now going to analyze the input and classify it as an integer, a string, or a blank line.

```
# test for integer, string or empty line.
/[0-9]+$/ { print "That is an integer" }
/[A-z]+/ { print "This is a string" }
/^$/     { print "This is a blank." }
```

The general idea is that if a line of input matches any of these patterns, the associated **print** statement will be executed. The + metacharacter is part of the extended set and means "one or more." Therefore, a line consisting of a sequence of one or more digits will be considered an integer. Here's a sample run, taking input from standard input:

```
% awk -f awkscr
4
That is an integer
t
This is a string
4T
That is an integer
This is a string
<CR>
This is a blank.
44
That is an integer
CTRL-D
%
```

Note that input "4T" was identified as both an integer and a string. A line can match more than one rule. You can write a stricter rule set to prevent a line from matching more than one rule. You can also write actions that are designed to skip other parts of the script.

We will be exploring the use of pattern matching rules throughout this chapter.

Describing Your Script

Adding comments as you write the script is a good practice. A comment begins with the "#" character and end at a newline. Unlike sed, awk allows comments anywhere in the script.

NOTE

Do not use a single quote in a comment. The shell interprets it and causes the program to stop.

As we begin writing scripts, we'll use comments to describe the action:

```
#  blank.awk -- Print message for each blank line.
/^$/ { print "This is a blank line" }
```

This comment offers the name of the script **blank.awk** and briefly describes what the script does. A particularly useful comment for longer scripts is one that identifies the expected structure of the input file. For instance, in the next section, we are going to look at writing a script that reads a file containing names and phone numbers. The introductory comments for this program should be:

```
# blocklist.awk -- print name and address in block form.
# fields: name, company, street, city, state and zip, phone
```

It is useful to embed this information in the script because the script won't work unless the structure of the input file corresponds to that expected by the person who wrote the script.

As awk interprets a script at run-time, there is undoubtedly some small penalty incurred by placing comments in scripts. However, in most cases, that should not have significant impact on awk applications.* One approach to take in those circumstances is to document the program in another file.

---

*I have found a couple of circumstances where larger scripts failed, reporting syntax errors that I could not track down. Removing all the comments made the program run fine. I concur from this that the size of the program was the problem, which seemed to be a machine-specific limitation of awk. The program, comments included, ran fine on two other systems.

Records and Fields

Awk makes the assumption that its input is structured and not just an endless string of characters. In the simplest case, it takes each input line as a record and each word, delimited by blank spaces or tabs, as a field. The following record in the file *names* has three fields, separated by either a blank space or a tab.

```
John Robinson   666-555-1111
```

Two or more consecutive blank spaces are counted as a single delimiter.

Awk allows you to reference fields in actions using the field operator $. This operator is followed by a literal or a variable that identifies the position of a field by number. "$1" refers to the first field, "$2" to the second field and so on. $0 refers to the entire input record. The following example displays the last name first, the first name second, followed by the phone number.

```
% awk '{ print $2, $1, $3 }' names
Robinson John 666-555-1111
```

$1 refers to the first name, $2 to the last name, and $3 to the phone number. The commas that separate each argument in the print statement cause a blank space to be output between the values. (Later on, we'll discuss the output field separator (OFS), whose value the comma outputs and which is by default a space.) In this example, a single input line forms one record containing three fields: there is a space between the first and last names and a tab between the last name and the phone number. If you wanted to grab the first and last name as a single field, you could set the field separator explicitly so that only tabs are recognized. Then, awk would recognize two fields for this record.

You can change the field separator with the **-F** option on the command line. It is followed immediately by the delimiter character. In the following example, the field separator is changed to a tab.

```
% awk -F"\t" '{ print $2 }' names
666-111-5555
```

"\t" is a valid escape sequence that indicates a tab. You can also enter a tab by pressing the TAB key. In any case, you must surround the tab by single or double quotes.

Commas delimit fields in the following two address records.

```
John Robinson,Koren Inc.,978 4th Ave.,Boston,MA 01760,696-0987
Phyllis Chapman,GVE Corp.,34 Sea Drive,Amesbury,MA 01881,879-0900
```

An awk program can print the name and address in block format.

```
# blocklist.awk -- print name and address in block form.
# input file -- name, company, street, city, state and zip, phone
{    print ""   #output blank line
     print $1   #name
     print $2   #company
     print $3   #street
     print $4, $5    #city, state zip
}
```

The first **print** statement specifies a null string ("") (remember, **print** by itself outputs the current line). This is used to separate each record in the report by a blank line. We can invoke this script and specify that the field separator is a comma using the following command:

```
awk -F, -f blocklist.awk names
```

The following report is produced:

```
John Robinson
Koren Inc.
978 4th Ave.
Boston   MA 01760

Phyllis Chapman
GVE Corp.
34 Sea Drive
Amesbury   MA 01881
```

It is usually a better practice, and more convenient, to specify the field separator in the script itself. The system variable **FS** can be defined to change the field separator. Because this must be determined before the first input line is read, we must assign this variable in an action controlled by the **BEGIN** rule.

```
BEGIN { FS = "," }
```

Now let's use it in a script to print out the names and phone numbers.

```
# phonelist.awk -- print name and phone number.
# input file -- name, company, street, city, state and zip, phone

BEGIN { FS = "," }  #comma-delimited fields

{ print $1 ", " $6 }
```

Notice that we use blank lines in the script itself to improve readability. The **print** statement puts a comma followed by a space between the two output fields. This script can be invoked from the command line:

```
% awk -f phonelist.awk names
John Robinson, 696-0987
Phyllis Chapman, 879-0900
```

This gives you a basic idea of how awk can be used to work with data that has a recognizable structure. This particular script is designed to print all lines of input, but we could modify the single action by writing a pattern-matching rule that selected only certain names or addresses. For instance, if we had a large listing of names, we might want to select only the names of people residing in a particular state. We could write:

```
/MA/ { print $1 ", " $6 }
```

where MA would match the postal state abbreviation for Massachusetts. However, we could possibly match a company name or some other field in which the letters "MA" appeared. We can test a specific field for a match. The tilde (˜) operator allows you to test a regular expression against a field.

```
$5 ˜ /MA/    { print $1 ", " $6 }
```

You can reverse the meaning of the rule by using bang-tilde (!˜).

```
$5 !˜ /MA/    { print $1 ", " $6 }
```

This rule would match all those records whose fifth field did not have "MA" in it. A more challenging pattern-matching rule would be one that matches only long-distance phone numbers. The following regular expression looks for an area code.

```
$6 ˜ /1?(-| )*\(?[0-9]+(\) ?|-)*[0-9]+-[0-9]+/
```

This rule matches any of the following forms:

```
707-724-0000
(707) 724-0000
(707)724-0000
1-707-724-0000
1 707-724-0000
1(707)724-0000
```

The regular expression can be deciphered by breaking down its parts. "1?" means zero or one occurrences of "1". "(-|)*" looks for either a hyphen or a space in the next position, or nothing at all. "\(?" looks for zero or one left parenthesis; the backslash prevents the interpretation of "(" as the grouping metacharacter. "[0-9]+" looks for one or more digits; note that we took the lazy way out and specified one or more digits rather than exactly three. In the next position, we are looking for either a right parenthesis or a hyphen, or again nothing at all. Then we look for one or more digits "[0-9]+" followed by a hyphen followed by one or more digits "[0-9]+".

Expressions

The use of expressions in which you can store, manipulate and retrieve data is quite different from anything you can do in sed, yet it is a common feature of most programming languages.

An expression is evaluated and returns a value. An expression consists of any combination of numeric and string constants, variables, operators, functions, and regular expressions. We covered regular expressions in detail in Chapter 2, *Understanding Basic Operations*, and we'll look at them later in this chapter. Functions will be discussed fully in Chapter 9, *Functions*. In this section, we will look at expressions consisting of constants, variables, and operators.

There are two types of constants: string or numeric ("red" or 1). A string must be quoted in an expression. Strings can make use of the escape sequences listed in Table 7-1.

Table 7-1. Escape Sequences

Sequence	Description
\a	Alert character, usually ASCII BEL character*
\b	Backspace
\f	Formfeed
\n	Newline
\r	Carriage return
\t	Horizontal tab
\v	Vertical tab*
\ddd	Character represented as 1 to 3 digit octal value*
\xhex	Character represented as hexadecimal value*
\c	Any literal character c (\" for ")

A *variable* is an identifier that references a value. To define a variable, you only have to name it and assign it a value. The name must not contain spaces or periods. Variables are not declared; that is, you do not have to tell awk what *type* of value will be stored in a variable. Each variable has a string value and a numeric

---

*Escape sequences found in nawk and gawk. \a, \v, and \x were introduced in gawk and later added to nawk.

value, and awk uses the appropriate value based on the context of the expression. (Strings that do not consist of numbers have a numeric value of 0.) Variables do not have to be initialized. The following expression assigns a value to **x**:

```
x = 1
```

x is the name of the variable, = is an assignment operator, and **1** is a numeric constant.

The following expression assigns the string "Hello" to the variable "z":

```
z = "Hello"
```

A blank space is the string concatenation operator. The expression:

```
z = "Hello" "World"
```

concatenates the two strings and assigns "HelloWorld" to the variable **z**.

The dollar sign ($) operator is used to reference fields. The following expression assigns the value of the first field of the current input record to the variable **w**:

```
w = $1
```

A variety of operators can be used in expressions. Arithmetic operators are listed in Table 7-2.

Table 7-2: Arithmetic Operators

Operator	Description
+	Addition
-	Subtraction
*	Multiplication
/	Division
%	Modulo
^	Exponentiation

Once a variable has been assigned a value, that value can be referenced using the name of the variable. The following expression adds 1 to the value of **x** and assigns it to the variable **y**:

```
y = x + 1
```

That is, evaluate **x**, add 1 to it, and put the result into the variable **y**. The statement:

```
print y
```

prints the value of **y**. If the following sequence of statements appear in a script:

```
x = 1
y = x + 1
print y
```

then the value of **y** is 2.

We could reduce these three statements to two:

```
x = 1
print x + 1
```

Notice, however, that after the **print** statement the value of x is still 1. We didn't change the value of x; we simply added 1 to it and printed that value. In other words, if a third statement "print x" followed, it would output 1. If, in fact, we wished to accumulate the value in x, we could use an assignment operator +=. This operator combines two operations; it adds 1 to x and assigns the new value to x. Table 7-3 lists the assignment operators used in awk expressions.

Table 7-3: Assignment Operators

Operator	Description
+=	Assign result of addition.
++	Add 1 to variable.
--	Subtract 1 from variable.
-=	Assign result of subtraction.
*=	Assign result of multiplication.
/=	Assign result of division.
%=	Assign result of modulo.

Look at the following example which counts each blank line in a file.

```
# Count blank lines.
/^$/ {
        print x += 1
        }
```

Although we didn't initialize the value of x, we can safely assume that its value is 0 up until the first blank line is encountered. The expression "x += 1" is evaluated each time a blank line is matched and the value of x is incremented by 1. The **print** statement prints the value returned by the expression.

There are different ways to write expressions, some more terse than others. The expression "x += 1" is more concise than the following equivalent expression:

```
x = x + 1
```

But both of these expressions are not as terse as the following expression:

```
++x
```

"++" is the increment operator. ("--" is the decrement operator.) Each time the expression is evaluated the value of the variable is incremented by one. The increment and decrement operators can appear on either side of the operand, as *prefix* or *postfix* operators. The position has a different effect.

```
++x    increment x before returning value (prefix)
x++    increment x after returning value (postfix)
```

For instance, if our example was written:

```
/^$/ {
      print x++
      }
```

When the first blank line is matched, the expression returns the value "0"; the second blank line returns "1" and so on. If we put the increment operator before x, then the first time the expression is evaluated, it will return "1".

Let's implement that expression in our example. In addition, instead of printing a count each time a blank line is matched, we'll accumulate the value of x and print only the total number of blank lines. The **END** pattern is the place to put the **print** that displays the value of x after the last input line is read.

```
# Count blank lines.
/^$/ {
      ++x
}
END {
      print x
}
```

Let's try it on the sample file which has three blank lines in it.

```
% awk -f awkscr test
3
```

The script outputs the number of blank lines.

Averaging Student Grades

Let's look at another example, one in which we sum a series of student grades and then calculate the average. Here's what the input file looks like:

```
john 85 92 78 94 88
andrea 89 90 75 90 86
jasper 84 88 80 92 84
```

There are five grades following the student's name. Here is the script that will give us each student's average:

```
# average five grades
{ total = $2 + $3 + $4 + $5 + $6
  avg = total / 5
  print $1, avg }
```

This script adds together fields 2 through 6 to get the sum total of the five grades. The value of **total** is divided by 5 and assigned to the variable **avg**. ("/" is the operator for division.) The **print** statement outputs the student's name and average. Note that we could have skipped the assignment of **avg** and instead calculated the average as part of the **print** statement, as follows:

```
print $1, total / 5
```

All in all, this script shows how relatively easy it is to write programs in awk. awk parses the input into fields and records. You are spared having to read individual characters and declaring data types. Awk does this for you, transparently.

Let's see a sample run of the script that calculates student averages:

```
% awk -f grades.awk grades
john 87.4
andrea 86
jasper 85.6
```

System Variables

There are a number of system or built-in variables defined by awk. Awk has two types of system variables. The first type defines values whose default can be changed, such as the default field and record separators. The second type defines values that can be used in reports or processing, such as the number of fields found in the current record, the count of the current record, and others.

There are a set of default values that affect the recognition of records and fields on input and their display on output. The system variable **FS** defines the field separator. By default, it is a space or a tab. Earlier, we changed the field separator to a comma in order to read a list of names and addresses. With nawk, if you specify more than a single character as the field separator, it will be interpreted as a regular expression. That is, the field separator will be the "leftmost longest non-null and nonoverlapping" substring* that matches the regular expression. You can see the difference between specifying:

```
FS = "\t"
```

which causes each tab to be interpreted as a field separator, and:

```
FS = "\t+"
```

which specifies that one or more consecutive tabs delimit a field. Using the first specification, the following line would have three fields:

```
abc\t\tdef
```

whereas the second specification would only recognize two fields. Using a regular expression allows you to specify several characters to be used as delimiters:

```
FS = "[':\t]"
```

Any of the three characters in brackets will be interpreted as the field separator.

The output equivalent of **FS** is **OFS**, which is a space by default. We'll see an example of redefining **OFS** shortly. Awk defines the variable **NF** to the number of fields for the current input record. This value can't be changed but it is useful to access to determine how many fields there are.

Awk also defines **RS**, the record separator, as a newline. Its output equivalent is **ORS**, which is also a newline by default. In the section "Working With Multi-line Records," we'll show how to change the default record separator. Awk sets the variable **NR** to the number of the current input record. It can be used to number records in a list. The variable **FILENAME** contains the name of the current input file. Nawk also defines the variable **FNR**. It is useful when multiple files are open as it provides the number of the current record relative to the current input file.

Typically, the field and record separators are defined in the **BEGIN** procedure because you want these values redefined before the first input line is read. However, you can redefine these values anywhere in the script, but you should test whether it affects the current input line. (With nawk, setting the field separator causes the current input line to be re-evaluated using the new value. With gawk and awk, this has no effect on the current input line; rather it affects the next input line.)

---

*The AWK Programming Language [Aho], p. 60.

Now let's look at some examples, beginning with the **NR** variable. Here's a revised **print** statement for the script that calculates student averages:

```
print NR ".", $1, avg
```

Running the revised script produces the following output:

```
1. john 87.4
2. andrea 86
3. jasper 85.6
```

After the last line of input is read, **NR** contains the number of input records that were read. It can be used in the **END** action to provide a report summary. Here's a revised version of the **phonelist.awk** script.

```
# phonelist.awk -- print name and phone number.
# input file -- name, company, street, city, state and zip, phone

BEGIN { FS = "," }   #comma-delimited fields

{ print $1 ", " $6 }

END {      print
        print NR "records printed." }
```

This program changes the default field separator and uses **NR** to print the total number of records printed. This program produces the following output:

```
John Robinson, 696-0987
Phyllis Chapman, 879-0900

2 records printed.
```

The output field separator (**OFS**) is generated when a comma is used to separate the arguments in a **print** statement. You may have wondered what effect the comma has in the following expression:

```
print NR ".", $1, avg
```

By default, the comma causes a blank space (the default **OFS**) to be output. For instance, you could redefine the **OFS** to be a tab in a **BEGIN** action. Then the preceding **print** statement would produce the following output:

```
1.      john    87.4
2.      andrea  86
3.      jasper  85.6
```

This is especially useful if the input consists of tab-separated fields and you want to generate the same kind of output. The **OFS** can be redefined to be a sequence of characters, such as a comma followed by a space.

Another commonly used system variable is **NF**, which is set to the number of fields for the current record. As we'll see in the next section, you can use **NF** to check that a record has the same number of fields that you expect. You can also use **NF** to reference the last field of each record. Using the "$" field operator and **NF** produces that reference. If there are six fields, then "$NF" is the same as "$6." Given a list of names, such as the following:

```
John Kennedy
Lyndon B. Johnson
Richard Milhouse Nixon
Gerald R. Ford
Jimmy Carter
Ronald Reagan
```

you will note that the last name is not the same field number for each record. You could print the last name of each President using "$NF."

These are the basic system variables, the ones most commonly used. There are more of them, as listed in Appendix B, and we'll introduce new system variables as needed in the chapters that follow. With nawk, there are several new system variables.

Working with Multi-line Records

All of our examples have used input files whose records consisted of a single line. In this section, we show how to read a record where each field consists of a single line.

Earlier, we looked at an example of processing a file of names and addresses. Let's suppose that the same data is stored on file in block format. Instead of having all the information on one line, the person's name is on one line, followed by the company's name on the next line and so on. Here's a sample record:

```
John Robinson
Koren Inc.
978 Commonwealth Ave.
Boston
MA 01760
696-0987
```

This record has six fields. After each record, a blank line is output.

To process this data, we can specify a multi-line record by defining the field separator to be a newline, represented as "\n"; and set the record separator to null, which stands for a blank line.

```
BEGIN { FS = "\n"; RS = "" }
```

We can print the first and last fields using the following script:

```
# block.awk - print first and last fields
# $1 = name; $NF = phone number

BEGIN { FS = "\n"; RS = "" }

{ print $1, $NF }
```

Here's a sample run:

```
% awk -f block.awk phones.block
John Robinson 696-0987
Phyllis Chapman 879-0900
Jeffrey Willis 914-636-0000
Alice Gold (707) 724-0000
Bill Gold 1-707-724-0000
```

The two fields are printed on the same line because the default output separator (**OFS**) remains a single space. If you want the fields to be output on separate lines, change **OFS** to a newline. While you're at it, you probably want to preserve the blank space between records so you must specify the output record separator **ORS** to be two newlines.

```
OFS = "\n"; ORS = "\n\n"
```

Balance the Checkbook

This is a simple application that processes items in your check register. While not necessarily the easiest way to balance the checkbook, it is amazing how quickly you can build something useful with awk.

This program presumes you have entered in a file the following information:

```
1000
125        Market              125.45
126        Hardware Store      34.95
127        Video Store         7.45
128        Book Store          14.32
129        Gasoline            16.10
```

The first line contains the beginning balance. Each of the other lines represent information from a single check: the check number, a description of where it was spent, and the amount of the check. Each of the three fields are separated by tabs.

The core task of the script is that it must get the beginning balance and then deduct the amount of each check from that balance. We can provide detail lines for each check to compare against the check register. Finally, we can print the ending balance. Here it is:

```
# checkbook.awk
BEGIN { FS = "\t" }
#1 Expect the first record to have the starting balance.
NR == 1 { print "Beginning Balance: \t" $1
    balance = $1
    next
}
#2 Apply to each check record, subtracting amount from balance.
{    print $1, $2, $3
    print balance -= $3
}
```

Let's run this program and look at the results:

```
% awk -f checkbook.awk checkbook.test
Beginning Balance:       1000
125 Market 125.45
874.55
126 Hardware Store 34.95
839.6
127 Video Store 7.45
832.15
128 Book Store 14.32
817.83
129 Gasoline 16.10
801.73
%
```

The report is difficult to read, but later we will learn to fix the format using the **printf** statement. What's important is to confirm that the script is doing what we want. It seems important to emphasize that getting this far takes only a few minutes in awk. In a programming language such as C, it would take you much longer to write this program; for one thing, you might have many more lines of code; and you'd be programming at a much lower level. There are any number of refinements that you'd want to make to this program to improve it, and refining a program takes much longer. The point is that with awk you are able to isolate and implement the basic functionality quite easily.

Relational and Boolean Operators

Relational and boolean operators allow you to make comparisons between two expressions. The relational operators are found in Table 7-4.

Table 7-4. Relational Operators

Operator	Description
<	Less than
>	Greater than
<=	Less than or equal to
>=	Greater than or equal to
==	Equal to
!=	Not equal to
~	Matches
!~	Does not match

A relational expression can be used in place of a pattern to control a particular action. For instance, if we wanted to limit the records selected for processing to those that have five fields, we could use the following expression:

```
NF == 5
```

This relational expression compares the value of **NF** (the number of fields for each input record) to five. If it is true, the action will be executed; otherwise, it will not.

NOTE

Make sure you notice that the relational operator "==" ("is equal to") is not the same as the assignment operator "=" ("equals"). It is a common syntax error to use "=" instead of "==" to test an expression.

We can use a relational expression to validate the *phonelist* database before attempting to print out the record.

```
NF == 6 { print $1, $6 }
```

Then only lines with six fields will be printed.

The opposite of "==" is "!=" ("is not equal to"). Similarly, you can compare one expression to another to see if it is greater than (>) or less than (<) or greater than or equals to (>=) or less than or equals to (<=). The following expression:

```
NR > 1
```

tests whether the number of the current record is greater than 1. As we'll see in the next chapter, relational expressions are typically used in conditional (**if**) statements and are evaluated to determine whether or not a particular statement should be executed.

Regular expressions must be enclosed in slashes except when used with the relational operators ˜ ("match") and !˜ ("no match"). These operators assume that the right hand side of the expression specifies a regular expression. We've already seen an example of this expression used as a pattern-matching rule for the phone database:

```
$5 ˜ /MA/    { print $1 ",  " $6 }
```

where the value of field 5 is compared against the regular expression "MA". The slashes are optional because awk interprets any string to the right of the "˜" operator as a regular expression.

With nawk, regular expressions can be supplied through variables. For instance, in the *phonelist* script, we could replace "/MA/" with **state** and have a procedure that defines the value of state.

```
$5 ˜ state
```

This makes the script much more general to use because a pattern can change dynamically during execution of the script. For instance, it allows us to get the value of **state** from a command-line parameter. We will talk about passing command-line parameters into a script later in this chapter. The original awk made it difficult to use patterns dynamically because they had to be fixed when the script was interpreted. (You can sometimes get around this limitation by passing a variable from the command line to the program using a shell variable. Because the shell variable was expanded before the script was executed, awk only saw a fixed regular expression. This approach has its limitations as well because you can't then change the pattern within the program.)

Boolean operators allow you to combine a series of comparisons. They are listed in Table 7-5.

Table 7-5. Boolean Operators

Operator	Description
||	Logical OR
&&	Logical AND

Given two or more expressions, || specifies that *either* one of them can return true (1) for the whole expression to be true. && specifies that *both* of the expressions must be true to return true. The following expression:

```
NF == 6 && NR > 1
```

states that the number of fields must be equal to 6 *and* that the **NR** of the record must be greater than 1.

&& has higher precedence than ||. Can you tell how the following expression will be evaluated?

```
NR > 1 && NF >= 2 || $1 ~ /\t/
```

The parentheses in the next example show which expression would be evaluated first based on the rules of precedence.

```
(NR > 1 && NF >= 2) || $1 ~ /\t/
```

In other words, both of the expressions in parentheses must be true *or* the right hand side must be true. You can use parentheses to override the rules of precedence, as in the following example which specifies that two conditions must be true.

```
NR > 1 && (NF >= 2 || $1 ~ /\t/)
```

The first condition must be true *and* either of two other conditions must be true.

Getting Information About Files

Now we are going to look at a couple of scripts that process the output of a UNIX command, **ls**. The following is a sample of the long listing produced by the command **ls -l:***

```
% ls -l
-rw-rw-rw-   1 dale      project    6041 Jan  1 12:31 com.tmp
-rwxrwxrwx   1 dale      project    1778 Jan  1 11:55 combine.idx*
-rw-rw-rw-   1 dale      project    1446 Feb 15 22:32 dang
-rwxrwxrwx   1 dale      project    1202 Jan  2 23:06 format.idx*
```

This listing is a report in which data is presented in rows and columns. Each file is presented across a single row. The file listing consists of nine columns. The file's permissions appear in the first column, the size of the file in bytes in the fifth column, and the filename is found in the last column. Because one or more spaces separate the data in columns, we can treat each column as a field.

---

*Note that on a Berkeley UNIX system, **ls -l** produces an eight-column report; use **ls -lg** to get the same report format shown here.

In our first example, we're going to pipe the output of this command to an awk script that prints selected fields from the file listing. To do this, we'll create a shell script so that we can make the pipe transparent to the user. Thus, the structure of the shell script is:

```
ls -l $* | awk 'script' -
```

The $* variable is used by the shell and expands to all arguments passed from the command line. (We could use $1 here, which would pass the first argument, but passing *all* the arguments provides greater flexibility.) These arguments can be the names of files or directories or additional options to the **ls** command. If no arguments are specified, the "$*" will be ignored and the current directory will be listed. Thus, the output of that command will be directed to awk, and we've specified "-" in place of a filename to indicate standard input.

We'd like our awk script to print the size and name of the file. That is, print field 5 ($5) and field 9 ($9).

```
ls -l $* | awk '{
    print $5,"\t", $9 }
}' -
```

If we put the above lines in a file named *fls* and make that file executable, we can enter **fls** as a command.

```
% fls
6041       com.tmp
1778       combine.idx
1446       dang
1202       format.idx
% fls com*
6041       com.tmp
1778       combine.idx
```

So what our program does is take the long listing and reduce it to two fields. Now, let's add new functionality to our report by producing some information that the **ls -l** listing does not provide. We can store the size of each file and accumulate it to produce the total number of bytes used by all files in the listing. We can also keep track of the number of files and produce that total. There are two parts to adding this functionality. The first is to accumulate the totals for each input line. We create the variable **sum** to accumulate the size of files and the variable **filenum** to accumulate the number of files in the listing.

```
{
    sum += $5
    ++filenum
    print $5,"\t", $9
}
```

The first expression uses the assignment operator +=. It adds the value of field 5 to the present value of the variable **sum**. The second expression increments the present value of the variable **filenum**. This variable is used as a *counter*, and each time the expression is evaluated, 1 is added to the count.

The action we've written will be applied to all input lines. The totals that are accumulated in this action must be printed after awk has read all the input lines. Therefore, we write an action that is controlled by the **END** rule.

```
END { print "Total: ", sum, "(" filenum " files)"
    }
```

We can also use the **BEGIN** rule to add column headings to the report.

```
BEGIN { print "BYTES" "" "FILE"
     }
```

Now we can put this script in an executable file named *filesum* and execute it as a single-word command.

```
% filesum c*
BYTES       FILE
882         ch01
1771        ch03
1987        ch04
6041        com.tmp
1778        combine.idx
Total:  12459 bytes (5 files)
```

What's nice about this command is that it allows you to determine the size of all files in a directory or any group of files.

While the basic mechanism works, there are a few problems to be taken care of. The first problem occurs when you list the entire directory using the **ls -l** command. The listing contains a line that specifies the total number of blocks in the directory. The partial listing (all files beginning with "c") in the previous example does not have this line. But the following line would be included in the output if the full directory was listed:

```
total 555
```

The block total does not interest us because the program displays the total file size in bytes. Currently, **filesum** does not print this line; however, it does read this line and cause the **filenum** counter to be incremented.

There is also a problem with this script in how it handles subdirectories. Look at the following line from an **ls -l**:

```
drwxrwxrwx   3 dale     project         960 Feb  1 15:47 sed
```

"d" as the first character in column 1 (file permissions) indicates that the file is a subdirectory. The size of this file (960 bytes) does not indicate the size of files in that subdirectory and therefore, it is slightly misleading to add it to the file size totals. Also, it might be helpful to indicate that it is a directory.

If you want to list the files in subdirectories, supply the **-R** option on the command line. It will be passed to the **ls** command. However, the listing is slightly different as it identifies each directory. For instance, to identify the subdirectory *old*, the **ls -lR** listing produces a blank line followed by:

```
./old:
```

Our script ignores that line and a blank line preceding it but nonetheless they increment the file counter. Fortunately, we can devise rules to handle these cases. Let's look at the revised, commented script:

```
ls -l $* | awk '
# filesum: list files and total size in bytes
# input: long listing produced by "ls -l"

#1 output column headers
BEGIN { print "BYTES" "" "FILE"
}
#2 test for 9 fields; files begin with "-"
NF == 9 && /^-/ {
        sum += $5       # accumulate size of file
        ++filenum       # count number of files
        print $5,"\t", $9       # print size and filename
}

#3 test for 9 fields; directory begins with "d"
NF == 9 && /^d/ {
        print "<dir>", "\t", $9  #print <dir> and name
}

#4 test for ls -lR line ./dir:
$1 ~ /^..*:$/ {
        print "\t" $0 # print that line preceded by tab
}

#5 once all is done,
END {
        #print total file size and number of files
    print "Total: ", sum, "bytes (" filenum " files)"
}' -
```

The rules and their associated actions have been numbered to make it easier to discuss them. The listing produced by **ls -l** contains nine fields for a file. Awk supplies the number of fields for a record in the system variable **NF**. Therefore, rules 2 and 3 test that **NF** is equal to 9. This helps us avoid matching odd blank lines or the line stating the block total. Because we want to handle directories and files differently, we use another pattern to match the first character of the line. In rule 2 we test for "-" in the first position on the line, which indicates a file. The associated action increments the file counter and adds the file size to the previous total. In rule 3, we test for a directory, indicated by "d" as the first character. The associated action prints "<dir>" in place of the file size. Rules 2 and 3 are *compound* expressions, specifying two patterns that are combined using the && operator. Both patterns must be matched for the expression to be true.

Rule 4 tests for the special case produced by the **ls -lR** listing ("./old:"). There are a number of patterns that we can write to match that line, using regular expressions or relational expressions:

```
NF == 1                If the number of fields equals 1 ...
/^\..*:$/              If the line begins with a period
                       followed by any number of characters and
                       ends in a colon...
$1 ~ /^\..*:$/         If field 1 matches the regular expression...
```

We used the latter expression because it seems to be the most specific. It employs the match operator (~) to test the first field against a regular expression. The associated action consists of only a **print** statement.

Rule 5 is the **END** pattern and its action is only executed once, printing the sum of file sizes as well as the number of files.

The **filesum** program demonstrates many of the basic constructs used in awk. What's more, it gives you a pretty good idea of the process of developing a program (although syntax errors produced by typos and hasty thinking have been gracefully omitted.) If you wish to tinker with this program, you might add a counter for a directories, or a rule that handles symbolic links.

Formatted Printing

Many of the scripts that we've written so far perform the data processing tasks just fine, but the output has not been formatted properly. That is because there is only so much you can do with the basic **print** statement. And since one of awk's most common functions is to produce reports, it is crucial that we be able to format our reports in an orderly fashion. The **filesum** program performs the arithmetic tasks well but the report lacks an orderly format.

Awk offers an alternative to the **print** statement, **printf**, which is borrowed from the C programming language. The **printf** statement can output a simple string just like the **print** statement.

```
awk '{ printf ("Hello, world") }' -
```

The main difference that you will notice at the outset is that, unlike the **print** statement, **printf** does not automatically supply a newline. You must specify it explicitly as **\n**.

The full syntax of the **printf** statement has two parts:

printf ([*format-expression*], *arguments*)

The parentheses are optional. The first part is an expression that describes the format specifications; usually this is supplied as a string constant in quotes. The second part is an argument list, such as a list of variable names, that correspond to the format specifications. A format specification is preceded by a percent sign (%) and the specifier is one of the characters shown in Table 7-6. The two main format specifiers are **s** for strings and **d** for decimal integers.

Table 7-6: Format Specifiers Used in printf

Character	Description
c	ASCII character.
d	Decimal integer.
e	Floating point format ([-]*d.precision*E[+-]*dd*).
f	Floating point format ([-]*ddd.precision*).
g	**e** or **f** conversion, whichever is shortest, with trailing zeros removed.
o	Unsigned octal value.
s	String.
x	Unsigned hexadecimal number.
%	Literal %.

The following example uses the **printf** statement to produce the output for rule 2 in the **filesum** program. It outputs a string and decimal value found in two different fields.

```
printf("%d\t%s\n", $5, $9)
```

The value of **$5** is to be output, followed by a tab (\t) and **$9** and then a newline (\n). For each format specification, you must supply a corresponding argument.

This **printf** statement can be used to specify the width and alignment of output fields. A format expression can take three optional modifiers following "%" and preceding the format specifier:

%-width.precision format-specifier

The *width* of the output field is a numeric value. When you specify a field width, the contents of the field will be right justified by default. You must specify "-" to get left-justification. Thus, "%-20s" outputs a string left-justified in a field 20 characters wide. If the string is less than 20 characters, the field will be padded with white space to fill. In the following examples, a "|" is output to indicate the actual width of the field. The first example right-justifies the text:

```
printf("|%10s|", "hello")
```

It produces:

```
|     hello|
```

The next example left-justifies the text:

```
printf("|%-10s|", "hello")
```

It produces:

```
|hello     |
```

The *precision* modifier, used for decimal or floating point values, controls the number of digits that appear to the right of the decimal point. Note that the default precision for the output of numeric values is "%.6g." In nawk, the default can be changed by setting the system variable **OFMT**. This affects the precision used by the **print** statement when outputting numbers. For instance, if you are using awk to write reports that contain dollar values, you might prefer to change **OFMT** to "%.2d."

Using the full syntax of the format expression can solve the problem with **filesum** of getting fields and headings properly aligned. One reason we output the file size before the filename was that the fields had a greater chance of aligning themselves if they were output in that order. The solution that **printf** offers us is the ability to fix the width of output fields; therefore, each field begins in the same column.

Let's rearrange the output fields in the **filesum** report. We want a minimum field width so that the second field begins at the same position. You specify the field width place between the % and the conversion specification. **%-15s** specifies a minimum field width of fifteen characters in which the value is left-justified. **%10d**, without the minus sign, is right-justified, which is what we want for a decimal value.

```
printf("%-15s\t%10d\n", $9, $5)        # print filename and size
```

This will produce a report in which the data is aligned in columns and the numbers are right justified. Look at how the **printf** summary is used in the **END** action:

```
printf("Total: %d bytes  (%d files)\n", sum, filenum)
```

With the use of the **printf** statement, **filesum** now produces the following output:

```
% filesum g*
FILE                BYTES
g                      23
gawk                 2237
gawk.mail            1171
gawk.test              74
gawkro                264
gfilesum              610
grades                 64
grades.awk            231
grepscript              6
Total: 4680 bytes  (9 files)
```

Passing Parameters into a Script

One of the more confusing subtleties of programming in awk is passing parameters into a script. A parameter assigns a value to a variable that can be accessed within the awk script. The variable can be set on the command line, after the script and before the filename.

> **awk** *'script' var=value inputfile*

Each parameter must be interpreted as a single argument. Therefore, spaces are not permitted on either side of the equals sign. Multiple parameters can be passed this way. For instance, if you wanted to define the variables "high" and "low" from the command line, you could invoke awk as follows:

```
% awk -f scriptfile high=100 low=60 datafile
```

Inside the script, these two variables are available and can be accessed as any awk variable. If you were to put this script in a shell script wrapper, then you could pass the shell's command-line arguments as values. (The shell makes available command-line arguments in the positional variables—$1 for the first parameter, $2 for the second and so on.) For instance, look at the shell script version of the previous command:

```
awk -f scriptfile high=$1 low=$2 datafile
```

If this shell script were named "awket," it could be invoked as:

```
% awket 100 60
```

"100" would be $1 and passed as the value assigned to the variable **high**.

In addition, environment variables or the output of a command can be passed as the value of a variable. Here are two examples:

```
directory=$cwd
directory='pwd'
```

"$cwd" returns the value of the variable **cwd** which is the current working directory. The second example uses backquotes to execute the **pwd** command and assign its result to the variable **directory**.

You can also use command-line parameters to define system variables, as in the following example:

```
awk '{print NR, $0 }' OFS='. ' names
1. Tom 656-5789
2. Dale 653-2133
3. Mary 543-1122
4. Joe 543-2211
```

The output field separator is re-defined to be a period followed by a space.

An important restriction on command-line parameters is that they are not available in the **BEGIN** procedure. That is, they are not available until *after* the first line of input is read. Why? Well, here's the confusing part. A parameter passed from the command line is treated as though it were a filename. The assignment does not occur until the parameter, if it were a filename, is actually evaluated.

Look at the following script that sets a variable **n** as a command-line parameter.

```
awk ' BEGIN { print n }
{
if (n == 1) print "Reading file first time"
if (n == 2) print "Reading file second time"
}' n=1 test n=2 test2
```

There are four command-line parameters: "n=1", "test", "n=2", and "test2."

Now, if you remember that a **BEGIN** procedure is "what we do before processing input," you'll understand why the reference to n in the **BEGIN** procedure returns nothing. So the **print** statement will print a blank line. If the first parameter were a file and not a variable assignment, the file would not be opened until the **BEGIN** procedure had been executed.

The variable **n** is given an initial value of 1 from the first parameter. The second parameter supplies the name of the file. Thus, for each line in *test*, the conditional "n == 1" will be true. After the input is exhausted from *test*, the third parameter is evaluated, and it sets **n** to 2. Finally, the fourth parameter supplies the name of a second file. Now the conditional "n == 2" in the main procedure will be true.

One consequence of the way parameters are evaluated is that you cannot use the **BEGIN** procedure to test or verify parameters that are supplied on the command line. They are only available after a line of input has been read. You can get around this limitation by composing the rule "NR == 1" and using its procedure to verify the assignment. Another way is to test the command-line parameters in the shell script before invoking awk.

Nawk's -v option

Nawk provides a solution to the problem of defining parameters before any input is read. The -v option* specifies command-line arguments that you want available in the **BEGIN** procedure (i.e., before the first line of input is read.) The -v option must be specified before the script or the -f *progfile* arguments. For instance, the following command uses the -v option to set the record separator for multi-line records.

```
% nawk -F"\n" -v RS="\n\n" '{print}' phones.block
```

A separate -v option is required for each argument passed to the program.

Nawk also creates the system variables **ARGC** and **ARGV**, which will be familiar to C programmers. Because this requires an understanding of arrays, we will discuss this feature in Chapter 10, *The Bottom Drawer*.

---

*Judging from release notes distributed with the version of nawk by the UNIX Toolchest, the -v option was added in the summer of 1989. It was not supported on a version of nawk running under System V Release 3 (Interactive Systems V/386) that I tested. However, it does appear in the System V Release 4 documentation for nawk.

Berkeley 4.2 awk

Apparently, the version of the original awk that runs under Berkeley 4.2 has a few additional problems to watch out for when using command-line parameters, according to several postings on the net by David P. Huelsbeck.*

I don't find these problems occurring in System V or Sun 4.0 versions of awk that I have tested or with nawk or gawk.

The first problem that Huelsbeck cites is that you shouldn't use command-line parameters to set the input field and record separators. That is because the first line of input has already been read and parsed by the time the assignment is made. It would take effect for the second record and those that follow. You can, however, set the output field or record separators because it does not impact the parsing of lines. Thus, the script shown earlier that sets the output field separator from the command line will work fine.

The second problem that Huelsbeck cites is the handling of string values when passed as a parameter. The string value must be quoted when awk interprets it, and therefore, the quotes must be protected from the shell by preceding the quote with a backslash. Thus, to define the variable **name** to be "Mr. Magoo," the parameter would be as follows:

```
name=\"Mr. Magoo\"
```

As I said, I did not find this necessary to do using the versions of awk that I tested.

Information Retrieval

An awk program can be used to retrieve information from a database, the database basically being any kind of text file. The more structured the text file, the easier it is to work with, although the structure might be no more than a line consisting of individual words.

The list of acronyms below is a simple database.

```
$ cat acronyms
BASIC          Beginner's All-Purpose Symbolic Instruction Code
CICS           Customer Information Control System
COBOL          Common Business Orientated Language
DBMS           Data Base Management System
```

---

*<7754@lanl.ARPA>, <7759@lanl.ARPA>, and <10025@beta.UUCP>. Huelsbeck has also written a good article on awk, "Awk Power Plays," in *UNIX Papers* (ed. Mitchell Waite, Howard W. Sams & Company, 1987) which features an unusual spreadsheet calculator.

```
GIGO            Garbage In, Garbage Out
GIRL            Generalized Information Retrieval Language
```

A tab is used as the field separator. We're going to look at a program that takes an acronym as input and displays the appropriate line from the database as output. (In the next chapter, we're going to look at two other programs that use the acronym database. One program reads the list of acronyms and then finds occurrences of these acronyms in another file. The other program locates the first occurrence of these acronyms in a text file and inserts the description of the acronym.)

The shell script that we develop is named **awkro**. It takes the first argument from the command line (the name of the acronym) and passes it to the awk script. The **awkro** script follows:

```
$ cat awkro
:
# assign shell's $1 to awk search variable
awk '$1 == search' search=$1 acronyms
```

The first token specified on the shell command line ($1) is assigned to the variable named **search**; this variable is passed as a parameter into the awk program. Parameters passed to an awk program are specified *after* the script section. (This gets somewhat confusing, because **$1** inside the awk program represents the first field of each input line, while **$1** in the shell represents the first argument supplied on the command line.)

The example below demonstrates how this program can be used to find a particular acronym on our list.

```
$ awkro CICS
CICS Customer Information Control System
```

Notice that we tested the parameter as a string (**$1 == search**). The original version of awk does not allow us to use a variable in a regular expression. If you are using nawk, then you can write a regular expression (**$1 ˜ search**).

Importing Shell Variables into an Awk Script

If you are using the original version of awk, you can get around the problem of not being able to pass a variable as a regular expression by importing a shell variable inside an awk program. The value of the shell variable will be interpreted by awk as a constant. Here's an example:

```
$ cat awkro2
:
# assign shell's $1 to awk search variable
search=$1
awk '$1 ˜ /'"$search"'/' acronyms
```

The first line of the script makes the variable assignment before awk is invoked. To get the shell to expand the variable inside the awk procedure, we enclose it within single, then double, quotation marks. Thus, awk never sees the shell variable and evaluates it as a constant string.

Here's another version which makes use of the Bourne shell variable substitution feature. Using this feature gives us an easy way to specify a default value for the variable if, for instance, the user does not supply a command line argument.

```
search=$1
awk '$1 ~ /'"${search:-.*}"'/' acronyms
```

The expression "${search:-.*}" tells the shell to use the value of **search** if it is defined; if not, use ".*" as the value. Here, ".*" is regular expression syntax specifying any string of characters; therefore, all entries are printed if no entry is supplied on the command line.

We have shown a number of different techniques for passing values dynamically into a script. As an exercise, re-write the script that queries the telephone database, allowing the user to specify a name and get the person's phone number in response.

Finding a Glitch

A recent net posting was forwarded to me by mail because it contained a problem that could be solved using awk. Here's the original posting by Emmett Hogan:

> I have been trying to rewrite a sed/tr/fgrep script that we use quite a bit here in Perl, but have thus far been unsuccessful...hence this posting. Having never written anything in perl, and not wishing to wait for the Nutshell Perl Book, I figured I tap the knowledge of this group.
>
> Basically, we have several files which have the format:
>
> item info line 1
> info line 2
> .
> .
> .
> info line n
>
> Where each info line refers to the item and is indented by either spaces or tabs. Each item "block" is separated by a blank line.
>
> What I need to do, is to be able to type:
>
> info glitch filename
>
> Where info is the name of the perl script, glitch is what I want to find out about, and filename is the name of the file with the

information in it. The catch is that I need it to print the entire
"block" if it finds glitch anywhere in the file, i.e.:

machine   Sun 3/75
                   8 meg memory
                   Prone to memory glitches
                   more info
                   more info

would get printed if you looked for "glitch" along with any other
"blocks" which contained the word glitch.

Currently we are using the following script:

```
#!/bin/csh -f
#
sed 'r Ns/r/@/r $2 | tr '\012@' '@\012' | fgrep -i $1 | tr '@' '\012'
```
Which is in a word....SLOW.

I am sure Perl can do it faster, better, etc...but I cannot figure it out.

Any, and all, help is greatly appreciated.

Thanks in advance,
Emmett

--

Emmett Hogan   Computer Science Lab, SRI International

I worked on the problem and sent him a solution based on awk. You may want to
try to tackle the problem yourself before reading any further. The solution relies
on awk's multi-line record capability and requires that you be able to pass the
search string as a command-line parameter.

Here's the **info** script using awk:

```
search=$1
awk 'BEGIN { FS = "\n"; RS = "" }

$0 ~ /'"$search"'/ { print $0 }' $2
```

Here's the **info** script using nawk:

```
awk 'BEGIN { FS = "\n"; RS = "" }

$0 ~ search { print $0 }' search=$1 $2
```

Given a test file with multiple entries, I tested **info** to see if it could find the word
"glitch."

```
% info glitch glitch.test

machine         Sun 3/75
                8 meg memory
                Prone to memory glitches
                more info
                more info
```

In the next chapter, we look at conditional and looping constructs, arrays and multi-line records.

8

Conditionals, Loops, and Arrays

Conditional Statements
Looping
Other Statements That Affect Flow
   Control
Arrays
An Acronym Processor
System Variables That Are Arrays (Nawk)

This chapter covers some fundamental programming constructs. It covers all the control statements in the awk programming language. It also covers arrays, variables that allow you to store a series of values. If this is your first exposure to such constructs, you'll recognize that even sed provided conditional and looping capabilities. In awk, these capabilities are much more generalized and the syntax is much easier to use. In fact, the syntax of awk's conditional and looping constructs is borrowed from the C programming language. Thus, by learning awk and the constructs in this chapter, you are also on the way to learning the C language.

Conditional Statements

A conditional statement allows you to make a test before performing an action. In the previous chapter, we saw examples of pattern matching rules that were essentially conditional expressions affecting the main input loop. In this section, we look at conditional statements used primarily within actions.

A conditional statement is introduced by **if** and evaluates an expression placed in parentheses. The syntax is:

> **if** (*expression*)
>   *action1*
> [**else**
>   *action2*]

If *expression* evaluates as true (non-zero), *action1* is performed. When an **else** clause is specified, *action2* is performed if *expression* evaluates to false (zero). An expression might contain arithmetic, relational, or boolean operators discussed in Chapter 7, *Writing Scripts for Awk*.

Perhaps the simplest conditional expression that you could write is one that tests whether a variable contains a non-zero value.

```
if ( x ) print x
```

If "x" is zero (or undefined), the **print** statement will not be executed. If "x" has a value, that value will be printed. You can also test whether "x" equals another value:

```
if ( x == y ) print x
```

Remember that "==" is a relational operator and "=" is an assignment operator. We can also test whether "x" matches a pattern using the pattern-matching operator "~":

```
if ( x ~ /[yY](es)*/ ) print x
```

Here are a few additional syntactical points:

• If any action consists of more than one statement, the action is enclosed within a pair of braces.

> **if** (*expression*) {
>   *statement1*
>   *statement2*
>   }

Awk is not very particular about the placement of braces and statements (unlike sed). The opening brace is placed after the conditional expression, either on the same line or on the the next line. The first statement can follow the opening brace or be placed on the line following it. The closing brace is put after the last statement, either on the same line or after it. Spaces or tabs are allowed before or after the braces. The indentation of statements is not required but is recommended to improve readability.

- A newline is optional after the close parenthesis, and after **else**.

    if (*expression*) *action1*
    [**else** *action2*]

- A newline is also optional after *action1*, providing that a semicolon ends *action1*.

    if (*expression*) *action1*; [**else** *action2*]

- You cannot avoid using braces by using semicolons to separate multiple statements on a single line.

In the previous chapter, we saw a script that averaged student grades. We could use a conditional statement to tell us whether the student passed or failed. Presuming that an average of 65 or above is a passing grade, we could write the following conditional:

```
if ( avg >= 65 )
    grade = "Pass"
else
    grade = "Fail"
```

The value assigned to **grade** depends upon whether the expression "avg >= 65" evaluates to true or false.

Multiple conditional statements can be used to test whether one of several possible conditions is true. For example, perhaps the students are given a letter grade instead of a pass-fail mark. Here's a conditional that assigns a letter grade based on a student's average:

```
if (avg >= 90)   grade="A"
else if (avg >= 80) grade="B"
else if (avg >= 70) grade="C"
else if (avg >= 60) grade="D"
else grade="F"
```

The important thing to recognize is that the successive conditionals are evaluated until one of them returns true; once that occurs, the rest of the conditionals are skipped. If none of the conditional expressions evaluates to true, the last **else** is accepted, constituting the default action; in this case, it assigns "F" to **grade**.

Conditional Operator (nawk)

Nawk provides a conditional operator that is found in the C programming language. Its form is:

    expr ? *action1* : *action2*

The previous **if/else** condition can be written using the conditional operator:

```
avg >= 65 ? grade = "Pass" : grade = "Fail"
```

This form has the advantage of brevity and is appropriate for simple conditionals such as the one shown here. However, unless your program uses other features that require nawk, using the conditional operator makes a program unnecessarily incompatible with the original awk.

Looping

A loop is a construct that allows us to perform one or more actions again and again. In awk, a loop can be specified using a **while** or **for** statement.

While Loop

The syntax of a **while** loop is:

> **while** (*condition*)
> *action*

The newline is optional after the right parenthesis. The conditional expression is evaluated at the top of the loop and, if true, the action is performed. If the expression is never true, the action is not performed. Typically, the conditional expression evaluates to true and the action changes a value such that the conditional expression eventually returns false and the loop is exited. For instance, if you wanted to perform an action four times, you could write the following loop:

```
i = 1
while ( i <= 4 ) {
    print $i
    ++i
}
```

Like the **if** statement, an action consisting of more than one statement must be enclosed in braces. Note the role of each statement. The first statement assigns an initial value to **i**. The expression "i <= 4" compares **i** to 4 to determine if the action should be executed. The action consists of two statements, one that simply prints the value of a field referenced as **$i** and another that increments **i**. **i** is a counter variable and is used to keep track of how many times we go through the loop. If we did not increment the counter variable or if the comparison would never evaluate to false (e.g., i > 0), then the action would be repeated without end.

Do Loop (nawk)

Nawk provides a **do** loop, which is a variation of the **while** loop. The syntax of a **do** loop is:

> **do**
> > *action*
> **while** (*condition*)

The newline is optional after **do**. It is also optional after *action* providing the statement is terminated by a semicolon.

The main feature of this loop is that the conditional expression appears *after* the action. Thus, the action is performed at least once.

Look at the following **do** loop.

```
BEGIN {
     do {
            ++i
            print i
     } while ( i <= 4 )
}
```

In this example, the value of **i** is set in the body of the loop using the auto-increment operator. The body of the loop is executed once and the expression is evaluated. In the previous example of a **while** loop, the initial value of **i** was set before the loop. The expression was evaluated first, then the body of the loop was executed once. Note the value of **i** when we run this example:

```
% gawk -f do.awk -
1
2
3
4
5
```

Before the conditional expression is first evaluated, **x** is incremented to 1. The body of the loop is executed five times, not four; when **x** equals 4, the conditional expression is true and the body of the loop is executed again, incrementing **x** to 5 and printing its value. Only then is the conditional expression evaluated to false and the loop exited. By changing the operator from "<=" to "<", or less than, the body of the loop will be executed four times.

To keep in mind the difference between the **do** loop and the **while** loop, remember that the **do** loop always executes the body of the loop *at least once*. At the bottom of the procedure, you decide if you need to execute it again.

For an example, let's look at a program that loops through the fields of a record, reading as many fields as necessary until their cumulative value exceeds 100. The reason we use a **do** loop is that we will read at least one of the fields. We read the field and if its value exceeds 100 we don't read any other fields. We read the second field only if the first field is less than 100. Its value is added to the total and if the total exceeds 100 then we exit the loop. If it is still less 100, we execute the loop once again.

```
{
total = i = 0
do {
      ++i
      total += $i
} while ( total <= 100 )
print i, ":", total
}
```

The first line of the script initializes the value of two variables: **total** and **i**. The loop increments the value of **i** and uses the field operator to reference a particular field. Each time through the loop, it refers to a different field. When the loop is executed for the first time, the field reference gets the value of field one and assigns it to the variable **total**. The conditional expression at the end of the loop evaluates whether **total** exceeds 100. If it does, the loop is exited. Then the value of **i**, the number of fields that we're read, and the total are printed. (This script assumes that each record totals at least 100; otherwise, we'd have to check that **i** does not exceed the number of fields for the record. We construct such a test in the example presented in next section to show the **for** loop.)

Here's a test file containing a series of numbers:

```
% cat test.do
45 25 60 20
10 105 50 40
33 5 9 67
108 3 5 4
```

Running the script on the test file produces the following:

```
% nawk -f do.awk test.do
3 : 130
2 : 115
4 : 114
1 : 108
```

For each record, only as many fields are read as needed for the total to exceed 100.

For Loop

A **for** statement offers a more compact syntax that achieves the same result as a **while** loop. Although it looks more difficult, this syntax is much easier to use and makes sure that you provide all the required elements of a loop. The syntax of a **for** loop is:

for (*set_counter*; *test_counter*; *increment_counter*)
    action

The newline after the right parenthesis is optional. The **for** loop consists of three expressions:

set_counter	Sets the initial value for a counter variable.
test_counter	States a condition that is tested at the top of the loop.
increment_counter	Increments the counter each time at the top of the loop.

Look at this rather common **for** loop that reads each field on the input line.

```
for ( i = 1; i <= NF; i++ )
    print $i
```

As in the previous example, **i** is a variable that is used to reference a field using the field operator. The system variable **NF** contains the number of fields for the current input record, and we test it to determine if **i** has reached the last field on the line. The value of **NF** is the maximum number of times to go through the loop. Inside the loop, the **print** statement is executed, printing each field on its own line. A script using this construct can print each word on a line by itself, which can then be run through **sort -u** to get word distribution statistics for a file.

You can also write a loop to read from the last field to the first.

```
for ( i = NF; i >= 1; i--)
    print $i
```

Each time through the loop the counter is decremented. You could use this to reverse the order of fields.

The **grades.awk** script that we showed earlier determined the average of five grades. We can make the script much more useful by averaging any number of grades. That is, if you were to run this script throughout the school year, the number of grades to average would increase. Rather than revising the script to accommodate the specific number of fields, we can write a generalized script that loops to read however many fields as there are. Our earlier version of the program calculated the average of 5 grades using these two statements:

```
total = $2 + $3 + $4 + $5 + $6
avg = total / 5
```

We can revise that using a **for** loop to read each field in the record.

```
total = 0
for (i = 2; i <= NF; ++i)
     total += $i
avg = total / (NF - 1)
```

We initialize the variable **total** because we don't want its value to accumulate from one record to the next. At the beginning of the **for** loop, the counter **i** is initialized to 2 because the first numeric field is field 2. Each time through the loop the value of the current field is added to **total**. When the last field has been read (**i** is greater than **NF**), then we break out of the loop and calculate the average. For instance, if the record consists of 4 fields, the first time through the loop, we assign the value of $2 to **total**. At the bottom of the loop, **i** is incremented by 1, then compared to **NF**, which is 4. The expression evaluates to true and **total** is incremented by the value of $3.

Notice how we divide the total by the number of fields minus 1 to remove the student name from the count. The parentheses are required around "NF - 1" because the precedence of operators would otherwise divide **total** by **NF** and then subtract 1, instead of subtracting 1 from **NF** first.

Deriving Factorials

The factorial of a number is the product of successively multiplying that number by one less than that number. The factorial of 4 is 4 x 3 x 2 x 1 or 24. The factorial of 5 is 5 times the factorial of 4 or 5 x 24 or 120. Deriving a factorial for a given number can be expressed using a loop as follows:

```
fact = number
for (x = number - 1 ; x > 1; x--)
     fact *= x
```

where **number** is the number for which we will derive the factorial **fact**. Let's say that **number** equals 5. The first time through the loop **x** is equal to 4. The action evaluates "5 * 4" and assigns the value to **fact**. The next time through the loop, **x** is 3 and 20 is multiplied by it. We go through the loop until **x** equals 0.

Here is the above fragment incorporated into a standalone script that prompts the user for a number and then prints the factorial of that number.

```
awk '# factorial: return factorial of user-supplied number
BEGIN {
      # prompt user; use printf, not print, to avoid the newline
      printf("Enter number: ")
}

# check that user enters a number
$1 ~ /[0-9]+/ {
      # assign value of $1 to number & fact
      number = $1
      fact = number
      # loop to multiple fact*x until x = 0
      for (x = number - 1 ; x > 1; x--)
            fact *= x
      printf("The factorial of %d is %g\n", number, fact)
      # exit -- saves user from typing CRTL-D.
      exit
}

# if not a number, prompt again.
$1 !~ /[0-9]+/ { printf("\nInvalid entry. Enter a number: ")
}' -
```

This is an interesting example of a main input loop that prompts for input and reads the reply from standard input. The **BEGIN** rule is used to prompt the user to enter a number. Because we have specified that input is to come not from a file but from standard input, the program will halt after putting out the prompt and then wait for the user to type a number. The first rule checks that a number has been entered. If not, the second rule will be applied, prompting the user again to re-enter a number. We set up an input loop that will continue to read from standard input until a valid entry is found. See the **lookup** program in the next section for another example of constructing an input loop.

Here's an example of how the **factorial** program works:

```
% factorial
Enter number: 5
The factorial of 5 is 120
```

Note that the result uses "%g" as the conversion specification format in the **printf** statement. This permits floating point notation to be used to express very large numbers. Look at the following example:

```
% factorial
Enter number: 33
The factorial of 33 is 8.68332e+36
```

Other Statements That Affect Flow Control

The **if, while,** and **for** statements allow you to change the normal flow through a procedure. In this section, we look at several statements that also effect a change in flow control.

There are two statements that affect the flow control of a loop, **break** and **continue.** The **break** statement, as you'd expect, breaks out of the loop at that point, such that no more iterations of the loop are performed. The **continue** statement stops the current iteration before reaching the bottom of the loop and starts a new iteration at the top.

Consider what happens in the following program fragment:

```
for ( x = 1; x <= NF; ++x )
    if ( y == $x ) {
        print x, $x
        break
    }
print
```

A loop is set up to examine each field of the current input record. Each time through the loop, the value of **y** is compared to the value of a field referenced as $i. If the result is true, we print the field number and its value and then break from the loop. The next statement to be executed is **print.** The use of **break** means that we are interested only in the first match on a line and that we don't want to loop through the rest of the fields.

Here's a similar example using the **continue** statement:

```
for ( x = 1; x <= NF; ++x ){
    if ( x == 3 )
        continue
    print x, $x
}
```

This example loops through the fields of the current input record, printing the field number and its value. However, (for some reason), we want to avoid printing the third field. The conditional statement tests the counter variable and if it is "3," the **continue** statement is executed. The **continue** statement passes control back to the top loop where the counter variable is incremented again. It avoids executing the **print** statement for that iteration. The same result could be achieved by simply re-writing the conditional to execute **print** as long as x is not equal to 3. The point is that you can use the **continue** statement to avoid hitting the bottom of the loop on a particular iteration.

There are two statements that affect the main input loop, **next** and **exit**. The **next** statement causes the next line of input to be read and then resumes execution at the top of the script. This allows you to avoid applying other procedures on the current input line. A typical use of the **next** statement is to continue reading input from a file, ignoring the other actions in the script until that file is exhausted. The system variable FILENAME provides the name of the current input file. Thus, a pattern can be written:

```
FILENAME == "acronyms" { action
                 next
}
{ print }
```

This causes the action to be performed for each line in the file *acronyms*. After the action is performed, the next line of input is read. Control does not pass to the **print** statement until the input is taken from a different source.

The **exit** statement exits the main input loop and passes control to the **END** rule, if there is one. If the **END** rule is not defined, or the **exit** statement is used in the **END** rule, then the script terminates. We used the **exit** statement earlier in the **factorial** program to exit after reading one line of input.

An **exit** statement can take an expression as an argument. The value of this expression will be returned as the exit status of awk. If the expression is not supplied, the exit status is 0.

You will come across examples that use these flow-control statements in upcoming sections.

Arrays

An array is a variable that can be used to store a set of values. Usually the values are related in some way. The following statement assigns a value to an element of an array:

array[*subscript*] = *value*

In awk, you don't have to declare the size of the array; you only have to load the array (before referencing it). For instance, the following example assigns the string "cherry" to an element of the array named **flavor**.

```
flavor[1] = "cherry"
```

The index or subscript of this element of the array is "1". The following statement prints the string "cherry":

```
print flavor[1]
```

Loops can be used to load and extract elements from arrays. For instance, if the array **flavor** has five elements, then you can write a loop to print each element as follows:

```
flavor_count = 5
for (x = 1; x <= flavor_count; ++x)
    print flavor[x]
```

One way that arrays are used in awk is to store a value from each record, using the record number as the index to the array. Let's suppose we wanted to keep track of the averages calculated for each student and come up with a class average. Each time a record is read we make the following assignment.

```
class_avg[NR] = avg
```

The system variable **NR** is used as the subscript for the array because it is incremented for each record. When the first record is read, the value of **avg** is placed in **class_avg[1]**; for the second record, the value is placed in **class_avg[2]**, and so on. After we have read all of the records, we have a list of averages in the array **class_avg**. In an **END** rule, we can average all of these grades by writing a loop to get the total of the grades and then dividing them by the value of **NR**. Then we can compare each student average to the class average to collect totals for the number of students at or above average and the number below.

```
END {
for( x = 1; x <= NR; x++ )
        class_avg_total += class_avg[x]

class_average =  class_avg_total / NR

for( x = 1; x <= NR; x++ )
        if (class_avg[x] >= class_average)
                ++above_average
        else
                ++below_average

print "Class Average: ", class_average
print "At or Above Average: ", above_average
print "Below Average: ", below_average
}
```

There are two **for** loops for reading the elements of the array. The first one totals the averages so that it can be divided by the number of student records. The next loop retrieves each student average so that it can be compared to the class average. If it is above average, we increment the variable **above_average**; otherwise, we increment **below_average**.

Associative Arrays

In awk, all arrays are *associative* arrays. What makes an associative array unique is that its index can be a string or a number.

In most programming languages, the indices of arrays are exclusively numeric. In these implementations, an array is a sequence of locations where values are stored. The indices of the array are derived from the order in which the values are stored. There is no need to keep track of indices. For instance, the index of the first element of an array is "1" or the first location in the array.

An associative array makes an "association" between the indices and the elements of an array. For each element of the array, a pair of values is maintained: the index of the element and the value of the element. The elements are not stored in any particular order as in a conventional array. Thus, even though you can use numeric subscripts in awk, the numbers do not have the same meaning that they do in other programming languages—they do not necessarily refer to sequential locations. However, with numeric indices, you can still read all the elements of an array in sequence, as we did in previous examples. You can create a loop to increment a counter that references the elements of the array in order.

Sometimes, the distinction between numeric and string indices is important. For instance, if you use "04" as the index to an element of the array, you cannot reference that element using "4" as its subscript. You'll see how to handle this problem in a sample program **romanum**, shown later in this chapter.

Associative arrays are a distinctive feature of awk, and a very powerful one that allows you to use a string as an index to another value. For instance, you could use a word as the index to its definition. If you know the word, you can retrieve the definition.

For example, you could use the first field of the input line as the index to the second field with the following assignment:

```
array[$1] = $2
```

Using this technique, we could take our list of acronyms and load it into an array named **acro**.

```
acro[$1] = $2
```

Each element of the array would be the description of an acronym and the subscript used to retrieve the element would be the acronym itself. The following expression:

```
acro["BASIC"]
```

produces:

```
Beginner's All-purpose Symbolic Instruction Code
```

There is a special looping syntax for reading all the elements of an associative array. It is a version of the **for** loop.

> **for** (*variable* **in** *array*)
>   *action array*[*variable*]

The *array* is the name of an array, as it was defined. The *variable* is any variable, which you can think of as a temporary variable similar to a counter that is incremented in a conventional **for** loop. This variable is set to a particular subscript each time through the loop. (Because *variable* is an arbitrary name, you often see item used, regardless of what variable name was used for the subscript when the array was loaded.) For example, the following **for** loop prints the name of the acronym "item" and the definition referenced by that name, "acro[item]."

```
for ( item in acro )
    print item, acro[item]
```

In this example, the print statement prints the current subscript ("BASIC", for instance) followed by the element of the **acro** array referenced by the subscript ("Beginner's All-purpose Symbolic Instruction Code").

This syntax can be applied to arrays with numeric subscripts. However, with the original awk, the order in which the items are retrieved is somewhat random (i.e., not necessarily in the order in which they were stored.) With nawk, this order is "implementation dependent," according to the *The AWK Programming Language*. My experience with nawk and gawk indicates that it works in a predictable manner. The following script demonstrates the problem so that you can test your implementation.

```
# load first field of each record into an array
{
    array[NR] = $1
}
# now print array
END {
    for (item in array)
        print array[item]
}
```

The array indexes the first field of each record by its record number. The **END** procedure is used to print all of the elements of the array. Each time through the loop, the variable **item** is set to the next element in the array. The input file consists of three lines:

```
% cat array.test
1
2
3
```

Now let's see what happens using the original awk.

```
% awk -f array.awk array.test
2
3
1
```

The items are not output in the same order in which they were read into the array. This can present problems if your script depends upon retrieving data in a particular order. Fortunately, nawk and gawk seem to solve this problem.

```
% gawk -f array.awk array.test
1
2
3
```

Now let's return to our student grade program for an example. Let's say that we wanted to report how many students got an A, how many got a "B" and so on. Once we determined the grade, we could increment a counter for that grade. We could set up individual variables for each letter grade and then test which one to increment.

```
if ( grade == "A" )
    ++gradeA
else if (grade == "B" )
    ++gradeB
```

However, an array makes this task much easier. We can define an array called **class_grade**, and simply use the letter grade (A through F) as the index to the array.

```
++class_grade[grade]
```

Thus, if the grade is an "A" then the value of **class_grade["A"]** is incremented by one. At the end of the program, we can print out these values in the **END** rule using the special **for** loop:

```
for (letter_grade in class_grade)
    print letter_grade ":", class_grade[letter_grade]
```

The variable **letter_grade** references a single subscript of the array **class_grade** each time through the loop. Since this is the last addition we make to the grades.awk script, we can look at the full listing.

```
# grades.awk -- average student grades and determine
# letter grade as well as class averages.
# $1 = student name; $2 - $NF = test scores.

# set output field separator to tab.
BEGIN { OFS = "" }

# action applied to all input lines
{
  # add up grades
     total = 0
     for (i = 2; i <= NF; ++i)
     total += $i
  # calculate average
     avg = total / (NF - 1)
  # assign student's average to element of array
     class_avg[NR] = avg
  # determine letter grade
     if (avg >= 90)   grade="A"
     else if (avg >= 80) grade="B"
     else if (avg >= 70) grade="C"
     else if (avg >= 60) grade="D"
     else grade="F"
  # increment counter for letter grade array
     ++class_grade[grade]
  # print student name, average and letter grade
     print $1, avg, grade
}
# print out class statistics
END {
  # calculate class average
     for( x = 1; x <= NR; x++)
         class_avg_total += class_avg[x]
     class_average =  class_avg_total / NR
  # determine how many above/below average
     for( x = 1; x <= NR; x++)
         if (class_avg[x] >= class_average)
                 ++above_average
         else
                 ++below_average
  # print results
     print ""
     print "Class Average: ", class_average
     print "At or Above Average: ", above_average
     print "Below Average: ", below_average
  # print number of students per letter grade
     for (letter_grade in class_grade)
         print letter_grade ":", class_grade[letter_grade]
}
```

Here's a sample run:

```
% cat grades.test
mona 70 77 85 83 70 89
john 85 92 78 94 88 91
andrea 89 90 85 94 90 95
jasper 84 88 80 92 84 82
dunce 64 80 60 60 61 62
ellis 90 98 89 96 96 92
% awk -f grades.awk grades.test
mona      79        C
john      88        B
andrea    90.5      A
jasper    85        B
dunce     64.5      D
ellis     93.5      A

Class Average:   83.4167
At or Above Average:      4
Below Average:   2
A:        2
B:        2
C:        1
D:        1
```

Testing for Membership in an Array (Nawk)

In nawk, **in** is actually an operator that can be used in a conditional expression to test that a subscript is a *member* of an array. The expression:

```
item in array
```

returns 1 if **array[item]** exists and 0 if it does not. For example, the following conditional statement is true if the string "BASIC" is a subscript of the array **acro**.

```
if ( "BASIC" in acro )
    print "Found BASIC"
```

This is true if "BASIC" is a subscript used to access an element of **acro**. This syntax cannot tell you whether "BASIC" is an element of "acro." This expression is the same as writing a loop to check that such a subscript exists, although the above expression is much easier to write.

A Glossary Lookup Script

This program reads a series of glossary entries from a file named *glossary* and puts them into an array. The user is prompted to enter a glossary term and if it is found, the definition of the term is printed.

Here's the **lookup** program:

```
awk '# lookup -- reads local glossary file and prompts user for query

#0
BEGIN { FS ="\t"; OFS = "\t"
     # prompt user
     printf ("Enter a glossary term: ")
}

#1 read local file named glossary
FILENAME == "glossary"{
          #load each glossary entry into an array
          entry[$1] = $2
          next
}
#2 scan for command to exit program
$0 ~ /^(quit|[qQ]|exit|[Xx])$/ { exit }

#3 process any non-empty line
$0 != "" {
     foundit = 0
     # loop through items in array
     for ( term in entry )
          # compare user input against entry for term
          if ($0 == term) {
               # if found, print definition
               print entry[term]
               foundit = 1
               # now exit this loop
               break
               }
     # check to see if we never found the term.
     if (foundit == 0)
          print $0 " not found"
}
#4 prompt user again for another term
{
printf ("Enter another glossary term (q to quit): ")
}' glossary -
```

The pattern-matching rules are numbered to make this discussion easier. As we look at the individual rules, we'll discuss them in the order in which they are encountered in the flow of the script. Because awk's rules are not always executed in sequence, it is important to understand this order. Rule #0 is the **BEGIN** rule which is performed only once before any input is read. It sets the **FS** and

OFS to a tab and then prompts the user to enter a glossary item. The response will come from standard input, but that is read after the *glossary* file.

Rule #1 tests to see if the current filename (FILENAME) is "glossary" and is therefore only applied while reading input from this file. This rule loads the glossary entries into an array.

```
entry[term] = defintion
```

where $1 is the term and $2 is the definition. The **next** statement at the end of rule #1 is used to skip other rules in the script and causes a new line of input to be read. So, until all the entries in the *glossary* file are read, no other rule is evaluated.

Once input from *glossary* is exhausted, awk reads from standard input because "-" is specified on the command line. Standard input is where the user's response comes from. Rule #3 tests that the input line ($0) is not empty. This rule should match whatever the user types. The action associated with this rule loops through the array to see if there is an entry that matches the user's input. If there is, the entry is found, and that element of the array is printed (i.e., the definition of the term). Once we find a match, we break from the **for** loop and process the next statement. The last statement is a conditional that tests to see if a flag (**foundit**) was set to indicate that a successful match was made. If this flag is 0, its initial value, we want to tell the user that no valid entry was found.

After rule #3, rule #4 will be evaluated. This rule simply prompts the user for another entry. Note that regardless of whether a valid entry was processed in rule #3, rule #4 is executed. The prompt also tells the user how to quit the program. After this rule, awk looks for the next line of input.

If the user chooses to quit by entering "q" as the next line of input, rule #2 will be matched. The pattern looks for a complete line consisting of alternative words or single letters that the user might enter to quit. The "^" and "$" are important, signifying that the input line contains no other characters but these; otherwise a "q" appearing in a glossary entry would be matched. Note that the placement of this rule in the sequence of rules is significant. It must appear before rules #3 and #4 because these rules will match anything, including the words "quit" and "exit."

Let's look at how the program works. For this example, we will make a copy of the *acronyms* file and use it as the *glossary* file.

```
% lookup
Enter a glossary term: GIGO
Garbage in, garbage out
Enter another glossary term (q to quit): BASIC
Beginner's All-Purpose Symbolic Instruction Code
Enter another glossary term (q to quit): q
```

As you can see, the program is set up to prompt the user for additional items until the user enters "q".

Note that this program can be easily revised to read a glossary anywhere on the file system, including the user's home directory. The shell script that invokes awk could handle command line options that allow the user to specify the glossary filename. You could also read a shared glossary file and then read a local one by writing separate rules to process the entries.

Using split to Create Arrays

The built-in function **split** can parse any string into elements of an array. This function can be useful to extract "subfields" from a field. The syntax of the **split** function is:

$$n = \textbf{split}(\textit{string}, \textit{array}, \textit{separator})$$

string is the input string to be parsed into elements of the named *array*. The elements will be split based on the specified *separator* character. If a delimiter is not specified, then the field separator is used. The value of n is the number of elements in the array.

For example, if you had a record in which the first field consisted of the person's full name, you could use the **split** function to extract the person's first and last names. The following statement breaks up the first field into elements of the array **fullname**:

```
sizeOfArray = split($1,fullname," ")
```

A blank space is specified as the delimiter. The person's first name can be referenced as:

```
fullname[1]
```

and the person's last name can be referenced as:

```
fullname[z]
```

because z contains the number of elements in the array. This works, regardless of whether the person's full name contains a middle name. If z is the value returned by split, you can write a loop to read all the elements of this array.

```
z = split($1,array,":")
for (i = 1; i <= z; ++i)
     array[i]
```

The next section contains additional examples of using the **split** function.

Making Conversions

This section looks at two examples that demonstrate similar methods of converting output from one format to another.

When working on the index program shown in Chapter 9, *Functions*, I needed a quick way to assign roman numerals to volume numbers. In other words, volume 4 needed to be identified as "IV" in the index. Since there was no immediate prospect of the number of volumes exceeding 10, I wrote a script that took as input a number between 1 and 10 and converted it to a roman numeral.

This shell script takes the first argument from the command line and echoes it as input to the awk program.

```
echo $1 |
awk '# romanum -- convert number 1-10 to roman numeral

# define romanlist as list of roman numerals 1-10
BEGIN {
     romanlist = "I,II,III,IV,V,VI,VII,VIII,IX,X"
     # create array named numerals from romanlist
     split(romanlist,numerals,",")
}

# look for number between 1 and 10
$1 > 0 && $1 < 10 {
     # print specified element
     print numerals[$1]
     exit
     }
{    print "invalid number"
     exit
}' -
```

This script defines a list of ten roman numerals, then uses **split** to load them into an array named **numerals**. This is done in the **BEGIN** action because it only needs to be done once.

The second rule checks that the first field of the input line contains a number between 1 and 10. If it does, this number is used as the index to the **numerals** array, retrieving the corresponding element. The **exit** statement terminates the program. The last rule is executed only if there is no valid entry.

Here's an example of how it works:

```
% romanum 4
IV
```

Following along on the same idea, here's a script that converts dates in the form "mm-dd-yy" or "mm/dd/yy" to "month day, year."

```
awk '# date-month -- convert mm/dd/yy to month day, year

# build list of months and put in array.
BEGIN {
    # the 2-step assignment is done for printing in book
    listmonths="January,February,March,April,May,June,"
    listmonths=listmonths "July,August,September,November,December"
    split( listmonths,month,"," )
}

# check that there is input
$1 != "" {

# split on "/" the first input field into elements of array
    sizeOfArray = split($1,date,"/")

# check that only one field is returned
    if (sizeOfArray == 1)
        # try to split on "-"
        sizeOfArray = split($1,date,"-")

# must be invalid
    if (sizeOfArray == 1)
        exit

# add 0 to number of month to coerce numeric type
    date[1] += 0

# print month day, year
    print month[date[1]], date[2]", 19" date[3]
}' -
```

This script reads from standard input. The **BEGIN** action creates an array named **month** whose elements are the names of the months of the year. The second rule verifies that we have a non-empty input line. The first statement in the associated action splits the first field of input looking for "/" as the delimiter. **sizeOfArray** contains the number of elements in the array. If awk was unable to parse the string, it creates the array with only one element. Thus, we can test the value of **sizeOfArray** to determine if we have several elements. If we do not, we assume that perhaps "-" was used as the delimiter. If that fails to produce an array with multiple elements, we assume the input is invalid, and exit. If we have success-fully parsed the input, "date[1]" contains the number of the month. This value can be used as the index to the array **month**, nesting one array inside another. However, before using **date[1]**, we coerce the type of **date[1]** by adding 0 to it. While awk will correctly interpret "11" as a number, leading zeros may cause a number to treated as a string. Thus, "06" might not be recognized properly without type coercion. The element referenced by **date[1]** is used as the subscript for **month**.

Here's a sample run:

```
% echo "5/11/55" | date-month
May 11, 1955
```

Deleting Elements of an Array (nawk)

Nawk provides a statement for deleting an element of an array. The syntax is:

> **delete** *array*[*subscript*]

This has basically the same effect as assigning null to that element, which is how you would do it using the original awk. For instance:

```
delete glossary[term]
```

is equivalent to

```
glossary[term] = ""
```

In other words, a reference to that element returns null. However, the subscript still exists. See the **lotto** script in the next chapter for an example of using the **delete** statement.

An Acronym Processor

Now let's look at a program that scans a file for an acronym, and prints the acronym, with the description as well. If a line refers to BASIC, we'd like to replace it with the description "Beginner's All-Purpose Symbolic Instruction Code" and put the acronym in parentheses afterwords. (I doubt this is a useful program in and of itself, but the techniques used in the program are generalized and have many such uses.)

We can design this program for use as a filter that prints all lines, regardless of whether a change has been made. We'll call it **awkro**.

```
awk '# awkro - expand acronyms
# load acronyms file into array "acro"
FILENAME == "acronyms" {
    split($0,entry,"")
    acro[entry[1]]=entry[2]
    next
}
```

```
# read any input line containing caps
$0 ~ /[A-Z][A-Z]+/ {
# loop through acronyms
   for ( acronym in acro )
      # compare each field to acronym
      for (i = 1; i <- NF; i++)
            if ( $i == acronym ) {
                # if it matches, add description
                $i = acro[acronym] " (" $i ")"
            }
}
{
# print all lines
print $0
}' acronyms  $*
```

Let's first see it in action. Here's a sample input file.

```
$ cat sample
The USGCRP is a comprehensive
research effort that includes applied
as well as basic research.
The NASA program Mission to Planet Earth
represents the principal space-based component
of the USGCRP and includes new initiatives
such as EOS and Earthprobes.
```

Now we run the program on the sample file.

```
% awkro sample
The U.S. Global Change Research Program (USGCRP) is a comprehensive
research effort that includes applied
as well as basic research.
The National Aeronautic and Space Administration (NASA) program
Mission to Planet Earth
represents the principal space-based component
of the U.S. Global Change Research Program (USGCRP) and includes new
initiatives
such as Earth Observing System (EOS) and Earthprobes.
```

We'll look at this program in two parts. The first part reads records from the
acronyms file.

```
# load acronyms file into array "acro"
FILENAME == "acronyms" {
     split($0,entry,"")
     acro[entry[1]]=entry[2]
     next
}
```

The two fields from these records are loaded into an array using the first field as
the subscript and assigning the second field to an element of the array. In other
words, the acronym itself is the index to its description.

Note that we did not change the field separator, but instead used the **split** function to create the array **entry**. This array is then used in creating an array named **acro.**

The second half of the program looks like:

```
# read any input line containing caps
$0 ~ /[A-Z][A-Z]+/ {
# loop through acronyms
   for ( acronym in acro )
      # compare each field to acronym
      for (i = 1; i <= NF; i++)
            if ( $i == acronym ) {
                  # if it matches, add description
                  $i = acro[acronym] " (" $i ")"
                  }
}
{
# print all lines
print $0
}
```

Only lines that contain more than one consecutive capital letter are processed by the first of the two actions shown here. This action loops through the elements of the array and the fields for each record. At the heart of this section is the conditional statement that tests if the current field (**$i**) is equal to the subscript of the array (**acronym**). If the value of the field and the subscript are equal, we replace the original value of the field with the array element and the original value in parentheses. Note that the insertion of the description of the acronym results in lines that may be too long. See the next chapter for a discussion of the **length** function, which can be used to determine the length of a string so you can divide it up if it is too long.

Finally, it should be clear why we make the comparison between **$i** and **acronym**, and not **acro[acronym]**; the latter refers to an element, while the former refers to the subscript, the name of the acronym.

Up to now the program will run using awk or nawk or gawk. We're going to make one change to it that makes use of a feature found in nawk. Then we'll show how to implement it using awk, and how much more difficult the code becomes.

We're going to change the program so it makes a replacement only the first time an acronym appears. After we've found it, we don't want to search for that acronym any more. Using nawk, we can simply delete that acronym from the array.

```
delete acro[acronym]
```

Using awk, we have to redefine that element in the array after we've used it. One way is to make the element equal to the subscript. Thus, **acro["BASIC"]** is equal to "Beginner's All-Purpose Symbolic Instruction Code" at the beginning of the procedure, and equal to "BASIC" if a match has been made. There are two places where we test the element against the subscript. The first place is after the **for** loop has read in a new element from **acro**; a conditional statement ensures that we don't scan the next input record for an acronym that has already been found. The second place is when we test **$i** to see if it matches **name**; this test ensures that we don't make another match for the same acronym on that line. This conditional statement evaluates a compound expression. The **&&** (and) boolean operator states a condition that both expressions have to be true for the entire expression to be true. Here's the code:

```
for ( name in acro )
    if (acro[name] != name)
        for (i = 1; i <= NF; i++)
            if ($i == name && acro[name] != name) {
            $i = acro[name] " (" $i ")"
                acro[name] = name
            }
}
```

There are other changes that would be good to make. In running the **awkronym** program, I soon discovered that it failed to match the acronym if it was followed by a punctuation mark. My solution using the original awk was was not to handle it in awk at all. Instead, I used two sed scripts, one before processing:

```
sed 's/\(..*\)\([.,;:!]\)/\1 @@@\2/g'
```

and one after:

```
sed 's/ @@@\([.,;:!]\)/\1/g'
```

A sed script, run prior to invoking awk, could simply insert a blank space before any punctuation mark, causing it to be interpreted as a separate field. A string of garbage characters (@@@) were also added so we'd be able to easily identify and restore the punctuation mark.

This kind of solution, using another tool in the UNIX toolbox, demonstrates that not everything needs to be done as an awk procedure. awk is all the more valuable because it is situated in the UNIX environment.

However, with the new awk, we can implement a different solution, one that uses a regular expression to match the acronym. We will see that solution in the next chapter when we look at the **match** and **sub** functions.

Multi-dimensional Arrays (nawk)

Awk supports linear arrays in which the index to each element of the array is a single subscript. If you imagine a linear array as a row of numbers, a two-dimensional array represents rows and columns of numbers. You might refer to the element in the second column of the third row as "array[3,2]. Two-dimensional and three-dimensional arrays are examples of multi-dimensional arrays. Nawk does not support multi-dimensional arrays but instead offers a syntax for subscripts that appear as though you were referencing a multi-dimensional array. For instance, you could write the following expression:

```
file_array[NR,i] = $i
```

where each field of an input record is indexed by its record number and field number. Thus, the following reference:

```
file_array[2,4]
```

would produce the value of the fourth field of the second record.

This syntax does not create a multi-dimensional array. The syntax is converted into a string that uniquely identifies the element in a linear array. The components of a multi-dimensional subscript are interpreted as individual strings ("2" and "4", for instance) and concatenated together separated by the value of the system variable **SUBSEP**. The subscript-component separator is defined as "\034" by default, a value rarely found in ASCII text. Thus, nawk maintains a linear array and the subscript for our previous example would actually be "2\0344". The main consequence, I believe, of this simulation of multi-dimensional arrays is the larger the array, the slower it is to access individual elements.

Here is a sample awk script named **bitmap.awk** that shows how to load and output the elements of a multi-dimensional array. This array represents a two-dimensional bitmap that is 12 characters in width and height.

```
BEGIN { FS = ","   # comma-separated fields
     # assign width and height of bitmap
     WIDTH = 12
     HEIGHT = 12
     # loop to load entire array with "O"
     for (i = 1; i <= WIDTH; ++i)
          for (j = 1; j <= HEIGHT; ++j)
               bitmap[i,j] = "O"
}
# read input of the form x,y.
{
     # found that bitmap[$0] would not work, so assign to variables.
     coordx = $1
     coordy = $2
     # assign "X" to that element of array
```

```
        bitmap[coordx,coordy] = "X"
}
# at end output multidimensional array
END {
      for (i = 1; i <= WIDTH; ++i){
            for (j = 1; j <= HEIGHT; ++j)
                  printf ("%s", bitmap[i,j] )
            # after each row, print newline
            printf("\n")
      }
}
```

Before any input is read, the **bitmap** array is loaded with O's. This array has 144 elements. The input to this program is a series of coordinates, one per line.

```
% cat bitmap.test
1,1
2,2
3,3
4,4
5,5
6,6
7,7
8,8
9,9
10,10
11,11
12,12
1,12
2,11
3,10
4,9
5,8
6,7
7,6
8,5
9,4
10,3
11,2
12,1
```

For each coordinate, the program will put an "X" in place of an "O" as that element of the array. At the end of the script, the same kind of loop that loaded the array, now outputs it. The following example reads the input from the file *bitmap.test*.

```
% gawk -f bitmap.awk bitmap.test
XOOOOOOOOOOX
OXOOOOOOOOXO
OOXOOOOOXOO
OOOXOOOOXOOO
OOOOXOOXOOOO
OOOOOXXOOOOO
OOOOOXXOOOOO
OOOOXOOXOOOO
OOOXOOOOXOOO
OOXOOOOOXOO
OXOOOOOOOOXO
XOOOOOOOOOOX
```

The multi-dimensional array syntax is also supported in testing for array membership. The subscripts must be placed inside parentheses.

```
if ((i,j) in array)
```

This tests whether the subscript *i,j* (actually, **I SUBSEP J**) exists in the specified array.

Looping over a multidimensional array is the same as with one-dimensional arrays.

```
for (item in array)
```

You must use the **split** function to access individual subscript components. Thus:

```
split(item,subscr,SUBSEP)
```

creates the array **subscr** from the subscript **item**.

Note that we needed to use the loop-within-a-loop to output the two-dimensional bitmap array in the previous example because we needed to maintain rows and columns.

System Variables That Are Arrays (nawk)

Nawk provides several two system variables that are arrays:

ARGV   An array of command-line arguments, excluding the script itself and any options specified with the invocation of awk. The number of elements in this array is available in **ARGC**. The index of the first element of the array is 0 (unlike all other arrays in awk but consistent with C) and the last is ARGC - 1.

ENVIRON   An array of environment variables. Each element of the array is the value in the current environment and the index is the name of the environment variable.

An Array of Command Line Parameters

You can write a loop to read all the elements of the **ARGV** array.

```
# argv.awk - test command-line parameters
BEGIN { for (x = 0; x < ARGC; ++x)
        print ARGV[x]
      print ARGC
}
```

This example also prints out the value of **ARGC**, the number of command-line arguments. Here's an example of how it works on a sample command line:

```
% nawk -f argv.awk 1234 "John Wayne" Westerns n=44 -
nawk
1234
John Wayne
Westerns
n=44
-
6
```

As you can see, there are six elements in the array. The first element is the name of the command that invoked the script. This could be useful, strangely enough, if you wanted to make use of gawk features in a script but provide workarounds if nawk runs the program. The last argument, in this case, is the filename, "-," for standard input. Note the "-f argv.awk" does not appear in the parameter list.

Generally, the value of **ARGC** will be at least 2. If you don't want to read the program name or the filename, you can initialize the counter to 1 and then test against **ARGC - 1** to avoid reading the last parameter.

Remember that if you invoke awk from a shell script, the command line parameters are passed to the shell script and not to awk. You have to pass the shell script's command-line parameters to the awk program inside the shell script. For instance, you can pass all command line parameters from the shell script to awk, using "$*." Look at the following shell script:

```
nawk '
# argv.sh - test command-line parameters
BEGIN { for (x = 0; x < ARGC; ++x)
        print ARGV[x]
      print ARGC
}' $*
```

This shell script works the same as the first example of invoking awk.

One practical use is to test the command-line parameters in the **BEGIN** rule using a regular expression. The following example tests that all the parameters, except the first and last, are integers.

```
# number.awk - test command-line parameters
BEGIN { for (x = 1; x < ARGC - 1; ++x)
           if ( ARGV[x] !~ /[0-9]+/ ){
           print ARGV[x] " is not an integer."
           exit
           }
}
```

If the parameters contain any character that is not a digit, the program will print the message and quit.

After testing the value, you can, of course, assign it to a variable. For instance, we could write a **BEGIN** procedure of a script that checks the command-line parameters before prompting the user. Let's look at the following shell script that uses the phone and address database from the previous chapter:

```
nawk '# phone - find phone number for person
# supply name of person on command line or at prompt.
BEGIN { FS ="," 
     # look for parameter
     if ( ARGC > 2 ){
          name = ARGV[1]
          delete ARGV[1]
     }
     else{
          # loop until we get a name
          while (! name) {
               printf "Enter a name?"
               getline name <"-"
          }
     }
}
$1 ~ name { print $1, $NF
}' $* phones.data
```

We test the **ARGC** variable to see if there are more than two parameters. By specifying "$*", we can pass several parameters from the shell command line inside to the awk command line. If this parameter has been supplied, we assume the second parameter "ARGV[1]" is the one we want and it is assigned to the variable **name**. Then that parameter is deleted from the array. This is very important if the parameter that is supplied on the command line is not of the form "*var=value*; otherwise, it will later be interpreted as a filename. If additional parameters are supplied, they will be interpreted as filenames of alternative phone databases. If there are not more than two parameters, then we prompt for the name. The **getline** function is discussed in Chapter 10, *The Bottom Drawer*. Using this syntax, it reads the next line from standard input. This particular syntax is not available in the original awk.

Here are several examples of this script in action:

```
% phone John
John Robinson 696-0987
% phone
Enter a name?Alice
Alice Gold (707) 724-0000
% phone Alice /usr/central/phonebase
Alice Watson (617) 555-0000
Alice Gold (707) 724-0000
```

The first example supplies the name on the command line, the second prompts the user, and the third takes two command-line parameters and uses the second as a filename. (The script will not allow you to supply a filename without supplying the person's name on the command line. You could devise a test that would permit this syntax, though.)

Because you can add to and delete from the **ARGV** array, there is the potential for doing a lot of interesting manipulation. You can place a filename at the end of the **ARGV** array, for instance, and it will be opened as though it were specified on the command line. Similarly, you can delete a filename from the array and it will never be opened.

An Array of Environment Variables

The **ENVIRON** array was introduced in System V Release 4 nawk and added to gawk. It allows you to access variables in the environment. The following script loops through the elements of the **ENVIRON** array and prints them.

```
# environ.awk - print environment variable
BEGIN {
        for (env in ENVIRON)
                print env "=" ENVIRON[env]
        }
```

The index of the array is the variable name. The script generates the same output produced by the **env** command (**printenv** on some systems).

```
% nawk -f environ.awk -
DISPLAY=scribe:0.0
FRAME=Shell 3
LOGNAME=dale
MAIL=/usr/mail/dale
PATH=:/bin:/usr/bin:/usr/ucb:/work/bin:/mac/bin:/work/src/awkcc/bin:.
TERM=mac2cs
HOME=/work/dale
SHELL=/bin/csh
TZ=PST8PDT
EDITOR=/usr/bin/vi
```

You can reference any element, using the variable name as the index of the array:

```
ENVIRON["LOGNAME"]
```

You can also change any element of the ENVIRON array.

```
ENVIRON["LOGNAME"] = "Tom"
```

However, this change does not affect the user's actual environment (i.e., when awk is done, the value of LOGNAME will not be changed) nor does it affect the environment inherited by programs that are invoked from awk via the **getline** or system() functions, which are described in Chapter 10.

This chapter has covered many important programming constructs. You will continue to see examples in upcoming chapters that make use of these constructs. If programming is new to you, be sure you take the time to run and modify the programs in this chapter, and write small programs of your own. It is essential, like learning how to conjugate verbs, that these constructs become familiar and predictable to you.

9

Functions

Arithmetic Functions
String Functions
Writing Your Own Functions (nawk)

A function is a self-contained routine that accepts a number of arguments as input and returns some value. Originally, awk had twelve built-in functions in two groups: arithmetic and string functions. Nawk added several new functions, but more importantly introduced user-defined functions. This is the single most important capability of nawk: it allows you to expand upon the built-in functions provided by awk by writing your own.

In this chapter, many examples are produced using gawk in order to make the point that it works the same as nawk.

Arithmetic Functions

Six of the original built-in functions can be classified as arithmetic functions. Nawk adds three new functions. Most of them take a numeric argument and return a numeric value. Table 9-1 summarizes these arithmetic functions.

Table 9-1: Awk's Built-in Arithmetic Functions

Awk Function	Description
cos(x)	Returns cosine of x in radians.
exp(x)	Returns exponent of x.
int(x)	Returns truncated value of x.
log(x)	Returns logarithm of x.
sin(x)	Returns sine of x in radians.
sqrt(x)	Returns square root of x.

Nawk Function	Description
atan2(y,x)	Returns arctangent of y/x in the range $-\pi$ to π.
rand()	Returns pseudo-random number r, where $0 <= r < 1$.
srand(x)	Establishes new seed for **rand()**. If no seed is specified, uses time of day.

Trigonometric Functions

I must confess that I do not use the trigonometric functions in the kinds of scripts that I write. Therefore, I will simply mention them here, and hope their application is apparent to those who need to use them.

The trigonometric functions **cos()**, and **sin()** work the same way, taking a single argument that is the size of an angle in radians and returning the cosine or sine for that angle. (To convert from degrees to radians, multiply the number by $\pi/180$.) The new trigonometric function **atan2()** takes two arguments and returns the arctangent. The expression:

```
atan2(0,-1)
```

produces π.

The function **exp()** uses the natural exponential, which is also known as base-*e* exponentiation. The following expression:

```
exp(1)
```

returns the natural number 2.71828, the base of the natural logarithm that is referred to as *e*. Thus, **exp(x)** is *e* to the *x*-th power.

The **log(x)** function gives the inverse of the **exp()** function, the natural logarithm of *x*. The **sqrt()** function takes a single argument and returns the square root of that argument.

Integer Function

The **int()** function truncates a numeric value by removing digits to the right of the decimal point. Look at the following two statements:

```
print 100/3
print int(100/3)
```

The output from these statements is shown below:

```
33.3333
33
```

The **int()** function simply truncates; it does not round up or down.

Random Number Generation (nawk)

The **rand()** function generates a pseudo-random floating point number between 0 and 1. The **srand()** function sets the seed or starting point for random number generation. If **srand()** is called without an argument, it uses the time of day to generate the seed. With an argument *x*, **srand()** uses *x* as the seed. Ideally, *x* should be a number that will vary when the program is run. If you call **rand()** without calling **srand()** first, then it will produce the same value whenever you run the program. Look at the following script:

```
# rand.awk -- test random number generation
BEGIN {
        print rand()
        print rand()
        srand()
        print rand()
        print rand()
}
```

We print the result of the **rand()** function twice, and then call the **srand()** function before printing the result of the **rand()** function two more times. Let's run the script.

```
% nawk -f rand.awk -
0.513871
0.175726
0.760277
0.263863
```

Four random numbers are generated. Now look what happens when we run the program again:

```
% nawk -f rand.awk -
0.513871
0.175726
0.787988
0.305033
```

The first two "random" numbers are identical to the numbers generated in the previous run of the program while the last two numbers are different. The last two numbers are different because we provided the **rand()** function with a new seed. The return value of the **srand()** function is the seed it was using. This can be used to keep track of sequences of random numbers.

Pick 'em

To show how to use **rand()**, we'll look at a script that implements a "quick-pick" for a lottery game. This script, named **lotto**, picks *x* numbers from a series of numbers 1 to *y*. Two arguments can be supplied on the command line: how many numbers to pick (the default is 6) and the highest number in the series (the default is 30). Using the default values for *x* and *y*, the script generates 6 unique random numbers between 1 and 30. The numbers are sorted for readability from lowest to highest and output. Before looking at the script itself, let's run the program:

```
% lotto
Pick 6 of 30
9 13 25 28 29 30
% lotto 7 35
Pick 7 of 35
1 6 9 16 20 22 27
```

The first example uses the default values to print 6 random numbers from 1 to 30. The second example prints 7 random numbers out of 35.

The full **lotto** script is fairly complicated, so before looking at the entire script, let's look at a smaller script that generates a single random number in a series:

```
echo "Do it once" | gawk '# pick1 - pick x random numbers out of y
# main routine
{
# seed random number using time of day
    srand()
# get a random number
    select = 1 + int(rand() * TOPNUM)
# print pick
    print select

}' TOPNUM=$1
```

What is labeled the main routine is executed for every input line. The **echo** command pipes a single line of input to awk. The contents of the line are insignificant. The line simply triggers the program into action. The shell script expects a single argument from the command line and this is passed into the program as "TOPNUM=$1."

The main routine first calls the **srand()** function to seed the random number generator. Then we get a random number by calling the **rand()** function:

```
select = 1 + int(rand() * TOPNUM)
```

It might be helpful to see this expression broken up so each part of it is obvious.

Statement	Result
print r = rand()	0.467315
print r * TOPNUM	14.0195
print int(r * TOPNUM)	14
print 1 + int(r * TOPNUM)	15

Because the **rand()** function returns a number between 0 and 1, we multiply it by **TOPNUM** to get a number between 0 and **TOPNUM**. We then truncate the number to remove decimal values and then add 1 to the number. The latter is necessary because **rand()** could return 0. In this example, the random number that is generated is 15. You could use this program to print any single number, such as picking a number between 1 and 100.

```
% pick1 100
83
```

The **lotto** script must "pick one" multiple times. Basically, we need to set up a **for** loop to execute the **rand()** function as many times as needed. One of the reasons this is difficult is that we have to worry about duplicates. In other words, it is possible for a number to be picked again; therefore we have to keep track of the numbers already picked.

Here's the **lotto** script:

```
echo "Do it once" | gawk '# lotto - pick x random numbers out of y
# main routine
{
# test command line args; NUM = $1, how many numbers to pick
#                     TOPNUM = $2, last number in series
     if ( NUM <= 0)
          NUM = 6
     if ( TOPNUM <= 0 )
          TOPNUM = 30
# print "Pick x of y"
     printf("Pick %d of %d\n", NUM, TOPNUM)
```

```
# load TOPNUM numbers into array
    for ( k = 1; k <= TOPNUM; ++k )
        range[k] = k
# seed random number using time and date; do this once
    srand()
# loop until we have NUM selections
    for ( j = 1; j <= NUM; ++j ) {
        select = 1 + int(rand() * TOPNUM)
        # this conditional checks for duplicates
        if ( range[select] == "") {
            --j
            continue
        }
        pick[j] = select
        delete range[select]
    }

# loop through array and print picks.
    for ( j = 1; j <= NUM; ++j )
        printf("%s ", pick[j])
    printf("\n")

}' NUM=$1 TOPNUM=$2
```

Unlike the previous program, this one looks for two command line arguments, indicating *x* numbers out of *y*. The main routine looks to see if these numbers were supplied and if not, assigns default values.

Notice that there are two arrays: **range** and **pick**. The **range** array is set up to hold the range of numbers that we can select from. The **pick** array is set up to hold the random numbers that are selected. The heart of the script is a loop that occurs **NUM** times to assign **NUM** elements to the **pick** array.

The reason for maintaining the **range** array is that we can delete the elements from it that correspond to the random numbers that are selected. For instance, when the range is 1 to 30, **range[29]** equals 29. To get a new non-duplicate random number, we test to see if the selection exists in the **range** array. If **range[select]** == **select**, then we assign **select** to an element of the **pick** array. If **range[select]** == "" (the corresponding element has been deleted), then the selection is a duplicate and we reject the selection. We reset the counter variable **j** and and use **continue** to go through the loop again to get another number.

There's another way to do this. Once you have a selection, you could loop through the elements of the **pick** array to see if you have already picked the number. However, the extra looping requires many more lookups than the version shown above and seems to run more slowly, especially as the number of picks increases.

Finally, the program loops through the **pick** array and prints the elements. This version of the **lotto** script leaves one thing out. See if you can tell what it is if we run it again:

```
% lotto 7 35
Pick 7 of 35
5 21 9 30 29 20 2
```

That's right, the numbers are not sorted. We'll defer showing the code for the sort routine until we discuss user-defined functions. While it's not necessary to have written this code as a function, it makes a lot of sense. One reason is that you can tackle a more generalized problem and retain the solution for use in other programs. Later on, we will write a function that sorts the elements of an array.

Earlier we said that the main input loop of the **lotto** is set up to read a single line of input ("Do this now."). The input itself is not dealt with. You could, however, revise this script to read a list of names from a file and for each name generate a "quick-pick".

String Functions

The built-in string functions are much more significant and interesting than the numeric functions. Because awk is essentially designed as a string processing language, a lot of its power derives from these functions. Table 9-2 lists the string functions found in awk along with those introduced by nawk and gawk.

Table 9-2. Awk's Built-In String Functions

Awk Function	Description
index(s,t)	Returns position of substring t in string s or zero if not present.
length(s)	Returns length of string s.
split(s,a,sep)	Parses string s into elements of array a using field separator sep; returns number of elements. If sep is not supplied, **FS** is used.
sprintf("fmt",$expr$)	Uses **printf** format specification for **expr**.
substr(s,p,n)	Returns substring of string s at beginning position p up to a maximum length of n. If n is not supplied, the rest of the string from p is used.

Nawk Function	Description
gsub(*r,s,t*)	Globally substitutes *s* for each match of the regular expression *r* in the string *t*. Returns the number of substitutions. If *t* is not supplied, defaults to **$0**.
match(*s,r*)	Returns either the position in *s* where the regular expression *r* begins, or 0 if no occurrences are found. Sets the value of **RSTART** and **RLENGTH**.
sub(*r,s,t*)	Substitutes *s* for first match of the regular expression *r* in the string *t*. Return 1 if successful; 0 otherwise. If *t* is not supplied, defaults to **$0**.

Gawk Function	Description
tolower(*s*)	Translates all uppercase characters in string *s* to lowercase and returns the new string.
toupper(*s*)	Translates all lowercase characters in string *s* to uppercase and returns the new string.

The **split()** function was introduced in the previous chapter in the discussion on arrays.

The **sprintf()** function uses the same format specification as **printf()**, which is discussed in Chapter 7. It allows you to apply the format specifications on a string. Instead of printing the result, **sprintf()** returns a value that can be assigned to a variable. It can do specialized processing of input records or fields, such as performing character conversions. For instance, the following example uses the **sprintf()** function to convert a number into an ASCII character.

```
for ( i = 97; i <= 122; ++i) {
    nextletter = sprintf("%c", i)
}
```

A loop supplies numbers from 97 to 122, which produce ASCII characters from a to z.

That leaves us with three basic built-in string functions to discuss: **index()**, **substr()**, and **length()**.

Substrings

The **index()** and **substr()** functions both deal with substrings. Given a string s, **index**(*s,t*) returns the leftmost **position** where string *t* is found in *s*. Look at the following example:

```
pos = index("Mississippi", "is")
```

The value of **pos** is 2. If the substring is not found, the **index** function returns 0.

Given a string **s**, **substr**(*s,p*) returns the characters beginning at position *p*. The following example creates a phone number without an area code.

```
phone = substr("707-555-1111",5)
```

You can also supply a third argument which is the number of characters to return. The next example returns just the area code:

```
area_code = substr("707-555-1111",1,3)
```

The two functions can be and are often used together as in the next example. This example capitalizes the first letter of the first word for each input record.

```
awk '# caps - capitalize 1st letter of 1st word

# initialize strings
BEGIN { upper="ABCDEFGHIJKLMNOPQRSTUVWXYZ"
        lower="abcdefghijklmnopqrstuvwxyz"
            }
# for each input line
{
# get first character of first word
    FIRSTCHAR = substr($1,1,1)
# get position of FIRSTCHAR in lowercase array; if 0, ignore
    if (CHAR = index(lower,FIRSTCHAR))
        # change $1, using position to retrieve
        # uppercase character
        $1 = substr(upper,CHAR,1) substr($1,2)
# print record
    print $0
}' -
```

This script creates two variables, **upper** and **lower**, consisting of uppercase and lowercase letters. Any character that we find in **lower** can be found at the same position in **upper**. The first statement of the main procedure extracts a single character, the first one, from the first field. The conditional statement tests to see if that character can be found in **lower** using the **index** function. If CHAR is not 0, then CHAR can be used to extract the uppercase character from **upper**. There are two **substr** function calls: the first one retrieves the capitalized letter and the second call gets the rest of the first field, extracting all characters, beginning with the second character. The values returned by both **substr** functions are con-catenated and assigned to $1. Making an assignment to a field* as we do here is a new twist, but it has the added benefit that the record can be output normally. (If the assignment was made to a variable, you'd have to output the variable and then output the record's remaining fields.) The print statement prints the changed record. Let's see it in action:

```
% caps
root user
Root user
dale
Dale
Tom
Tom
```

You could revise this program so it changed all characters in a string from lower to uppercase or vice versa. If you are using gawk there are built-in functions to do that: **tolower(s)** and **toupper(s)** where *s* is a string. These functions return the converted string. In some versions of nawk, these functions are undocumented† but they do exist.

String Length

When presenting the **awkro** program in the previous chapter, we noted that the program was likely to produce lines that exceed 80 characters. After all, the descriptions are quite long. We can find out how many characters are in a string, using a built-in awk function, **length**. For instance, to evaluate the length of the current input record, we specify **length($0)**. (This particular function without an argument returns the length of the input record.)

Below is a procedure that evaluates the length of the current input record to deter-mine if we need to break the line.

```
if (length($0) > 70){
    if (i > 2)
        $i = "\n" $i
    if (i+1 < NF )
        $(i+1) = "\n" $(i+1)
    }
```

---

*David Huelsbeck in "Awk Power Plays" in *UNIX Papers* (ed., Mitchell Waite, Howard W. Sams, Inc., 1987) comments that in Berkeley 4.2 awk an assignment to a field does not cause the record to change. This assignment works fine with awk, gawk, and nawk under System V and with awk under SunOS 4.0 where I tested it. If it does not work on your system, you'll have to revise the script.

†Nawk's FIXES file has a note from a peeved maintainer of the program that says: "Reluctantly added toupper and tolower functions. Subject to rescinding without notice."

If the record is greater than 70 characters, then two conditions test where to put the newline. The newline precedes the field in each of these operations. Putting it at the end of the field would result in a new line that begins with a space output with the next field.

Another way to handle the line break, perhaps more efficiently, is to use the **length** function to return a value for each field. By accumulating that value, we could specify a line break when a new field causes the total to exceed a certain number.

Chapter 12, *A Miscellany of Scripts*, contains a script that uses the **length**() function to break lines greater than 80 columns wide.

Substitution Functions (nawk)

It was a real weakness in the original awk that it didn't offer a simple regular expression-based substitution capability, similar to the s command in sed.

Nawk provides two substitutions functions: **sub**() and **gsub**(). The difference between them is that **gsub**() performs its substitution globally on the input string whereas **sub**() makes only the first substitution possible. This makes **gsub**() equivalent to the sed substitution command with the **g** (global) flag.

Both functions take at least two arguments. The first is a regular expression (surrounded by slashes) that matches a pattern and the second argument is a string that replaces what the pattern matches. The regular expression can be supplied by a variable in which case the slashes are omitted. An optional third argument specifies the string which is the target of the substitution. If there is no third argument, the substitution is made for the current input record ($0).

The substitution functions change the specified string directly. (You might expect, given the way functions work, that the function returns the new string created when the substitution is made.) The substitution functions actually return the *number* of substitutions made. **sub**() will always return 1 if successful; both return 0 if not successful. Thus, you can test the result to see if a substitution was made.

For example, the following example uses **gsub**() to replace all occurrences of "UNIX" with "POSIX".

```
if (gsub(/UNIX/,"POSIX"))
     print
```

The conditional statement tests the return value of **gsub**() such that the current input line is printed only if a change is made.

As with sed, if an & appears in the substitution string, it will be replaced by the string matched by the regular expression. Use "\&" to output an ampersand. Because the backslash is used to escape the meaning of the ampersand, you must use two backslashes to output a backslash. Also, note that awk does not "remember" the previous regular expression, as does sed, so you cannot use the syntax "//" to refer to the last regular expression.

The following example surrounds any occurrence of UNIX with the **troff** font-change escape sequences.

```
gsub(/UNIX/,"\\fB&\\fR")
```

If the input is "the UNIX operating system," the output is "the \fBUNIX\fR operating system."

In Chapter 4, *Writing Sed Scripts*, we presented the following sed script named **do.outline**:

```
sed -n '
s/"//g
s/^\.Se /Chapter /p
s/^\.Ah / A. /p
s/^\.Bh /      B.   /p' $*
```

Now here's that script re-written using the substitution functions:

```
gawk '
{
gsub(/"/,"")
if (sub(/^\.Se /,"Chapter ")) print
if (sub(/^\.Ah /,"\tA. ")) print
if (sub(/^\.Bh /,"\t\tB.   ")) print
}' $*
```

The two scripts are exactly equivalent, printing out only those lines that are changed. I used **timex** to compare the run-time of both scripts and as I expected the awk script was slower. However, we have the capabilities in awk to make the script do more things. For instance, instead of using letters of the alphabet, we could number the headings. Here's the revised awk script:

```
gawk '# do.outline -- number headings in chapter.
{
gsub(/"/,"")
}
/^\.Se/ {
    sub(/^\.Se /, "Chapter ")
    ch = $2
    ah = 0
    bh = 0
    print
    next
```

```
      }
/^\.Ah/ {
      sub(/^\.Ah /,"\t  " ch "." ++ah " ")
      bh = 0
      print
      next
      }
/^\.Bh/ {
      sub(/^\.Bh /,"\t\t  " ch "."   ah "." ++bh " ")
      print
      }' $*
```

In this version, we break out each heading into its own pattern matching rule. This is not necessary but seems more efficient since we know that once a rule is applied, we don't need to look at the others.

The chapter number is read as the first argument to the .Se macro and is thus the second field on that line. The numbering scheme is done by incrementing a variable each time the substitution is made. The action associated with the chapter-level heading initializes the section-heading counters to zero. The action associated with the top-level heading ".Ah" zeroes the second-level heading counter. Obviously, you can create as many levels of heading as you need. Note how we can specify a combination of strings and variables as a single argument to the sub() function.

```
% do.outline ch02
Chapter 2 Understanding Basic Operations
            2.1 Understanding Basic Operations
                  2.1.1 Syntax
                  2.1.2 Scripts
                  2.1.3 A Sample Mailing List
            2.2 Using grep
            2.3 Using sed
                  2.3.1 Interactive Command Lines
                  2.3.2 Script Files
            2.4 Using awk
            2.5 Using Sed and Awk
```

If you wanted the option of choosing either numbers or letters, you could maintain both programs and construct a shell wrapper that uses some flag to determine which program should be invoked.

Match Function (nawk)

The **match()** function allows you to determine if a regular expression matches a specified string. It takes two arguments, the string and the regular expression. (I frequently have to look this one up because the regular expression is in the second position, whereas it is in the first position for the substitution functions.)

The **match()** function returns the starting position of the substring that was matched by the regular expression. You might consider it a close relation to the **index** function. In the following example, the regular expression matches any sequence of capital letters in the string "the UNIX operating system."

```
match("the UNIX operating system",/[A-Z]+/)
```

The value returned by this function is 5, the character position of "U," the first capital letter in the string.

The **match** function also sets two system variables: **RSTART** and **RLENGTH**. **RSTART** contains the same value returned by the function, the starting position of the substring. **RLENGTH** contains the length of the string in characters (not the ending position of the substring). In the previous example, **RSTART** is equal to 5 and **RLENGTH** is equal to 4. (Adding them together gives you the ending position.)

Let's look at a rather simple example that prints out a string matched by a specified regular expression, demonstrating the "extent of the match," as discussed in Chapter 3, *Understanding Regular Expression Syntax*. The following shell script takes two command-line arguments: the regular expression, which should be specified in quotes, and the name of the file to search.

```
gawk '# match -- print string that matches line
# for lines match pattern
match($0, pattern) {
        # extract string matching pattern using
        # starting position and length of string in $0
        # print string
        print substr($0, RSTART, RLENGTH)
}' pattern="$1" $2
```

The first command-line parameter is passed as the value of **pattern**. Note that $1 is surrounded by quotes, necessary to protect any spaces that might appear in the regular expression. The **match()** function appears in a conditional expression that controls execution of the only procedure in this awk script. The **match()** function returns 0 if the pattern is not found, and a positive value (**RSTART**) if it is found. If the current record matches the pattern, then the string is extracted from $0, using the values of **RSTART** and **RLENGTH** in the **substr** function to specify the starting position of the substring to be extracted and its length. The substring is printed. This procedure only matches the first occurrence in $0.

Here's a trial run, given a regular expression that matches "emp" and any number of characters up to a blank space:

```
% match "emp[^ ]*" personnel.txt
employees
employee
employee.
```

```
employment,
employer
employment
employee's
employee
```

The **match** script could be a useful tool in improving your understanding of regular expressions.

The next script uses the **match()** function to locate any sequence of uppercase letters so that they can be converted to lowercase. Compare it to the **caps** program shown earlier in the chapter.

```
gawk '# lower - change upper case to lower case
# initialize strings
BEGIN { upper="ABCDEFGHIJKLMNOPQRSTUVWXYZ"
      lower="abcdefghijklmnopqrstuvwxyz"
}
# for each input line
{
# see if there is a match for all caps
      while (match($0,/[A-Z]+/))
            # get each cap letter
            for ( x = RSTART; x <= RLENGTH+RSTART; ++x) {
                 CAP = substr($0, x, 1)
                 if (CHAR = index(upper,CAP))
                      # substitute lowercase for upper
                      gsub(CAP, substr(lower,CHAR,1))
            }

# print record
      print $0
}' $*
```

In this script, the **match()** function appears in a conditional expression that determines whether a **while** loop will be executed. By placing this function in a loop, we apply the body of the loop as many times as the pattern occurs in the current input record.

The regular expression matches any sequence of uppercase letters in $0. If a match is made, a **for** loop does the lookup of each character in the substring that was matched, similar to what we did in the **caps** sample program, shown earlier in this chapter. What's different here is how we use the system variables **RSTART** and **RLENGTH**. RSTART initializes the counter variable x. It is used in the substr function to extract one character at a time from $0, beginning with the first character that matched the pattern. By adding **RLENGTH** to **RSTART**, we get the position of the last character that matched the pattern. At the end, we use

gsub to replace the uppercase letter with the corresponding lowercase letter. Notice that we use **gsub()** instead of **sub()** because it offers us the advantage of making several substitutions if there are multiple instances of the same letter on the line.

```
% cat test
Every NOW and then, a WORD I type appears in CAPS.
% lower test
every now and then, a word i type appears in caps.
```

Note that you could change the regular expression to avoid matching individual capital letters by matching a sequence of two or more uppercase characters: "/[A-Z][A-Z]+/." This would also require revising the way the lowercase conversion was made using **gsub**, since it matches a single character on the line.

In our discussion of the sed substitution command, you saw how to save and recall a portion of a string matched by a pattern, using \(and \) to surround the pattern to be saved and \n to recall the saved string in the replacement pattern. Unfortunately, awk's substitution functions offer no equivalent syntax. The **match()** function can come in handy, though, in many situations where you might have used sed's save and recall syntax.

For instance, if you match a string using the **match()** function, you can single out characters or a substring at the head or tail of the string. Given the values of **RSTART** and **RLENGTH**, you can use the **substr()** function to extract the characters. In the following example, we replace the second of two colons with a semicolon. We can't use **gsub()** to make the replacement because "/:/" matches the first colon and "/:.*:/" matches a string of characters. We can, however, use **match()** to match the string of characters and to extract the last character of the string.

```
# replace 2nd colon with semicolon using match, substr
if (match($1, /:.*:/)){
     before = substr($1,1,(RSTART+RLENGTH-2))
     after = substr($1,(RSTART+RLENGTH))
        $1 = before ";" after
        }
```

The **match()** function is placed within a conditional statement that tests that a match was found. If there is a match, we use the **substr()** function to extract the substring before the second colon as well as the substring after it. Then we concatenate **before**, the literal ";", and **after**, assigning it to $1.

You can see examples of the **match()** function in use in Chapter 11, *Full-Featured Applications*.

Writing Your Own Functions (nawk)

With the addition of user-defined functions, nawk allows the awk programmer to take another step towards C programming by writing programs that make use of self-contained functions. When you write a function properly, you have defined a program component that can be re-used in other programs. The real benefit of modularity becomes apparent as programs grow in size or in age, and as the number of programs you write increases significantly.

A function definition can be placed anywhere in a script that a pattern-action rule appears. Typically, we put the function definitions at the top of the script before the pattern-action rules. A function is defined using the following syntax:

> **function** *name*(*parameter-list*) {
> > *statements*
> }

The newlines after the left parenthesis and before the right parenthesis are optional.

The *parameter-list* is a comma-separated list of variables that are passed as arguments into the function when it is called. The body of the function consists of one or more statements. The function typically contains a **return** statement that returns control to that point in the script where the function was called; it often has an expression that returns a value as well.

> **return** *expression*

The following example shows the definition for an **insert**() function:

```
function insert(STRING,POS,INS) {
        before_tmp = substr(STRING,1,POS)
        after_tmp = substr(STRING,POS+1)
        return before_tmp INS after_tmp
}
```

This function takes three arguments, inserting one string **INS** in another string **STRING** after the character at position **POS**. The body of this function uses the **substr**() function to divide the value of **STRING** into two parts. The **return** statement returns a string that is the result of concatenating the first part of **STRING**, the **INS** string, and the last part of **STRING**. A function call can appear anywhere that an *expression* can. Thus, the following statement:

```
print insert($1,4,"XX")
```

If the value of $1 is "Hello," then this functions returns "HellXXo." Note that there can be no blank spaces between the function name and the left parenthesis.

This is not true of built-in functions.

It is important to understand the notion of local and global variables. A local variable is a variable that is local to a function and cannot be accessed outside of it. A global variable, on the other hand, can be accessed or changed anywhere in the script. There can be potentially damaging side effects of global variables if a function is changing a variable that is used elsewhere in the script. Therefore, it is usually a good idea to eliminate global variables in a function.

When we call the **insert()** function, and specify $1 as the first argument, then a copy of that variable is passed to the function, where it is manipulated as a local variable named **STRING**. All the variables in the function definition's parameter list are local variables and their values are not accessible outside the function. Similarly, the arguments in the function call are not changed by the function itself. When the **insert()** function returns, the value of $1 is not changed.

However, the variables defined in the body of the function are global variables, by default. Given the above definition of the **insert()** function, the temporary variables **before_tmp** and **after_tmp** are visible outside the function. Nawk provides what its developers call an "inelegant" means of declaring variables local to a function, and that is by specifying those variables in the parameter list. By convention, the local temporary variables are put at the end of the parameter list, separated by several spaces. For example, here's how to define the insert function with two local variables:

```
function insert (STRING, POS, INS,    before_tmp, after_tmp) {
        body
```

If this seems confusing,* seeing how the following script works might help:

```
function insert (STRING, POS, INS,  before_tmp) {
    before_tmp = substr (STRING, 1, POS)
    after_tmp = substr (STRING, POS+1)
    return before_tmp INS after_tmp
}
# main routine
{
print "Function returns", insert ($1, 4, "XX")
print "The value of $1 after is:", $1
print "The value of STRING is:", STRING
print "The value of before_tmp:", before_tmp
print "The value of after_tmp:", after_tmp
}
```

Notice that we specify **before_tmp** in the parameter list. In the main routine, we call the **insert()** function and print its result. Then we print different variables to

---

*The documentation calls it a syntactical botch.

see what their value is, if any. Now let's run the above script and look at the output:

```
% echo "Hello" | gawk -f insert.awk -
Function returns HellXXo
The value of $1 after is: Hello
The value of STRING is:
The value of before_tmp:
The value of after_tmp: o
```

The **insert()** function returns "HellXXo," as expected. The value of $1 is the same after the function was called as it was before. The variable STRING is local to the function and it does not have a value when called from the main routine. The same is true for **before_tmp** because its name was placed in the parameter list for the function definition. The variable **after_tmp** which was not specified in the parameter list does have a value, the letter "o."

As this example shows, $1 is passed "by value" into the function. This means that a copy is made of the value when the function is called and the function manipulates the copy, not the original. Arrays, however, are passed "by reference." That is, the function does not work with a copy of the array but is passed the array itself. Thus, any changes that the function makes to the array are visible outside of the function. This distinction between "scalar" variables and arrays holds true for functions written in the C language. The next section presents an example of a function that operates on an array.

Writing a Sort Function

Earlier in this chapter we presented the **lotto** script for picking *x* random numbers out of a series of *y* numbers. The script that we showed did not sort the list of numbers that were selected. In this section, we develop a **sort** function that sorts the elements of an array.

We define a function that takes two arguments, the name of the array and the number of elements in the array. This function can be called as such:

```
sort(pick,NUM)
```

The function definition lists the two arguments and three local variables used in the function.

```
# sort numbers in ascending order
function sort(ARRAY,ELEMENTS,    temp,i,j) {
        for ( i = 2; i <= ELEMENTS; ++i )
                for ( j = i; ARRAY[j-1] > ARRAY[j]; --j ) {
                        temp = ARRAY[j]
                        ARRAY[j] = ARRAY[j-1]
                        ARRAY[j-1] = temp
                }
        return
}
```

The body of the function implements an insertion sort. This sorting algorithm is very simple. We loop through each element of the array and compare it to the value preceding it. If the first element is greater than the second, the first and second elements are swapped. To actually swap the values, we use a temporary variable to hold a copy of the value while we overwrite the original. The loop continues swapping adjacent elements until all are in order. At the end of the function, we use the **return** to simply return control. It does not need to pass the array back to the main routine because the array itself is changed and it can be accessed directly.

Here's proof positive:

```
% lotto 7 35
Pick 7 of 35
6 7 17 19 24 29 35
```

In fact, many of the scripts that we developed in this chapter could be turned into functions. For instance, if we didn't have gawk, we might want to write our own **lower()** and **upper()** functions.

The value of writing the **sort()** function in a general fashion is that you can easily re-use it. To demonstrate this, we'll take the above sort function and use it to sort student grades. In the following script, we read all of the student grades into an array and then call **sort()** to put the grades in ascending order.

```
# grade.sort.awk -- script for sorting student grades
# input: student name followed by a series of grades

# sort function -- sort numbers in ascending order
function sort(ARRAY,ELEMENTS,       temp,i,j) {
     for ( i = 2; i <= ELEMENTS; ++i )
          for ( j = i; ARRAY[j-1] > ARRAY[j]; --j ) {
                temp = ARRAY[j]
                ARRAY[j] = ARRAY[j-1]
                ARRAY[j-1] = temp
          }
     return
}
# main routine
{
```

```
# loop through fields 2 through NF and assign values
# array named grades
for (i = 2; i <= NF; ++i)
    grades[i-1] = $i

# call sort function to sort elements

sort(grades,NF-1)

# print student name
printf ("%s: ", $1)

# output loop
for (j = 1; j <= NF-1; ++j)
    printf ("%d ", grades[j])
printf ("\n")
}
```

Note that the sort routine is identical to the previous version. In this example, once we've sorted the grades we simply output them:

```
% nawk -f grade.sort.awk grades.test
mona: 70 70 77 83 85 89
john: 78 85 88 91 92 94
andrea: 85 89 90 90 94 95
jasper: 80 82 84 84 88 92
dunce: 60 60 61 62 64 80
ellis: 89 90 92 96 96 98
```

However, you could, for instance, delete the first element of the sort array if you wanted to average the student grades after dropping the lowest grade.

As another exercise, you could write a version of the sort function that takes a third argument indicating an ascending or descending sort.

Maintaining a Function Library

You might want to put a useful function in its own file and store it in a central directory. Nawk permits multiple uses of the -f option to specify more than one program file. For instance, we could have written the previous example such that the sort function was placed in a separate file from the main program **grade.awk**. The following command specifies both program files:

```
% awk -f grade.awk -f /usr/local/lib/awk/sort.awk grades.test
```

This command assumes that **grade.awk** is in the working directory and that the sort function is defined in **sort.awk** in the directory */usr/local/lib/awk*.

NOTE

You cannot use the **-f** option to specify the filename for a script *and* specify a script also on the command line.

Sun's version of nawk does not seem to support multiple script files. Gawk allows you to specify an environment variable named **AWKPATH** that defines a search path for awk program files. By default, it is defined to be "*.:/usr/lib/awk:/usr/local/lib/awk*." Thus, when a filename is specified with the **-f** option, the three default directories will be searched, beginning with the current directory. Note that if the filename contains a "/," then no search is performed. Use of **AWKPATH** would permit us to omit the absolute pathname of **sort.awk** in the previous example.

Remember to document functions clearly so that you will understand how they work when you want to reuse them.

Another Sorted Example

Lenny, our production editor, is back with another request.

Dale:

The last section of each Xlib manpage is called "Related Commands" (that is the argument of a .SH) and it's followed by a list of commands (often ten or twenty) that are now in random order. It'd be more useful and professional if they were alphabetized. Currently, commands are separated by a a comma after each one except the last, which has a period.

The question is: could awk alphabetize these lists? We're talking about a couple of hundred manpages. Again, don't bother if this is a bigger job than it seems to someone who doesn't know what's involved.

Best to you and yours,

Lenny

To see what he is talking about, a simplified version of the Xlib manpage is shown below:

```
.SH "Name"
XSubImage \(em create a subimage from part of an image.
    .
    .
    .
```

```
.SH "Related Commands"
XDestroyImage, XPutImage, XGetImage,
XCreateImage, XGetSubImage, XAddPixel,
XPutPixel, XGetPixel, ImageByteOrder.
```

You can see that the names of related commands appear on several lines following the heading. You can also see that they are in no particular order.

To sort the list of related commands is actually fairly simple, given that we've already covered sorting. The structure of the program is somewhat interesting, as we must read several lines *after* matching the "Related Commands" heading. For additional interest, I'll offer this solution first for awk and then for nawk. It's a chance to see how the additional functionality in nawk affects how you attack a problem.

Looking at the input, it is obvious that the list of related commands is the last section in the file. All other lines except these we want to print as is. The key is to match all lines from the heading "Related Commands" to the end of the file. Our script can consist of four rules, that match:

1. The "Related Commands" heading.

2. The lines following that heading.

3. All other lines.

4. After all lines have been read (**END**).

Most of the "action" takes place in the **END** procedure. That's where we sort and output the list of commands. Here's the awk version of the script:

```
# sorter.awk -- sort list of related commands -- awk version
# requires sort.awk as function in separate file
BEGIN { x = 0 }

#1 Match related commands; enable flag x
/.SH "Related Commands"/ { print
            x = 1
            next
            }
#2 Apply to lines following "Related Commands"
(x == 1){
      commandList = commandList $0
}
#3 Print all other lines, as is.
(x != 1) { print }
#4
END {
# split line into fields
sizeOfArray = split(commandList,comArray,",")
```

```
# remove leading blanks and final period.
for(i=1;i<=sizeOfArray;i++)
      if (substr(comArray[i],1,1) == " ")
          comArray[i] = substr(comArray[i],2)
      y = split(comArray[sizeOfArray],Last,".")
      if (y == 2)
          comArray[sizeOfArray] = Last[1]
# sort list of commands
for(i=2;i<=sizeOfArray;i++)
      for (j = i; j > 1 && comArray[j-1] > comArray[j]; j--){
          t = comArray[j-1]
          comArray[j-1] = comArray[j]
          comArray[j] = t
          }
# output list of commands
      for(i = 1; i < sizeOfArray; i++)
          printf("%s,\n", comArray[i])
      printf("%s.\n", comArray[i])
}' $*
```

Once the "Related Commands" heading is matched, we print that line and then set a flag, the variable **x**, which indicates that subsequent input lines are to be collected.* The second procedure actually collects each line into the variable **commandList**. The third procedure is executed for all other lines, simply printing them. Note that it must appear after the first two procedures. When all lines of input have been read, the **END** procedure is executed, and we know that our list of commands is complete. First, we use the **split()** function to create an array **comArray** from the variable **commandList** using a comma as the delimiter. Then we have to do a little housekeeping, looking for elements that begin with a space and removing the final period from the last element. This is necessary to achieve a clean sort. The sort code is nearly identical to the previous version. Finally, we loop through the array, printing its elements.

This program generates the following output:

```
% awk -f sorter.awk test
.SH "Name"
XSubImage \(em create a subimage from part of an image.
.SH "Related Commands"
ImageByteOrder,
XAddPixel,
XCreateImage,
XDestroyImage,
XGetImage,
XGetPixel,
```

---

*In the next chapter, the **getline** function is introduced and it provides a simpler way to control reading input lines.

```
XGetSubImage,
XPutImage,
XPutPixel.
```

The nawk version differs only in the **END** procedure:

```
# now sort and output list of commands
END {
# remove leading blanks and final period.
    gsub(/, */, ",", commandList)
    gsub(/\. *$/, "," commandList)
# split list into array
    sizeOfArray = split(commandList,comArray,",")

# sort
    sort(comArray, sizeOfArray)
# output elements
    for(i = 1; i < sizeOfArray; i++)
        printf("%s,\n", comArray[i])
    printf("%s.\n", comArray[i])
}
```

This script achieves the same result but is arguably simpler. The most notable difference is that the housekeeping tasks are performed using the **gsub()** function. Before splitting up the commands into fields, we remove any number of spaces following a comma. Next we remove the final period. Compare these two lines of code to the more complex way of handling this problem shown in the awk version. Handling this problem with a substitution command is much more straightforward, nearly a no-brainer.

Finally, we create the array **comArray** using the **split()** function. This array is passed as an argument to the **sort()** function. Once again, the virtue of calling a function to do the sort versus writing or copying the code to do the same task is that the function is a module that's been tested previously and has a standard interface. That is, you know that it works and you know how it works. When you come upon the same sort code in the awk version, which uses different variable names, you have to scan it to verify that it works the same way as other versions. Even if you were to copy the lines into another program, you would have to make changes to accommodate the new circumstances. With a function, all you need to know is what kind of arguments it expects and their calling sequence. Using a function reduces the chance for error by reducing the complexity of the problem that you are solving.

Because this script presumes that the **sort()** function exists in a separate file, it must be invoked using the **-f** option:

```
% nawk -f sort.awk -f sorter.awk test
```

where the **sort()** function is defined in the file **sort.awk**.

10

The Bottom Drawer

The getline Function
The system() Function (Nawk)
A Menu-based Command Generator
Directing Output to Files and Pipes
Generating Columnar Reports
Gawk Talk
Debugging
Limitations
Invoking Awk Using the #! Syntax
A Trick for Mac Text Files
Using awkcc

This chapter is proof that not every thing has its place. Some things just don't seem to fit, no matter how you organize them. This chapter is a collection of such things. There is every temptation to label it "Advanced Topics," as if to explain its organization (or lack thereof) but some readers might feel they need to make more progress before reading it. I have therefore called it the "Bottom Drawer," thinking of the organization of a chest of drawers, with underwear, socks, and other day-to-day things in the top drawers and heavier things, like sweaters, that are less frequently used in the bottom drawers. All of it is equally accessible, but you have to bend over to get things in the bottom drawer. It requires a little more effort to get something, that's all.

In this chapter we cover a number of topics, including the following:

1. The getline function.
2. The system function.
3. Directing output to files and pipes.
4. Debugging awk scripts.
5. Using **awkcc**, an awk-to-C translator.

The getline Function

The **getline** function is used to read another line of input. This function is not documented for the original awk but does exist (at least on the versions I tested). Nawk extends the original by adding the ability to handle input from files and pipes.

As it works in the original version, the **getline** function is similar to awk's **next** statement. While both cause the next input line to be read, the **next** statement passes control back to the top of the script. The **getline** function gets the next line without changing control in the script. Possible return values are:

1   If it was able to read a line.

0   If it encounters the end-of-file.

-1   If it encounters an error.

NOTE

Although **getline** is called a function and it does return a value, its syntax resembles a statement. Do not write **getline( )**; its syntax does not permit parentheses.

In the previous chapter, we used a man page source file as an example. The **man** macros typically place the text argument on the next line. Although the macro is the pattern that you use to find the line, it is actually the next line that you process. For instance, to extract the name of the command from the man page, the following example matches the heading "Name", reads the next line and prints the first field of it:

```
# getline.awk -- test getline function
/\.SH '*Name'*/ {
        getline # get next line
            print $1 # print $1 of new line.
    }
```

The pattern matches any line with ".SH" followed by "Name", which might be enclosed in quotes. Once this line is matched, we use **getline** to read the next input line. When the new line is read, **getline** assigns it $0 and parses it into fields. The system variables **NF, NR** and **FNR** (nawk) are also set. Thus, the new line becomes the current line, and we are able to refer to "$1" and retrieve the first field. Note that the previous line is no longer available as $0. (In nawk, you can assign the line read by **getline** to a variable and avoid changing $0.)

Here's an example that shows how the previous script works, printing out the first field of the line following ".SH Name".

```
% awk -f getline.awk test
XSubImage
```

The **sorter** program that we demonstrated at the end of the previous chapter could have used **getline** to read all the lines after the heading "Related Commands". We can test the return value of **getline** in a **while** loop to read a number of lines from the input. The following procedure replaces the first two procedures in the **sorter** program:

```
# Match Related Commands' and collect them
/\.SH '*Related Commands'*/ {
 print
 while (getline > 0)
        commandList = commandList $0
 }
```

The expression "getline > 0" will be true as long as **getline** successfully reads an input line. When it gets to the end-of-file, **getline** returns 0 and the loop is exited.

Reading Input from Files (nawk)

Nawk's new and improved **getline** function allows you to read input from a file or a pipe. For instance, the following statement reads the next line from the file *data*:

```
getline <'data'
```

Although the filename can be supplied through a variable, it is typically specified as a string constant, which must be enclosed in quotes. The symbol "<" is the same as the shell's input redirection symbol and will not be interpreted as the "less than" symbol. We can use a **while** loop to read all the lines from a file, testing for an end-of-file to exit the loop. The following example opens the file *data* and prints all of its lines:

```
while ( getline <"data" > 0 )
     print
```

The input can also come from standard input. You can use **getline** following a prompt for the user to enter information:

```
BEGIN { printf "Enter your name:"
     getline <"-"
     print
     }
```

This sample code prints the prompt "Enter your name:"; **printf** is used because we don't want a carriage return after the prompt, and then calls **getline** to gather the user's response. The response is assigned to $0, and the **print** statement outputs that value.

Assigning the Input to a Variable (nawk)

Nawk's getline function allows you to assign the input record to a variable. The name of the variable is supplied as an argument. Thus, the following statement reads the next line of input into the variable **input**:

```
getline input
```

Assigning the input to a variable does not affect the current input line; that is, $0 is not affected. The new input line is not split into fields, and thus the variable NF is also unaffected. It also increments the record counters, **NR** and **FNR**.

The previous example demonstrated how to prompt the user. That example could be written as follows, assigning the user's response to the variable **name**.

```
BEGIN { printf "Enter your name:"
     getline name <"-"
     print Name
     }
```

Study the syntax for assigning the output to a variable because it is a common mistake to instead write:

```
name = getline # wrong
```

which assigns the return value of **getline** to the variable **name**.

Reading Input from a Pipe

You can execute a command and pipe the output into **getline**. For example, look at the following expression:

```
"who am i" | getline
```

That expression sets "$0" to the output of the **who am i** command.

```
dale        ttyC3        Jul 18 13:37
```

The line is parsed into fields and the system variable **NF** is set. Similarly, you can assign the result to a variable:

```
"who am i" | getline me
```

By assigning the output to a variable, you avoid setting $0, but the line is not split into fields.

The following script is a fairly simple example of piping the output of a command to **getline**. It uses the output from the **who am i** command to get the user's name. It then looks up the name in *letc/passwd*, printing out the fifth field of that file, the user's full name:

```
nawk '# getname - print user's fullname from /etc/passwd
BEGIN { "who am i" | getline
    name = $1
    FS=":"
}
name ~ $1 { print $5 }
' /etc/passwd
```

The command is executed from the **BEGIN** procedure, and it provides us with the name of the user that will be used to find the user's entry in *letc/passwd*. As explained above, **who am i** outputs a single line, which **getline** assigns to $0. $1, the first field of that output, is then assigned to **name**.

The field separator is set to a colon (:) to allow us to access individual fields in entries in the *letc/passwd* file. Notice that **FS** is set after **getline** or else the parsing of the command's output would be affected.

Finally, the main procedure is designed to test that the first field matches **name**. If it does, the fifth field of the entry is printed. For instance, when I run this script, it prints "Dale Dougherty".

When the output of a command is piped to **getline** and it contains multiple lines, **getline** reads a line at a time. The first time **getline** is called it reads the first line of output. If you call it again, it reads the second line. To read all the lines of output, you must set up a loop that executes **getline** until there is no more output. For instance, the following example uses a **while** loop to read each line of output and assign it to the next element of the array, **who_out**:

```
while ("who" | getline)
      who_out[++i]
```

Each time the **getline** function is called, it reads the next line of output. The **who** command, however, is executed only once.

The next example looks for "@date" in a document and replaces it with today's date:

```
# subdate.awk -- replace @date with todays date
$0 ~ /@date/ { "date +'%a., %h %d, 19%y'" | getline today
           gsub(/@date/, today)
           }
{print}
```

The **date** command, using its formatting options, provides the date and **getline** assigns it to the variable **today**. The **gsub()** function replaces each instance of "@date" with today's date: This script might be used to insert the date in a form letter:

```
To: Peabody
From: Sherman
Date: @date

I am writing you on @date to
remind you about our special offer
```

All lines of the input file would be passed through as is, except the lines containing "@date" which are replaced with today's date:

```
% nawk -f subdate.awk subdate.test
To: Peabody
From: Sherman
Date: Thu., Oct 04, 1990

I am writing you on Thu., Oct 04, 1990 to
remind you about our special offer
```

The Close Statement (nawk)

You can only have one pipe open at a time. (See the section "Limitations," which describes how such limitations can differ from system to system.) If you wish to open multiple pipes in a program, you must use the **close** statement to close a pipe before opening a new one. It takes a single argument which is the same expression used to create the pipe. Here's an example:

```
close("who")
```

You do not need to close a pipe if the program opens only one. You do, however, have to close a pipe, even if you have exhausted the input, before you can open another one.

The **close** statement is also used to close files that you've opened, as we'll see in the section "Working with Multiple Files."

The system() Function (nawk)

The **system()** function executes a command supplied as an expression. It does not, however, make the result of the command available within the program for processing. It returns the exit status of the command that was executed. The script waits for the command to finish before continuing execution.* The following example executes the **mkdir** command:

```
BEGIN { if ( system("mkdir dale") != 0)
           print "Command Failed"}
```

The **system** function is called from an **if** statement which tests for a non-zero exit status. Running the program twice produces one success and one failure:

```
% nawk -f system.awk
% ls dale
% nawk -f system.awk
mkdir: dale: File exists
Command Failed
```

The first run creates the new directory and **system** returns an exit status of 0 (success). The second time the command is executed, the directory already exists, so **mkdir** fails and produces an error message. The "Command Failed" message is produced by awk.

The Berkeley UNIX command set has a small but useful command for **troff** users named **soelim**, named because it "eliminates" ".so" lines from a **troff** input file.

---

* The system() function is modeled after a standard C library function of the same name.

(.so is a request to source in the contents of the named file.) Because this command is not typically found under System V, you can use the following nawk script to create it:

```
$1 ~ /^.so/ { gsub(/"/,"", $2)
              system("cat " $2)
              next
              }
{print}
```

This script looks for ".so" at the beginning of a line, removes any quotation marks, and then uses **system()** to execute the **cat** command and output the contents of the file. This output merges with the rest of the lines in the file, which are simply printed to standard output:

```
% cat soelim.test
This is a test
.so test1
This is a test
.so test2
This is a test.
% nawk -f soelim.awk soelim.test
This is a test
first:second
one:two
This is a test
three:four
five:six
This is a test.
```

We don't explicitly test the exit status of the command. Thus, if the file does not exist, the error messages merge with the output:

```
% nawk -f soelim.awk soelim.test
This is a test
first:second
one:two
This is a test
cat: cannot open test2
This is a test.
```

We might want to test the return value of the **system()** function and generate an error message for the user.

The next example is a function that prompts the user to enter a filename. It uses the **system()** function to execute the **test** command to verify that the file exists and is readable.

```
# getFilename function -- prompts user for filename,
#    verifies that file exists and returns absolute pathname.
function getFilename(    file) {
    while (! file) {
```

```
    printf "Enter a filename:"
    getline <"-" # get response
    file = $0
    # check that file exists and is readable
    # test returns 1 if file does not exist.
    if (system("test -r " file)) {
        print file " not found"
        file = ""
    }
}
if (file !~ /^\//) {
"pwd" | getline # get current directory
file = $0 "/" file
}
return file
}
```

This function returns the absolute pathname of the file specified by the user. It places the prompting and verification sequence inside a **while** loop in order to allow the user to make a different entry if the previous one is invalid.

The **test** command is something of an oddball; it returns 1 if the file does not exist and 0 if it does. Once it is determined that the filename is valid, then we test the filename to see if it begins with a "/", which would indicate that the user supplied an absolute pathname. If that test fails, we use the **getline** command to get the output of the **pwd** command and prepend it to the filename. (Admittedly, the script makes no attempt to deal with "./" or "../" entries, although tests can be easily devised to match them.) Note the two uses of the **getline** function: the first gets the user's response and the second executes the **pwd** command.

A Menu-based Command Generator

In this section, we look at a general use of the **system()** and **getline** functions to implement a menu-based command generator. The object of this program is to give unsophisticated users a simple way to execute long or complex UNIX commands. A menu is used to prompt the user with a description of the task to be performed, allowing the user to choose by number any selection of the menu to execute.

This program is designed as a kind of interpreter that reads from a file the descriptions that appear in the menu and the actual command lines that are executed. That way, multiple menu-command files can be used, and they can be easily modified by awk-less users without changing the program.

The format of a menu-command file contains the menu title as the first line in the file. Subsequent lines contain two fields: the first is the description of the action to be performed and the second is the command line that performs it. An example is shown below:

```
% cat uucp_commands
UUCP Status Menu
Look at files in PUBDIR:find /usr/spool/uucppublic -print
Look at recent status in LOGFILE:tail /usr/spool/uucp/LOGFILE
Look for lock files:ls /usr/spool/uucp/*.LCK
```

The first part of implementing the menu-based command generator is to read the menu-command file. We read the first line of this file and assign it to a variable named **title**. The rest of the lines contain two fields and are read into two arrays, one for the menu items and one for the commands to be executed. A **while** loop is used, along with **getline**, to read one line at a time from the file.

```
BEGIN { FS = ":"
while (getline < CMDFILE > 0 ) {
    # read title
    if (! title) {
        title = $1
        continue
    }
    # load array
    ++sizeOfArray
    # array of menu items
    menu[sizeOfArray] = $1
    # array of commands associated with items
    command[sizeOfArray] = $2
    }
...
}
```

Look carefully at the syntax of the expression tested by the **while** loop.

```
getline < CMDFILE > 0
```

The variable **CMDFILE** is the name of the menu-command file, which is passed as a command-line parameter. The two angle-bracket symbols have completely different functions. The "<" symbol is interpreted by **getline** as the input redirection character. Then the value returned by **getline** is tested to see if it is greater than (>) 0. If it helps to make the syntax clearer, you can use parentheses, as follows:

```
while ((getline < CMDFILE) > 0)
```

In other words, "getline < **CMDFILE**" is evaluated first and then its return value is compared to 0.

This procedure is placed in the **BEGIN** pattern. However, there is one catch. Because we intended to pass the name of the menu file as a command-line parameter, the variable **CMDFILE** would not normally be defined and available in the **BEGIN** pattern. Nawk provides a new -v option to handle just such a case. In other words, the following command will *not* work:

```
nawk script CMDFILE="uucp_commands" -
```

because the **CMDFILE** variable will not be defined until the first line of input is read. Using the -v option makes sure that the variable is set immediately and thus available in the **BEGIN** pattern.

```
nawk -v CMDFILE="uucp_commands" script
```

If your version of awk doesn't have the -v option, you can pass the value of **CMDFILE** as a shell variable. Create a shell script to execute awk and in it define **CMDFILE**. Then change the line that reads **CMDFILE** in the **invoke** script as follows:

```
while (getline < "'$CMDFILE'" > 0 ) {
```

Once the menu-command file is loaded, the program must display the menu and prompt the user. This is implemented as a function because we need to call it in two places: from the **BEGIN** pattern to prompt the user initially, and after we have processed the user's response so that another choice can be made. Here's the **display_menu**() function:

```
function display_menu() {
    # clear screen -- comment out if clear does not work
    system("clear")
    # print title, list of items, exit item, and prompt
    print "\t" title
    for ( i = 1; i <= sizeOfArray; ++i)
        print "\t" i ". " menu[i]
    print "\t" i ". Exit"
    printf("Choose one:")
}
```

The first thing we do is use the **system**() function to call a command to clear the screen. (On my system, **clear** does this; on others it may be **cls** or some other command. Comment out the line if you cannot find such a command.) Then we print the title and each of the items in a numbered list. The last item is always "Exit". Finally, we prompt the user for a choice.

The program will take standard input so that the user's answer to the prompt will be the first line of input. Our reading of the menu-command file was done within the program and not as part of the input stream. Thus, the main procedure of the program is to respond to the user's choice and execute a command. Here's that part of the program:

```
# Applies to user response to prompt
{
   # test value of user response
   if ($1 > 0 && $1 <= sizeOfArray) {
      # print command that is executed
      printf ("Executing ...")
      print command[$1]
      # then execute it.
      system(command[$1])
      printf("<Press RETURN to continue>")
      # wait for input before displaying menu again
      getline
   }
   else
      exit
   # re-display menu
   display_menu()
}
```

First, we test the range of the user's response. If the response falls outside the range, we simply exit the program. If it is a valid response, then we retrieve the command from the array **commands**, display it, and then execute it using the system() function. The user sees the result of the command on the screen followed by the message "Press RETURN to continue". The purpose of this message is to wait for the user to finish before clearing the screen and redisplaying the menu. The **getline** function causes the program to wait for a response. Note that we don't do anything with the response. The **display_menu()** function is called at the end of this procedure to redisplay the menu and prompt for another line of input.

Here's the **invoke** program in full:

```
nawk -v CMDFILE="uucp_commands" '# invoke -- menu-based \
                                  # command generator
# first line in CMDFILE is the title of the menu
# subsequent lines contain: $1 - Description; \
# $2 Command to execute
BEGIN { FS = ":"
# process CMDFILE, reading items into menu array
   while (getline < CMDFILE > 0 ) {
      # read title
      if (! title) {
         title = $1
         continue
      }
      # load array
      ++sizeOfArray
```

```
        # array of menu items
        menu[sizeOfArray] = $1
        # array of commands associated with items
        command[sizeOfArray] = $2
        }
    # call function to display menu items and prompt
    display_menu()
}
# Applies to user response to prompt
{
    # test value of user response
    if ($1 > 0 && $1 <= sizeOfArray) {
        # print command that is executed
        printf ("Executing ...")
        print command[$1]
        # then execute it.
        system(command[$1])
        printf("<Press RETURN to continue>")
        # wait for input before displaying menu again
        getline
    }
    else
        exit
    # re-display menu
    display_menu()
}

function display_menu() {
        # clear screen -- if clear does not work, try "cls"
        system("clear")
        # print title, list of items, exit item, and prompt
        print "\t" title
        for ( i = 1; i <= sizeOfArray; ++i)
            print "\t" i ". " menu[i]
        print "\t" i ". Exit"
        printf("Choose one:")
}' -
```

When a user runs the program, the following output is displayed:

```
UUCP Status Menu
    1. Look at files in PUBDIR
    2. Look at recent status in LOGFILE
    3. Look for lock files
    4. Exit
Choose one:
```

The user is prompted to enter the number of a menu selection. Anything other than a number between 1 and 3 exits the menu. For instance, if the user enters "1" to see a list of files in *uucp*'s public directory, then the following result is displayed on the screen:

```
Executing ...find /usr/spool/uucppublic -print
/usr/spool/uucppublic
/usr/spool/uucppublic/dale
/usr/spool/uucppublic/HyperBugs
<Press RETURN to continue>
```

When the user presses the RETURN key, the menu is re-displayed on the screen. The user can quit from the program by choosing "4".

This program is really a shell for executing commands. Any sequence of commands (even other awk programs) can be executed by modifying the menu-command file. In other words, the part of the program that might change the most is extracted from the program itself and maintained in a separate file. This allows the menu list to be changed and extended very easily by a non-technical user.

Directing Output to Files and Pipes

The output of any **print** or **printf** statement can be directed to a file, using output redirection operators ">" or ">>." For example, the following statement writes the current record to the file *data.out*:

```
print > "data.out"
```

The filename can be any expression that evaluates to a legal filename. A file is opened by the first use of the redirection operator, and subsequent uses append data to the file. The difference between ">" and ">>" is the same as between the shell redirection operators. A right-angle bracket (>) clears the file when opening it while ">>" preserves whatever the file contains and appends data to it.

Because the redirection operator ">" is the same as the relational operator, there is the potential for confusion when you specify an expression as an argument to the **print** command. The rule is that ">" will be interpreted as a redirection operator when it appears in an argument list for any of the print statements. To use ">" as a relational operator in an expression that appears in the argument list, put either the expression or the argument list in parentheses. For example, the following example uses parentheses around the conditional expression to make sure that the relational expression is evaluated properly:

```
print $1, ($3 > $2 ? $2, $3 : $3, $2) > "data.out"
```

The conditional expression evaluates whether $3 is greater than $2; if it is, then $2 is output before $3; otherwise $3 is output before $2. Thus, $1 and the result of the conditional expression are written to the file *data.out*.

Directing Output to a Pipe (nawk)

You can also direct output to a pipe. The following command:

```
print | command
```

opens a pipe the first time it is executed and sends the current record as input to that command. In other words, the command is only invoked once, but each execution of the **print** command supplies another line of input.

The following script strips **troff** macros and requests from the current input line and then sends the line as input to **wc** to determine how many words are in the file:

```
{# words.awk - strip macros then get word count
gsub(/^\.../,"")
print | "wc -w"
}
```

By removing formatting codes, we get a truer word count.

In most cases, I prefer to use a shell script to pipe the output of the awk command to another command rather than do it inside the awk script. For instance, I'd write the previous example as a shell script invoking awk and piping its output to **wc**:

```
nawk '{ # words -- strip macros
gsub(/^\.../,"")
print
}' $* |
# get word count
wc -w
```

This method seems to me simpler and easier to understand. Nonetheless, the other method has the advantage of accomplishing the same thing without creating a shell script.

Remember that you can only have one pipe open at a time. Use the **close** statement to close the pipe before opening another.

Special Filenames

With any version of awk, you can write directly to the special UNIX file, */dev/tty*, that is a name for the user's terminal. This can be used to direct prompts or messages to the user's attention when the output of the program is directed to a file:

```
printf "Enter your name:" >"/dev/tty"
```

In gawk, there are several special filenames, as listed in Table 10-1.

Table 10-1. Special Filenames: Gawk

Filename	Description
/dev/stdin	Standard input.
/dev/stdout	Standard output.
/dev/stderr	Standard error.
/dev/fd/*n*	The file referenced as file descriptor *n*.

You can use file descriptor 0 for standard input, 1 for standard output, and 2 for for standard error. Note that a special filename, like any filename, must be quoted when specified as a string constant.

A printerr Function

Error messages inform users about problems often related to missing or incorrect input. You can simply inform the user with a **print** statement. However, if the output of the program is redirected to a file, the user won't see it. Therefore, it is good practice to specify explicitly that the error message be sent to the terminal.

The following **printerr()** function helps to create consistent user error messages. It prints the word "ERROR" followed by a supplied message, the record number, and the current record. The following example directs output to */dev/tty*:

```
function printerr ( message ) {
        # print message, record number and record
        print "ERROR:" message " (" NR ") " $0 > "/dev/tty"
}
```

If the output of the program is sent to the terminal screen, then error messages will be mixed in with the output. Outputting "ERROR" will help the user recognize error messages.

In UNIX, the standard destination of error messages is standard error. The rationale for writing to standard error is the same as above. To write to standard error explicitly, you must use the convoluted syntax "cat 1>&2" as in the following example:

```
print "ERROR" | "cat 1>&2"
```

This directs the output of the **print** statement to a pipe which executes the **cat** command. You can also use the **system( )** function to execute a UNIX command such as **cat** or **echo** and direct its output to standard error.

In gawk, the special file */dev/stderr* is available and much more easily used:

```
print "ERROR" > "/dev/stderr"   #gawk only
```

Working with Multiple Files

A file is opened whenever you read from or write to a file. The original awk allowed you to open up to 10 files. The new awk ups this number to 15 but more importantly provides a **close** statement so that you can close an open file.

A common use for directing output to files is to split up a large file into a number of smaller files. Although UNIX provides several utilities, **split** and **csplit**, that do a similar job, they do not have the ability to give the new file a useful filename. Similarly, sed can be used to write to a file, but you must specify a fixed filename. With awk, you can use a variable to specify the filename and pick up the value from a pattern in the file. For instance, if $1 provided a string that could be used as a filename, you could write a script to output each record to its own file:

```
print $0 > $1
```

You should perhaps test the filename, either to determine its length or to look for characters that cannot be used in a filename.

Using the original awk to write this kind of program meant that you were limited to splitting up a file into ten or fewer smaller ones. The example we are going to look at works for awk or nawk but it uses the **close** statement* so that when using nawk you will not run into open-file limitation.

---

*The original awk does not gripe about the presence of the **close** statement, although it has no effect. Thus, the script example will run, as is, under awk or nawk.

The following script was used to split up a large file containing dozens of man pages. Each man page began by setting a number register and ended with a blank line:

```
.nr X 0
```

(Although they use the **man** macros for the most part, the beginning of a man page was strangely coded, making things a little harder.) The line that provides the filename looks like this:

```
.if \nX=0 .ds x}  XDrawLine "" "Xlib - Drawing Primitives"
```

The fifth field on this line, "XDrawLine," contains the filename. Perhaps the only difficulty in writing the script is that the first line is not the one that provides the filename. Therefore, we collect the lines in an array until we get a filename. Once we get the filename, we output the array, and from that point on we simply write each input line to the new file. Here's the **man.split** script:

```
# man.split -- split up a file containing X man pages.
BEGIN {file=0;i=0;filename = ""}
# First line of new man page is ".nr X 0"
# Last line is blank
/\.nr X 0/,/^$/ {
    # this conditional collects lines until we get a filename.
    if ( file == 0){
        ++i
        line[i]=$0
        }
    else
        print $0 > filename

    # this matches line that gives us the filename
    if ($4 ~ /x}/) {
        # now we have a filename
        filename = $5
        file = 1
        # output name to screen
        print filename
        # print any lines collected
        for (x=1;x<=i;++x){
            print line[x] > filename
            }
        i = 0
        }

    # close up and clean up for next one
```

```
if ($0 ~ /^$/){
    close(filename)
    filename = ""
    file = 0
    i = 0
    }
}
```

As you can see, we use the variable **file** as a flag to convey whether or not we have a valid filename and can write to the file. Initially, **file** is 0, and the current input line is stored in an array. The variable *i* is a counter used to index the array. When we encounter the line that sets the filename, then we set **file** to 1. The name of the new file is printed to the screen so that the user can get some feedback on the progress of the script. Then we loop through the array and output it to the new file. When the next input line is read, **file** will be set to 1 and the **print** statement will output it to the named file.

I should add that there are several workarounds if you only have access to the original awk and need to break up a very large file. The one I used most frequently was to use **csplit** to break up the file. The result is a series of sequentially numbered files. Then write a script to process these files and rename them.

Here's a shell script that automates running **csplit**:

```
count=`grep -c "\.nr X" testfile`
count=`expr $count - 1`
echo $count
csplit -f man $1 '/^$/' {$count}
```

The **csplit** command needs to know how many times you want to apply the pattern that is used to break up the file. We run **grep -c** to get the count, subtract 1 from it and supply it as an argument to the **csplit** command. "$1" supplies the name of the large file and the **-f** option allows us to specify a prefix for the filename. The files generated by **csplit** will begin with **man** and be followed by digits. The **man.split** script can be modified to process each *man** file and create a new file with a reasonable name.

Generating Columnar Reports

This section describes a small-scale business application that produces reports with dollar amounts. While this application doesn't introduce any new material, it does emphasize the data processing and reporting capabilities of awk. (Surprisingly, some people do use awk to write small business applications.)

It is presumed that a script exists for data entry. The data-entry script has two jobs: the first is to enter the customer's name and mailing address for later use in building a mailing list; the second is to record the customer's order of any of seven items, the number of items ordered, and the price per item. The data collected for the mailing list and the customer order were written to separate files.

Here are two sample customer records from the customer order file:

```
Charlotte Webb
P.O  N61331 86 Y 045      Date: 03/14/86
#1 3   7.50
#2 3   7.50
#3 1   7.50
#4 1   7.50
#7 1   7.50

Martin S. Rossi
P.O  NONE      Date: 03/14/86
#1 2   7.50
#2 5   6.75
```

Each order covers multiple lines, and a blank line separates one order from another. The first two lines supply the customer's name, purchase order number and the date of the order. Each subsequent line identifies an item by number, the number ordered, and the price of the item.

Let's write a simple program that multiplies the number of copies by the price. The script can ignore the first two lines of each record. We only want to read the lines where an item is specified:

```
awk '/^#/ {
         amount = $2 * $3
         printf "%s %6.2f\n", $0, amount
         next
     }
{print}' $*
```

The main procedure only affects lines that match the pattern. It multiplies the second field by the third field, assigning the value to the variable **amount**. The **printf** conversion %f is used to print a floating point number; "2" specifies a minimum field width of six and a precision of 2. Precision is the number of digits to the right of the decimal point; the default for %f is six. We print the current record along with the value of the variable **amount**. If a line is printed within this procedure, the next line is read from standard input. Lines not matching the pattern are simply passed through. Let's look at how **addem** works:

```
% addem orders
Charlotte Webb
P.O  N61331 86 Y 045      Date: 03/14/86
#1 3   7.50   22.50
```

```
#2 3  7.50   22.50
#3 1  7.50    7.50
#4 1  7.50    7.50
#7 1  7.50    7.50

Martin S. Rossi
P.O  NONE     Date: 03/14/86
#1 2  7.50   15.00
#2 5  6.75   33.75
```

This program did not need to access the customer record as a whole; it simply acted on the individual item lines. Now, let's design a program that reads multi-line records and accumulates order information for display in a report. This report should display for each item the total number of copies and the total amount. We also want totals reflecting all copies ordered and the sum of all orders.

Our new script will begin by setting the field and record separators:

```
BEGIN { FS = "\n"; RS = "" }
```

Each record has a variable number of fields, depending upon how many items have been ordered. First, we check that the input record has at least three fields. Then a **for** loop is built to read all of the fields beginning with the third field.

```
NF >= 3 {
for (i = 3; i <= NF; ++i)
```

In database terms, each field has a value and each value can be further broken up as subvalues. That is, if the value of a field in a multi-line record is a single line, subvalues are the words that are on that line. We can use the **split** function to divide a field into subvalues.

The following part of the script splits each field into subvalues. **$i** will supply the value of the current field which will be divided into elements of the array **order**:

```
sv = split($i, order)
    if (sv == 3) {
            procedure
    }
    else print "Incomplete Record"
```

The number of elements returned by the function is saved in a variable sv. This allows us to test that there are three subvalues. If there are not, the **else** statement is executed, printing the error message to the screen.

Next we assign the individual elements of the array to a specific variable. This is mainly to make it easier to remember what each element represents:

```
title = order[1]
copies = order[2]
price = order[3]
```

Then a group of arithmetic operations are performed on these values:

```
amount = copies * price
total_vol += copies
total_amt += amount
vol[title] += copies
amt[title] += amount
```

These values are accumulated until the last input record is read. The **END** procedure prints the report.

Here's the complete program:

```
% cat addemup
:
#addemup -- total customer orders
awk ' BEGIN { FS = "\n"; RS = "" }
NF >= 3 {
for (i = 3; i <= NF; ++i){
   sv = split($i, order)
       if (sv == 3){
           title = order[1]
           copies = order[2]
           price = order[3]
           amount = copies * price
           total_vol += copies
           total_amt += amount
           vol[title] += copies
           amt[title] += amount
               }
       else print "Incomplete Record"
       }
}
     END {
   printf "%5s\t%10s\t%6s\n\n", "TITLE", "COPIES SOLD", "TOTAL"
   for (title in vol)
       printf "%5s\t%10d\t$%7.2f\n", title, vol[title], amt[title]
   printf "%s\n", "--------------"
   printf "\t%s%4d\t$%7.2f\n", "Total ", total_vol, total_amt }' $*
```

We have defined two arrays that have the same subscript. We only need to have one **for** loop to read both arrays.

addemup, an order report generator, produces the following output:

```
% addemup orders.today
  TITLE       COPIES SOLD       TOTAL

    #1             5        $   37.50
    #2             8        $   56.25
    #3             1        $    7.50
    #4             1        $    7.50
    #7             1        $    7.50
  -------------
         Total    16        $  116.25
```

This section reviews a few of the enhancements available in gawk but not in awk or nawk. The list of features unique to gawk is getting smaller because some features have migrated over to nawk. Examples of gawk features now supported in nawk are:

1. The escape sequences \a, \v, and \x are now supported.

2. The **toupper()** and **tolower()** functions are there, but because they are not documented, it is not clear whether they are supported.

The following gawk features are found only in gawk:

1. The additional special filenames, such as */dev/stderr* and */dev/stdout*.

2. The **AWKPATH** environment variable that gives a directory search path for awk to use when the **-f** specifies a file not found in the current directory.

3. The **IGNORECASE** variable for case-independent pattern matching.

We have presented all of the gawk-specific features except **IGNORECASE**.

All pattern matching in awk and nawk is case sensitive. Gawk introduced the **IGNORECASE** variable so that you can specify that regular expressions can be interpreted without regard for uppercase or lowercase characters.

The default value of **IGNORECASE** is zero, which means that pattern matching is performed the same as awk and nawk. If **IGNORECASE** is set to a non-zero value, then case distinctions are ignored. This applies to all places where regular expressions are used, including the field separator **FS**.

Debugging

No aspect of programming is more frustrating or more essential than debugging. In this section, we'll look at ways to debug awk scripts and offer advice on how to correct an awk program that fails to do what it is supposed to do.

Nawk is a significant improvement on awk in reporting syntax errors in a way that helps you locate the problem. As mentioned earlier, awk's standard error message ("bailing out") is hardly any help. But even with improved error detection, it is often difficult to isolate the problem. The techniques for discovering the source of the problem are a modest few and are fairly obvious.

There are two classes of problems with a program. The first is really a bug in the program's logic. The program runs—that is, it finishes without reporting any error messages, but it does not produce the result you wanted. For instance, perhaps it does not create any output. This bug could be caused by failing to use a **print** statement to output the result of a calculation. Program errors are mental errors, if you will.

The second class of error is one in which the program fails to execute or complete execution. This could result from a syntax error and cause awk to spit code at you that it is unable to interpret. Many syntax errors are the result of a typo or a missing brace or parenthesis. Syntax errors usually generate error messages that help direct you to the problem. Sometimes, however, a program may fail (or "core dump") without producing any reasonable error message. This may be also caused by a syntax error, but there could be problems specific to the machine. I have had a few larger scripts that dumped core on one machine while they ran without a problem on another. You could, for instance, be running up against limitations set for awk for that particular implementation. See the section "Awk's Limitations."

You should be clear in your mind which type of program bug you are trying to find: an error in the script's logic or an error in its syntax.

Make a Copy

Before you begin debugging a program, make a copy of it. This is extremely important. To debug an awk script, you have to change it. These modifications may point you to the error but many changes will have no effect or may introduce new problems. It's good to be able to restore changes that you make. However, it is bothersome to restore each change that you make, so I like to continue making changes until I have found the problem. When I know what it is, I go back to the original and make the change. In effect, that restores all the other inconsequential changes that were made in the copy.

It is also helpful to view the process of creating a program as a series of stages. Look at a core set of features as a single stage. Once you have implemented these features and tested them, make a copy of the program before going to the next stage to develop new features. That way, you can always return to the previous stage if you have problems with the new code that you added.

Before and After Photos

What is difficult in debugging awk is that you don't always know what is happening during the course of the program. You can inspect the input and the output, but there is no way to stop the program in mid-course and examine its state. Thus, it is difficult to know which part of the program is causing a problem.

A common problem is determining when or where in the program the assignment of a variable takes place. The first method of attack is to use the **print** statement to print the value of the variable at various points in the program. For instance, it is common to use a variable as a flag to determine that a certain condition has occurred. At the beginning of the program, the flag might be set to 0. At one or more points in the program, the value of this flag might be set to 1. The problem is to find where the change actually occurs. If you want to check the flag at a particular part of the program, use **print** statements before and after the assignment. For instance:

```
print flag, "before"
if (! $1 ) {
        .
        .
        .
        flag = 1
}
print flag, "after"
```

If you are unsure about the result of a substitution command or any function, print the string before and after the function is called:

```
print $2
sub(/ *\(/,"(", $2)
print $2
```

The value of printing the value before the substitution command is to make sure that the command sees the value that you think should be there. A previous command might have changed that variable. The problem may turn out to be that the format of the input record is not as you thought. Checking the input carefully is a very important step in debugging. In particular, use **print** statements to verify that the sequence of fields is as you expect. When you find that input is causing the problem, you can either fix the input or write new code to accommodate it.

Finding Out Where the Problem Is

The more modular a script is—that is, the more it can be broken down into separate parts, the easier it is to test and debug the program. One of the advantages of writing functions is that you can isolate what is going on inside the function and test it without affecting other parts of the program. You can omit an entire action and see what happens.

If a program has a number of branching constructs, you might find that an input line falls through one of branches. Test that the input reaches part of a program. For instance, when debugging the **masterindex** program, I wanted to know if an entry containing the word "retrieving" was being handled in a particular part of the program. I inserted the following line in the part of the program where I thought it should be encountered:

```
if ($0 ~ /retrieving/) print ">> retrieving" > "/dev/tty"
```

When the program runs, if it encounters the string "retrieving", it will print the message. I like to use some pair of characters that will instantly call my attention to the output. Here I use ">>" but "!!" is also a good one.

Sometimes you might not be sure which of several **print** statements are causing a problem. Insert identifiers into the **print** statement that will alert you to the **print** statement being executed. In the following example, we simply put use the variable name to identify what is printed with a label:

```
if (PRIMARY)
    print (">>PRIMARY:%s", PRIMARY)
else
    if (SECONDARY)
        print (">>SECONDARY:%s", SECONDARY)
    else
        print (">>TERTIARY:%s", TERTIARY)
```

This technique is also useful for investigating whether or not parts of the program are executed at all. Some programs get to be like remodeled homes: a room is added here, a wall is taken down there. Trying to understand the basic structure can be difficult. You might wonder if each of the parts is truly needed or indeed if it is ever executed at all.

If an awk program is part of a pipeline of several programs, even other awk programs, you can use the **tee** command to re-direct output to a file, while also piping the output to the next command. For instance, look at the shell script for running the **masterindex** program, as shown in Chapter 11, *Full-featured Applications*:

```
$INDEXDIR/input.idx $FILES |
sort -bdf -t:  +0 -1 +1 -2 +3 -4 +2n -3n | uniq |
$INDEXDIR/pagenums.idx | tee page.tmp |
$INDEXDIR/combine.idx |
$INDEXDIR/format.idx
```

By adding "tee page.tmp", we are able to capture the output of the **pagenums.idx** program in a file named *page.tmp*. The same output is also piped to **combine.idx**.

Commenting Out Loud

Another technique is simply commenting out a series of lines that may be causing problems. This is useful in determining which lines are really causing the problem.

I recommend developing a consistent two-character symbol such as "#%" to comment out lines temporarily. Then you will notice them on subsequent editing and remember to deal with them. It also becomes easier to remove the symbols and restore the lines with a single editing command that does not affect program comments:

```
#% if ( thisFails )
      print "I give up"
```

Using the comment here eliminates the conditional, so the **print** statement is executed unconditionally.

Slash and Burn

When all else fails, arm yourself with your editor's delete command and begin deleting portions of the program until the error disappears. Of course, make a copy of the program and delete lines from the temporary copy. This is a very crude technique, but an effective one to use before giving up altogether or starting over from scratch. It is sometimes the only way to discover what is wrong when the only result you get is that the program dumps core. The idea is the same as above, to isolate the problem code. Remove a function, for instance, or a *for* loop to see if it is the cause of the problem. Be sure to cut out complete units: for instance, all the statements within braces and the matching braces. If the problem persists—the program continues to break— then cut out another large section of the program. Sooner or later, you will find the line that is causing the problem.

You can use "slash and burn" to learn how a program works. First, run the original program on sample input, saving the output. Begin by removing a part of the program that you don't understand. Then run the modified program on sample input and compare the output to the original. Look to see what changed.

Getting Defensive About Your Script

There are all types of input errors and inconsistencies that will turn up bugs in your script. You probably didn't consider that *user* errors will be pointed to as problems with *your* program. Therefore, it is a good idea to surround your core program with "defensive" procedures designed to trap inconsistent input records and prevent the program from failing unexpectedly. For instance, you might want to verify each input record before processing it, making sure that the proper number of fields exist or that the kind of data that you expect is found in a particular field.

Another aspect of incorporating defensive techniques is error handling. In others words, what do you want to have happen once the program detects an error? While in some cases you can have the program continue, in other cases it may be preferable that the program print an error message and/or halt if such an error is encountered.

It is also appropriate to recognize that awk scripts are typically confined to the realm of quick fixes, programs that solve a particular problem rather solving a class of problems encountered by many different users. Because of the nature of these programs, it is not really necessary that they be professional quality. Thus, it is not necessary to write 100% user-proof programs. For one thing, defensive programming is quite time-consuming and frequently tedious. Secondly, as amateurs, we are at liberty to write programs that perform the way we expect them to; a professsional has to write for an audience and must account for their expectations. In brief, if you are writing the script for others to use, consider the possible uses and problems possibly encountered by users before considering the program complete. If not, maybe the fact that the script works—even for a very narrow set of circumstances—is good enough and all there is time for.

Limitations

There are fixed limits within any awk implementation. The only trouble is that the documentation seldom reports them. Figure 10-1 lists the limitations as described in *The AWK Programming Language*. These limitations are implementation-specific but they are good ballpark figures for most systems.

Number of fields per record	100
Characters per input record	3000
Characters per output record	3000
Characters per field	1024
Characters per printf string	3000
Characters in literal string	400
Characters in character class	400
Files open	15
Pipes open	1

Figure 10-1. Limitations

In terms of numeric values, awk uses double-precision floating point numbers that are limited in size by the machine's architecture.

Running into these limits can cause unanticipated problems with scripts. In developing examples for this book, I thought I'd write a search program that could look for a word or sequence of words in a single paragraph. The idea was to read a document as a series of multi-line records and if any of the fields contained the search term, I'd print the record, which was a paragraph. It could be used to search through mail files where blank lines delimit paragraphs. The resulting program worked for small test files. However, when I tried it on larger files, the program dumped core because it encountered a paragraph that was longer than the maximum input record size, which is 3000 characters. (Actually, the file contained an included mail message where blank lines within the message were prefixed by ">"). Thus, when reading multiple lines as a single record, you better be sure that you don't anticipate records longer than 3000 characters. By the way, there is no particular error message that alerts you to the fact that the problem is the size of the current record.

Invoking Awk Using the #! Syntax

The "#!" syntax is an alternative syntax for invoking awk from a shell script. It has the advantage of allowing you to specify awk parameters and filenames on the shell-script command line. The "#!" syntax is recognized on BSD UNIX systems, but is not typically found in System V. The best way to use this syntax is to put the following line as the first line of the shell script:

```
#!/bin/awk -f
```

"#!" is followed by the pathname that locates awk (or nawk or gawk) and then the **-f** option. After this line, you specify the awk script:

```
#!/bin/awk -f
{ print $1 }
```

Note that no quotes are necessary around the script. All lines in the file after the first one will be executed as though they were specified in a separate script file.

A couple of years ago, there was an interesting discussion on the net about the use of the "#!" syntax that clarified how it works. The discussion was prompted by a 4.2BSD user's observation that the shell script below failed:

```
#!/bin/awk
{ print $1 }
```

while the one below works:

```
#!/bin/sh
/bin/awk '{ print $1 }'
```

The two responses that I saw were by Chris Torek and Guy Harris and I will try to summarize their explanation. The first script fails because it passes the filename of the script as the first parameter (argv[1]) and awk interprets it as the input file and not the script file. Because no script has been supplied, awk produces a syntax error message. In other words, if the name of the shell script is "myscript", then the first script executes as:

```
/bin/awk myscript
```

If the script was changed to add the **-f** option, it executes as follows:

```
#!/bin/awk -f
{ print $1 }
```

Then you enter the following command:

```
% myscript myfile
```

It then executes as though you had typed:

```
/bin/awk -f myscript myfile
```

The "#!" syntax allows you to create shell scripts that pass command-line parameters transparently to awk. In other words, you can pass awk parameters from the command line that invokes the shell script. For instance, we demonstrate passing parameters by changing our sample awk script to expect a parameter **n**:

```
{ print $1*n }
```

Assuming that we have a test file in which the first field contains a number that can be multiplied by **n**, we can invoke the program, as follows:

```
% myscript n=4 myfile
```

This spares us from having to pass "$1" as a shell variable and assigning it to **n** as an awk parameter inside the shell script.

The **masterindex** program in the next chapter uses the "#!" syntax to invoke awk. If your system does not support this syntax, you can change the script by removing the "#!", placing single quotes around the entire script, and ending the script with "$*" which expands to all shell command-line parameters.

A Trick for Mac Text Files

Macintosh text files are delimited by carriage returns instead of newlines. This means, for instance, that you can't open a Macintosh text file using **vi** without getting the message "Line too long".

You can read a Mac text file using awk if you change the record separator to a carriage return:

```
RS = "\r"
```

"\r" is the escape sequence for a carriage return. A simple conversion script for a Mac text file to a UNIX text file is shown below:

```
RS = "\r"
{ print }
```

Remember that **RS** is the input record separator; the output record separator remains a linefeed (\n) and thus the records are output followed by linefeeds rather than carriage returns.

If you wanted to process the Mac text file without changing it to a UNIX file, set the output field separator to a carriage return.

I've only begun testing using this syntax to make changes in a Microsoft Word file. I have not found a way to pass the binary information through, but I can extract and manipulate the text (providing it was not saved using the Fast Save option.)

Using awkcc

The **awkcc*** program is an awk-to-C translator. It takes an awk script and produces a C source program. This source is automatically compiled to produce an executable program that is generally much faster at accomplishing the same task as the original awk script. The author of the program writes that "increases of a factor of 2 and 6 are common." I have just begun using it, but it seems to live up to those claims.

To run **awkcc** requires a special library file named *libAWK.a*, various header files, the program **awkcc**, and the shell script **awkcc.sh**. The basic syntax of invoking **awkcc** is:

> **awkcc** [**-o** *output*] [**-c** *progfile*] *awkprog*

Awkcc reads the program *awkprog* and generates a C source code file named *awker.c*. When this file is compiled, an executable file named *a.out* is created. You can name the source code file using the **-c** option or the output file using the **-o** option. (There are also several technically-oriented options.)

The following example runs **awkcc** on the **lotto.awk** script:

```
% awkcc lotto.awk
```

It occasionally spits out some warning messages but I haven't been able to tell whether they should be regarded. An executable file named **a.out** is created. We can run it, directing input from a file named *blank* that contains a single blank line:

```
% a.out < blank
Pick 6 of 30
10 18 20 25 26 28
```

Now let's compare the speed of the compiled awk script with its original. We use the **timex** command to give us the statistics. First, let's see the compiled script:

```
% timex a.out < blank
Pick 6 of 30
4 5 12 14 29 30

real       0.25
user       0.06
sys        0.06
```

---

*This program is not part of standard UNIX. It was written by J. Christopher Ramming and is distributed through AT&T's UNIX Toolchest. Ordering information can be found in the Preface.

The real or elapsed time was .25 seconds. The actual time spent processing was 6 hundredths of a second. Now let's look at the original awk version:

```
% timex nawk -f lotto.awk < blank
Pick 6 of 30
12 17 23 24 25 30

real       1.08
user       0.36
sys        0.35
```

The elapsed time was over a second and the actual system time was nearly six times as long.

We can run another time trial using one of the modules from the indexing program presented in the next chapter. It is a larger program and we will have it process a file that contains 1689 lines of index entries. This time, we'll let nawk go first:

```
% timex nawk -f combine.awk tmp > /dev/null

real      54.03
user      45.51
sys        5.05
```

It takes almost a minute in real time but only 5 seconds of system time. Now, the chance for **awkcc**:

```
% awkcc -o combine.out combine.awk
% timex combine.out tmp > /dev/null

real      11.48
user       9.60
sys        1.21
```

It takes just under 12 seconds of real time and over 1 second of actual processing time. This is quite a significant speed-up.

The numbers in these time trials are not absolutes, but are rather intended to show you the difference in speed between running an interpreted script and a compiled program. It is best to look at **awkcc** as a way to optimize an existing program that you expect to use frequently. It does not make sense to compile simple scripts or to compile a script that might change, for instance, if you are still developing it.

We have pointed out several times the similarities between programming in awk and programming in C, enough so that I hope you will want to take the next step and begin learning C. However, let me caution you that trying to read the C source code produced by **awkcc** is not a good place to start. By no means does it represent a mere translation from awk to C. It is quite complicated and I'm not sure even experienced C programmers would set out to modify it.

Well, I think I've quite nearly cleaned out this bottom drawer. The material in this chapter has a lot to do with how awk interfaces with the UNIX operating system, invoking other utilities, opening and closing files, and using pipes. We have also discussed some of the admittedly crude techniques for debugging awk scripts. Finally, we looked at a new tool, **awkcc**, which is not part of the standard UNIX distribution.

And so we have covered all of the features of the awk programming language and differences among its implementations (awk, gawk and nawk). The next chapter is devoted to breaking down two large, complex applications: a document spellchecker and an indexing program. Chapter 12, *A Miscellany of Scripts*, presents a variety of user-contributed programs that provide additional examples of how to write programs.

11

Full-featured Applications

An Interactive Spell Checker
Generating a Formatted Index
Spare Details of the Masterindex Program

This chapter presents two complex applications that integrate most features of the awk programming language. The first program, **spellcheck**, provides an interactive interface to the UNIX **spell** program. The second application, **masterindex**, is a batch program for generating an index for a book or a set of books. Even if you are not interested in the particular application, you should study these larger programs to get a feel for the scope of the problems that an awk program can solve.

An Interactive Spell Checker

The UNIX **spell** program does an adequate job of catching spelling errors in a document. For most people, however, it only does half the job. It doesn't help you correct the misspelled words. First-time users of **spell** find themselves jotting down the misspelled words and then using the text editor to change the document. More skilled users build a sed script to make the changes automatically. The **spellcheck** program offers another way—it shows you each word that **spell** has found and asks if you want to correct the word. You can change each occurrence of the word after seeing the line on which it occurs, or you can correct the spelling error globally. The user can also choose to add any word that **spell** turns up to a local dictionary file.

Before describing the program, let's have a demonstration of how it works. The user enters **spellcheck**, a shell script that invokes awk, and the name of the document file.

```
% spellcheck ch00
Use local dict file? (y/n)y
```

If a dictionary file is not specified on the command line, and a file named *dict* exists in the current directory, then the user is asked if the local dictionary should be used. **spellcheck** then runs **spell** using the local dictionary.

```
Running spell checker ...
```

Using the list of "misspelled" words turned up by **spell**, **spellcheck** prompts the user to correct them. Before the first word is displayed, a list of responses is shown that describe what actions are possible.

```
Responses:
     Change each occurrence,
     Global change,
     Add to Dict,
     Help,
     Quit
     CR to ignore:
1 - Found SparcStation (C/G/A/H/Q/):a
```

The first word found by **spell** is "SparcStation." A response of "a" (followed by a carriage return) adds this word to a list that will be used to update the dictionary. The second word is clearly a misspelling and a response of "g" is entered to make the change globally:

```
2 - Found languauge (C/G/A/H/Q/):g
Globally change to:language
Globally change languauge to language? (y/n):y
> and a full description of its scripting language.
1 lines changed. Save changes? (y/n)y
```

After prompting the user to enter the correct spelling and confirming the entry, the change is made and each line affected is displayed, preceded by a ">." The user is then asked to approve these changes before they are saved. The third word is also added to the dictionary:

```
3 - Found nawk (C/G/A/H/Q/):a
```

The fourth word is a misspelling of "utilities."

```
4 - Found utlitities (C/G/A/H/Q/):c
These utlitities have many things in common, including
      ^^^^^^^^^^
Change to:utilities
Change utlitities to utilities? (y/n):y
Two other utlitities that are found on the UNIX system
          ^^^^^^^^^^
Change utlitities to utilities? (y/n):y

>These utilities have many things in common, including
>Two other utilities that are found on the UNIX system
2 lines changed. Save changes? (y/n)y
```

The user enters "c" to change each occurrence. This response allows the user to see the line containing the misspelling and then make the change. After the user has made each change, the changed lines are displayed and the user is asked to confirm saving the changes.

It is unclear whether the fifth word is a misspelling or not, so the user enters "c" to view the line.

```
5 - Found xvf (C/G/A/H/Q/):c
tar xvf filename
    ^^^
Change to:<CR>
```

After determining that it is not a misspelling, the user enters a carriage return to ignore the word. Generally, **spell** turns up a lot of words that are not misspellings so a carriage return means to ignore the word.

After all the words in the list have been processed, or if the user quits before then, the user is prompted to save the changes made to the document and the dictionary.

```
Save corrections in ch00 (y/n)? y
Make changes to dictionary (y/n)? y
```

If the user answer "n," the original file and the dictionary are left unchanged.

Now let's look at the **spellcheck.awk** script, which can be divided into four sections:

1. The **BEGIN** procedure, that processes the command line arguments and executes the **spell** command to create a word list.

2. The main procedure, that reads one word at a time from the list and prompts the user to make a correction.

3. The **END** procedure, that saves the working copy of the file, overwriting the original. It also appends words from the exception list to the current dictionary.

4. Supporting functions, that are called to make changes in the file.

We will look at each of these sections of the program.

BEGIN Procedure

The **BEGIN** procedure for **spellcheck.awk** is large. It is also somewhat unusual.

```
# spellcheck.awk -- interactive spell checker
#
# AUTHOR: Dale Dougherty
#
# Usage: nawk -f spellcheck.awk [+dict] file
# (Use spellcheck as name of shell program)
# SPELLDICT = "dict"
# SPELLFILE = "file"

# BEGIN actions perform the following tasks:
#    1) process command line arguments
#    2) create temporary filenames
#    3) execute spell program to create wordlist file
#    4) display list of user responses
BEGIN {
# Process command line arguments
# Must be at least two args -- nawk and filename
   if (ARGC > 1) {
   # if more than two args, second arg is dict
      if (ARGC > 2) {
      # test to see if dict is specified with "+"
      # and assign ARGV[1] to SPELLDICT
         if (ARGV[1] ~ /^\+.*/)
            SPELLDICT = ARGV[1]
         else
            SPELLDICT = "+" ARGV[1]
      # assign file ARGV[2] to SPELLFILE
         SPELLFILE = ARGV[2]
      # delete args so awk does not open them as files
         delete ARGV[1]
         delete ARGV[2]
      }
   # not more than two args
      else {
      # assign file ARGV[1] to SPELLFILE
         SPELLFILE = ARGV[1]
      # test to see if local dict file exists
         if (! system ("test -r dict")) {
```

```
            # if it does, ask if we should use it
               printf ("Use local dict file? (y/n)")
               getline reply <"-"
            # if reply is yes, use "dict"
               if (reply ~ /[yY](es)*/){
                   SPELLDICT = "+dict"
               }
            }
      }
   } # end of processing args > 1
   # if args not > 1, then print shell-command usage
   else {
      print "Usage: spellcheck [+dict] file"
      exit
   }
# end of processing command line arguments

# create temporary file names, each begin with sp_
   wordlist = "sp_wordlist"
   spellsource = "sp_input"
   spellout = "sp_out"

# copy SPELLFILE to temporary input file
   system("cp " SPELLFILE " " spellsource)

# now run spell program; output sent to wordlist
   print "Running spell checker ..."
   if (SPELLDICT)
      SPELLCMD = "spell " SPELLDICT " "
   else
      SPELLCMD = "spell "
   system(SPELLCMD spellsource " > " wordlist )

# test wordlist to see if misspelled words turned up
   if ( system("test -s " wordlist ) ) {
   # if wordlist is empty, (or spell command failed), exit
      print "No misspelled words found."
      exit
   }

# assign wordlist file to ARGV[1] so that awk will read it.
   ARGV[1] = wordlist

# display list of user responses
   responseList = "Responses: \n\tChange each occurrence,"
   responseList = responseList "\n\tGlobal change,"
   responseList = responseList "\n\tAdd to Dict,"
   responseList = responseList "\n\tHelp,"
   responseList = responseList "\n\tQuit"
   responseList = responseList "\n\tCR to ignore: "
   printf("%s", responseList)

} # end of BEGIN procedure
```

The first part of the **BEGIN** procedure processes the command line arguments. It checks that **ARGC** is greater than one for the program to continue. That is, in addition to "nawk," a filename must be specified. This file specifies the document that **spell** will analyze. An optional dictionary filename can be specified as the second argument. The **spellcheck** script follows the command line interface of **spell**, although none of the obscure **spell** options can be invoked from the **spellcheck** command line. If a dictionary is not specified, then the script executes a **test** command to see if the file *dict* exists. If it does, the prompt asks the user to approve using it as the dictionary file.

Once we've processed the arguments, we delete them from the **ARGV** array. This is to prevent their being interpreted as filename arguments.

The second part of the **BEGIN** procedure sets up some temporary files, because we do not want to work directly with the original file. At the end of the program, the user will have the option of saving or discarding the work done in the temporary files. The temporary files all begin with "sp_" and are removed before exiting the program.

The third part of the program executes **spell** and creates a word list. We test to see that this file exists and that there is something in it before proceeding. If for some reason the **spell** program fails, or there are no misspelled words found, the **wordlist** file will be empty. If this file does exist, then we assign the filename as the second element in the **ARGV** array. This is an unusual but valid way of supplying the name of the input file that awk will process. Note that this file did not exist when awk was invoked! The name of the document file, which was specified on the command line, is no longer in the **ARGV** array. We will not read the document file using awk's main input loop. Instead, a **while** loop reads the file to find and correct misspelled words.

The last task in the **BEGIN** procedure is to define and display a list of responses that the user can enter when a misspelled word is displayed. This list is displayed once at the beginning of the program as well as when the user enters "Help" at the main prompt. Putting this list in a variable allows us to access it from different points in the program, if necessary, without maintaining duplicates. The assignment of **responseList** could be done more simply, but the long string would not be printable in this book. (You can't break a string over two lines.)

Main Procedure

The main procedure is rather small in that it displays a misspelled word and prompts the user to enter an appropriate response. This procedure is executed for each misspelled word.

One reason this procedure is short is because the central action—correcting a misspelled word—is handled by two larger user-defined functions, which we'll see in the last section.

```
# main procedure, executed for each line in wordlist.
#    Purpose is to show misspelled word and prompt user
#    for appropriate action.

{
# assign word to misspelling
   misspelling = $1
   response = 1
   ++word
# print misspelling and prompt for response
   while (response !~ /(^[cCgGaAhHqQ])|^$/ ) {
       printf("\n%s - Found %s (C/G/A/H/Q/):", word, misspelling)
       getline response <"-"
   }
# now process the user's response
# CR - carriage return ignores current word
# Help
   if (response ~ /[Hh](elp)*/) {
   # Display list of responses and prompt again.
       printf("%s", responseList)
       printf("\n%s - Found %s (C/G/A/Q/):", word, misspelling)
       getline response <"-"
   }
# Quit
   if (response ~ /[Qq](uit)*/) exit
# Add to dictionary
   if ( response ~ /[Aa](dd)*/) {
       dict[++dictEntry] = misspelling
   }
# Change each occurrence
   if ( response ~ /[cC](hange)*/) {
   # read each line of the file we are correcting
       newspelling = ""; changes = ""
       while( getline < spellsource > 0){
       # call function to show line with misspelled word
       # and prompt user to make each correction
           make_change($0)
       # all lines go to temp output file
           print > spellout
       }
   # all lines have been read
   # close temp input and temp output file
```

```
            close(spellout)
            close(spellsource)
    # if change was made
        if (changes){
        # show changed lines
            for (j = 1; j <= changes; ++j)
                print changedLines[j]
            printf ("%d lines changed. ", changes)
        # function to confirm before saving changes
            confirm_changes()
        }
    }
# Globally change
    if ( response ~ /[gG](lobal)*/) {
    # call function to prompt for correction
    # and display each line that is changed.
    # Ask user to approve all changes before saving.
        make_global_change()
    }
} # end of Main procedure
```

The first field of each input line from **wordlist** contains the misspelled word and it is assigned to **misspelling**. We construct a **while** loop inside which we display the misspelled word to the user and prompt for a response. Look closely at the regular expression that tests the value of **response**:

```
while (response !~ /(^[cCgGaAhHqQ])|^$/ )
```

The user can only get out of this loop by entering any of the specified letters *or* by entering a carriage return—an empty line. The use of regular expressions for testing user input helps tremendously in writing a simple but flexible program. The user can enter a single letter "c" in lower or uppercase or a word beginning with "c" such as "ch" or "Change."

The rest of the main procedure consists of conditional statements that test for a specific response and perform a corresponding action. The first response is "help" which displays the list of responses again and then re-displays the prompt.

The next response is "quit." The action associated with quit is **exit**, which drops out of the main procedure and goes to the **END** procedure.

If the user enters "add," the misspelled word is put in the array **dict** and will be added as an exception in a local dictionary.

The "Change" and "Global" responses cause the program's real work to begin. It's important to understand how they differ. When the user enters "c" or "change," the first occurrence of the misspelled word in the document is displayed. Then the user is prompted to make the change. This happens for each occurrence in the document. When the user enters "g" or "global," the user is prompted to make the change right away, and all the changes are made at once without prompting the user to confirm each one. This work is largely handled by two functions **make_change()** and **make_global_change()**, which we'll look at in the last section.

These are all the valid responses, except one. A carriage return means to ignore the misspelled word and get the next word in the list. This is the default action of the main input loop, so no conditional need be set up for it.

End Procedure

The **END** procedure, of course, is reached in one of the following circumstances:

1. The **spell** command failed or did not turn up any misspellings.
2. The list of misspelled words is exhausted.
3. The user has entered "quit" at a prompt.

The purpose of the **END** procedure is to allow the user to confirm any permanent change to the document or the dictionary.

```
# END procedure makes changes permanent.
# It overwrites the original file, and adds words
# to the dictionary.
# It also removes the temporary files.

END {
# if we got here after reading only one record,
# no changes were made, so exit.
   if (NR <= 1) exit
# user must confirm saving corrections to file
   while (saveAnswer !~ /([yY](es)*)|([nN]o*)/ ) {
       printf "Save corrections in %s (y/n)? ", SPELLFILE
       getline saveAnswer <"-"
   }
# if answer is yes then mv temporary input file to SPELLFILE
   if (saveAnswer ~ /^[yY]/)
       system("mv " spellsource " " SPELLFILE)
# if answer is no then rm temporary input file
   if (saveAnswer ~ /^[nN]/)
       system("rm " spellsource)

# if words have added to dictionary array, then prompt
# to confirm saving in current dictionary.
   if (dictEntry) {
       printf "Make changes to dictionary (y/n)? "
       getline response <"-"
       if (response ~ /^[yY]/){
       # if no dictionary defined, then use "dict"
           if (! SPELLDICT) SPELLDICT="dict"
```

```
        # loop through array and append words to dictionary
            sub(/^\+/,"",SPELLDICT)
            for ( item in dict )
               print dict[item] >> SPELLDICT              •
        # sort dictionary file
            system("sort " SPELLDICT "> tmp_dict")
            system("mv " "tmp_dict " SPELLDICT)
         }
      }
   # remove word list.
      system("rm" " sp_wordlist")
   } # end of END procedure
```

The **END** procedure begins with a conditional statement that tests that the number of records is less than or equal to 1. This occurs when the **spell** program does not generate a word list or when the user enters "quit" after seeing just the first record. If so, the **END** procedure is exited as there is no work to save.

Next, we create a **while** loop to ask the user about saving the changes made to the document. It requires the user to respond "y" or "n" to the prompt. If the answer is "y," the temporary input file replaces the original document file. If the answer is "n," the temporary file is removed. No other responses are accepted.

Next, we test to see if the **dict** array has something in it. Its elements are the words to be added to the dictionary. If the user approves adding them to the dictionary, these words are appended to the current dictionary, as defined above, or if not, to a local "dict" file. Because the dictionary must be sorted to be read by **spell**, a **sort** command is executed with the output sent to a temporary file that is afterwards copied over the original file.

Supporting Functions

There are three supporting functions, two of which are large and do the bulk of the work of making changes in the document. The third function supports that work by confirming that the user wants to save the changes that were made.

When the user wants to "Change each occurrence" in the document, the main procedure has a **while** loop that reads the document one line at a time. (This line becomes $0.) It calls the **make_change** function to see if the line contains the misspelled word. If it does, the line is displayed and the user is prompted to enter the correct spelling of the word.

```
# make_change -- prompt user to correct misspelling
#       for current input line.  Calls itself
#         to find other occurrences in string.
#     stringToChange -- initially $0; then unmatched substring of $0
```

```
#     len -- length from beginning of $0 to end of matched string
# Assumes that misspelling is defined.

function make_change (stringToChange,len,  line, OKmakechange) {

# match misspelling in stringToChange; otherwise do nothing
  if ( match(stringToChange, misspelling) ){
  # Display matched line
   printstring = $0
   gsub(/\t/," ",printstring)
   print printstring
   carets = "^"
   for (i = 1; i < RLENGTH; ++i)
      carets = carets "^"
   if (len)
      FMT = "%" len+RSTART+RLENGTH-2 "s\n"
   else
      FMT = "%" RSTART+RLENGTH-1 "s\n"
   printf(FMT, carets)
  # Prompt user for correction, if not already defined
   if (! newspelling) {
      printf "Change to:"
      getline newspelling <"-"
   }
  # A carriage return falls through
  # If user enters correction, confirm
   while (newspelling && ! OKmakechange) {
      printf ("Change %s to %s? (y/n):", misspelling, newspelling)
      getline OKmakechange <"-"
      madechg = ""
   # test response
      if (OKmakechange ~ /[yY](es)*/ ) {
      # make change (first occurrence only)
         madechg = sub(misspelling, newspelling, stringToChange)
      }
      else if ( OKmakechange ~ /[nN]o*/ ){
         # offer chance to re-enter. correction
         printf "Change to:"
         getline newspelling <"-"
         OKmakechange = ""
      }
   } # end of while loop

   # if len, we are working with substring of $0
   if (len) {
   # assemble it
      line = substr($0,1,len-1)
      $0 = line stringToChange
   }
   else {
      $0 = stringToChange
      if (madechg) ++changes
   }
```

```
# put changed line in array for display
if (madechg)
    changedLines[changes] = ">" $0

# create substring so we can try to match other occurrences
len = len+RSTART + RLENGTH
part1 = substr($0,1,len-1)
part2 = substr($0,len)
# calls itself to see if misspelling is found in remaining part
 make_change(part2,len)

} # end of if

} # end of make_change()
```

If the misspelled word is not found in the current input line, nothing is done. If it is found, this function shows the line containing the misspelling and asks the user if it should be corrected. Underneath the display of the current line is a row of carets that indicates the misspelled word.

```
Two other utlitities that are found on the UNIX system
         ^^^^^^^^^^
```

The current input line is copied to **printstring** because it is necessary to change the line for display purposes. If the line contains any tabs, the tab in this copy of the line is temporarily replaced by a single space. This solves a problem of aligning the carets when tabs were present. (A tab counts as a single character when determining the length of a line but actually occupies greater space when displayed, usually five to eight characters long.)

After displaying the line, the function prompts the user to enter a correction. It then follows up by displaying what the user has entered and asks for confirmation. If the correction is approved, the **sub** function is called to make the change. If not approved, the user is given another chance to enter the correct word.

Remember that the **sub** function only changes the first occurrence on a line. The gsub function changes all occurrences on a line, but we want to allow the user to confirm *each* change. Therefore, we have to try to match the misspelled word against the remaining part of the line. And we have to be able to match the next occurrence regardless of whether or not the first occurrence was changed.

To do this, **make_change()** is designed as a recursive function; it calls itself to look for additional occurrences on the same line. In other words, the first time **make_change()** is called, it looks at all of $0 and matches the first misspelled word on that line. Then it splits the line into two parts—the first part contains the characters up to the end of the first occurrence and the second part contains the characters that immediately follow up to the end of the line. Then it calls itself to try and match the misspelled word in the second part. When called recursively, the function takes two arguments.

```
make_change(part2, len)
```

The first is the string to be changed, which is initially $0 when called from the main procedure but each time thereafter is the remaining part of $0. The second argument is **len** or the length of the first part, which we use to extract the substring and re-assemble the two parts at the end.

The **make_change** function also collects an array of lines that were changed.

```
# put changed line in array for display
        if (madechg)
                changedLines[changes] = ">" $0
```

The variable **madechg** will have a value if the **sub** function was successful. "$0" (the two parts have been rejoined) is assigned to an element of the array. When all of the lines of the document have been read, the main procedure loops through this array to display all the changed lines. Then it calls the **confirm_changes** function to ask if these changes should be saved. It copies the temporary output file over the temporary input file, keeping intact the corrections made for the current misspelled word.

If a user decides to make a "Global change," the **make_global_change**() function is called to do it. This function is similar to the **make_change** function. It is made easier because we can make the change globally on each line.

```
# make_global_change --
#       prompt user to correct misspelling
#       for all lines globally.
#               Has no arguments
# Assumes that misspelling is defined.

function make_global_change(    newspelling, OKmakechange, changes)\
 {

# prompt user to correct misspelled word
   printf "Globally change to:"
   getline newspelling <"-"

# carriage return falls through
# if there is an answer, confirm
   while (newspelling && ! OKmakechange) {
       printf ("Globally change %s to %s? (y/n):", misspelling,\
               newspelling)
       getline OKmakechange <"-"
   # test response and make change
       if (OKmakechange ~ /[yY](es)*/ ) {
       # open file, read all lines
```

```
        while( getline < spellsource > 0){
        # if match is found, make change using gsub
        # and print each changed line.
            if ($0 ~ misspelling) {
                madechg = gsub(misspelling, newspelling)
                print ">", $0
                changes += 1   # counter for line changes
            }
        # write all lines to temp output file
            print > spellout
        } # end of while loop for reading file

    # close temporary files
        close(spellout)
        close(spellsource)
    # report the number of changes
        printf ("%d lines changed. ", changes)
    # function to confirm before saving changes
        confirm_changes()
    } # end of if (OKmakechange ~ y)

# if correction not confirmed,  prompt for new word
    else if ( OKmakechange ~ /[nN]o*/ ){
        printf "Globally change to:"
        getline newspelling <"-"
        OKmakechange = ""
    }

    } # end of while loop for prompting user for correction

} # end of make_global_change()
```

This function prompts the user to enter a correction. A **while** loop is set up to read all the lines of the document and apply the **gsub** function to make the changes. The main difference is that all the changes are made at once—the user is not prompted to confirm them. When all lines have been read, the function displays the lines that were changed and calls **confirm_changes** to get the user to approve this batch of changes before saving them.

The **confirm_changes** function is a routine called to get approval of the changes made when the **make_change** or **make_global_change** function is called.

```
# confirm_changes --
#       confirm before saving changes

function confirm_changes(  savechanges) {
# prompt to confirm saving changes
    while (! savechanges ) {
        printf ("Save changes? (y/n)")
        getline savechanges <"-"
    }
```

```
# if confirmed, mv output to input
   if (savechanges ~ /[yY](es)*/)
      system("mv " spellout " " spellsource)
}
```

The reason for creating this function is to prevent the duplication of code. Its purpose is simply to require the user to acknowledge the changes before replacing the old version of the document file (**spellsource**) with the new version (**spellout**).

The spellcheck Shell Script

To make it easy to invoke this awk script, we create the **spellcheck** shell script (say *that* 3 times fast). It contains the following lines:

```
AWKLIB=/user/awklib
nawk -f $AWKLIB/spellcheck.awk $*
```

This script sets up a shell variable **AWKLIB** that specifies the location of the **spellcheck.awk** script. The symbol "$*" expands to all command line parameters following the name of the script. These parameters are then available to awk.

One of the things that is interesting about this spell checker is how little is done in the shell script.* All of the work is done in the awk programming language, including executing ten UNIX commands. I'm using a consistent syntax and the same constructs by doing it all in awk. When you have to do some of your work in the shell and some in awk, it can get confusing. For instance, you have to remember the differences in the syntax of **if** conditionals and how to reference variables. The new version of awk provides a true alternative to the shell for executing commands and interacting with a user.

The full listing for **spellcheck.awk** is found in Appendix C, *Supplement for Chapter 11*.

---

*UNIX Text Processing (Dougherty and O'Reilly, Howard W. Sams, 1987) presents a sed-based spell checker that relies heavily upon the shell. It is interesting to compare the two versions.

Generating a Formatted Index

The process of generating an index usually involves three steps:

1. Code the index entries in the document.

2. Format the document, producing index entries with page numbers.

3. Process the index entries to sort them, combining entries that differ only in page number, and then preparing the formatted index.

This process remains pretty much the same whether using **troff**, other coded batch formatters, or a WYSIWYG formatter such as *Frame*, although the steps are not as clearly separated with the latter. However, I will be describing how we use **troff** to generate an index such as the one for this book.

We code the index using the following macros:

Macro	Description
.XX	Produces general index entries.
.XN	Creates "see" or "see also" cross references.
.XB	Creates bold page entry indicating primary reference.
.XS	Begins range of pages for entry.
.XE	Ends range of pages for entry.

The quoted argument can take one of several forms, indicating primary, secondary or tertiary keys:

"*primary*[:*secondary*[;*tertiary*]]"

A colon is used as the separator between the primary and secondary keys. To support an earlier coding convention, the first comma is interpreted as the separator if no colon is used. A semicolon indicates the presence of a tertiary key. The page number is always associated with the last key.

Here is an entry with only a primary key:

```
.XX "XView"
```

The next two entries specify a secondary key:

```
.XX "XView: reserved names"
.XX "XView, packages"
```

The most complex entries contain tertiary keys:

```
.XX "XView: objects; list"
.XX "XView: objects; hierarchy of"
```

Finally, there are two types of cross references:

```
.XN "error recovery: (see error handling)"
.XX "mh mailer: (see also xmh mailer)"
```

The "see" entry refers a person to another index entry. The "see also" is typically used when there are entries for, in this case, "mh mailer," but there is relevant information catalogued under another name. Only "see" entries do not have page numbers associated with them.

When the document is processed by **troff**, the following index entries are produced with page numbers.

```
XView            42
XView: reserved names     43
XView, packages 43
XView: objects; list of 43
XView: objects; hierarchy of44
XView, packages 45
error recovery: (See error handling)
mh mailer: (see also xmh mailer)46
```

These entries serve as input to the indexing program. Each entry consists of the key and a page number. In other words, the entry is divided into two parts and the first part, the key, can also be divided into three parts. When these entries are processed by the indexing program and the output is formatted, the entries for "XView" are combined as follows:

```
XView, 42
                    objects; hierarchy of, 44;
                       list of, 43
                    packages, 43,45
                    reserved names, 43
```

To accomplish this, the indexing program must:

1. Sort the index by key and page number.
2. Merge entries that differ only in the page number.
3. Merge entries that have the same primary and/or secondary keys.
4. Look for consecutive page numbers and combine as a range.
5. Prepare the index in a format for display on screen or for printing.

This is what the index program does if you are processing the index entries for a single book. It also allows you to create a master index, an overall index for a set of volumes. To do that, an awk script appends either a roman numeral or an abbreviation after the page number. Each file then contains the entries for a particular book and those entries are uniquely identified. If we chose to use roman numerals to identify the volume, then the above entries would be changed to:

```
XView       42:I
XView: reserved names    43:I
XView: objects; list of 43:I
```

With multi-volume entries, the final index that is generated might look like the following:

```
XView, I:42; II:55,69,75
    objects; hierarchy of, I:44;
         list of, I:43; II: 56
    packages, I:43,45
    reserved names, I:43
```

For now, it's only important to recognize that the index entry used as input to the awk program can have a page number or a page number followed by a volume identifier.

The masterindex* Program

Because of the length and complexity of this indexing application, my description presents the larger structure of the program. Use the comments in the program itself to understand what is happening in the program line-by-line.

After describing each of the program modules, there is a final section that discusses a few remaining details. For the most part, these are code fragments that deal with nitty-gritty, input-related problems that had to be solved along the way. The shell script **masterindex**† allows the user to specify a number of different command-line options to specify what kind of index to make and it invokes the

---

*The origins of this indexing program are traced back to a copy of an indexing program written in awk by Steve Talbott. I learned this program by taking it apart and made some changes to it to support consecutive page numbering in addition to section-page numbering. That was the program I described in *UNIX Text Processing*. Knowing that program, I wrote an indexing program that could deal with index entries produced by Microsoft Word and generate an index using section-page numbering. Later, we needed a master index for several books in our X Window System Series. I took it as an opportunity to rethink our indexing program, and rewrite it using nawk, so that it supports both single book and multiple-book indices. *The AWK Programming Language* contains an example of an index program, which is smaller than the one shown here and might be a place to start if you find this one too complicated. It does not, however, deal with keys.

†This shell script along with the documentation for the program are presented in Appendix C. You might want to first read the documentation to get an understanding of using the program.

necessary awk programs to do the job. The operations of the **masterindex** program can be broken into five separate programs or modules that form a single pipe.

```
input.idx | sort | pagenums.idx | combine.idx | format.idx
```

All but one of the programs are written using nawk. For sorting the entries, we rely upon **sort**, a standard UNIX utility. Here's a brief summary of what each of these programs do:

input.idx   Standardizes the format of entries as well as rotate entries.

sort   Sorts entries by key, volume and page number.

pagenums.idx   Merges entries with same key, creating a list of page numbers.

combine.idx   Combines consecutive page numbers into a range.

format.idx   Prepares the formatted index for the screen or processing by **troff**.

We will discuss each of these steps in a separate section.

Standardizing Input

This **input.idx** script looks for different types of entries and standardizes them for easier processing by subsequent programs. Additionally, it automatically rotates index entries containing a tilde (˜). (See "Rotating Two Parts" in the "Details" section.)

The input to the **input.idx** program consists of two tab-separated fields, as described earlier. The program produces output records with three colon-separated fields. The first field contains the primary key; the second field contains the secondary and tertiary keys, if defined; and the third field contains the page number. Here's the code for **input.idx** program:

```
#!/work/bin/nawk -f
# ---------------------------------------------------
# input.idx -- standardize input before sorting
# Author:  Dale Dougherty
# Version 1.1   7/10/90
#
# input is "entry" tab "page_number"
# ---------------------------------------------------
BEGIN { FS="\t"; OFS="" }

#1 Match entries that need rotating that contain a single tilde
    # $1 ˜ /˜[^˜]/  # regexp does not work and I do not know why
$1 ˜ /˜/ && $1 !˜ /˜˜/ {
    # split first field into array named subfield
    n = split($1,subfield,"˜")
```

```
        if (n == 2) {
        # print entry without "~" and then rotated
           printf("%s %s::%s\n", subfield[1], subfield[2], $2)
           printf("%s:%s:%s\n", subfield[2], subfield[1], $2)
           next
           }
        next
}# End of 1


#2 Match entries that contain two tildes
$1 ~ /~~/ {
    # replace ~~ with ~
    gsub(/~~/,"~",$1)
} # End of 2


#3  Match entries that use "::" for literal ":".
$1 ~ /::/ {
    # substitute octal value for "::"
    gsub(/::/, "\3a", $1)
}# End of 3


#4 Clean up entries
{
    # look for second colon, which might be used instead of ";"
    if (sub(/:.*:/, "&;",$1)) {
        sub(/:;/,";",$1)
    }
    # remove blank space if any after colon.
    sub(/: */,":",$1)
    # if comma is used as delimiter, convert to colon.
    if ( $1 !~ /:/ ){
    # On see also & see, try to put delimiter before "("
        if ($1 ~ /\([sS]ee/) {
            if (sub(/, *.*\(/,":&",$1))
                sub(/:, */, ":", $1)
            else
                sub(/ *\(/,":(",$1)
            }
        else{ # otherwise, just look for comma
            sub(/, */,":",$1)
        }
    }
    else
        # added to insert semicolon in "See"
        if ($1 ~ /:[^;]+ *\([sS]ee/)
            sub(/ *\(/,";(",$1)

}# End of 4


#5 match See Alsos and fix for sort at end
$1 ~ / *\([Ss]ee [Aa]lso/ {
  # add "~zz" for sort at end
  sub(/\([Ss]ee [Aa]lso/,"~zz(see also",$1)
```

```
      if ($1 ~ /:[^; ]+ *~zz/) {
          sub(/ *~zz/,"; ~zz",$1)
      }
   # if no page number
      if ($2 == "") {
          print $0 ":"
          next
      }
      else {
      # output two entries:
      # print See Also entry w/out page number
          print $1 ":"
      # remove See Also
          sub(/ *~zz\(see also.*$/,"", $1)
          sub(/;/,"", $1)
      # print as normal entry
          if ( $1 ~ /:/ )
              print $1 ":" $2
          else
              print $1 "::" $2
          next
      }
}# End of 5

#6 Process entries without page number (See entries)
(NF == 1 || $2 == "" || $1 ~ /\([sS]ee/) {
   # if a "See" entry
      if ( $1 ~ /\([sS]ee/ ) {
          print $1 ":"
      }
      else # if not a See entry, generate error
          printerr("No page number")
      next
}# End of 6

#7 If the colon is used as the delimiter
$1 ~ /:/ {
   # output entry:page
      print $1 ":" $2
      next
}# End of 7

#8  Match entries with only primary keys.
{
      print $1 "::" $2
}# End of 8

# supporting functions
```

```
#
# printerr -- print error message and current record
#      Arg: message to be displayed

function printerr ( message ) {
    # print message, record number and record
    print "ERROR:" message " (" NR ") " $0 > "/dev/tty"
}
```

This script consists of a number of pattern-matching rules to recognize different types of input. Note that an entry could match more than one rule unless the action associated with a rule calls the **next** statement.

As we describe this script, we will be referring to the rules by number. Rule 1 rotates entries containing a tilde and produces two output records. The **split()** function creates an array named **subfield** that contains the two parts of the compound entry. The two parts are printed in their original order and then swapped to created a second output record in which the secondary key becomes a primary key.

Because we are using the tilde as a special character, we must provide some way of actually entering a tilde. We have implemented the convention that two consecutive tildes are translated into a single tilde. Rule 2 deals with that case, but notice that the pattern for rule 1 makes sure that the first tilde it matches is not followed by another tilde.* The order of rules 1 and 2 in the script is significant. We can't replace "~~" with "~" until after the procedure for rotating the entry.

Rule 3 does a similar job as rule 2; it allows "::" to be used to output a literal ":" in the index. However, since we use the colon as an input delimiter throughout the input to the program, we cannot allow it to appear in an entry as finally output until the very end. Thus, we replace the sequence "::" with the colon's ASCII value in octal. (The **format.idx** program will reverse the replacement.)

Beginning with rule 4, we attempt to recognize various ways of coding entries— giving the user more flexibility. However, to make writing the remaining programs easier, we must reduce this variety to a few basic forms.

In the "basic" syntax, the primary and secondary keys are separated by a colon. The secondary and tertiary keys are separated by a semicolon. Nonetheless the program also recognizes a second colon, in place of a semicolon, as the delimiter between the secondary and tertiary keys. It also recognizes that if no colon is specified as a delimiter, then a comma can be used as the delimiter between primary and secondary keys. (In part, this was done to be compatible with an earlier program that used the comma as the delimiter.) The **sub** function looks for the

---

*For extra credit, please send me mail if you can figure out why the commented regular expression just before rule 1 does not do the job. I used the compound expression as a last resort.

first comma on the line and changes it to a colon. This rule also tries to standardize the syntax of "see" and "see also" entries. For entries that are colon-delimited, rule 4 removes blank spaces after the colon. All of the work is done using the **sub** function.

Rule 5 deals with "see also" entries. We prepend the arbitrary string "~zz" to the "see also" entries so that they will sort at the end of the list of secondary keys. The **pagenume** script, later in the pipeline, will remove "~zz" after the entries have been sorted.

Rule 6 matches entries that do not specify a page number. The only legal entry without a page number contains a "see" reference. This rule outputs "see" entries with ":" at the end to indicate an empty third field. All other entries generate an error message via the **printerr** function. This function notifies the user that a particular entry does not have a page number and will not be included in the output. This is one method of standardizing input—throwing out what you can't interpret properly. However, it is critical to notify the user so that he or she can correct the entry.

Rule 7 outputs entries that contain the colon-delimiter. Its action uses **next** to avoid reaching rule 8.

Finally, rule 8 matches entries that contain only a primary key. In other words, there is no delimiter. We output "::" to indicate an empty second field.

Here's a portion of the contents of our *test* file. We'll be using it to generate examples in this section.

```
% cat test
XView: programs; initialization 45
XV_INIT_ARGS~macro        46
Xv_object~type    49
Xv_singlecolor~type        80
graphics: (see also server image)
graphics, XView model    83
X Window System: events 84
graphics, CANVAS_X_PAINT_WINDOW 86
X Window System, X Window ID for paint window    87
toolkit (See X Window System).
graphics: (see also server image)
Xlib, repainting canvas 88
Xlib.h~header file    89
```

When we run this file through **input.idx**, it produces:

```
% input.idx test
XView:programs; initialization:45
XV_INIT_ARGS macro::46
macro:XV_INIT_ARGS:46
Xv_object type::49
```

```
type:Xv_object:49
Xv_singlecolor type::80
type:Xv_singlecolor:80
graphics:~zz(see also server image):
graphics:XView model:83
X Window System:events:84
graphics:CANVAS_X_PAINT_WINDOW:86
X Window System:X Window ID for paint window:87
graphics:~zz(see also server image):
Xlib:repainting canvas:88
Xlib.h header file::89
header file:Xlib.h:89
```

Each entry now consists of three colon-separated fields. In the sample output, you can find examples of entries with only a primary key, those with primary and secondary keys, and those with primary, secondary, and tertiary keys. You can also find examples of rotated entries, duplicate entries, and "see also" entries.

The only difference in this output for multi-volume entries is that each entry would have a fourth field that contains the volume identifier.

Sorting the Entries

Now the output produced by **input.idx** is ready to be sorted. The easiest way to sort the entries is to use the standard UNIX **sort** program rather than write a custom script. In addition to sorting the entries, we want to remove any duplicates and for this task we use the **uniq** program. Here's the command line we use:

```
sort -bdf -t: +0 -1 +1 -2 +3 -4 +2n -3n | uniq
```

As you can see, we use a number of options with the **sort** command. The first option, **-b**, specifies that leading blanks be ignored. The **-d** option specifies a dictionary sort in which symbols and special characters are ignored. **-f** specifies that lowercase and uppercase letters are to be *folded* together; in other words, they are to be treated as the same character for purposes of the sort. The next argument is perhaps the most important; **-t:** tells the program to use a colon as a field delimiter for sort keys. The + options that follow specify the number of fields to skip from the beginning of the line. Therefore, to specify the first field as the primary sort key, we use "+0." Similarly, the - options specify the end of a sort key. "-1" specifies that the primary sort key ends at the first field, or the beginning of the second field. The second sort field is the secondary key. The fourth field ("+3") if it exists, contains the volume number. The last key to sort is the page number; this requires a numeric sort (if we did not tell sort that this key consists of numbers, then the number 1 would be followed by 10, instead of 2). Notice that we sort page numbers after sorting the volume numbers. Thus, all the page numbers for Volume I are sorted in order before the page numbers before Volume II. Finally, we pipe the output to **uniq** to remove identical entries. Processing the output from **input.idx**, the **sort** command produces:

```
X Window System:Xlib:6
XFontStruct structure::317
Xlib::6
Xlib:repainting canvas:88
Xlib.h header file::89
Xlib.h header file::294
Xv_Font type::310
XView::18
XView:about:3
XView:about:7
XView:about:10
XView:as object-oriented system:17
XView:compiling programs:41
```

Handling Page Numbers

The **pagenums.idx** program looks for entries that differ only in page number and creates a list of page numbers for a single entry.

The input to this program is four colon-separated fields:

PRIMARY:SECONDARY:PAGE:VOLUME

The fourth is optional. For now, we consider only the index for a single book, in which there are no volume numbers. Remember that the entries are now sorted.

The heart of this program compares the current entry to the previous one and determines what to output. The conditionals that implement the comparison can be extracted and expressed in pseudocode as follows:

```
PRIMARY = $1
SECONDARY = $2
PAGE = $3

if (PRIMARY == prevPRIMARY)
     if (SECONDARY == prevSECONDARY)
          print PAGE
     else
          print PRIMARY:SECONDARY:PAGE
else
     print PRIMARY:SECONDARY:PAGE

prevPRIMARY = PRIMARY
prevSECONDARY = SECONDARY
```

Let's see how this code handles a series of entries, beginning with:

```
XView::18
```

The primary key does not match the previous primary key, so the line is output as is:

```
XView::18
```

The next entry is:

```
XView:about:3
```

When we compare the primary key of this entry to the previous one, they are the same. When we compare secondary keys, they differ and we output the record as is:

```
XView:about:3
```

The next entry is:

```
XView:about:7
```

Because both the primary and secondary keys match the keys of the previous entry, we simply output the page number. (The **printf** function is used instead of **print** so that there is no automatic newline.) This page number is appended to the previous entry so that it looks like this:

```
XView:about:3,7
```

The next entry also matches both keys:

```
XView:about:10
```

Again, only the page number is output so that entry now looks like:

```
XView:about:3,7,10
```

In this way, three entries that differ only in page number are combined into a single entry.

The full script adds an additional test to see if the volume identifier matches. Here's the full **pagenums.idx** script:

```
#!/work/bin/nawk -f
# ----------------------------------------------------
# pagenums.idx -- collect pages for common entries
# Author:  Dale Dougherty
# Version 1.1   7/10/90
#
# input should be PRIMARY:SECONDARY:PAGE:VOLUME
# ----------------------------------------------------

BEGIN { FS=":"; OFS=""}
```

```
# main routine -- apply to all input lines
{
    # assign fields to variables
    PRIMARY = $1
    SECONDARY = $2
    PAGE = $3
    VOLUME = $4

    # check for a see also and collect it in array
    if (SECONDARY ~ /\([Ss]ee [Aa]lso/) {
    # create tmp copy & remove "~zz" from copy
        tmpSecondary = SECONDARY
        sub(/~zz\([Ss]ee [Aa]lso */,"",tmpSecondary)
        sub(/\) */,"",tmpSecondary)
    # remove secondary key along with "~zz"
        sub(/^.*~zz\([Ss]ee [Aa]lso */,"",SECONDARY)
        sub(/\) */,"",SECONDARY)
    # assign to next element of seeAlsoList
        seeAlsoList[++eachSeeAlso] = SECONDARY "; "
        prevPrimary = PRIMARY
    # assign copy to previous secondary key
        prevSecondary = tmpSecondary
        next
    } # end test for see also

    # Conditionals to compare keys of current record to previous
    #   record.  If Primary and Secondary keys are the same, only
    #   the page number is printed.

    # test to see if each PRIMARY key matches previous key
    if (PRIMARY == prevPrimary) {
    # test to see if each SECONDARY key matches previous key
        if (SECONDARY == prevSecondary)
        # test to see if VOLUME matches;
        # print only VOLUME:PAGE
            if (VOLUME == prevVolume)
                printf (",%s", PAGE)
            else{
                printf ("; ")
                volpage(VOLUME, PAGE)
            }
        else{
        # if array of see alsos, output them now
            if (eachSeeAlso) outputSeeAlso(2)
        # print PRIMARY:SECONDARY:VOLUME:PAGE
            printf ("\n%s:%s:", PRIMARY, SECONDARY)
            volpage(VOLUME, PAGE)
        }
    } # end of test for PRIMARY == prev
    else { # PRIMARY != prev
        # if we have an array of see alsos, output them now
        if (eachSeeAlso) outputSeeAlso(1)
```

```
            if (NR != 1)
                printf ("\n")
            if (NF == 1){
                printf ("%s:", $0)
                }
            else{
                printf ("%s:%s:", PRIMARY, SECONDARY)
                volpage(VOLUME, PAGE)
                }
        }
    prevPrimary = PRIMARY
    prevSecondary = SECONDARY
    prevVolume = VOLUME

} # end of main routine

# at end, print newline
END {
    # in case last entry has "see also"
if (eachSeeAlso) outputSeeAlso(1)
printf("\n")
}

    # outputSeeAlso function -- list elements of seeAlsoList
function outputSeeAlso(LEVEL) {
    # LEVEL - indicates which key we need to output
    if (LEVEL == 1)
        printf ("\n%s:(See also ", prevPrimary)
    else {
        sub(/;.*$/,"",prevSecondary)
        printf ("\n%s:%s; (See also ", prevPrimary, prevSecondary)
    }
    sub(/; $/,".):", seeAlsoList[eachSeeAlso])
    for (i = 1; i <= eachSeeAlso; ++i)
        printf ("%s", seeAlsoList[i])
    eachSeeAlso=0
}
    # volpage function -- determine whether to print volume info
    #     two args: volume & page

function volpage(v,p) {

    # if VOLUME is empty then print PAGE only
    if (v == "" )
        printf ("%s", p)
    else
    # otherwise print VOLUME^PAGE
        printf ("%s^%s",v, p)
}
```

Remember, first of all, that the input to the program is sorted by its keys. The page numbers are also in order, such that an entry for "graphics" on page 7 appears in the input before one on page 10. Similarly, entries for Volume I appear in the input before Volume II. Therefore, this program need do no sorting; it simply compares the keys and if they are the same, appends the page number to a list. In this way, the entries are reduced.

This script also handles "see also" entries. Since the records are now sorted, we can remove the special sorting sequence "~zz." We also handle the case where we might encounter consecutive "see also" entries. We don't want to output:

```
Toolkit (see also Xt) (See also XView) (See also Motif).
```

Instead we'd like to combine them into a list such that they appear as:

```
Toolkit (see also Xt; XView; Motif)
```

To do that, we create an array named **seeAlsoList**. From **SECONDARY**, we remove the parentheses, the secondary key if it exists and the "see also" and then assign it to an element of **seeAlsoList**. We make a copy of **SECONDARY** with the secondary key and assign it to **prevSecondary** for making comparisons to the next entry.

The function **outputSeeAlso** is called to read all the elements of the array and print them. The function **volpage** is also simple and determines whether or not we need to output a volume number. Both of these functions are called from more than one place in the code, so the main reason for defining them as functions is to reduce duplication.

Here's an example of what it produces for a single-book index:

```
X Window System:Xlib:6
XFontStruct structure::317
Xlib::6
Xlib:repainting canvas:88
Xlib.h header file::89,294
Xv_Font type::310
XView::18
XView:about:3,7,10
XView:as object-oriented system:17
```

Here's an example of what it produces for a master index:

```
reserved names:table of:I^43
Xt:example of programming interface:I^44,65
Xt:objects; list of:I^43,58; II^40
Xt:packages:I^43,61; II^42
Xt:programs; initialization:I^45
Xt:reserved names:I^43,58
Xt:reserved prefixes:I^43,58
Xt:types:I^43,54,61
```

The "^" is used as a temporary delimiter between the volume number and the list of page numbers.

Merging Entries with the Same Keys

The **pagenums.idx** program reduced entries that were the same except for the page number. Now we are going to process entries that share the same primary key. We also want to look for consecutive page numbers and combine them in ranges.

The **combine.idx** is quite similar to the **pagenums.idx** script, making another pass through the index, comparing entries with the same primary key. The following pseudocode abstracts this comparison similar to **pagenums.idx**. (To make this discussion easier, we will omit tertiary keys and show how to compare primary and secondary keys.) After the entries are processed by **pagenums.idx**, no two entries exist which share the same primary and secondary keys. Therefore, we don't have to compare secondary keys.

```
PRIMARY = $1
SECONDARY = $2
PAGE = $3

if (PRIMARY == prevPRIMARY)
     print :SECONDARY:
else
     print PRIMARY:SECONDARY

prevPRIMARY = PRIMARY
prevSECONDARY = SECONDARY
```

If the primary keys match, we output only the secondary key. For instance, if there are three entries:

```
XView:18
XView:about:3, 7, 10
XView:as object-oriented system:17
```

they will be output as:

```
XView:18
:about:3, 7, 10
:as object-oriented system:17
```

We drop the primary key when it is the same. The actual code is a little more difficult because there are tertiary keys. We have to test primary and secondary keys to see if they are unique or the same, but we don't have to test tertiary keys. (We only need to know that they are there.)

You no doubt noticed that the above pseudocode does not output page numbers. The second role of this script is to examine page numbers and combine a list of consecutive numbers. The page numbers are a comma-separated list that can be loaded into an array, using the **split** function.

To see if numbers are consecutive, we loop through the array comparing each element to 1+ the previous element.

```
eachpage[j-1]+1 == eachpage[j]
```

In other words, if adding 1 to the previous element produces the current element, then they are consecutive. The previous element becomes the first page number in the range and the current element becomes the last page in the range. This is done within a **while** loop until the conditional is not true, and the page numbers are not consecutive. Then we output the first page number and the last page number separated by a hyphen:

```
23-25
```

The actual code looks more complicated than this because it is called from a function that must recognize volume and page number pairs. It has to first split the volume from the list of page numbers and then it can call the function (**rangeOfPages**) to process the list of numbers.

The full listing of **combine.idx** follows:

```
#!/work/bin/nawk -f
# ---------------------------------------------------
# combine.idx -- merge keys with same PRIMARY key
#       and combine consecutive page numbers
# Author:  Dale Dougherty
# Version 1.1   7/10/90
#
# input should be PRIMARY:SECONDARY:PAGELIST
# ---------------------------------------------------

BEGIN   { FS = ":"; OFS=""}

# main routine -- applies to all input lines
#   It compares the keys and merges the duplicates.
{
    # assign first field
    PRIMARY=$1
    # split second field, getting SEC and TERT keys.
    sizeOfArray = split ($2, array, ";")
    SECONDARY=array[1]
    TERTIARY=array[2]
    # test that tertiary key exists
    if (sizeOfArray > 1) {
    # tertiary key exists
       isTertiary=1
    # two cases where ";" might turn up
    # check SEC key for list of "see also"
       if (SECONDARY ~ /\([sS]ee also/){
           SECONDARY = $2
           isTertiary=0
       }
```

```
            # check TERT key for "see also"
               if (TERTIARY ~ /\([sS]ee also/){
                  TERTIARY = substr($2,(index($2,";")+1))
               }
            }
         else # tertiary key does not exist
               isTertiary=0
         # assign third field
         PAGELIST = $3

         # Conditional to compare primary key of this entry to that of
         #  of previous entry. Then compare secondary keys.  This
         #  determines which non-duplicate keys to output.

         if (PRIMARY == prevPrimary){
            if (isTertiary && SECONDARY == prevSecondary)
               printf (";\n::%s", TERTIARY)
            else
               if (isTertiary)
                  printf ("\n:%s; %s", SECONDARY, TERTIARY)
               else
                  printf ("\n:%s", SECONDARY)
         }
         else {
            if (NR != 1)
               printf ("\n")
            if ($2 != "")
               printf ("%s:%s", PRIMARY, $2)
            else
               printf ("%s", PRIMARY)

            prevPrimary = PRIMARY
         }
   prevSecondary = SECONDARY
   } # end of main procedure

   # routine for "See" entries (primary key only)
   NF == 1 { printf ("\n") }

   # routine for all other entries
   #   It handles output of the page number.

   NF > 1  {
      if (PAGELIST)
      # calls function numrange to look for
         #  consecutive page numbers.
         printf (":%s", numrange(PAGELIST))
      else
         if (! isTertiary || (TERTIARY && SECONDARY))  printf (":")

   } # end of NF > 1

   # END procedure outputs newline
```

```
END {
printf ("\n") }

# Supporting Functions

# numrange -- read list of Volume^Page numbers, detach Volume
#       from Page for each Volume and call rangeOfPages
#       to combine consecutive page numbers in the list.
#    PAGE = volumes separated by semicolons; volume and page
#       separated by ^.

function numrange(PAGE,      listOfPages, sizeOfArray) {

  # Split up list by volume.
     sizeOfArray = split (PAGE, howManyVolumes,";")
  # Check to see if more than 1 volume.
     if ( sizeOfArray > 1)

       # if more than 1 volume, loop through list
       for (i = 1; i <= sizeOfArray; ++i){
         # for each Volume^Page element, detach Volume
         # and call rangeOfPages function on Page to separate page
         # numbers and compare to find consecutive numbers.
           if (split (howManyVolumes[i],volPage,"^") == 2 )
             listOfPages=volPage[1] "^" rangeOfPages(volPage[2])
         # collect output in listOfPages
         if (i == 1)
            result=listOfPages
         else {
            result=result ";" listOfPages
         }
     } # end for loop

       else { # not more than 1 volume

       # check for single volume index with volume number
       #  if so, detach volume number.
       #  Both call split page on the list of page numbers.
           if (split (PAGE,volPage,"^") == 2 )
       # if Volume^Page, detach volume and then call rangeOfPages
          listOfPages=volPage[1] "^" rangeOfPages(volPage[2])
       else # No volume number involved
          listOfPages=rangeOfPages(volPage[1])
       result=listOfPages
       } # end of else

return result   # Volume^Page list

} # End of numrange function

# rangeOfPages -- read list of comma-separated page numbers,
#       load them into an array, and compare each one
#       to the next, looking for consecutive numbers.
```

```
#    PAGENUMBERS = comma-separated list of page numbers

function rangeOfPages (PAGENUMBERS, pagesAll,sizeOfArray,pages,
                          listOfPages,d,p,j) {
    # close-up space on troff-generated ranges
    gsub(/ - /,",-",PAGENUMBERS)

    # split list up into eachpage array.
    sizeOfArray = split (PAGENUMBERS, eachpage, ",")
    # if more than 1 page number
    if (sizeOfArray > 1){
    # for each page number, compare it to previous number + 1
        p=0  # flag indicates assignment to pagesAll
    # for loop starts at 2
        for (j=2; j-1 <= sizeOfArray; ++j){
    # start by saving first page in sequence (firstpage)
    # and loop until we find last page (lastpage)
            firstpage=eachpage[j-1]
            d=0  # flag indicates consecutive numbers found
    # loop while page numbers are consecutive
            while ((eachpage[j-1]+1) == eachpage[j] ||
                        eachpage[j] ~/^-/) {
    # remove "-" from troff-generated range
                if (eachpage[j] ~ /^-/){
                    sub(/^-/,"",eachpage[j])
                    }
                lastpage=eachpage[j]
    # increment counters
                ++d
                ++j
            } # end of while loop
    # use values of firstpage and lastpage to make range.
            if (d >= 1){
    # there is a range
                pages=firstpage "-" lastpage
            }
            else # no range; only read firstpage
                pages=firstpage
    # assign range to pagesAll
            if (p == 0){
                pagesAll=pages
                p=1
                }
            else {
                pagesAll=pagesAll "," pages
                }
        }# end of for loop

    # assign pagesAll to listofPages
        listOfPages = pagesAll

    } # end of sizeOfArray > 1
```

```
      else # only one page
         listOfPages = PAGENUMBERS

      # remove space following comma
      gsub(/,/, ", ", listOfPages)
      # return changed list of page numbers
      return listOfPages
   } # End of rangeOfPages function
```

This script consists of minimal **BEGIN** and **END** procedures. The main routine does the work of comparing primary and secondary keys. The first part of this routine assigns the fields to variables. The second field contains the secondary and tertiary keys and we use **split** to separate them. Then we test that there is a tertiary key and set the flag **isTertiary** to either 1 or 0.

The next part of the main procedure contains the conditional expressions that look for identical keys. As we said in our discussion of the pseudocode for this part of the program, entries with wholly identical keys have already been removed by the **pagenums.idx**.

The conditionals in this procedure determine what keys to output based on whether or not it is unique. If the primary key is unique, it is output, along with the rest of the entry. If the primary key matches the previous key, we compare secondary keys. If the secondary key is unique, then it is output, along with the rest of the entry. If the primary key matches the previous primary key, and the secondary key matches the previous primary key, then the tertiary key must be unique. Then we only output the tertiary key, leaving the primary and secondary keys blank. The different forms are shown below:

> primary
> primary:secondary
> :secondary
> :secondary:tertiary
> ::tertiary
> primary:secondary:tertiary

The main procedure is followed by two additional routines. The first of them is executed only when **NF** equals one. It deals with the first of the forms on the list above. That is, there is no page number so we must output a newline to finish the entry.

The second procedure deals with all entries that have page numbers. This is the procedure where we call a function to take apart the list of page numbers and look for consecutive pages. It calls the **numrange** function whose main purpose is to deal with a multi-volume index where a list of page numbers might look like:

```
I^35,55; II^200
```

This function calls **split** using a semicolon delimiter to separate each volume. Then we call **split** using a "^" delimiter to detach the volume number from the list of page numbers. Once we have the list of pages, we call a second function **rangeOfPages** to look for consecutive numbers. On a single book index, such as the sample shown in this chapter, the **numrange** function really does nothing but call **rangeOfPages**. We discussed the meat of the **rangeOfPages** function earlier. The **eachpage** array is created and a **while** loop is used to go through the array comparing an element to the one previous. This function returns the list of pages.

Sample output from this program follows:

```
Xlib:6
:repainting canvas:88
Xlib.h header file:89, 294
Xv_Font type:310
XView:18
:about:3, 7, 10
:as object-oriented system:17
:compiling programs:41
:concept of windows differs from X:25
:data types;  table of:20
:example of programming interface:44
:frames and subframes:26
:generic functions:21
:Generic Object:18, 24
:libraries:42
:notification:10, 35
:objects:23-24;
:: table of:20;
:: list of:43
:packages:18, 43
:programmer's model:17-23
:programming interface:41
:programs;  initialization:45
:reserved names:43
:reserved prefixes:43
:structure of applications:41
:subwindows:28
:types:43
:window objects:25
```

In particular, notice the entry for "objects" under "XView." This is an example of a secondary key with multiple tertiary keys. It is also an example of an entry with a consecutive page range.

Formatting the Index

The previous scripts have done nearly all of the the processing such that the list of entries are in good order. The **format.idx** script, probably the easiest of the scripts, reads the list of entries and generates a report in two different formats, one for display on a terminal screen and one to send to **troff** for printing on a laser printer. Perhaps the only difficulty is that we output the entries grouped by each letter of the alphabet.

A command-line argument sets the variable **FMT** that determines which of the two output formats is to be used.

Here's the full listing for **format.idx**:

```
#!/work/bin/nawk -f
# ---------------------------------------------------
# format.idx -- prepare formatted index
# Author:  Dale Dougherty
# Version 1.1   7/10/90
#
# input should be PRIMARY:SECONDARY:PAGE:VOLUME
# Args:  FMT = 0 (default) format for screen
#        FMT = 1 output with troff macros
#        MACDIR = pathname of index troff macro file
# ---------------------------------------------------
BEGIN {    FS=":"
       upper="ABCDEFGHIJKLMNOPQRSTUVWXYZ"
       lower="abcdefghijklmnopqrstuvwxyz"
}


# Output initial macros if troff FMT
NR == 1 && FMT == 1 {
       if (MACDIR)
          printf (".so %s/indexmacs\n", MACDIR)
       else
          printf (".so indexmacs\n")
       printf (".Se \"\" \"Index\"\n")
       printf (".XC\n")
} # end of NR == 1


# main routine - apply to all lines
# determine which fields to output
{
    # convert octal colon to "literal" colon
    # make sub for each field, not $0, so that fields are not parsed
    gsub(/\3a/,":",$1)
    gsub(/\3a/,":",$2)
    gsub(/\3a/,":",$3)

    # assign field to variables
```

```
        PRIMARY = $1
        SECONDARY = $2
        TERTIARY = ""
        PAGE = $3
        if (NF == 2) {
            SECONDARY = ""
            PAGE = $2
        }
    # Look for empty fields to determine what to output
    if (! PRIMARY) {
    if (! SECONDARY) {
        TERTIARY = $3
        PAGE = $4
        if (FMT == 1)
            printf (".XF 3 \"%s", TERTIARY)
        else
            printf ("   %s", TERTIARY)
    }
    else
    if (FMT == 1)
        printf (".XF 2 \"%s", SECONDARY)
    else
        printf ("   %s", SECONDARY)
}
else { # if primary entry exists

    # extract first char of primary entry
    firstChar = substr($1,1,1)
    # see if it is in lower string.
    char = index(lower,firstChar)
    # char is an index to lower or upper letter
    if (char == 0)
    # if char not found, see if it is upper
        char = index(upper,firstChar)
        if ( char == 0 )
            char = prevChar
    # if new char, then start group for new letter of alphabet
    if (char != prevChar)
        {
        if (FMT == 1)
            printf(".XF A \"%s\"\n", substr(upper,char,1))
        else
            printf("\n\t\t%s\n", substr(upper,char,1))
        prevChar = char
        }
    # now output primary and secondary entry
    if (FMT == 1)
        if (SECONDARY)
            printf (".XF 1 \"%s\" \"%s", PRIMARY, SECONDARY)
        else
            printf (".XF 1 \"%s\" \"", PRIMARY)
    else
        if (SECONDARY)
```

```
            printf ("%s, %s", PRIMARY, SECONDARY)
        else
            printf ("%s", PRIMARY)
}

# if page number, call pageChg to replace "^" with ":"
#   for multi-volume page lists.
if (PAGE) {
    if (FMT == 1) {
        # added to omit comma after bold entry
        if (! SECONDARY && ! TERTIARY)
            printf ("%s\"", pageChg(PAGE))
        else
            printf (", %s\"", pageChg(PAGE))
    }
    else
        printf (", %s", pageChg(PAGE))
}
else if (FMT == 1) printf("\"")

printf ("\n")

} # End of main routine

# Supporting function

# pageChg -- convert "^" to ":" in list of volume^page
#   Arg: pagelist -- list of numbers

function pageChg(pagelist){
    gsub(/\^/,":",pagelist)
    if (FMT == 1) {
        gsub(/[1-9]+\*/,"\\fB&\\fP", pagelist)
        gsub(/\*/,"",pagelist)
    }
    return pagelist
}# End of pageChg function
```

The **BEGIN** procedure defines the field separator and the strings **upper** and **lower**. The next procedure is one that outputs the name of the file that contains the **troff** index macro definitions. The name of the macro directory can be set from the command line as the second argument.

The main procedure begins by converting the "hidden" colon to a literal colon. Note that we apply the **sub** function to each field rather than the entire line because doing the latter would cause the line to be re-evaluated and the current order of fields would be disturbed.

Next we assign the fields to variables and then test to see whether the field is empty. If the primary key is not defined, then we see if the secondary key is defined. If it is, we output it. If it is not, then we output a tertiary key. If the primary key is defined, then we extract the first character of it and then see if we find it in the **lower** string.

```
firstChar = substr($1,1,1)

char = index(lower,firstChar)
```

The **char** variable holds the position of the letter in the string. If this number is greater than 1, then we also have an index into the **upper** string. We compare each entry and while **char** and **prevChar** are the same, the current letter of the alphabet is unchanged. Once they differ, first we check for the letter in the **upper** string. If **char** is a new letter, we output a centered string that identifies that letter of the alphabet.

Then we look at outputting the primary and secondary entries. Finally, the list of page numbers is output, after calling the **pageChg** function to replace the "^" in volume-page references to a colon.

Sample screen output produced by **format.idx** is shown below:

```
     X
   X Protocol, 6
   X Window System, events, 84
      extensibility, 9
      interclient communications, 9
      overview, 3
      protocol, 6
      role of window manager, 9
      server and client relationship, 5
      software hierarchy, 6
      toolkits, 7
      X Window ID for paint window, 87
      Xlib, 6
   XFontStruct structure, 317
   Xlib, 6
      repainting canvas, 88
   Xlib.h header file, 89, 294
   Xv_Font type, 310
   XView, 18
      about, 3, 7, 10
      as object-oriented system, 17
      compiling programs, 41
      concept of windows differs from X, 25
      data types; table of, 20
      example of programming interface, 44
      frames and subframes, 26
      generic functions, 21
      Generic Object, 18, 24
```

Sample **troff** output produced by **format.idx** is shown below:

```
.XF A "X"
.XF 1 "X Protocol" "6"
.XF 1 "X Window System" "events, 84"
.XF 2 "extensibility, 9"
.XF 2 "interclient communications, 9"
.XF 2 "overview, 3"
.XF 2 "protocol, 6"
.XF 2 "role of window manager, 9"
.XF 2 "server and client relationship, 5"
.XF 2 "software hierarchy, 6"
.XF 2 "toolkits, 7"
.XF 2 "X Window ID for paint window, 87"
.XF 2 "Xlib, 6"
.XF 1 "XFontStruct structure" "317"
.XF 1 "Xlib" "6"
.XF 2 "repainting canvas, 88"
.XF 1 "Xlib.h header file" "89, 294"
.XF 1 "Xv_Font type" "310"
.XF 1 "XView" "18"
.XF 2 "about, 3, 7, 10"
.XF 2 "as object-oriented system, 17"
```

This output must be formatted by **troff** to produce a printed version of the index.
The index of this book was done using the **masterindex** program.

The masterindex Shell Script

The **masterindex** shell script is the glue that holds all of these scripts together
and invokes them with the proper options based on the user's command line. For
instance, the user enters:

```
% masterindex -s -m volume1 volume2
```

to specify that a master index be created from the files *volume1* and *volume2* and
that the output be sent to the screen.

The **masterindex** shell script is presented in Appendix C with the documentation.

Spare Details of the Masterindex Program

This section presents a few interesting details of the **masterindex** program that
might otherwise escape attention. The purpose of this section is to extract some
interesting program fragments and show how they solve a particular problem.

How to Hide a Special Character

Our first fragment is from the **input.idx** script, whose job it is to standardize the index entries before they are sorted. This program takes as its input a record consisting of two tab-separated fields: the index entry and its page number. A colon is used as part of the syntax for indicating the parts of an index entry.

Because the program uses a colon as a special character, we must provide a way to pass a literal colon through the program. To do this, we allow the indexer to specify two consecutive colons in the input. However, we can't simply convert the sequence to a literal colon because the rest of the program modules called by **masterindex** read three colon-separated fields. The solution is to convert the colon to its octal value using the **gsub** function.

```
#< from input.idx
# convert literal colon to octal value
$1 ~ /::/ {
        # substitute octal value for "::"
        gsub(/::/, "\3a", $1)
```

"\3a" represents the octal value of a colon. (You can find this value by scanning a table of hexadecimal and octal equivalents in the file */usr/pub/ascii*.) In the last program module, we use **gsub** to convert the octal value back to a colon. Here's the code from **format.idx**.

```
#< from format.idx
# convert octal colon to "literal" colon
# make sub for each field, not $0, so that fields are not parsed
        gsub(/\3a/,":",$1)
        gsub(/\3a/,":",$2)
        gsub(/\3a/,":",$3)
```

The first thing you notice is that we make this substitution for each of the three fields separately, instead of having one substitution command that operates on $0. The reason for this is because the input fields are colon-separated. When awk scans an input line, it breaks the line into fields. If you change the contents of $0 at any point in the script, nawk will re-evaluate the value of $0 and parse the line into fields again. Thus, if you have three fields prior to making the substitution, and the substitution makes one change, adding a colon to $0, then nawk will recognize four fields. By doing the substitution for each field, we avoid having the line parsed again into fields.

Rotating Two Parts

Above we talked about the colon syntax for separating the primary and secondary keys. With some kinds of entries, it makes sense to classify the item under its secondary key as well. For instance, we might have a group of program statements or user commands, such as "sed command." The indexer might create two entries: one for "sed command" and one for "command: sed." To make coding this kind of entry easier, we implemented a coding convention that uses a tilde (˜) character to mark the two parts of this entry so that the first and second part can be swapped to create the second entry automatically.* Thus, coding the following index entry:

```
.XX "sed˜command"
```

produces two entries:

```
sed command     43
command: sed    43
```

Here's the code that rotates entries.

```
#> from input.idx
# Match entries that need rotating that contain a single tilde
$1 ˜ /˜/ && $1 !˜ /˜˜/ {
    # split first field into array named subfield
    sizeOfArray = split($1,subfield,"˜")
    if (sizeOfArray == 2) {
        # print entry without "˜" and then rotated
        printf("%s %s::%s\n", subfield[1], subfield[2], $2)
        printf("%s:%s:%s\n", subfield[2], subfield[1], $2)
        next
        }
}
```

The pattern-matching rule matches any entry containing a tilde but not two consecutive tildes, which indicate a literal tilde. The procedure uses the **split** function to break the first field into two "subfields." This gives us two substrings, one before and one after the tilde. The original entry is output and then the rotated entry is output, both using the **printf** statement.

Because the tilde is used as a special character, we use two consecutive tildes to represent a literal tilde in the input. The following code occurs in the program after the code that swaps the two parts of an entry.

---

*The idea of rotating index entries was derived from *The AWK Programming Language*. They, however, automatically rotate an entry where a blank is found; the tilde is used to prevent a rotation by "filling in" the space. Rather than have rotation be the default action, I use a different coding convention, where the tilde indicates where the rotation should occur.

```
#> from input.idx
# Match entries that contain two tildes
$1 ~ /~~/ {
    # replace ~~ with ~
    gsub(/~~/,"~",$1)
}
```

Unlike the colon, which retained a special meaning throughout the **masterindex** program, the tilde has no significance after this module so we can simply output a literal tilde.

Finding a Replacement

The next fragment also comes from **input.idx**. The problem was to look for two colons separated by text and change the second colon to a semicolon. If the input line contains:

```
class: class initialize: (see also methods)
```

Then the result is:

```
class: class initialize; (see also methods)
```

The problem is fairly simple to formulate—we want to change the second colon, not the first one. It is pretty easy to solve in sed because of the ability to select and recall a portion of what is matched in the replacement section (using \(\) to surround the portion to match and \1 to recall the first portion). Lacking the same ability in awk, you have to be more clever. Here's one possible solution:

```
#< from input.idx
#   replace 2nd colon with semicolon
if (sub(/:.*:/,"&;",$1))
        sub(/:;/,";",$1)
```

The first substitution matches the entire span between two colons. It makes a replacement with what is matched (&) followed by a semicolon. This substitution occurs within a conditional expression that evaluates the return value of the **sub** function. Remember this function returns 1 if a substitution is made. (I always have to remind myself that it does not return the resulting string.) In other words, if we make the first substitution, then we make the second one. The second substitution replaces ":;" with ";". Because we can't make the replacement directly, we do it indirectly by making the context in which the second colon appears distinct.

A Function For Reporting Errors

The purpose of the **input.idx** is to allow variations (or less kindly, inconsistencies) in the coding of index entries. By reducing these variations to one basic form, the other programs are made easier to write.

The other side is that if the **input.idx** program cannot accept an entry, it must report it to the user and drop the entry so that it does not affect the other programs. The **input.idx** program has a function used for error reporting called **printerr**, as shown below:

```
function printerr ( message ) {
        # print message, record number and record
        print "ERROR:" message " (" NR ") "   $0 > "/dev/tty"
}
```

This function makes it easier to report errors in a standard manner. It takes as an argument a **message**, which is usually a string that describes the error. It outputs this message along with the record number and the record itself. The output is directed to the user's terminal "/dev/tty." This is a good practice since the standard output of the program might be, as it is in this case, directed to a pipe or to a file. We could also send the error message to standard error.

In the program, the **printerr** function is called as follows:

```
printerr("No page number")
```

When this error occurs, the user sees the following error message:

```
ERROR:No page number (612) geometry management:set_values_almost
```

Handling See Also Entries

One type of index entry is a "see also." Like a "see" reference, it refers the reader to another entry. However, a "see also" entry may have a page number as well. In other words, this entry contains information of its own but refers the reader elsewhere for additional information. Here are a few sample entries.

```
error procedure     34
error procedure (see also XtAppSetErrorMsgHandler)     35
error procedure (see also XtAppErrorMsg)
```

The first entry in this sample has a page number while the last one does not. When the **input.idx** program finds a "see also" entry, it checks to see if a page number ($2) is supplied. If there is one, it outputs two records, the first of which is the entry without the page number and the second of which is an entry and page number without the "see also" reference.

```
#< input.idx
#if no page number
        if ($2 == "") {
                print $0 ":"
                next
        }
        else {
#  output two entries:
#  print see also entry w/out page number
                print $1 ":"
#  remove see also
                sub(/ *~zze also.*$/,"", $1)
                sub(/;/,"", $1)
#  print as normal entry
                if ( $1 ~ /:/ )
                        print $1 ":" $2
                else
                        print $1 "::" $2
                next
        }
```

The next problem to be solved was how to get the entries sorted in the proper order. The **sort** program, using the options we gave it sorted the secondary keys for "see also" entries together under "s." (The **-d** option causes the parenthesis to be ignored.) To change the order of the sort, we alter the sort key by adding the sequence "~zz" to the front of it.

```
#< input.idx
#  add "~zz" for sort at end
        sub(/\([Ss]ee [Aa]lso/,"~zz(see also",$1)
```

The tilde is not interpreted by the sort but it helps us identify the string later when we remove it. Adding "~zz" assures us of sorting to the end of the list of secondary or tertiary keys.

The **pagenums.idx** script removes the sort string from "see also" entries. However, as we described earlier, we look for a series of "see also" entries for the same key and create a list. Therefore, we also remove that which is the same for all entries, and put the reference itself in an array:

```
#< pagenums.idx
        sub(/^.*~zz\([Ss]ee [Aa]lso */,"",SECONDARY)
        sub(/\) */,"",SECONDARY)
#  assign to next element of seeAlsoList
        seeAlsoList[++eachSeeAlso] = SECONDARY "; "
```

There is a function that outputs the list of "see also" entries, separating each of them by a semicolon. Thus, the output of the "see also" entry by **pagenums.idx** looks like:

```
error procedure:(see also XtAppErrorMsg; XtAppSetErrorHandler.)
```

Alternative Ways to Sort

In this program, I chose not to support **troff** font and point size requests in index entries. If you'd like to support special escape sequences, one way to do so is shown in *The AWK Programming Language*. For each record, take the first field and prepend it to the record as the sort key. Now that there is a duplicate of the first field, remove the escape sequences from the sort key. Once the entries are sorted, you can remove the sort key. This process prevents the escape sequences from disturbing the sort.

Yet another way is do something similar to what we did for "see also" entries. Because special characters are ignored in the sort, we could use the **input.idx** program to convert a **troff** font change sequence such as "\fB" to "~~~" and "fI" to "~~~," or any convenient escape sequence. This would get the sequence through the **sort** program without disturbing the sort. (This technique was used by Steve Talbott in his original indexing script.)

The only additional problem that needs to be recognized in both cases is that two entries for the same term, one with font information and one without, will be treated as different entries when one is compared to the other.

12

A Miscellany of Scripts

This chapter contains a miscellany of contributed scripts. These scripts were contributed by USENET users who responded to my request for sed or awk scripts.

Here is a summary of the scripts in this chapter:

uutot.awk	Report UUCP statistics.
phonebill	Track phone usage.
combine	Extract multi-part uuencoded binaries.
mailavg	Check size of mail boxes.
adj	Adjust lines for text files.
readsource	Format program source files for **troff**.
gent	Get a termcap entry.
plpr	**lpr** preprocessor.
transpose	Perform a matrix transposition.

Each program is introduced with a brief description by the program's author. Any comments of mine are placed inside brackets [like this]. Then the full program listing is shown. If the author did not supply an example, I generated one on my system and describe it after the listing. Finally, in a section called "Program Notes," I talk briefly about the program and some points that I find interesting.

---

uutot.awk—Report UUCP statistics

Contributed by Roger A. Cornelius

Here's something I wrote in nawk in response to all the C versions of the same thing which were posted to *alt.sources* awhile back. Basically, it summarizes statistics of **uucp** connections (connect time, throughput, files transmitted, etc.). It only supports HDB-style log files, but will show statistics on a site-by-site, or on an overall (all sites) basis. [I find that it also works with */usr/spool/uucp/SYS-LOG*.]

I use a shell wrapper which calls "awk -f" to run this, but it's not necessary. Usage information is in the header. (Sorry about the lack of comments.)

```
# @(#) uutot.awk - display uucp statistics - requires new awk
# @(#) Usage: awk -f uutot.awk [site ...]
#                 /usr/spool/uucp/.Admin/xferstats
# Author:  Roger A. Cornelius (rac@sherpa.uucp)

# dosome[];           # site names to work for - all if not set
# remote[];           # array of site names
# bytes[];            # bytes xmitted by site
# time[];             # time spent by site
# files[];            # files xmitted by site
BEGIN {
     doall = 1;
     if (ARGC > 2) {
          doall = 0;
          for (i = 1; i < ARGC-1; i++) {
               dosome[ ARGV[i] ];
               ARGV[i] = "";
          }
     }

     kbyte = 1024    # 1000 if you're not picky
     bang = "!";
     sending = "->";
     xmitting = "->" "|" "<-";

     hdr1 = "Remote       KB    KB    KB " \
         "Hr:Mn:Sc Hr:Mn:Sc AvCPS AvCPS     #     #\n";
     hdr2 = "Site         Recv      Xmit       Total     " \
         "Recv    Xmit  Recv  Xmit Recv Xmit\n";
     hdr3 = "------ ----- ------ ------- -------- ---------" \
         "-------- ----- ----- ---- ----";
     fmt1 = "%-8.8s %9.3f %9.3f %9.3f %2d:%02d:%02.0f " \
         "%2d:%02d:%02.0f %5.0f %5.0f %4d %4d\n";
     fmt2 = "Totals   %9.3f %9.3f %9.3f %2d:%02d:%02.0f " \
         "%2d:%02d:%02.0f %5.0f %5.0f %4d %4d\n";
```

```
}
{
        if ($6 !~ xmitting)        # should never be
                next;
        direction = ($6 == sending ? 1 : 2)

        site = substr($1,1,index($1,bang)-1);
        if (site in dosome || doall) {
                remote[site];
                bytes[site,direction] += $7;
                time[site,direction] += $9;
                files[site,direction]++;
        }
}
END {
        print hdr1 hdr2 hdr3;
        for (k in remote) {
                rbyte += bytes[k,2];      sbyte += bytes[k,1];
                rtime += time[k,2];       stime += time[k,1];
                rfiles += files[k,2];     sfiles += files[k,1];
                printf(fmt1, k, bytes[k,2]/kbyte, bytes[k,1]/kbyte,
                        (bytes[k,2]+bytes[k,1])/kbyte,
                        time[k,2]/3600, (time[k,2]%3600)/60, time[k,2]%60,
                        time[k,1]/3600, (time[k,1]%3600)/60, time[k,1]%60,
                        bytes[k,2] && time[k,2] ? bytes[k,2]/time[k,2] : 0,
                        bytes[k,1] && time[k,1] ? bytes[k,1]/time[k,1] : 0,
                        files[k,2], files[k,1]);
        }

        print hdr3
        printf(fmt2, rbyte/kbyte, sbyte/kbyte, (rbyte+sbyte)/kbyte,
                rtime/3600, (rtime%3600)/60, rtime%60,
                stime/3600, (stime%3600)/60, stime%60,
                rbyte && rtime ? rbyte/rtime : 0,
                sbyte && stime ? sbyte/stime : 0,
                rfiles, sfiles);
}
```

I generated a test file on my system to test Cornelius' program. Here are a few lines extracted from */usr/spool/uucp/.Admin/xferstats* (because each line in this file is too long to print on a page, we have broken the line following the directional arrow for display purposes only):

```
isla!nuucp S (8/3-16:10:17) (C,126,25) [ttyi1j]->
                1131/4.880 secs, 231 bytes/sec
isla!nuucp S (8/3-16:10:20) (C,126,26) [ttyi1j]->
                149/0.500 secs, 298 bytes/sec
isla!sue S (8/3-16:10:49) (C,126,27) [ttyi1j]->
                646/25.230 secs, 25 bytes/sec
isla!sue S (8/3-16:10:52) (C,126,28) [ttyi1j]->
                145/0.510 secs, 284 bytes/sec
uunet!uisla M (8/3-16:15:50) (C,951,1) [cuila]->
                1191/0.660 secs, 1804 bytes/sec
```

```
uunet!uisla M (8/3-16:15:53) (C,951,2) [cuila]->
                   148/0.080 secs, 1850 bytes/sec
uunet!uisla M (8/3-16:15:57) (C,951,3) [cuila]->
                   1018/0.550 secs, 1850 bytes/sec
uunet!uisla M (8/3-16:16:00) (C,951,4) [cuila]->
                   160/0.070 secs, 2285 bytes/sec
uunet!daemon M (8/3-16:16:06) (C,951,5) [cuila] <-
                   552/2.740 secs, 201 bytes/sec
uunet!daemon M (8/3-16:16:09) (C,951,6) [cuila] <-
                   102/1.390 secs, 73 bytes/sec
```

Note that there are 12 fields, however, the program really only uses fields 1, 6, 7, and 9. Running the program on the sample input produces the following results:

```
% nawk -f uutot.awk uutot.test
```

Remote Site	KB Recv	KB Xmit	KB Total	Hr:Mn:Sc Recv	Hr:Mn:Sc Xmit	AvCPS Recv	AvCPS Xmit	# Recv	# Xmit
uunet	0.639	2.458	3.097	0:00:04	0:00:01	158	1851	2	4
isla	0.000	2.022	2.022	0:00:00	0:00:31	0	67	0	4
Totals	0.639	4.480	5.119	0:00:04	0:00:32	158	141	2	8

Program notes for uutot.awk. This nawk application is an excellent example of a clearly written awk program. It is also a typical example of using awk to change a rather obscure UNIX log into a useful report.

Although Cornelius apologizes for the lack of comments that explain the logic of the program, the usage of the program is clear from the initial comments. Also, he uses variables to define search patterns and the report's layout. This helps to simplify conditional and print statements in the body of the program. It also helps that the variables have names which aid in immediately recognizing their purpose.

This program has a three-part structure, as we emphasized in Chapter 7, *Writing Scripts for Awk*. It consists of a **BEGIN** procedure, in which variables are defined; the body, in which each line of data from the log file is processed; and the **END** procedure, in which the output for the report is generated.

phonebill—Track phone usage

Contributed by Nick Holloway

The problem is to calculate the cost of phone calls made. In the United Kingdom, charges are made for the number of "units" used during the duration of the call (no free local calls). The length of time a "unit" lasts depends on the charge band (linked to distance) and the charge rate (linked to time of day). You get charged a whole unit as soon as the time period begins.

The input to the program is four fields. The first field is the date (not used). The second field is "band/rate" and is used to look up the length a unit will last. The third field is the length of the call. This can either be "ss," "mm:ss," or "hh:mm:ss". The fourth field is the name of the caller. We keep a stopwatch (old cheap digital), a book, and a pen. Come bill time this is fed through my awk script. This only deals with the cost of the calls, not the standing charge.

The aim of the program was to enable the minimum amount of information to be entered by the callers, and the program could be used to collect together the call costs for each user in one report. It is also written so that if British Telecom changes its costs, these can be done easily in the top of the source (this has been done once already). If more charge bands or rates are added, the table can be simply expanded (wonders of associative arrays). There are no real sanity checks done on the input data. The usage is:

phonebill [*file* ...]

Here is a (short) sample of input and output.

Input:

```
29/05    b/p       5:35    Nick
29/05    L/c    1:00:00    Dale
01/06    L/c      30:50    Nick
```

Output:

```
Summary for Dale:
     29/05    L/c  1:00:00  11 units
Total: 11 units @ 5.06 pence per unit = $0.56

Summary for Nick:
     29/05    b/p       5:35  19 units
     01/06    L/c      30:50   6 units
Total: 25 units @ 5.06 pence per unit = $1.26
```

The listing for **phonebill** follows:

```
#!/bin/awk -f
#-------------------------------------------------------------------
#   Awk script to take in phone usage - and calculate cost for each
#   person
#-------------------------------------------------------------------
#   Author: N.Holloway (alfie@uk.ac.warwick.cs)
#   Date  : 27 January 1989
#   Place : University of Warwick
#-------------------------------------------------------------------
#   Entries are made in the form
#     Date    Type/Rate    Length  Name
#
#   Format:
#     Date       : "dd/mm"      - one word
#     Type/Rate  : "bb/rr"    (e.g. L/c)
#     Length        : "hh:mm:ss", "mm:ss", "ss"
#     Name       : "Fred"    - one word (unique)
#-------------------------------------------------------------------
#   Charge information kept in array 'c', indexed by "type/rate",
#   and the cost of a unit is kept in the variable 'pence_per_unit'
#   The info is stored in two arrays, both indexed by the name. The
#   first 'summary' has the lines that hold input data, and number
#   of units, and 'units' has the cumulative total number of units
#   used by name.
#-------------------------------------------------------------------

BEGIN \
    {
    # --- Cost per unit
    pence_per_unit  = 4.40          # cost is 4.4 pence per unit
    pence_per_unit *= 1.15          # VAT is 15%

    # --- Table of seconds per unit for different bands/rates
    #     [ not applicable have 0 entered as value ]
    c ["L/c"] = 330 ;  c ["L/s"] = 85.0;  c ["L/p"] = 60.0;
    c ["a/c"] =  96 ;  c ["a/s"] = 34.3;  c ["a/p"] = 25.7;
    c ["b1/c"]= 60.0;  c ["b1/s"]= 30.0;  c ["b1/p"]= 22.5;
    c ["b/c"] = 45.0;  c ["b/s"] = 24.0;  c ["b/p"] = 18.0;
    c ["m/c"] = 12.0;  c ["m/s"] = 8.00;  c ["m/p"] = 8.00;
    c ["A/c"] = 9.00;  c ["A/s"] = 7.20;  c ["A/p"] = 0   ;
    c ["A2/c"]= 7.60;  c ["A2/s"]= 6.20;  c ["A2/p"]= 0   ;
    c ["B/c"] = 6.65;  c ["B/s"] = 5.45;  c ["B/p"] = 0   ;
    c ["C/c"] = 5.15;  c ["C/s"] = 4.35;  c ["C/p"] = 3.95;
    c ["D/c"] = 3.55;  c ["D/s"] = 2.90;  c ["D/p"] = 0   ;
    c ["E/c"] = 3.80;  c ["E/s"] = 3.05;  c ["E/p"] = 0   ;
    c ["F/c"] = 2.65;  c ["F/s"] = 2.25;  c ["F/p"] = 0   ;
    c ["G/c"] = 2.15;  c ["G/s"] = 2.15;  c ["G/p"] = 2.15;
    }

    {
    spu = c [ $2 ]                  # look up charge band
```

```
        if ( spu == "" || spu == 0 ) {
            summary [ $4 ] = summary [ $4 ] "\n\t" \
                    sprintf ( "%4s  %4s  %7s   ? units",\
                                 $1, $2, $3 ) \
                    " - Bad/Unknown Chargeband"
        } else {
            n = split ( $3, t, ":" )   # calculate length in seconds
            seconds = 0
            for ( i = 1; i <= n; i++ )
             seconds = seconds*60 + t[i]
            u = seconds / spu    # calculate number of seconds
            if ( int( u ) == u )    # round up to next whole unit
             u = int( u )
            else
             u = int( u ) + 1
            units [ $4 ] += u    # store info to output at end
            summary [ $4 ] = summary [ $4 ] "\n\t" \
                    sprintf ( "%4s  %4s  %7s %3d units",\
                                 $1, $2, $3, u )
        }
    }

END \
    {
     for ( i in units ) {                    # for each person
         printf ( "Summary for %s:", i ) # newline at start \
                                           # of summary
         print summary [ i ]              # print summary details
         total = int ( units[i] * pence_per_unit + 0.5 ) \
                                           # calc cost
         printf ( "Total: %d units @ %.2f pence per unit =\
             $%d.%02d\n\n", \
                     units [i], pence_per_unit, total/100, \
                                         # total%100 )
     }
    }
```

Program notes for phonebill. This program is another example of generating a report that consolidates information from a simple record structure.

This program also follows the three-part structure. The **BEGIN** procedure defines variables that are used throughout the program. This makes it easy to change the program, as phone companies are known to "upwardly revise" their rates. One of the variables is a large array named **c** in which each element is the number of seconds per unit, using the band over the rate as the index to the array.

The main procedure reads each line of the user log. It uses the second field, which identifies the band/rate, to get a value from the array **c**. It checks that a positive value was returned and then processes that value by the time specified in $3. The number of units for that call is then stored in array named **units**, indexed by the name of the caller ($4). This value accumulates for each caller.

Finally, the **END** routine prints out the values in the **unit** array, producing the report that tells how many units were used by a caller and what the total cost of the calls were.

---

combine—Extract multi-part uuencoded binaries

Contributed by Rahul Dhesi

Of all the scripts I have ever written, the one I am most proud of is the "combine" script.

While I was moderating *comp.binaries.ibm.pc*, I wanted to provide users a simple way of extracting multi-part uuencoded binaries. I added **BEGIN** and **END** headers to each part to enclose the uuencoded part and provided users with the following script:

```
cat $*  |  sed '/^END/,/^BEGIN/d' |  uudecode
```

This script will accept a list of filenames (in order) provided as command-line arguments. It will accept accept concatenated articles as standard input.

This script invokes **cat** in a very useful way that is well known to expert shell script users but not enough used by most others. This allows the user the choice of either providing command-line arguments or standard input.

The script invokes sed to strip out superfluous headers and trailers, except for headers in the first input file and trailers in the last input file. The final result is that the uuencoded part of the multiple input files is extracted and uudecoded. Each input file (see postings in *comp.binaries.ibm.pc*) has the following form:

```
headers
BEGIN
END
```

I have lots of other shell stuff, but the above is simplest and has proved useful to several thousand *comp.binaries.ibm.pc* readers.

Program notes for combine. This one is pretty obvious but accomplishes a lot. For those who might not understand the use of this command, let me explain. A USENET newsgroup such as *comp.binaries.ibm.pc* distributes public domain programs and such. Binaries, the object code created by the compiler, cannot be distributed using as news articles unless they are "encoded". A program named **uuencode** converts the binary to an ASCII representation which can be easily distributed. It is the program that inserts the **BEGIN** and **END** to mark the representation. Furthermore, there are limits on the size of news articles and large binaries are broken up into a series of articles (1 of 3, 2 of 3, 3 of 3, for example).

A reader of these articles might save each article in a file. Dhesi's script automates the process of combining these articles and removing extraneous information such as the article header as well as the extra **BEGIN** and **END** headers. His script removes lines from the first **END** up to and including the next **BEGIN** pattern. It combines all the separate encoded parcels and directs them to uudecode, which converts the ASCII representation to binary.

One has to appreciate the amount of manual editing work avoided by a simple one-line script.

---

mailavg—Check size of mail boxes

Contributed by Wes Morgan

While tuning our mail system, we needed to take a "snapshot" of the users' mailboxes at regular intervals over a 30-day period. This script simply calculates the average size and prints the arithmetic distribution of user mailboxes.

```
:
#
# mailavg - average size of files in /usr/mail
#
# Written by Wes Morgan, morgan@engr.uky.edu, 2 Feb 90
ls -Fs /usr/mail | awk '
    { if(NR != 1) {
        total += $1;
        count += 1;
        size = $1 + 0;
        if(size == 0) zercount+=1;
        if(size > 0 && size <= 10) tencount+=1;
        if(size > 10 && size <= 19) teencount+=1;
        if(size > 20 && size <= 50) uptofiftycount+=1;
        if(size > 50) overfiftycount+=1;
        }
    }
    END { printf("/usr/mail has %d mailboxes using %d blocks,",\
                    count,total)
        printf("average is %6.2f blocks\n", total/count)
        printf("\nDistribution:\n")
        printf("Size        Count\n")
        printf(" 0          %d\n",zercount)
        printf("1-10        %d\n",tencount)
        printf("11-20       %d\n",teencount)
        printf("21-50       %d\n",uptofiftycount)
        printf("Over 50     %d\n",overfiftycount)
    }'
exit 0
```

I ran Morgan's program on our system in Cambridge, MA.

```
% mailavg
/usr/mail has 47 mailboxes using 5116 blocks,
average is 108.85 blocks

Distribution:
Size        Count
  O           1
1-10         13
11-20         1
21-50         5
Over 50      27
```

Program notes for mailavg. This administrative program is similar to the **filesum** program in Chapter 7, *Writing Scripts for Awk*. It processes the output of the **ls** command.

The conditional expression "NR != 1" could have been put outside the main procedure as a pattern. While the logic is the same, using the expression as a pattern clarifies how the procedure is accessed. It would make the program easier to understand.

In that procedure, Morgan uses a series of conditionals that allow him to collect distribution statistics on the size of each user's mailbox.

---

adj—Adjust lines for text files

Contributed by Norman Joseph

[Given that the author used his program to format his mail message before sending it, I'm preserving the linebreaks and indented paragraphs in presenting it here as the program's example. This program is similar to the BSD **fmt** program.]

Well, I decided to take you up on your offer. I'm sure there are more sophisticated gurus out there than me, but I do have a nawk script that I'm kind of fond of, so I'm sending it in.

Ok, here's the low down. When I'm writing e-mail, I often make a lot of changes to the text (especially if I'm going to post on the net). So what starts out as a nicely adjusted letter or posting usually ends up looking pretty sloppy by the time I'm done adding and deleting lines. So I end up spending a lot of time joining and breaking lines all through my document so as to get a nice right-hand margin. So I say to myself, "This is just the kind of tedious work a program would be good for."

Now, I know I can use **nroff** to filter my document through and adjust the lines, but it has lousy defaults (IMHO) for simple text like this. So, with a view to sharpening my nawk skills I wrote **adj.nawk** and the accompanying shell script wrapper **adj**.

Here's the syntax for the nawk filter **adj**:

    adj [-l|c|r|b] [-w n] [-i *n*] [*files* ...]

The options are:

    -l   Lines are left adjusted, right ragged (default).

    -c   Lines are centered.

    -r   Lines are right adjusted, left ragged.

    -b   Lines are left and right adjusted.

    -w n Sets line width to *n* characters (default is 70).

    -i n Sets initial indent to *n* characters (default is 0).

So, whenever I'm finished with this letter (I'm using **vi**) I will give the command **: %!adj -w73** (I like my lines a little longer) and all the breaking and joining will be done by a program (the way the Good Lord intended :-). Indents and blank lines are preserved, and two spaces are given after any end-of-sentence punctuation.

The program is naive about tabs, and when computing line lengths, it considers a tab character to be one space wide.

The program is notable for its use of command-line parameter assignment, and some of the newer features of awk (nawk), such as the match and split built-in functions, and for its use of support functions.

```
:
#
# adj - adjust text lines
#
# usage: adj [-l|c|r|b] [-w n] [-i n] [files ...]
#
# options:
#     -l     - lines are left adjusted, right ragged (default)
#     -c     - lines are centered
#     -r     - lines are right adjusted, left ragged
#     -b     - lines are left and right adjusted
#     -w n   - sets line width to <n> characters (default: 70)
#     -i n   - sets initial indent to <n> characters (default: 0)
#
# note:
#     output line width is -w setting plus -i setting
#
# author:
#     Norman Joseph (amanue!oglvee!norm)

adj=l
wid=70
ind=0

set -- `getopt lcrbw:i: $*`
if test $? != 0
then
    printf 'usage: %s [-l|c|r|b] [-w n] [-i n] [files ...]' $0
    exit 1
fi

for arg in $*
do
    case $arg in
    -l) adj=l;  shift;;
    -c) adj=c;  shift;;
    -r) adj=r;  shift;;
    -b) adj=b;  shift;;
    -w) wid=$2;  shift 2;;
    -i) ind=$2;  shift 2;;
    --) shift;  break;;
    esac
done

exec nawk -f adj.nawk type=$adj linelen=$wid indent=$ind $*
```

Here's the **adj.nawk** script that's called by the shell script **adj.**

```
# adj.nawk -- adjust lines of text per options
#
# NOTE:  this nawk program is called from the shell script "adj"
#     see that script for usage & calling conventions
#
# author:
#     Norman Joseph (amanue!oglvee!norm)

BEGIN   {
    FS = "\n"
    blankline  = "^[ \t]*$"
    startblank = "^[ \t]+[^ \t]+"
    startwords = "^[^ \t]+"
}

$0 ~ blankline {
    if ( type == "b" )
        putline( outline "\n" )
    else
        putline( adjust( outline, type ) "\n" )
    putline( "\n" )
    outline = ""
}

$0 ~ startblank {
    if ( outline != "" ) {
        if ( type == "b" )
            putline( outline "\n" )
        else
            putline( adjust( outline, type ) "\n" )
    }

    firstword = ""
    i = 1
    while ( substr( $0, i, 1 ) ~ "[ \t]" ) {
        firstword = firstword substr( $0, i, 1 )
        i++
    }
    inline = substr( $0, i )
    outline = firstword

    nf = split( inline, word, "[ \t]+" )

    for ( i = 1;  i <= nf;  i++ ) {
        if ( i == 1 ) {
            testlen = length( outline word[i] )
        } else {
            testlen = length( outline " " word[i] )
            if ( match( ".!?:;", "\\" substr( outline, length
                ( outline ), 1 )) )
                testlen++
```

```
            }

        if ( testlen > linelen ) {
            putline( adjust( outline, type ) "\n" )
            outline = ""
        }

        if ( outline == "" )
            outline = word[i]
        else if ( i == 1 )
            outline = outline word[i]
        else {
            if ( match( ".!?:;", "\\" substr( outline, length
                    ( outline ), 1 )) )
                outline = outline "  " word[i]      # 2 spaces
            else
                outline = outline " " word[i]       # 1 space
        }
    }
}

$0 ~ startwords  {
    nf = split( $0, word, "[ \t]+" )

    for ( i = 1;  i <= nf;  i++ ) {
        if ( outline == "" )
            testlen = length( word[i] )
        else {
            testlen = length( outline " " word[i] )
            if ( match( ".!?:;", "\\" substr( outline, length
                    ( outline ), 1 )) )
                testlen++
        }

        if ( testlen > linelen ) {
            putline( adjust( outline, type ) "\n" )
            outline = ""
        }

        if ( outline == "" )
            outline = word[i]
        else {
            if ( match( ".!?:;", "\\" substr( outline, length
                    ( outline ), 1 )) )
                outline = outline "  " word[i]      # 2 spaces
            else
                outline = outline " " word[i]       # 1 space
        }
    }
}

END  {
    if ( type == "b" )
```

332

```
            putline( outline "\n" )
        else
            putline( adjust( outline, type ) "\n" )
}


#
# -- support functions --
#

function putline( line,     fmt )
{
    if ( indent ) {
        fmt = "%" indent "s%s"
        printf( fmt, " ", line )
    } else
        printf( "%s", line )
}


function adjust( line, type,     fill, fmt )
{
    if ( type != "l" )
        fill = linelen - length( line )

    if ( fill > 0 ) {
        if          ( type == "c" ) {
            fmt = "%" (fill+1)/2 "s%s"
            line = sprintf( fmt, " ", line )
        } else if ( type == "r" ) {
            fmt = "%" fill "s%s"
            line = sprintf( fmt, " ", line )
        } else if ( type == "b" ) {
            line = fillout( line, fill )
        }
    }

    return line
}


function fillout( line, need, i, newline, nextchar, blankseen )
{
    while ( need ) {
        newline = ""
        blankseen = 0

        if ( dir == 0 ) {
            for ( i = 1;  i <= length( line ); i++ ) {
                nextchar = substr( line, i, 1 )
                if ( need ) {
                    if ( nextchar == " " ) {
                        if ( ! blankseen ) {
```

```
                                      newline = newline " "
                                      need--
                                      blankseen = 1
                          }
                    } else {
                          blankseen = 0
                    }
              }
              newline = newline nextchar
        }

    } else if ( dir == 1 ) {
        for ( i = length( line ); i >= 1;  i-- ) {
            nextchar = substr( line, i, 1 )
            if ( need ) {
                if ( nextchar == " " ) {
                    if ( ! blankseen ) {
                          newline = " " newline
                          need--
                          blankseen = 1
                    }
                } else {
                    blankseen = 0
                }
            }
            newline = nextchar newline
        }
    }

    line = newline

    dir = 1 - dir
}

return line
}
```

Program notes for adj. This small text formatter is a nifty program for those of us who use text editors. It allows you to set the maximum line width and justify paragraphs and thus can be used to format mail messages or simple letters.

The **adj** shell script does all the option setting, although it could have been done by reading **ARGV[]** in the **BEGIN** action. Using the shell to establish command-line parameters is probably easier for for those who are already familiar with the shell.

The lack of comments in the **adj.awk** script makes this script more difficult to read than some of the others. The **BEGIN** procedure assigns three regular expressions to variables: **blankline, startblank, startwords**. This is a good technique (one that you'll see used in **lex** specifications) because regular expressions can be difficult to read and the name of the variable makes it clear what it matches. Remember it is a new feature of nawk that you can test a variable that contains a regular expression using the match operator (˜).

There are three main procedures, which can be named by the variable they match. The first is **blankline**, which handles collected text once a blank line is encountered. The second is **startblank**, which handles lines that begin with blanks spaces or tabs. The third is **startwords**, which handles a line of text. The basic procedure is to read a line of text and determine how many of the words in that line will fit, given the line width, and outputting those that will fit and save those that will not in the variable **outline**. When the next input line is read, the contents of **outline** must be output before that line is output.

The **adjust** function does the work of justifying the text based on a command-line option specifying the format type. All types except "l" (left-adjusted, right-ragged) need to be filled. Therefore, the first thing this function does is figure out how much "fill" is needed by subtracting the length of the current line from the specified line length. It makes excellent use of the **sprintf** function to actually do the positioning of the text. For instance, to center text, the value of **fill** (plus 1) is divided by 2 to determine the amount of padding needed on each side of the line. This amount is passed through the **fmt** variable as the argument to **sprintf**:

```
fmt = "%" (fill+1)/2 "s%s"
line = sprintf( fmt, " ", line )
```

Thus, the blank space will be used to pad a field that is the length of half the amount of fill needed.

If right-justified, the value of **fill** itself is used to pad the field. Finally, if the format type is "b" (block), then the function **fillout** is called to determine where to add blanks that will fill out the line.

In looking over the design of the program, you can see, once again, how the use of functions helps to clarify what a program is doing. It helps me to think of the main procedure as controlling the flow of input through the program while procedures handle the operations performed on the input. Separating the "operations" from the flow control makes the program readable and more easily maintained.

In passing, I'm not sure why **FS**, the field separator, is set to \n in the **BEGIN** procedure. This means that the field and record separators are the same (i.e., $0 and $1 are the same). The **split** function is called to break the line into fields using tabs or spaces as the delimiter.

```
nf = split( $0, word, "[ \t]+" )
```

It seems to me that the field separator could have been set to the same regular expression, as follows:

```
FS = "[ \t]+"
```

It would be more efficient to use the default field parsing.

readsource—Format program source files for troff

Contributed by Martin Weitzel

I am often preparing technical documents, especially for courses and training. In these documents, I often need to print source files of different kinds (C programs, **awk** programs, shell scripts, makefiles.) The problem is that the sources often change with time and I want the most recent version when I print. I also want to avoid typos in print.

As I'm using **troff** for text processing, it should be easy to include the original sources into the text of the document. But there are some characters (especially "\" and "." and "," at the beginning of a line) that I must escape to prevent interpretation by **troff**.

I often want excerpts from sources rather than a complete file. I also need a mechanism for setting page breaks. Well, perhaps I'm being a perfectionist, but I don't want to see a C function printed nearly complete on one page, but only the two last lines appear on the next. As I frequently change the documents, I cannot hunt for "nice" page breaks—this must be done automatically.

To solve these set of problems, I wrote a filter that preprocesses any source and for inclusion as text in **troff**. This is the **awk** program I send with this letter. [He didn't offer a name for it so I named it **readsource**.]

The whole process can be further automated through *makefiles*. I include a preprocessed version of the sources into my **troff** documents, and I make the formatting dependent on these preprocessed files. These files again are dependent on their originals, so if I "make" the document to print it, the preprocessed sources will be checked to see if they are still current; otherwise they will be generated new from their originals.

My program contains a complete description in form of comments. But as the description is more for me than for others, I'll give you some more hints. Basically, the program simply guards some characters, e.g., "\" is turned into "\e" and "\&" is written before every line. Tabs may be expanded to spaces (there's a switch for it), and you may even generate line numbers in front of every line (switch selectable). The format of these line numbers can be set through an environmental variable.

If you want only *parts* of a file to be processed, you can select these parts with two regular expressions (with another switch). You must specify the first line to be included and the first line not to be. I've found that this is often practical: If you want to show only a certain function of a C program, you can give the first line of the function definition and the first line of the next function definition. If the source is changed such that new functions are inserted between the two or the order is changed, the pattern matching will not work correctly. But this will accommodate the more frequently made, smaller changes in a program.

The final feature, getting the page breaks right, is a bit tricky. Here a technique has evolved that I call "here-you-may-break." Those points are marked by a special kind of line (I use "/*!" in C programs and "#!" in awk, shell, makefiles, etc.). How the points are marked doesn't matter too much, you may have your own conventions, but it must be possible to give a regular expression which matches exactly this kind of lines and no others (e.g., if your sources are written that a page break is acceptable wherever you have an empty line, you can specify this very easy, as all you need is the regular expression for empty lines).

Before all the marked lines, a special sequence will be inserted which again is given by an environmental variable. With **troff**, I use the technique of opening a "display" (.DS) before I include such preprocessed text, and inserting a close (.DE) and new open (.DS) display wherever I would accept a page break. After this, **troff** does the work of gathering as many lines as fit onto the current page. I suppose that suitable techniques for other text processors exist.

```
:
# Copyright 1990 by EDV-Beratung Martin Weitzel, D-6100 Darmstadt
# ====================================================================
# PROJECT:     Printing Tools
# SH-SCRIPT:   Source to Troff Pre-Formatter
# ====================================================================

#!
# --------------------------------------------------------------------
# This programm is a tool to preformat source files, so that they
# can be included (.so) within nroff/troff-input. Problems when
# including arbitrary files within nroff/troff-input occur on
# lines, starting with dot (.) or an apostrophe ('), or with the
# respective chars, if these are changed, furthermore from
# embedded backslashes. While changing the source so that non of
# the above will cause any problems, some other usefull things can
# be done, including line numbering and selecting interesting parts.
# --------------------------------------------------------------------
#!
    USAGE="$0 [-x d] [-n] [-b pat] [-e pat] [-p pat] [file ...]"
#
# SYNOPSIS:
# The following options are supported:
#     -x d  expand tabs to "d" spaces
#     -n    number source lines (see also: NFMT)
#     -b pat    start output on a line containing "pat",
#          including this line (Default: from beginning)
#     -e pat    end output on a line containing "pat"
#          excluding this line (Default: upto end)
```

```
#      -p pat     before lines containing "pat", page breaks
#            may occur (Default: no page breaks)
# "pat" may be an "extended regular expression" as supported by awk.
# The following variables from the environment are used:
#      NFMT specify format for line numbers (Default: see below)
#      PBRK string, to mark page breaks. (Default: see below)
#!
# PREREQUISITS:
# Common UNIX-Environment, including awk.
#
# CAVEATS:
# "pat"s are not checked before they are used (processing may have
# started, before problems are detected).
# "NFMT" must contain exactly one %d-format specifier, if -n
# option is used.
# In "NFMT" and "PBRK", embedded doublequotes must be guarded with
# a leading backslash.
# In "pat"s, "NFMT" and "PBRK" embedded TABs and NLs must be written
# as \t and \n. Backslashes that should "go thru" to the output as
# such, should be doubled. (The latter is only *required* in a few
# special cases, but it does no harm the other cases).
#
#!
# BUGS:
# Slow - but may serve as prototype for a faster implementation.
# (Hint: Guarding backslashes the way it is done by now is very
# expensive and could also be done using sed 's/\\/\\e/g', but tab
# expansion would be much harder then, because I can't imagine how
# to do it with sed. If you have no need for tab expansion, you may
# change the program. Another option would be to use gsub(), which
# would limit the program to environments with nawk.)
#
# Others bugs may be, please mail me.
#!
# AUTHOR: Martin Weitzel, D-6100 DA (martin@mwtech.UUCP)
#
# RELEASED:    25. Nov 1989, Version 1.00
# -----------------------------------------------------------------------
#! CSOPT
# -----------------------------------------------------------------------
#      check/set options
# -----------------------------------------------------------------------

xtabs=0 nfmt= bpat= epat= ppat=
for p
do
case $sk in
1) shift; sk=0; continue
esac
case $p in
-x)   shift;
      case $1 in
```

```
        [1-9]|1[0-9]) xtabs=$1; sk=1;;
        *) { >&2 echo "$0: bad value for option -x: $1"; exit 1; }
        esac
        ;;
-n)  nfmt="${NFMT:-<%03d>\      }"; shift ;;
-b)  shift; bpat=$1; sk=1 ;;
-e)  shift; epat=$1; sk=1 ;;
-p)  shift; ppat=$1; sk=1 ;;
--)  shift; break ;;
*)   break
esac
done


#! MPROC
# -----------------------------------------------------------------------
#    now the "real work"
# -----------------------------------------------------------------------

awk '
#. prepare for tab-expansion, page-breaks and selection
BEGIN {
    if (xt = '$xtabs') while (length(sp) < xt) sp = sp " ";
    PBRK = "'"${PBRK-'.DE\n.DS\n'}"'"
    '${bpat:+' skip = 1; '}'
}
#! limit selection range
{
    '${epat:+' if (!skip && $0 ~ /'"$epat"'/) skip = 1; '}'
    '${bpat:+' if (skip && $0 ~ /'"$bpat"'/) skip = 0; '}'
    if (skip) next;
}
#! process one line of input as required
{
    line = ""; ll = 0;
    for (i = 1; i <= length; i++) {
        c = substr($0, i, 1);
        if (xt && c == "\t") {
            # expand tabs
            nsp = 8 - ll % xt;
            line = line substr(sp, 1, nsp);
            ll += nsp;
        }
        else {
            if (c == "\\") c = "\\e";
            line = line c;
            ll++;
        }
    }
}
#! finally print this line
{
    '${ppat:+' if ($0 ~ /'"$ppat"'/) printf("%s", PBRK); '}'
    '${nfmt:+' printf("'"$nfmt"'", NR) '}'
```

```
       printf("\\&%s\n", line);
}
'  $*
```

For an example of how it works, I ran **readsource** to extract a part of its own program.

```
% readsource -x 3 -b "process one line" -e "finally print" readsource
\&#! process one line of input as required
\&{
\&    line = ""; ll = 0;
\&    for (i = 1; i <= length; i++) {
\&        c = substr($0, i, 1);
\&        if (xt && c == "\et") {
\&            # expand tabs
\&            nsp = 8 - ll % xt;
\&            line = line substr(sp, 1, nsp);
\&            ll += nsp;
\&        }
\&        else {
\&            if (c == "\e\e") c = "\e\ee";
\&            line = line c;
\&            ll++;
\&        }
\&    }
\&}
```

Program notes for readsource. This program is first of all quite useful, as it helped me prepare the listings in this book. The author does really stretch awk to its limits, using shell variables to pass information into the script. It gets the job done, but it is quite obscure.

The program does run slowly. I followed up on the author's suggestion and changed the way the program replaced tabs and backslashes. The original program uses an expensive character-by-character comparison, obtaining the character using the **substr** function. (It is the procedure that is extracted in the example above.) It points out how costly it is in awk to read a line one character at a time, something that is very simple in C.

Running **readsource** on itself produced the following times:

```
% timex readsource -x 3 readsource > /dev/null

real      16.76
user      13.18
sys        1.71
```

341

The procedure that changes the way tabs and backslashes are handled can be re-written in nawk to use the **gsub** function:

```
#! process one line of input as required
{
        if ( xt && $0 ~ "\t" )
                gsub(/\t/, sp)
        if ($0 ~ "\\")
                gsub(/\\/, "\\e")
}
```

The last procedure needs a small change, replacing the variable **line** with "$0". (We don't use the temporary variable **line**). The nawk version produces:

```
% timex readsource.2 -x 3 readsource > /dev/null
real        1.58
user        1.08
sys         0.36
```

The difference is pretty remarkable.

gent—Get a termcap Entry

Contributed by Tom Christiansen

Here's a sed script I use to extract a **termcap** entry. It works for any **termcap**-like file, such as disktab. For example:

```
% gent vt100
```

extracts the vt100 entry from termcap, while:

```
% gent eagle /etc/disktab
```

gets the eagle entry from disktab. Now I know it could have been done in C or perl, but I did it a long time ago. It's also interesting because of the way it passes options into the sed script. I know, I know: it should have been written in *sh* not *csh*, too.

```
#!/bin/csh -f

set argc = $#argv


set noglob
set dollar = '$'
set squeeze = 0
set noback="" nospace=""

rescan:
    if ( $argc > 0 && $argc < 3 ) then
        if ( "$1" =~ -* ) then
            if ( "-squeeze" =~ $1* ) then
                set noback='s/\\//g' nospace='s/^[   ]*//'
                set squeeze = 1
                shift
                @ argc --
                goto rescan
            else
                echo "Bad switch: $1"
                goto usage
            endif
        endif

        set entry = "$1"
        if ( $argc == 1 ) then
            set file = /etc/termcap
        else
            set file = "$2"
        endif
    else
```

```
          usage:
              echo "usage: `basename $0` [-squeeze] entry\
                      [termcapfile]"
              exit 1
      endif
```

```
sed -n -e \
"/^${entry}[|:]/ {\
    :x\
    /\\${dollar}/ {\
    ${noback}\
    ${nospace}\
    p\
    n\
    bx\
    }\
    ${nospace}\
    p\
    n\
    /^ / {\
        bx\
    }\
    }\
/^[^     ]*|${entry}[|:]/ {\
    :y\
    /\\${dollar}/ {\
    ${noback}\
    ${nospace}\
    p\
    n\
    by\
    }\
    ${nospace}\
    p\
    n\
    /^ / {\
        by\
    }\
    }" < $file
```

Program notes for gent. Once you get used to reading awk scripts, they seem so much easier to understand than all but the simplest sed script. It can be a painstaking task to figure out what a small sed script like the one shown here is doing.

This script does show how to pass shell variables into a sed script. Variables are used to pass optional sed commands into the script, such as the substitution commands that replace backslashes and spaces.

This script could be simplified in several ways. First of all, I can't see why the two regular expressions are necessary to match the entry. The first matches the name of the entry at the beginning of a line; the second matches it elsewhere on the line. The loops labeled **x** and **y** are identical and even if the two regular expressions were necessary, we could have them branch to the same loop.

plpr—lpr preprocessor

Contributed by Tom Van Raalte

I thought you might want to use the following script around the office. It is a preprocessor for **lpr** that sends output to the "best" printer. [This shell script is written for a BSD system and you would use this command in place of **lpr**. It reads the output of the **lpq** command to determine if a specific printer is available. If not, it tries a list of printers to see which one is available or which is the least busy. Then it invokes **lpr** to send the job to that printer.]

```
#!/bin/sh
#
#set up temp file
TMP=/tmp/printsum.$$
LASERWRITER=${LASERWRITER-ps6}
#Check to see if the default printer is free?
#
#
FREE=`lpq -P$LASERWRITER | awk '
{ if ($0 == "no entries")
   {
         val=1
print val
exit 0
   }
   else
   {
val=0
print val
exit 0
   }
}'`
#echo Free is $FREE
#
#If the default is free then $FREE is set, and we print and exit.
#
if [ $FREE -eq 1 ]
then
        SELECT=$LASERWRITER
#echo selected $SELECT
lpr -P$SELECT $*
        exit 0
fi
#echo Past the exit
#
#Now we go on to see if any of the printers in bank are free.
#
BANK=${BANK-$LASERWRITER}
```

```
#echo bank is $BANK
#
#If BANK is the same as LASERWRITER, then we have no choice.
#otherwise, we print on the one that is free, if any are free.
#
if [ "$BANK" = "$LASERWRITER" ]
then
        SELECT=$LASERWRITER
lpr -P$SELECT $*
exit 0
fi
#echo past the check bank=laserprinter
#
#Now we check for a free printer.
#Note that $LASERWRITER is checked again in case it becomes
#free during the check.
#
#echo now we check the other for a free one
for i in $BANK $LASERWRITER
do
FREE=`lpq -P$i | awk '
{ if ($0 == "no entries")
   {
        val=1
print val
exit 0
   }
   else
   {
val=0
print val
exit 0
   }
}' `
                if [ $FREE -eq 1 ]
then
#    echo in loop for $i
            SELECT=$i
#    echo select is $SELECT
#    if [ "$FREE" != "$LASERWRITER" ]
#    then
#            echo "Output redirected to printer $i"
#    fi
    lpr -P$SELECT $*
                    exit 0
fi
done
#echo done checking for a free one
#
#If we make it here then no printers are free.  So we
#print on the printer with the least bytes queued.
#
#
```

```
for i in $BANK $LASERWRITER
do
val=`lpq -P$i | awk ' BEGIN {
start=0;
}
/^Time/ {
start=1;
next;
}
(start == 1){
  test=substr($0,62,20);
  print test;
} ' | awk '
BEGIN {
summ=0;
}
{
summ=summ+$1;
}
END {
print summ;
}' `
echo "$i $val" >> $TMP
done

SELECT=`awk '(NR==1) {
      select=$1;
      best=$2
      }
      ($2 < best) {
      select=$1;
      best=$2}
END{
print select
}
' $TMP `
#echo $SELECT
#
rm $TMP
#Now print on the selected printer
#if [ $SELECT != $LASERWRITER ]
#then
#    echo "Output redirected to printer $i"
#fi
lpr -P$SELECT $*
trap 'rm -f $TMP; exit 99' 2 3 15
```

Program notes for plpr. For the most part, I've avoided scripts like these in which most of the logic is coded in the shell script. However, such a minimalist approach is representative of a wide variety of uses of awk. Here, awk is called to do only those things which the shell script can't do (or do as easily). Manipulating the output of a command and performing numeric comparisons is an example of such a task.

transpose—Perform a matrix transposition

Contributed by Geoff Clare

transpose performs a matrix transposition on its input. I wrote this when I saw a script to do this job posted to the net and thought it was horribly inefficient. I posted mine as an alternative with timing comparisons. If I remember rightly, the original one stored all the elements individually and used a nested loop with a **printf** for each element. It was immediately obvious to me that it would be much faster to construct the rows of the transposed matrix "on the fly."

My script uses '${1+"$@"}' to supply file names on the awk command line so that if no files are specified awk will read its standard input. This is much better than plain '$*' which can't handle file names containing white space.

```
:
# Transpose a matrix: assumes all lines have same number \
# of fields

exec awk '
NR == 1 {
      n = NF
      for (i = 1; i <= NF; i++)
            row[i] = $i
      next
}
{
      if (NF > n)
            n = NF
      for (i = 1; i <= NF; i++)
            row[i] = row[i] " " $i
}
END {
      for (i = 1; i <= n; i++)
            print row[i]
}' ${1+"$@"}
```

Here's a test file:

```
1 2 3 4
5 6 7 8
9 10 11 12
```

Now we run **transpose** on the file:

```
% transpose test
```

```
1  5  9
2  6  10
3  7  11
4  8  12
```

Program notes for transpose. This is a very simple but interesting script. It creates an array named **row** and appends each field into an element of the array. The **END** procedure outputs the array.

A

Sed Quick Reference
Command Line Syntax
Syntax of Sed Commands
Sed Command Summary

Command Line Syntax

The syntax for invoking sed has two forms:

> **sed** *[[-n][-e] 'command' file(s)*
> **sed** *[-n] -f scriptfile file(s)*

The first form allows you to specify an editing command on the command line, surrounded by single quotes. The second form allows you to specify a *scriptfile*, a file containing sed commands.

The following options are recognized:

-**n**   Only print lines specified with the **p** command or the **p** flag of the **s** command.

-e *cmd*   Next argument is an editing command. Useful if multiple scripts are specified.

-f *file*   Next argument is a file containing editing commands.

Frequently used sed scripts are usually invoked from a shell script. Since this is the same for sed or awk, see the section "Shell Wrapper for Invoking Awk" in Appendix B, *Awk Quick Reference*.

Syntax of Sed Commands

Sed commands have the general form:

> [*address*][,*address*][!]*command* [*arguments*]

Sed copies each line of input into a pattern space. Sed instructions consist of addresses and editing commands. If the address of the command matches the line in the pattern space, then the command is applied to that line. If a command has no address, then it is applied to each input line. If a command changes the contents of the space, subsequent command-addresses will be applied to the current line in the pattern space, not the original input line.

Pattern Addressing

An *address* can be either a line number or a *pattern*, enclosed in slashes (*/pattern/*). A pattern is described using a regular expression. Additionally, \n can be used to match any newline in the pattern space (resulting from the **N** command), but not the newline at the end of the pattern space.

If no pattern is specified, the command will be applied to all lines. If only one address is specified, the command will be applied to all lines matching that address. If two comma-separated addresses are specified, the command will be applied to a range of lines between the first and second addresses, inclusively. Some commands accept only one address: **a, i, r, q**, and **=**.

The **!** operator following an address causes sed to apply the command to all lines that do not match the address.

Braces ({ }) are used in sed to nest one address inside another or to apply multiple commands at the same address.

> [*/pattern/*][,*/pattern/*]{
> *command1*
> *command2*
> }

The opening curly brace must end a line, and the closing curly brace must be on a line by itself. Be sure there are no blank spaces after the braces.

Sed Regular Expression Metacharacters

The following table lists the pattern-matching metacharacters that were discussed in Chapter 3, *Understanding Regular Expression Syntax.*

Special Characters	Usage
.	Matches any single character except *newline*.
*	Matches any number (including zero) of the single character (including a character specified by a regular expression) that immediately precedes it.
[...]	Matches any one of the class of characters enclosed between the brackets. All other metacharacters lose their meaning when specified as members of a class. A circumflex (ˆ) as the first character inside brackets reverses the match to all characters except newline and those listed in the class. A hyphen (-) is used to indicate a range of characters. The close bracket (]) as the first character in class is a member of the class.
\{*n,m*\}	Matches a range of occurrences of the single character (including a character specified by a regular expression) that immediately precedes it. \{*n*\} will match exactly *n* occurrences, \{*n,*\} will match at least *n* occurrences, and \{*n,m*\} will match any number of occurrences between *n* and *m*. (sed and grep only).
ˆ	Locates regular expression that follows at the beginning of line.
$	Locates preceding regular expression at the end of line.
\	Escapes the special character that follows.
\(\)	Saves the pattern enclosed between "\(" and "\)" into a special holding space. Up to nine patterns can be saved in this way on a single line. They can be "replayed" in substitutions by the escape sequences "\1" to "\9".

Special Characters	Usage
\n	Matches the *n*th pattern previously saved by "\(" and "\)", where *n* is a number from 0 to 9 and previously saved patterns are counted from the left on the line.
&	Prints the entire search pattern when used in a replacement string.

Note that an empty regular expression "//" is the same as the previous regular expression.

Sed Command Summary

:   *:label*

Label a line in the script for the transfer of control by **b** or **t**. *label* may contain up to seven characters.

=   *[address]=*

Write to standard output the line number of addressed line.

a   *[address]*a\
     text

Append *text* following each line matched by *address*. If *text* goes over more than one line, newlines must be "hidden" by preceding them with a backslash. The *text* will be terminated by the first newline that is not hidden in this way. The *text* is not available in the pattern space and subsequent commands cannot be applied to it. The results of this command are sent to standard output when the list of editing commands is finished, regardless of what happens to the current line in the pattern space.

b   *[address1][,address2]*b*[label]*

Transfer control unconditionally to *:label* elsewhere in script. That is, the command following the *label* is the next command applied to the current line. If no *label* is specified, control falls through to the end of the script, so no more commands are applied to the current line.

c   [*address1*][,*address2*]c\
text

Replace the lines selected by the address with *text*. When a range of lines is specified, all lines as a group are replaced by a single copy of *text*. The newline following each line of *text* must be escaped by a backslash, except the last line. The contents of the pattern space are, in effect, deleted and no subsequent editing commands can be applied to it (or *text*).

d   [*address1*][,*address2*]d

Delete line from pattern space. Thus, the line is not passed to standard output. A new line of input is read and editing resumes with first command in script.

D   [*address1*][*address2*]D

Delete first part (up to embedded newline) of multi-line pattern space created by **N** command and resume editing with first command in script. If this command empties the pattern space, then a new line of input is read, as if the **d** had been executed.

g   [*address1*][,*address2*]g

Copy contents of hold space (see **h** or **H** command) into the pattern space, wiping out previous contents.

G   [*address1*][,*address2*]G

Append newline followed by contents of hold space (see **h** or **H** command) to contents of the pattern space. If hold space is empty, a newline is still appended to the pattern space.

h   [*address1*][,*address2*]h

Copy pattern space into hold space, a special temporary buffer. Previous contents of hold space are wiped out.

H   [*address1*][,*address2*]H

Append newline and contents of pattern space to contents of the hold space. Even if hold space is empty, this command still appends newline.

i   [*address1*]i\
text

Insert *text* before each line matched by *address*. (See **a** for details on *text*.)

l   *[address1][,address2]*l

List the contents of the pattern space, showing nonprinting characters as ASCII codes. Long lines are wrapped.

n   *[address1][,address2]*n

Read next line of input into pattern space. Current line is sent to standard output. New line becomes current line and increments line counter. Control passes to command following **n** instead of resuming at the top of the script.

N   *[address1][,address2]*N

Append next input line to contents of pattern space; the new line is separated from the previous contents of the pattern space by a newline. (This command is designed to allow pattern matches across two lines.) Using \n to match the embedded newline, you can match patterns across multiple lines.

p   *[address1][,address2]*p

Print the addressed line(s). Unless the **-n** command line option is used, this command will cause duplicate lines to be output. Also, it is typically used before commands that change flow control (**d**, **n**, **b**) and might prevent the current line from being output.

P   *[address1][,address2]*P

Print first part (up to embedded newline) of multi-line pattern space created by **N** command. Same as **p** if **N** has not been applied to a line.

q   *[address]*q

Quit when *address* is encountered. The addressed line is first written to output (if default output is not suppressed), along with any text appended to it by previous **a** or **r** commands.

r   *[address]*r *file*

Read contents of *file* and append after the contents of the pattern space. Exactly one space must be put between **r** and the filename.

s [*address1*][,*address2*]s/*pattern*/*replacement*/[*flags*]

Substitute *replacement* for *pattern* on each addressed line. If pattern addresses are used, the pattern // represents the last pattern address specified. The following flags can be specified:

    n   Replace *n*th instance of /*pattern*/ on each addressed line. *n* is any number in the range 1 to 512, and the default is 1.

    g   Replace all instances of /*pattern*/ on each addressed line, not just the first instance.

    p   Print the line if a successful substitution is done. If several successful substitutions are done, multiple copies of the line will be printed.

    w *file*   Write the line to a *file* if a replacement was done. A maximum of ten different *files* can be opened.

t [*address1*][,*address2*]t [*label*]

Test if successful substitutions have been made on addressed lines, and if so, branch to line marked by :*label*. (See **b** and :.) If label is not specified, control falls through to bottom of script.

w [*address1*][,*address2*]w *file*

Append contents of pattern space to *file*. This action occurs when the command is encountered rather than when the pattern space is output. Exactly one space must separate the **w** and the filename. A maximum of ten different files can be opened in a script. This command will create the file if it does not exist; if the file exists, its contents will be overwritten each time the script is executed. Multiple write commands that direct output to the same file append to the end of the file.

x [*address1*][,*address2*]x

Exchange contents of the pattern space with the contents of the hold space.

y [*address1*][,*address2*]y/*abc*/*xyz*/

Transform each character by position in string *abc* to its equivalent in string *xyz*.

Awk Quick Reference

Command Line Syntax
Awk Command Summary

This appendix describes the features of the awk scripting language.

Command Line Syntax

The syntax for invoking awk has two basic forms:

> **awk** [-F*c*] '*pattern { action }*' *var=value file(s)*
> **awk** [-F*c*] **-f** *scriptfile var=value file(s)*

An awk command line consists of the command, the script and the input filename. Input is read from the file specified on the command line. If there is no input file or "-" is specified, then standard input is read. The -F option sets the field separator (FS) to *c*.

Nawk provides a -v option that takes an argument *var=value*. This option sets the variable *var* to *value* before the script is executed. (See discussion below on command-line parameters.)

Gawk provides a "--" option that marks the end of command line options, per POSIX argument parsing conventions. Using this option, for instance, you could specify a *scriptfile* that begins with "-", which would otherwise be confused with command-line options.

You can specify a script consisting of *pattern* and *action* on the command line, surrounded by single quotes. Alternatively, you can place the script in a separate file and specify the name of the *scriptfile* on the command line with the -f option.

Parameters can be passed into awk by specifying them on the command line after the script. This includes setting system variables such as **FS**, **OFS** and **RS**. The *value* can be a literal, a shell variable ($*var*) or the result of command ('*cmd*'); it must be quoted if it contains blank spaces. Any number of parameters can be specified.

Command-line parameters are not available until the first line of input is read, and thus cannot be accessed in the BEGIN procedure. (Setting system variables seems to be an exception, but this might not be true of all implementations.) Parameters are evaluated in the order in which they appear on the command line up until a filename is recognized. Parameters appearing after that filename will be available when the next filename is recognized. (In nawk, you can use the -v option to assign the parameter before the script is read.)

Shell Wrapper for Invoking Awk

Typing a script at the system prompt is only practical for simple, one-line scripts. Any script that you might invoke as a command and re-use can be put inside a shell script. Using a shell script to invoke awk makes the script easy for others to use.

You can put the command line that invokes awk in a file, giving it a name that identifies what the script does. Make that file executable (using the **chmod** command) and put in a directory where local commands are kept. The name of the shell script can be typed on the command line to execute the awk script. This is preferred for easily used and re-used scripts.

On BSD UNIX systems, you can use the "#!" syntax to create self-contained awk scripts:

```
#!/usr/bin/awk -f
script
```

Awk parameters and the input filename can be specified on the command line that invokes the shell script.

Records and Fields

Each line of input is split into fields. The field delimiter is one or more blank spaces by default. You can change the field separator by using the -F command line option. The following command line changes the field separator to a colon:

```
awk -F: -f awkscr passwd
```

You can also assign the delimiter to the system variable **FS**. This is typically done in the BEGIN procedure, but can also be passed as a parameter on the command line.

```
awk -f awkscr FS=: /etc/passwd
```

Each input line forms a record containing any number of fields. Each field can be referenced by its position in the record. "$1" refers to the value of the first field; "$2" to the second field, and so on. "$0" refers to the entire record. The following action prints the first field of each input line:

```
{ print $1 }
```

The default record separator is a newline. The following procedure sets **FS** and **RS** so that awk interprets an input record as any number of lines up to a blank line.

```
BEGIN { FS = "\n"; RS = "" }
```

Format of a Script

An awk script is a set of of pattern-matching rules and *actions*:

> *pattern { action }*

An action is one or more statements that will be performed on those input lines that match the pattern. If no pattern is specified, the action is performed for every input line. The following example uses the **print** statement to print each line in the input file:

```
{ print }
```

If only a pattern is specified, then the default action consists of the **print** statement, as shown above.

In nawk, function definitions can also appear:

> **function** *name(parameter-list) { statements }*

This syntax defines the function *name*, making available the list of parameters for processing in the body of the function. Variables specified in the parameter-list are treated as local variables within the function. All other variables are global and can be accessed outside the function. No space is permitted between the name of the function and the opening parenthesis. This also applies to calling a user-defined function. User-defined functions are described in Chapter 9, *Functions*, as well.

Line Termination

A line in an awk script is terminated by a newline or a semicolon. Using semicolons to put multiple statements on a line, while permitted, reduces the readability of most programs. Blank lines are permitted between statements.

Program control statements (**do, if, for,** or **while**) continue on the next line, where a dependent statement is listed. If multiple dependent statements are specified, they must be enclosed within braces.

```
if (NF > 1){
    name = $1
    total += $2
}
```

You cannot use a semicolon to avoid using braces for multiple statements.

You can type a single statement over multiple lines by escaping the newline with a backslash (\). You can also break lines following any of the following characters:

```
, { ? : && ||
```

Strings cannot be broken across a line.

Comments

A comment begins with a "#" and ends with a newline. It can appear on a line by itself or at the end of a line. Comments are descriptive remarks that explain the operation of the script.

Patterns

A pattern can be any of the following:

> */regular expression/*
> *relational expression*
> BEGIN
> END

1. Regular expressions use the extended set of metacharacters and must be enclosed in slashes. For a full discussion of regular expressions, see Chapter 3, *Understanding Regular Expression Syntax.*

2. Relational expressions use the relational operators listed under "Expressions" later in this chapter.

3. The BEGIN pattern is applied before the first line of input is read and the END pattern is applied after the last line of input is read.

4. Use ! to negate the match; i.e., to handle lines not matching the pattern.

5. You can address a range of lines, just as in sed:

    pattern,pattern

    Patterns, except BEGIN and END, can be expressed in compound forms using the following operators:

    &&   Logical And
    || Logical Or*

    In addition, nawk and gawk define the C conditional operator ?: (*pattern* ? *pattern* : *pattern*).

6. Patterns can be placed in parentheses to ensure proper evaluation.

7. BEGIN and END patterns must be associated with actions. Gawk and nawk do not require that the END pattern appear as the last rule in the script, while awk does. If multiple BEGIN and END rules are written, as permitted in nawk, they are merged into a single rule before being applied.

Regular Expressions

Table B-1 summarizes regular expressions described in Chapter 3. The metacharacters are listed in order of precedence.

Table B-1. Regular Expressions Metacharacters

Special Characters	Usage
c	Matches any literal character *c* that is not a metacharacter.
\	Escapes any metacharacter that follows, including itself.
^	Locates regular expression that follows at the beginning of line.

---

*Sun's version of nawk (SunOs 4.1) does not seem to support logical OR.

Special Characters	Usage
$	Locates preceding regular expression at the end of line.
.	Matches any single character except *newline*.
[...]	Matches any *one* of the class of characters enclosed between the brackets. A circumflex (^) as the first character inside brackets reverses the match to all characters except newline and those listed in the class. A hyphen (-) is used to indicate a range of characters. The close bracket (]) as the first character in a class is a member of the class. All other metacharacters lose their meaning when specified as members of a class.
r1 | *r2*	Between two regular expressions, *r1* and *r2*, it allows either of the regular expressions to be matched.
(*r1*)(*r2*)	Used for concatenating regular expressions.
r*	Matches any number (including zero) of the regular expression that immediately precedes it.
r+	Matches one or more occurrences of the preceding regular expression.
r?	Matches 0 or 1 occurrences of the preceding regular expression.
(*r*)	Used for grouping regular expressions.

Regular expressions can also make use of the escape sequences for accessing special characters, as defined in the section "Escape Sequences" later in this chapter.

Expressions

An expression can be made up of constants, variables, operators and functions. A constant is a string (any sequence of characters) or a numeric value. A variable is a symbol that references a value. You can think of it as a piece of information that retrieves a particular numeric or string value.

Constants

There are two types of constants, string and numeric. A string constant must be quoted while a numeric constant is not.

Escape Sequences

Table B-2 can be used in strings and regular expressions.

Table B-2. Escape Sequences

Sequence	Description
\a	Alert character, usually ASCII BEL character.
\b	Backspace.
\f	Formfeed.
\n	Newline.
\r	Carriage return.
\t	Horizontal tab.
\v	Vertical tab.
ddd	Character represented as one- to three-digit octal value.
\x*hex*	Character represented as hexadecimal value.
c	Any literal character *c* (\" for ").

Variables

There are three kinds of variables: user-defined, built-in, and fields. By convention, built-in or system variables consist of all capital letters.

The name of a variable cannot start with a digit. Otherwise, it consists of letters, digits and underscores.

A variable does not need to be declared or initialized. A variable can contain either a string or numeric value. An unitialized variable has the null string ("") as its string value and 0 as its numeric value. Awk attempts to decide whether a value should be processed as a string or a number depending upon the operation.

The assignment of a variable has the form:

> *var=expr*

It assigns the value of expression to *var*. The following expression assigns a value of 1 to the variable x.

```
x = 1
```

The name of the variable is used to reference the value:

```
{ print x }
```

prints the value of the variable x. In this case, it would be 1.

See the section "System Variables" later in this chapter for information on built-in variables. A field variable is referenced using $n, where n is any number 0 to NF, that references the field by position. It can be supplied by a variable, such as $NF meaning the last field, or constant, such as $1 meaning the first field.

Arrays

An array is a variable that can be used to store a set of values. The following statement assigns a value to an element of an array:

> *array*[*index*] = *value*

In awk, all arrays are *associative* arrays. What makes an associative array unique is that its index can be a string or a number.

An associative array makes an "association" between the indices and the elements of an array. For each element of the array, a pair of values is maintained: the index of the element and the value of the element. The elements are not stored in any particular order as in a conventional array.

You can use the special **for** loop to read all the elements of an associative array.

> **for** *item* **in** *array*

The index of the array is available as *item*, while the value of an element of the array can be referenced as *array*[*item*].

In nawk, you can use the operator **in** to test that an element exists by testing to see if its index exists.

> **if** (*index* **in** *array*)

tests that *array*[*index*] is true but you cannot use it to test the value of the element referenced by *array*[*index*].

In nawk, you can also delete individual elements of the array using the **delete** statement.

System Variables

Awk defines a number of special variables that can be referenced or reset inside a program, as shown in Table B-3.

Table B-3. Awk System Variables

Version	Variable	Description
awk	**FILENAME**	Current filename.
	FS	Field separator (a blank).
	NF	Number of fields in current record.
	NR	Number of the current record.
	OFS	Output field separator (a blank).
	ORS	Output record separator (a newline).
	RS	Record separator (a newline).
nawk	**ARGC**	Number of arguments on command line.
	ARGV	An array containing the command-line arguments.
	FNR	Like NR, but relative to the current file.
	OFMT	Output format for numbers (%.6g).
	RSTART	First position in the string matched by **match** function.
	RLENGTH	Length of the string matched by **match** function.
	SUBSEP	Separator character for array subscripts (\034).
gawk	**ENVIRON**	An associative array of environment variables.
	IGNORECASE	If non-zero, pattern matches are case-independent.

Awk Reference

Operators

Table B-4 lists the operators in the order of precedence that are available in awk.

Table B-4. Operators

Operators	Description
= += -= *= /= %= ^=	Assignment.
?:	C conditional expression (nawk and gawk).
||	Logical OR.
&&	Logical AND.
~ !~	Match regular expression and negation.
< <= > >= != ==	Relational operators.
(blank)	Concatenation.
+ -	Addition, subtraction.
* / %	Multiplication, division, and modulus.
+ - !	Unary plus and minus, and logical negation.
^	Exponentiation.

Operators	Description
++ —	Increment and decrement, either prefix or postfix.
$	Field reference.

Statements and Functions

An action is enclosed in braces and consists of one or more statements and/or expressions. The difference between a statement and a function is that a function returns a value, and its argument list is specified within parentheses. (The formal syntactical difference does not always hold true: **printf** is considered a statement, but its argument list can be put in parentheses; **getline** is a function that does not use parentheses.)

Awk has a number of predefined arithmetic and string functions. A function is called as follows:

return = function(arg1,arg2)

where *return* is a variable created to hold what the function returns. Arguments to a function are specified as a comma-separated list. The left parenthesis follows after the name of the function. (With built-in functions, a space is permitted between the function name and the parentheses.)

Awk Command Summary

The following alphabetical list of statements and functions includes all that are available in awk, nawk, or gawk. Unless otherwise mentioned, the statement or function is found in all versions. New statements and functions introduced with nawk are also found in gawk.

atan2()   **atan2**(*y,x*)

Returns the arctangent of y/x in radians. (nawk)

break   Exit from a **while** or **for** loop.

close   **close**(*filename-expr*)

close(*command-expr*)

In most implementations of awk, you can only have ten files open simultaneously and one pipe. Therefore, nawk provides a **close** statement that allows you to close a file or an pipe. It takes as an argument the same expression that opened the pipe or file. (nawk)

continue   Begin next iteration of **while** or **for** loop.

cos()   **cos(***x***)**

Return cosine of *x*.

delete   **delete(***array[element]***)**

Delete element of array. (nawk)

do   **do**
        body
    while (*expr***)**

Looping statement. Execute statements in *body* then evaluate *expr* and if true, execute *body*a again. (nawk)

exit   Exit from script, reading no new input. An END rule will be executed.

exp()   **exp(***x***)**

Return exponent of *x*.

for   **for (***init-expr***; *test-expr***; *incr-expr***)**
      statement

C style looping construct. *init-expr* assigns the initial value of the counter variable. *test-expr* is a relational expression that is evaluated each time before executing the statement. When *test-expr* is false, the loop is exited. *incr-expr* is used to increment the counter variable after each pass.

for (*item-expr* **in** *array***)**
      statement

Special loop designed for reading associative arrays. For each element of the array, the *statement* is executed; the element can be referenced by **array[***item-expr***]**.

getline   Read next line of input. Original awk does not support the syntax to open multiple input streams.

getline [*var*] [*<file*]

command | **getline** [*var*]

The first form reads input from *file* and the second form reads the output of *command*. Both forms read one line at a time, and each time the statement is executed it gets the next line of input. The line of input is assigned to $0 and it is parsed into fields, setting **NF**, **NR** and **FNR**. If *var* is specified, the result is assigned to *var* and the $0 is not changed. Thus, if the result is assigned to a variable, the current line does not change. It is actually a function and it returns 1 if it reads a record successfully, 0 if end-of-line is encountered, and -1 if for some reason it is otherwise unsuccessful. (nawk)

gsub()   **gsub(***r,s,t***)**

Globally substitute *s* for each match of the regular expression *r* in the string *t*. Return the number of substitutions. If *t* is not supplied, defaults to $0. (nawk)

if   **if** (*expr*) *statement1*
[**else** *statement*]

Conditional statement. Evaluate *expr* and if true, execute *statement1*; if **else** clause is supplied, execute *statement* if *expr* is false.

index()   **index(***str, substr***)**

Return position of substring in string.

int()   **int(***x***)**

Return integer value of *x* by truncating any digits following a decimal point.

length()   **length(***str***)**

Return length of string.

log()   **log(***x***)**

Return logarithm of *x*.

match()   **match(***s,r***)**

Function that matches the pattern, specified by the regular expression *r*, in the string *s* and returns either the position in *s* where the match begins, or 0 if no occurences are found. Sets the value of **RSTART** and **RLENGTH**. (nawk)

next   Read next input line and begin executing script at first rule.

print   **print** [*output-expr*] [*dest-expr*]

Evaluate the *output-expr* and direct it to standard output followed by a newline. *dest-expr* is an optional expression that directs the output to a file or pipe. "> *file*" directs the output to a file, overwriting its previous contents. ">> *file*" appends the output to a file, preserving its previous contents. In both case, the file will be created it if it does not exist. "| *command*" directs the output as the input to a UNIX command.

printf   **printf** (*format-expr* [, *expr-list*]) [*dest-expr*]

An alternative print statement borrowed from the C language. It has the ability to produced formatted output. It can also be used to output data without automatically producing a newline. *format-expr* is a string of format specifications and constants; see next section for a list of format specifiers. *expr-list* is a list of arguments corresponding to format specifiers. See the **print** statement for a descripion of *dest-expr*.

rand()   **rand()**

Generate a random number between 0 and 1. This function returns the same number each time the script is executed, unless the random number generator is seeded using the **srand()** function. (nawk)

return   **return** [*expr*]

Used at end of user-defined functions to exit function, returning value of expression. (nawk)

sin()   **sin(**x**)**

Return sine of x.

split()   **split(***str,array,sep***)**

Function that parses string into elements of array using field separator, returning number of elements in array. Value of **FS** is used if no field separator is specified.

sprintf()   **sprintf** (*format-expr* [, *expr-list*])

Function that returns string formatted according to **printf** format specification. It formats data but does not output it. *format-expr* is a string of format specifications and constants; see next section for a list of format specifiers. *expr-list* is a list of arguments corresponding to format specifiers.

sqrt()   **sqrt(**x**)**

Return square root of x.

srand()   **srand(***expr***)**

Use *expr* to set a new seed for random number generator. Default is time of day. (nawk)

sub()   **sub(***r,s,t***)**

Substitute s for first match of the regular expression r in the string t. Return 1 if successful; 0 otherwise. If t is not supplied, defaults to $0. (nawk)

substr()	substr(*str,beg,len*)

Return substring of string at beginning position and the characters that follow to a maximum specified length.

system()	system(*command*)

Function that executes the specified *command* and returns its status. The status of the command that is executed typically indicates its success (1), completion (0) or unexpected error (-1). The output of the command is not available for processing within the awk script. Use "*command* | **getline**" to read the output of the command into the script. (nawk)

tolower()	tolower(*str*)

Translate all uppercase characters in *str* to lowercase and return the new string. (gawk)

toupper()	toupper(*str*)

Translate all lowercase characters in *str* to uppercase and return the new string. (gawk)

while	while (*expr*) *statement*

Looping construct. While *expr* is true, execute *statement*.

Format Expressions Used in Printf and Sprintf

A format expression can take three optional modifiers following "%" and preceding the format specifier:

> *%-width.precision format-specifier*

The *width* of the output field is a numeric value. When you specify a field width, the contents of the field will be right justified by default. You must specify "-" to get left-justification. Thus, "%-20s" outputs a string left-justified in a field 20 characters wide. If the string is less than 20 characters, the field will be padded with white space to fill.

The *precision* modifier, used for decimal or floating point values, controls the number of digits that appear to the right of the decimal point. Note that the default precision for the output of numeric values is "%.6g." In nawk, the default can be changed by setting the system variable **OFMT**. This affects the precision used by the **print** statement when outputting numbers. For instance, if you are using awk to write reports that contain dollar values, you might prefer to change **OFMT** to "%.2d."

The format specifiers, shown in Table B-5, are used with **printf** and **sprintf** statements.

Table B-5: Format Specifiers

Letter	Description
c	ASCII character.
d	Decimal integer.
e	Floating point format ([-]*d.precision*E[+-]*dd*).
f	Floating point format ([-]*ddd.precision*)
g	**e** or **f** conversion, whichever is shortest, with trailing zeros removed.
o	Unsigned octal value.
s	String.
x	Unsigned hexadecimal number.
%	Literal %.

C

Supplement for Chapter 11

Full Listing of spellcheck.awk
Listing of Masterindex Shell Script
Documentation for Masterindex

This appendix contains supplemental programs and documentation for the programs described in Chapter 11, *Full-featured Applications*.

Full Listing of spellcheck.awk

```
# spellcheck.awk -- interactive spell checker
#
# AUTHOR: Dale Dougherty
#
# Usage: nawk -f spellcheck.awk [+dict] file
# (Use spellcheck as name of shell program)
# SPELLDICT = "dict"
# SPELLFILE = "file"

# BEGIN actions perform the following tasks:
#    1) process command line arguments
#    2) create temporary filenames
#    3) execute spell program to create wordlist file
#    4) display list of user responses
```

```
BEGIN {
# Process command line arguments
# Must be at least two args -- nawk and filename
   if (ARGC > 1) {
   # if more than two args, second arg is dict
      if (ARGC > 2) {
      # test to see if dict is specified with "+"
      # and assign ARGV[1] to SPELLDICT
         if (ARGV[1] ~ /^\+.*/)
            SPELLDICT = ARGV[1]
         else
            SPELLDICT = "+" ARGV[1]
      # assign file ARGV[1] to SPELLFILE
         SPELLFILE = ARGV[2]
      # delete args so awk does not open them as files
         delete ARGV[1]
         delete ARGV[2]
      }
   # not more than two args
      else {
      # assign file ARGV[2] to SPELLFILE
         SPELLFILE = ARGV[1]
      # test to see if local dict file exists
         if (! system ("test -r dict")) {
         # if it does, ask if we should use it
            printf ("Use local dict file? (y/n)")
            getline reply <"-"
         # if reply is yes, use "dict"
            if (reply ~ /[yY](es)*/){
               SPELLDICT = "+dict"
            }
         }
      }
   } # end of processing args > 1
   # if args not > 1, then print shell-command usage
   else {
      print "Usage: spellcheck [+dict] file"
      exit
   }
# end of processing command line arguments

# create temporary file names, each begin with sp_
   wordlist = "sp_wordlist"
   spellsource = "sp_input"
   spellout = "sp_out"

# copy SPELLFILE to temporary input file
   system("cp " SPELLFILE " " spellsource)

# now run spell program; output sent to wordlist
   print "Running spell checker ..."
   if (SPELLDICT)
```

```
            SPELLCMD = "spell " SPELLDICT " "
        else
            SPELLCMD = "spell "
        system(SPELLCMD spellsource " > " wordlist )

    # test wordlist to see if misspelled words turned up
        if ( system("test -s " wordlist ) ) {
        # if wordlist is empty, (or spell command failed), exit
            print "No misspelled words found."
            exit
        }

    # assign wordlist file to ARGV[1] so that awk will read it.
        ARGV[1] = wordlist

    # display list of user responses
        responseList = "Responses: \n\tChange each occurrence,"
        responseList = responseList "\n\tGlobal change,"
        responseList = responseList "\n\tAdd to Dict,"
        responseList = responseList "\n\tHelp,"
            responseList = responseList "\n\tQuit"
        responseList = responseList "\n\tCR to ignore: "
        printf("%s", responseList)

} # end of BEGIN procedure

# main procedure, executed for each line in wordlist.
#    Purpose is to show misspelled word and prompt user
#    for appropriate action.

{
# assign word to misspelling
    misspelling = $1
    response = 1
    ++word
# print misspelling and prompt for response
    while (response !~ /(^[cCgGaAhHqQ])|^$/ ) {
        printf("\n%s - Found %s (C/G/A/H/Q/):", word, misspelling)
        getline response <"-"
    }
# now process the user's response
# CR - carriage return ignores current word
# Help
    if (response ~ /[Hh](elp)*/) {
    # Display list of responses and prompt again.
        printf("%s", responseList)
        printf("\n%s - Found %s (C/G/A/Q/):", word, misspelling)
        getline response <"-"
    }
# Quit
    if (response ~ /[Qq](uit)*/) exit
# Add to dictionary
    if ( response ~ /[Aa](dd)*/) {
```

```
            dict[++dictEntry] = misspelling
    }
# Change each occurrence
    if ( response ~ /[cC](hange)*/) {
    # read each line of the file we are correcting
        newspelling = ""; changes = ""
        while( getline < spellsource > 0){
        # call function to show line with misspelled word
        # and prompt user to make each correction
            make_change($0)
        # all lines go to temp output file
            print > spellout
        }
    # all lines have been read
    # close temp input and temp output file
        close(spellout)
        close(spellsource)
    # if change was made
        if (changes){
        # show changed lines
            for (j = 1; j <= changes; ++j)
                print changedLines[j]
            printf ("%d lines changed. ", changes)
        # function to confirm before saving changes
            confirm_changes()
        }
    }
# Globally change
    if ( response ~ /[gG](lobal)*/) {
    # call function to prompt for correction
    # and display each line that is changed.
    # Ask user to approve all changes before saving.
        make_global_change()
    }
} # end of Main procedure

# END procedure makes changes permanent.
# It overwrites the original file, and adds words
# to the dictionary.
# It also removes the temporary files.

END {
# if we got here after reading only one record,
# no changes were made, so exit.
    if (NR <= 1) exit
# user must confirm saving corrections to file
    while (saveAnswer !~ /([yY](es)*)|([nN]o*)/ ) {
        printf "Save corrections in %s (y/n)? ", SPELLFILE
        getline saveAnswer <"-"
    }
# if answer is yes then mv temporary input file to SPELLFILE
    if (saveAnswer ~ /^[yY]/)
        system("mv " spellsource " " SPELLFILE)
```

```awk
# if answer is no then rm temporary input file
   if (saveAnswer ~ /^[nN]/)
      system("rm " spellsource)

# if words have added to dictionary array, then prompt
# to confirm saving in current dictionary.
   if (dictEntry) {
      printf "Make changes to dictionary (y/n)? "
      getline response <"-"
      if (response ~ /^[yY]/){
      # if no dictionary defined, then use "dict"
         if (! SPELLDICT) SPELLDICT="dict"

      # loop through array and append words to dictionary
         sub(/^\+/,"",SPELLDICT)
         for ( item in dict )
            print dict[item] >> SPELLDICT
      # sort dictionary file
         system("sort " SPELLDICT "> tmp_dict")
         system("mv " "tmp_dict " SPELLDICT)
      }
   }
# remove word list.
   system("rm" " sp_wordlist")
} # end of END procedure

# function definitions

# make_change -- prompt user to correct misspelling
#        for current input line.  Calls itself
#        to find other occurrences in string.
#     stringToChange -- initially $0; then unmatched substring of $0
#     len -- length from beginning of $0 to end of matched string
# Assumes that misspelling is defined.

function make_change (stringToChange,len,  line, OKmakechange) {

# match misspelling in stringToChange; otherwise do nothing
   if ( match(stringToChange, misspelling) ){
   # Display matched line
   printstring = $0
   gsub(/\t/," ",printstring)
   print printstring
   carets = "^"
   for (i = 1; i < RLENGTH; ++i)
      carets = carets "^"
   if (len)
      FMT = "%" len+RSTART+RLENGTH-2 "s\n"
   else
      FMT = "%" RSTART+RLENGTH-1 "s\n"
   printf(FMT, carets)
   # Prompt user for correction, if not already defined
   if (! newspelling) {
```

```
        printf "Change to:"
        getline newspelling <"-"
}
# A carriage return falls through
# If user enters correction, confirm
  while (newspelling && ! OKmakechange) {
      printf ("Change %s to %s? (y/n):", misspelling, newspelling)
      getline OKmakechange <"-"
      madechg = ""
  # test response
      if (OKmakechange ~ /[yY](es)*/ ) {
      # make change (first occurrence only)
          madechg = sub(misspelling, newspelling, stringToChange)
      }
      else if ( OKmakechange ~ /[nN]o*/ ){
          # offer chance to re-enter correction
          printf "Change to:"
          getline newspelling <"-"
          OKmakechange = ""
      }
  } # end of while loop

  # if len, we are working with substring of $0
  if (len) {
  # assemble it
      line = substr($0,1,len-1)
      $0 = line stringToChange
  }
  else {
      $0 = stringToChange
      if (madechg) ++changes
  }

  # put changed line in array for display
  if (madechg)
      changedLines[changes] = ">" $0

  # create substring so we can try to match other occurrences
  len = len+RSTART + RLENGTH
  part1 = substr($0,1,len-1)
  part2 = substr($0,len)
  # calls itself to see if misspelling is found in remaining part
   make_change(part2,len)

  } # end of if

} # end of make_change()

# make_global_change --
#       prompt user to correct misspelling
#       for all lines globally.
#             Has no arguments
# Assumes that misspelling is defined.
```

```
function make_global_change(newspelling, OKmakechange, changes) {

# prompt user to correct misspelled word
    printf "Globally change to:"
    getline newspelling <"-"

# carriage return falls through
# if there is an answer, confirm
    while (newspelling && ! OKmakechange) {
        printf ("Globally change %s to %s? (y/n):", misspelling,\
                    newspelling)
        getline OKmakechange <"-"
    # test response and make change
        if (OKmakechange ~ /[yY](es)*/ ) {
        # open file, read all lines
            while( getline < spellsource > 0){
            # if match is found, make change using gsub
            # and print each changed line.
                if ($0 ~ misspelling) {
                    madechg = gsub(misspelling, newspelling)
                    print ">", $0
                    changes += 1  # counter for line changes
                }
            # write all lines to temp output file
                print > spellout
            } # end of while loop for reading file

        # close temporary files
            close(spellout)
            close(spellsource)
        # report the number of changes
            printf ("%d lines changed. ", changes)
        # function to confirm before saving changes
            confirm_changes()
        } # end of if (OKmakechange ~ y)

    # if correction not confirmed, prompt for new word
        else if ( OKmakechange ~ /[nN]o*/ ){
            printf "Globally change to:"
            getline newspelling <"-"
            OKmakechange = ""
        }

    } # end of while loop for prompting user for correction
} # end of make_global_change()

# confirm_changes --
#       confirm before saving changes

function confirm_changes( savechanges) {
# prompt to confirm saving changes
    while (! savechanges ) {
```

```
        printf ("Save changes? (y/n)")
        getline savechanges <"-"
    }
# if confirmed, mv output to input
    if (savechanges ~ /[yY](es)*/)
        system("mv " spellout " " spellsource)
}
```

Listing of Masterindex Shell Script

```
:
# 1.1 -- 7/9/90
MASTER=""
FILES=""
PAGE=""
FORMAT=1
INDEXDIR=/work/sedawk/awk/index
#INDEXDIR=/work/index
INDEXMACDIR=/work/macros/current
# Add check that all dependent modules are available.
sectNumber=1
useNumber=1
while [ "$#" != "0" ]; do
    case $1 in
    -m*)    MASTER="TRUE";;
    [1-9])   sectNumber=$1;;
    *,*)     sectNames=$1; useNumber=0;;
    -p*)    PAGE="TRUE";;
    -s*)    FORMAT=0;;
    -*)    echo $1 " is not a valid argument";;
        *) if [ -f $1 ]; then
                FILES="$FILES $1"
            else
                echo "$1: file not found"
            fi;;
    esac
    shift
done
if [ "$FILES" = "" ]; then
    echo "Please supply a valid filename."
    exit
fi
if [ "$MASTER" != "" ]; then
    for x in $FILES
    do
    if [ "$useNumber" != 0 ]; then
        romaNum=`$INDEXDIR/romanum $sectNumber`
        awk -F\t '
            NF == 1 { print $0 }
```

```
                NF > 1 { print $0 ":" volume }
            ' volume=$romaNum $x >>/tmp/index$$
            sectNumber=`expr $sectNumber + 1`
        else
            awk -F\t '
                NR==1 { split(namelist, names, ",");
                volname=names[volume]}
                NF == 1 { print $0 }
                NF > 1 { print $0 ":" volname }
            ' volume=$sectNumber namelist=$sectNames $x >>/tmp/index$$
            sectNumber=`expr $sectNumber + 1`
        fi
        done
        FILES="/tmp/index$$"
    fi
    if [ "$PAGE" != "" ]; then
        $INDEXDIR/page.idx $FILES
        exit
    fi
    $INDEXDIR/input.idx $FILES |
    sort -bdf -t:  +0 -1 +1 -2 +3 -4 +2n -3n | uniq |
    $INDEXDIR/pagenums.idx |
    $INDEXDIR/combine.idx |
    $INDEXDIR/format.idx FMT=$FORMAT MACDIR=$INDEXMACDIR
    if [ -s "/tmp/index$$" ]; then
        rm /tmp/index$$
    fi
```

Documentation for Masterindex

NAME **masterindex** – indexing program for single and multi-volume indexing.

SYNOPSIS **masterindex** [**–master** [*volume*]] [**–page**] [**–screen**] [*filename* ...]

DESCRIPTION **masterindex** generates a formatted index based on structured index entries output by **troff**. Unless you redirect output, it comes to the screen.

OPTIONS **–m** or **-master** indicates that you are compiling a multi-volume index. The index entries for each volume should be in a single file and the filenames should be listed in sequence. If the first file is not the first volume, then specify the volume number as a separate argument. The volume number is converted to a Roman numeral and pre-pended to all the page numbers of entries in that file.

–p or **-page** produces a listing of index entries for each page number. It can be used to proof the entries against hard copy.

–s or **-screen** specifies that the unformatted index will be viewed on the "screen". The default is to prepare output that contains **troff** macros for formatting.

FILES
/work/bin/masterindex   /work/bin/page.idx
/work/bin/pagenums.idx /work/bin/combine.idx
/work/bin/format.idx   /work/bin/rotate.idx
/work/bin/romanum   /work/macros/current/indexmacs

SEE   Note that these programs require "nawk" (new awk).

BUGS   The new index program is modular, invoking a series of smaller programs. This should allow me to connect different modules to implement new features as well as isolate and fix problems more easily.

Index entries should not contain any **troff** font changes. The program does not handle them.

Roman numerals greater than eight will not be sorted properly, thus imposing a limit of an eight-book index. (The sort program will sort the roman numerals 1-10 in the following order: I,II,III,IV,IX,V,VI,VII,VIII,X.)

Background Details

Tim recommends *The Joy of Cooking* (JofC) index as an ideal index. I examined the JofC index quite thoroughly and set out to write a new indexing program that duplicated its features. I did not wholly duplicate the JofC format as well, but this could be done fairly easily if it is ever desired. Please look at the JofC index yourself to examine its features.

I also tried to do a few other things to improve on the previous index program and provide more support for the person coding the index.

If the entry consists of primary and secondary sort keys, then we can code it as:

```
.XX "primary, secondary"
```

A comma delimits the two keys. We also have a .XN macro for generating "See" references without a page number. It is specified as:

```
.XN "entry (See anotherEntry)"
```

While these coding forms continue to work as they have, **masterindex** provides greater flexibility by allowing three levels of keys: primary, secondary and tertiary. You'd specify the entry like so:

```
.XX "primary: secondary; tertiary"
```

Note that the comma is not used as a delimiter. A colon delimits the primary and secondary entry; the semicolon delimits the secondary and tertiary entry. This means that commas can be a part of a key using this syntax. Don't worry, though, you can continue to use a comma to delimit the primary and secondary keys. (Be aware that the first comma in a line is converted to a colon, if no colon delimiter is found.) I'd recommend that new books be coded using the above syntax, even if you are only specifying a primary and secondary key.

Another feature is automatic rotation of primary and secondary keys if a tilde (˜) is used as the delimiter. So the following entry:

```
.XX "cat˜command"
```

is equivalent to the following two entries:

```
.XX "cat command"
.XX "command: cat"
```

You can think of the secondary key as a classification (command, attribute, function, etc.) of the primary entry. Be careful not to reverse the two, as "command cat" does not make much sense. To use a tilde in an entry, enter "˜˜".

I added a new macro .XB that is the same as .XX except that the page number for this index entry will be output in bold to indicate that it is the most significant page number in a range. Here is an example:

```
.XB "cat command"
```

When **troff** processes the index entries, it outputs the page number followed by an asterisk. This is how it appears when output is seen in screen format. When coded for **troff** formatting, the page number is surrounded by the bold font change escape sequences. By the way, in the JofC index, I noticed that they allowed having the same page number in Roman and in Bold. Also, this page number will not be combined in a range of consecutive numbers.

```
.XB "cat command"
```

When **troff** processes the index entries, it outputs the page number followed by an asterisk. This is how it appears when output is seen in screen format. When coded for **troff** formatting, the page number is surrounded by the bold font change escape sequences. By the way, in the JofC index, I noticed that they allowed having the same page number in Roman and in Bold. Also, this page number will not be combined in a range of consecutive numbers.

One other feature of the JofC index is that the very first secondary key appears on the same line with the primary key. The old index program placed any secondary key on the next line. The one advantage of doing it the JofC way is that entries containing only one secondary key will be output on the same line and look much better. Thus, you'd have "line justification, definition of" rather than having "definition of" indented on the next line. The next secondary key would be indented. Note that if the primary key exists as a separate entry (it has page numbers associated with it), the page references for the primary key will be output on the same line and the first secondary entry will be output on the next line.

To reiterate, while the syntax of the three-level entries is different, this index entry is perfectly valid:

```
.XX "line justification, definition of"
```

It also produces the same result as:

```
.XX "line justification: definition of"
```

(The colon disappears in the output.) Similarly, you could write an entry, such as:

```
.XX "justification, lines, defined"
```

or:

```
.XX "justification: lines, defined"
```

where the comma between "lines" and "defined" does not serve as a delimiter but is part of the secondary key.

The previous example could be written as an entry with three levels:

```
.XX "justification: lines; defined"
```

where the semicolon delimits the tertiary key. The semicolon is output with the key, and multiple tertiary keys may follow immediately after the secondary key.

The main thing, though, is that page numbers are collected for all primary, secondary, and tertiary keys. Thus, you could have output such as:

justification 4-9
  lines 4,6; defined, 5

Output Format

One thing I wanted to do that our previous program did not do is generate an index without the **troff** codes. **masterindex** has three output modes: **troff**, **screen**, and **page**.

The default output is intended for processing by **troff** (via **fmt**). It contains macros that are defined in */work/macros/current/indexmacs*. These macros should produce the same index format as before, which was largely done directly through **troff** requests. Here are a few lines off the top:

```
$ masterindex ch01
.so /work/macros/current/indexmacs
.Se "" "Index"
.XC
.XF A "A"
.XF 1 "applications, structure of  2;  program  1"
.XF 1 "attribute, WIN_CONSUME_KBD_EVENTS  13"
.XF 2 "WIN_CONSUME_PICK_EVENTS  13"
.XF 2 "WIN_NOTIFY_EVENT_PROC  13"
.XF 2 "XV_ERROR_PROC  14"
.XF 2 "XV_INIT_ARGC_PTR_ARGV  5,6"
```

The top two lines should be obvious. The .XC macro produces multi-column output. (It will print out two columns for smaller books. It's not smart enough to take arguments specifying the width of columns, but that should be done.) The .XF macro has three possible values for its first argument. An "A" indicates that the second argument is a letter of the alphabet that should be output as a divider. A "1" indicates that the second argument contains a primary entry. A "2" indicates that the entry begins with a secondary entry, which is indented.

When invoked with the **-s** argument, the program prepares the index for viewing on the screen (or printing as an ASCII file). Again, here are a few lines:

```
$ masterindex -s ch01

        A
applications, structure of  2;  program  1
attribute, WIN_CONSUME_KBD_EVENTS  13
   WIN_CONSUME_PICK_EVENTS  13
   WIN_NOTIFY_EVENT_PROC  13
   XV_ERROR_PROC  14
   XV_INIT_ARGC_PTR_ARGV  5,6
   XV_INIT_ARGS  6
   XV_USAGE_PROC  6
```

Obviously, this is useful for quickly proofing the index. The third type of format is also used for proofing the index. Invoked using **-p**, it provides a page-by-page listing of the index entries.

```
$ masterindex -p ch01

Page 1
     structure of XView applications
     applications, structure of; program
     XView applications
     XView applications, structure of
     XView interface
     compiling XView programs
     XView, compiling programs
Page 2
     XView libraries
```

Compiling a Master Index

A multi-volume master index is invoked by specifying **-m** option. Each set of index entries for a particular volume must be placed in a separate file.

```
$ masterindex -m -s book1 book2 book3
xv_init() procedure  II: 4; III: 5
XV_INIT_ARGC_PTR_ARGV attribute  II: 5,6
XV_INIT_ARGS attribute  I: 6
```

Files must be specified in consecutive order. If the first file is not Volume 1, you can specify the number as an argument.

```
$ masterindex -m 4 -s book4 book5
```

Index

About the Author

Dale Dougherty is an editor and writer for O'Reilly & Associates. He has either thought up, written, or edited many of the books published by O'Reilly. Among other books, Dale has written *sed & awk*, *DOS Meets UNIX* (with Tim O'Reilly), *Using UUCP & Usenet* (with Grace Todino), and *Guide to the Pick System*.

Dale is also manager of O'Reilly's Digital Media Group. He is responsible for developing books with companion CD-ROM disks as well as digital delivery of the information that O'Reilly has published in their UNIX and X books. He founded the Davenport Group, a group of over 30 UNIX system vendors, software vendors and book publishers working to standardize an interchange format for computer documentation.

Colophon

Our look is the result of reader comments, our own experimentation, and distribution channels.

Distinctive covers complement our distinctive approach to UNIX documentation, breathing personality and life into potentially dry subjects. UNIX and its attendant programs can be unruly beasts. Nutshell Handbooks help you tame them.

The animal featured on the cover of *sed & awk* is a slender loris. Lorises are nocturnal, tree-dwelling, tailless primates with thick, soft fur and large round eyes. They are found in India and Ceylon where they live in the trees, rarely descending to the ground. Lorises have been observed urinating on their hands and feet—it is thought that they do this to improve their grip while climbing or to leave a scent trail.

A small animal, the slender loris is generally between 7 and 10 inches in size and weighs 12 ounces or less. It subsists on a diet of fruit, leaves and shoots, and small animals which it captures by hand.

Edie Freedman designed this cover and the entire UNIX bestiary that appears on other Nutshell Handbooks. The beasts themselves are adapted from 19th-century engravings from the Dover Pictorial Archive.

The text of this book is set in Times Roman; headings are Helvetica; examples are Courier. Text was prepared using SortQuad's sqtroff text formatter. Figures are produced with a Macintosh. Printing is done on an Apple LaserWriter.

USING UNIX AND X

Books from O'Reilly & Associates, Inc.

UNIX Power Tools

By Jerry Peek, Mike Loukides, Tim O'Reilly, et al.
1st Edition March 1993
1162 pages, (includes CD-ROM)
Random House ISBN 0-679-79073-X

Ideal for UNIX users who hunger for technical—yet accessible—information, *UNIX Power Tools* consists of tips, tricks, concepts, and freeware (CD-ROM included). It also covers add-on utilities and how to take advantage of clever features in the most popular UNIX utilities.

This is a browser's book...like a magazine that you don't read from start to finish, but leaf through repeatedly until you realize that you've read it all. You'll find articles abstracted from O'Reilly Nutshell Handbooks®, new information that highlights program "tricks" and "gotchas", tips posted to the Net over the years, and other accumulated wisdom. The goal of *UNIX Power Tools* is to help you think creatively about UNIX and get you to the point where you can analyze your own problems. Your own solutions won't be far behind.

"Unix Power Tools is an encyclopedic work that belongs next to every serious Unix user's terminal. If you're already a Unix wizard, keep this book tucked under your desk for late-night reference when solving those difficult problems."
—Raymond GA Côté, *BYTE*, June 1993

SCO UNIX in a Nutshell

By Ellie Cutler & the staff of O'Reilly & Associates
1st Edition February 1994
590 pages, ISBN 1-56592-037-6

The desktop reference to SCO UNIX and Open Desktop, this version of *UNIX in a Nutshell* shows you what's under the hood of your SCO system. It isn't a scaled-down quick reference of common commands, but a complete reference containing all user, programming, administration, and networking commands.

Contents include:

- All commands and options
- Shell syntax for the Bourne, Korn, C, and SCO shells
- Pattern matching, with *vi, ex, sed*, and *aw*k commands
- Compiler and debugging commands for software development
- Networking with email, TCP/IP, NFS, and UUCP
- System administration commands and the SCO sysadmsh shell

This edition of *UNIX in a Nutshell* is the most comprehensive SCO quick reference on the market, a must for any SCO user. You'll want to keep *SCO UNIX in a Nutshell* close by as you use your computer: it'll become a handy, indispensible reference for working with your SCO system.

FOR INFORMATION: **800-998-9938**, 707-829-0515; **NUTS@ORA.COM**

Our UNIX in a Nutshell *guides are the most compre-*
hensive quick reference on the market—a must for
every UNIX *user. No matter what system you use,*
we've got a version to cover your needs.

UNIX in a Nutshell: System V Edition

By Daniel Gilly & the staff of O'Reilly & Associates
2nd Edition June 1992
444 pages, ISBN 1-56592-001-5

You may have seen UNIX
quick-reference guides, but
you've never seen anything
like *UNIX in a Nutshell.* Not
a scaled-down quick reference
of common commands, *UNIX*
in a Nutshell is a complete
reference containing all commands and options, along with
generous descriptions and examples that put the
commands in context. For all but the thorniest
UNIX problems, this one reference should be all
the documentation you need. Covers System V,
Releases 3 and 4, and Solaris 2.0.

"This book is the perfect desktop reference...
The authors have presented a clear and concisely
written book which would make an excellent
addition to any UNIX user's library."
—*SysAdmin,* Sept/Oct 1992

UNIX in a Nutshell: Berkeley Edition

By the staff of O'Reilly & Associates
1st Edition December 1986 (latest update October 1990)
272 pages, ISBN 0-937175-20-X

An alternate version of the quick-reference guide.
The latest update covers BSD 4.3.

"Whether you are setting up your first UNIX
system or adding your fiftieth user, these books
can ease you through learning the fundamentals
of the UNIX system."
—Michael J. O'Brien, Hardware Editor,
ABA/Unix/group Newsletter

Learning the UNIX Operating System

By Grace Todino, John Strang & Jerry Peek
3rd Edition August 1993
108 pages, ISBN 1-56592-060-0

If you are new to UNIX, this
concise introduction will tell
you just what you need to get
started and no more. Why
wade through a six-hundred-
page book when you can begin
working productively in a
matter of minutes? It's an ideal
primer for Mac and PC users
of the Internet who need to know a little bit about
UNIX on the systems they visit.

This book is the most effective introduction to
UNIX in print. The third edition has been updated
and expanded to provide increased coverage of
window systems and networking. It's a handy
book for someone just starting with UNIX, as well
as someone who encounters a UNIX system as a
visitor via remote login over the Internet.

"Once you've established a connection with the
network, there's often a secondary obstacle to
surmount.... *Learning the UNIX Operating*
System helps you figure out what to do next by
presenting in a nutshell the basics of how to deal
with the 'U-word.' Obviously a 92-page book isn't
going to make you an instant Unix guru, but it
does an excellent job of introducing basic operations in a concise nontechnical way, including
how to navigate through the file system, send and
receive E-mail and—most importantly—get
to the online help...."
—Michael L. Porter, associate editor,
Personal Engineering & Instrumentation News,
December 1993

Learning the vi Editor

By Linda Lamb
5th Edition October 1990
192 pages, ISBN 0-937175-67-6

A complete guide to text editing
with *vi*, the editor available
on nearly every UNIX system.
Early chapters cover the basics;
later chapters explain more
advanced editing tools, such
as ex commands and global
search and replacement.

Learning the GNU Emacs

By Debra Cameron & Bill Rosenblatt
1st Edition October 1991
442 pages, ISBN 0-937175-84-6

An introduction to the GNU Emacs editor, one of the most widely used and powerful editors available under UNIX. Provides a solid introduction to basic editing, a look at several important editing modes (special Emacs features for editing specific types of documents), and a brief introduction to customization and Emacs LISP programming. The book is aimed at new Emacs users, whether or not they are programmers.

"Authors Debra Cameron and Bill Rosenblatt do a particularly admirable job presenting the extensive functionality of GNU Emacs in well-organized, easily digested chapters.... Despite its title, *Learning GNU Emacs* could easily serve as a reference for the experienced Emacs user."
—Laura Branagan, Convex Computer Corporation

Learning the Korn Shell

By Bill Rosenblatt
1st Edition June 1993
363 pages, ISBN 1-56592-054-6

A thorough introduction to the Korn shell, both as a user interface and as a programming language. This book provides a clear explanation of the Korn shell's features, including *ksh* string operations, co-processes, signals and signal handling, and command-line interpretation. *Learning the Korn Shell* also includes real-life programming examples and a Korn shell debugger (*kshdb*).

"Readers still bending back the pages of Korn-shell manuals will find relief in...*Learning the Korn Shell*...a gentle introduction to the shell. Rather than focusing on syntax issues, the book quickly takes on the task of solving day-to-day problems with Korn-shell scripts. Application scripts are also shown and explained in detail. In fact, the book even presents a script debugger written for *ksh*. This is a good book for improving your knowledge of the shell."
—*Unix Review*, October 1993

Making TEX Work

By Norman Walsh
1st Edition April 1994
522 pages, ISBN 1-56592-051-1

TeX is a powerful tool for creating professional-quality typeset text and is unsurpassed at typesetting mathematical equations, scientific text, and multiple languages. Many books describe how you use TeX to construct sentences, paragraphs, and chapters. Until now, no book has described all the software that actually lets you build, run, and use TeX to best advantage on your platform. Because creating a TeX document requires the use of many tools, this lack of information is a serious problem for TeX users.

Making TEX Work guides you through the maze of tools available in the TeX system. Beyond the core TeX program there are myriad drivers, macro packages, previewers, printing programs, online documentation facilities, graphics programs, and many more. This book describes them all.

sed & awk

By Dale Dougherty
1st Edition November 1990
414 pages, ISBN 0-937175-59-5

For people who create and modify text files, *sed* and *awk* are power tools for editing. Most of the things that you can do with these programs can be done interactively with a text editor; however, using *sed* and *awk* can save many hours of repetitive work in achieving the same result.

"*sed* and *awk* is a must for UNIX system programmers and administrators, and even general UNIX readers will benefit. I have over a hundred UNIX and C books in my personal library at home, but only a dozen are duplicated on the shelf where I work. This one just became number twelve."
—*Root Journal*, January/February 1992

FOR INFORMATION: **800-998-9938**, 707-829-0515; **NUTS@ORA.COM**

MH & xmh: E-mail for Users & Programmers

By Jerry Peek
2nd Edition September 1992
728 pages, ISBN 1-56592-027-9

Customizing your email environment can save time and make communicating more enjoyable. *MH & xmh: E-Mail for Users & Programmers* explains how to use, customize, and program with the MH electronic mail commands available on virtually any UNIX system. The handbook also covers *xmh*, an X Window System client that runs MH programs. The second edition is updated for X Release 5 and MH 6.7.2. We added a chapter on mhook, sections explaining under-appreciated small commands and features, and more examples showing how to use MH to handle common situations.

"There is something for everyone who uses either MH or *xmh* in this book. [It] takes you from the basics through to some very useful routines quickly...packed full of useful tips and time-saving techniques...[and] is well researched and written in a language that all can understand."
—*Sun UK User,* August 1993

Using UUCP and Usenet

By Grace Todino & Dale Dougherty
1st Edition February 1986 (latest update October 1991)
210 pages, ISBN 0-937175-10-2

Shows users how to communicate with both UNIX and non-UNIX systems using UUCP and *cu* or *tip*, and how to read news and post articles. This handbook assumes that UUCP is already running at your site.

"Are you having trouble with UUCP? Have you torn out your hair trying to set the Dialers file? *Managing UUCP and Usenet* and *Using UUCP and Usenet* will give you the information you need to become an accomplished Net user. The companion book is *!%@:: A Directory of Electronic Mail Addressing & Networks*, a compendium of world networks and how to address and read them. All of these books are well written, and I urge you to take a look at them."
—*Root Journal,* September/October 1990

Volume 3: X Window System User's Guide

Standard Edition
By Valerie Quercia & Tim O'Reilly
4th Edition May 1993
836 pages, ISBN 1-56592-014-7

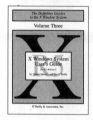

The *X Window System User's Guide* orients the new user to window system concepts and provides detailed tutorials for many client programs, including the *xterm* terminal emulator and window managers. Building on this basic knowledge, later chapters explain how to customize the X environment and provide sample configurations. The *Standard Edition* uses the *twm* manager in most examples and illustrations. Revised for X11 Release 5. This popular manual is available in two editions, one for users of the MIT software, and one for users of Motif. (see below).

"For the novice, this is the best introduction to X available. It will also be a convenient reference for experienced users and X applications developers."
—*Computing Reviews,* March 1991

Volume 3M: X Window System User's Guide

Motif Edition
By Valerie Quercia & Tim O'Reilly
2nd Edition January 1993
956 pages, ISBN 1-56592-015-5

This alternative edition of the *User's Guide* is revised for Motif 1.2 and X11 Release 5. It highlights the Motif window manager and graphical interface, including such new features as tear-off menus and drag-and-drop. It will be the first choice for users with the Motif graphical user interface. Material covered in the second edition (also covered in Volume 3 *Standard Edition*):

- Overview of the X Color Management System (Xcms)
- Creating your own Xcms color database
- Tutorials for two "color editors": *xcoloredit* and *xtici*
- Using the X font server
- Tutorial for *editres*, a resource editor
- Extensive coverage of the new implementations of *bitmap* and *xmag*
- Overview of internationalization features

GLOBAL NETWORK NAVIGATOR

The Global Network Navigator™ (GNN) is a unique kind of information service that makes the Internet easy and enjoyable to use. We organize access to the vast information resources of the Internet so that you can find what you want. We also help you understand the Internet and the many ways you can explore it.

Charting the Internet, the Ultimate Online Service

In GNN you'll find:

- *The Online Whole Internet Catalog*, an interactive card catalog for Internet resources that expands on the catalog in Ed Krol's best-selling book, *The Whole Internet User's Guide & Catalog*.

- *Newsnet*, a news service that keeps you up to date on what's happening on the Net.

- *The Netheads Department*, which features profiles of interesting people on the Internet and commentary by Internet experts.

- *GNN Metacenters*, special-interest online magazines aimed at serving the needs of particular audiences. GNN Metacenters not only gather the best Internet resources together in one convenient place, they also introduce new material from a variety of sources. Each Metacenter contains new feature articles, as well as columns, subject-oriented reference guides for using the Internet, and topic-oriented discussion groups. Travel, music, education, and computers are some of the areas that we cover.

All in all, GNN helps you get more value for the time you spend on the Internet.

 ## The Best of the Web

The *O'Reilly Resource Center* was voted "**Best Commercial Site**" by users participating in "Best of the Web' 94."

GNN received "Honorable Mention" for "**Best Overall Site**," "**Best Entertainment Service**," and "**Most Important Service Concept**."

The *GNN NetNews* received "Honorable Mention" for "**Best Document Design**."

Subscribe Today

GNN is available over the Internet as a subscription service. To get complete information about subscribing to GNN, send email to **info@gnn.com**. If you have access to a World Wide Web browser such as Mosaic or Lynx, you can use the following URL to register online: http://gnn.com/

If you use a browser that does not support online forms, you can retrieve an email version of the registration form automatically by sending email to **form@gnn.com**. Fill this form out and send it back to us by email, and we will confirm your registration.

BOOK INFORMATION
AT YOUR FINGERTIPS

O'Reilly & Associates offers extensive online information through a Gopher server (**gopher.ora.com**).
Here you can find detailed information on our entire catalog of books, tapes, and much more.

The O'Reilly Online Catalog

Gopher is basically a hierarchy of menus and files that can easily lead you to a wealth of information. Gopher is also easy to navigate; helpful instructions appear at the bottom of each screen (notice the three prompts in the sample screen below). Another nice feature is that Gopher files can be downloaded, saved, or printed out for future reference. You can also search Gopher files and even email them.

To give you an idea of our Gopher, here's a look at the top, or root, menu:

```
O'Reilly & Associates (The public Gopher server)
    1.  News Flash! -- New Products and Projects/
    2.  Feature Articles/
    3.  Product Descriptions/
    4.  Ordering Information/
    5.  Complete Listing of Titles
    6.  Errata for "Learning Perl"
    7.  FTP Archive and Email Information/
    8.  Bibliographies/


Press ? for Help, q to Quit, u to go up a menu
```

The heart of the O'Reilly Gopher service is the extensive information provided on all ORA products in menu item three, "Product Descriptions." For most books this usually includes title information, a long description, a short author bio, the table of contents, quotes and reviews, a gif image of the book's cover, and even some interesting information about the animal featured on the cover. (One of the benefits of a Gopher database is the ability to pack a lot of information in an organized, easy-to-find place.)

How to Order

Another important listing is "Ordering Information," where we supply information to those interested in buying our books. Here, you'll find instructions and an application for ordering O'Reilly products online, a listing of distributors (local and international), a listing of bookstores that carry our titles, and much more.

The item that follows, "Complete Listing of Titles," is helpful when it's time to order. This single file, with short one-line listings of all ORA products, quickly provides the essentials for easy ordering: title, ISBN, and price.

And More

One of the most widely read areas of the O'Reilly Gopher is "News Flash!," which focuses on important new products and projects of ORA. Here, you'll find entries on newly published books and audiotapes; announcements of exciting new projects and product lines from ORA; upcoming tradeshows, conferences, and exhibitions of interest; author appearances; contest winners; job openings; and anything else that's timely and topical.

"Feature Articles" contains just that—many of the articles and interviews found here are excerpted from the O'Reilly magazine/catalog *ora.com*.

The "Bibliographies" entries are also very popular with readers: providing critical, objective reviews on the important literature in the field.

"FTP Archive and Email Information" contains helpful ORA email addresses, information about our "ora-news" listproc server, and detailed instructions on how to download ORA book examples via FTP.

Other menu listings are often available. "Errata for 'Learning Perl,'" for example, apprised readers of errata found in the first edition of our book, and responses to this file greatly aided our campaign to ferret out errors and typos for the upcoming corrected edition (a nice example of the mutual benefits of online interactivity).

Come and Explore

Our Gopher is vibrant and constantly in flux. By the time you actually log onto this Gopher, the root menu may well have changed. The goal is to always improve, and to that end we welcome your input (email: **gopher@ora.com**). We invite you to come and explore.

Here are four basic ways to call up our Gopher online.

1) If you have a local Gopher client, type:
   ```
   gopher gopher.ora.com
   ```

2) For Xgopher:
   ```
   xgopher -xrm "xgopher.root\
   Server: gopher.ora.com"
   ```

3) To use telnet (for those without a Gopher client):
   ```
   telnet gopher.ora.com
   ```
   login: **gopher** (no password)

4) For a World Wide Web browser, use this URL:
   ```
   http://gopher.ora.com:70/
   ```

COMPLETE LISTING OF TITLES
from O'Reilly & Associates, Inc.

INTERNET

The Whole Internet User's Guide & Catalog
Connecting to the Internet: An O'Reilly Buyer's Guide
!%@:: A Directory of Electronic Mail
    Addressing & Networks
Smileys

USING UNIX AND X

UNIX Power Tools (with CD-ROM)
UNIX in a Nutshell: System V Edition
UNIX in a Nutshell: Berkeley Edition
SCO UNIX in a Nutshell
Learning the UNIX Operating System
Learning the vi Editor
Learning GNU Emacs
Learning the Korn Shell
Making TeX Work
sed & awk
MH & xmh: E-mail for Users & Programmers
Using UUCP and Usenet
X Window System User's Guide: Volume 3
X Window System User's Guide, Motif Edition: Volume 3M

SYSTEM ADMINISTRATION

Essential System Administration
sendmail
Computer Security Basics
Practical UNIX Security
System Performance Tuning
TCP/IP Network Administration
Learning Perl
Programming perl
Managing NFS and NIS
Managing UUCP and Usenet
DNS and BIND
termcap & terminfo
X Window System Administrator's Guide: Volume 8
    (available with or without CD-ROM)

UNIX AND C PROGRAMMING

ORACLE Performance Tuning
High Performance Computing
lex & yacc
POSIX Programmer's Guide
Power Programming with RPC
Programming with curses
Managing Projects with make
Software Portability with imake
Understanding and Using COFF
Migrating to Fortran 90
UNIX for FORTRAN Programmers
Using C on the UNIX System
Checking C Programs with lint
Practical C Programming
Understanding Japanese Information Processing

DCE (DISTRIBUTED COMPUTING ENVIRONMENT)

Distributing Applications Across DCE and Windows NT
Guide to Writing DCE Applications
Understanding DCE

BERKELEY 4.4 SOFTWARE DISTRIBUTION

4.4BSD System Manager's Manual
4.4BSD User's Reference Manual
4.4BSD User's Supplementary Documents
4.4BSD Programmer's Reference Manual
4.4BSD Programmer's Supplementary Documents
4.4BSD-Lite CD Companion

X PROGRAMMING

The X Window System in a Nutshell
X Protocol Reference Manual: Volume 0
Xlib Programming Manual: Volume 1
Xlib Reference Manual: Volume 2
X Toolkit Intrinsics Programming Manual: Volume 4
X Toolkit Intrinsics Programming Manual,
    Motif Edition: Volume 4M
X Toolkit Intrinsics Reference Manual: Volume 5
Motif Programming Manual: Volume 6A
Motif Reference Manual: Volume 6B
XView Programming Manual: Volume 7A
XView Reference Manual: Volume 7B
PEXlib Programming Manual
PEXlib Reference Manual
PHIGS Programming Manual (softcover or hardcover)
PHIGS Reference Manual
Programmer's Supplement for R5 of the X Window System

THE X RESOURCE

A quarterly working journal for X programmers
The X Resource: Issues 0 through 11

OTHER

Building a Successful Software Business
Love Your Job!

TRAVEL

Travelers' Tales Thailand

AUDIOTAPES

Internet Talk Radio's "Geek of the Week" Interviews
The Future of the Internet Protocol, 4 hours
Global Network Operations, 2 hours
Mobile IP Networking, 1 hour
Networked Information and Online Libraries, 1 hour
Security and Networks, 1 hour
European Networking, 1 hour

Notable Speeches of the Information Age
John Perry Barlow, 1.5 hours

O'REILLY WOULD LIKE TO HEAR FROM YOU

Please send me the following:

❏ *ora.com*

O'Reilly's magazine/catalog, containing behind-the-scenes articles and interviews on the technology we write about, and a complete listing of O'Reilly books and products.

❏ *Global Network Navigator™*

Information and subscription.

Please print legibly

Which book did this card come from?

_____

Where did you buy this book?
    ❏ Bookstore   ❏ Direct from O'Reilly
    ❏ Bundled with hardware/software   ❏ Class/seminar

Your job description: ❏ SysAdmin   ❏ Programmer

    ❏ Other_____

What computer system do you use?   ❏ UNIX
    ❏ MAC ❏ DOS(PC) ❏ Other_____

Name _____ Company/Organization Name _____

Address _____

City _____ State _____ Zip/Postal Code _____ Country _____

Telephone _____ Internet or other email address (specify network) _____

Nineteenth century wood engraving
of the horned owl from the O'Reilly
& Associates Nutshell Handbook®
Learning the UNIX Operating System

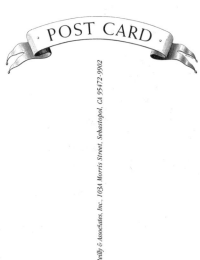

O'Reilly & Associates, Inc., 103A Morris Street, Sebastopol, CA 95472-9902

BUSINESS REPLY MAIL
FIRST CLASS MAIL   PERMIT NO. 80   SEBASTOPOL, CA

Postage will be paid by addressee

O'Reilly & Associates, Inc.
103A Morris Street
Sebastopol, CA 95472-9902